TRADE BARRIERS TO THE PUBLIC GOOD

Trade Barriers to the Public Good

Free Trade and Environmental Protection

ALEX C. MICHALOS

McGill-Queen's University Press
Montreal & Kingston • London • Ithaca

© McGill-Queen's University Press 2008

ISBN 978-0-7735-3352-3 (cloth)
ISBN 978-0-7735-3380-6 (paper)

Legal deposit second quarter 2008
Bibliothèque nationale du Québec

Printed in Canada on acid-free paper that is 100% ancient forest free
(100% post-consumer recycled), processed chlorine free

This book has been published with the help of a grant from the Canadian
Federation for the Humanities and Social Sciences, through the Aid to
Scholarly Publications Programme, using funds provided by the Social
Sciences and Humanities Research Council of Canada.

McGill-Queen's University Press acknowledges the support of the Canada
Council for the Arts for our publishing program. We also acknowledge
the financial support of the Government of Canada through the Book
Publishing Industry Development Program (BPIDP) for our publishing
activities.

Library and Archives Canada Cataloguing in Publication

Michalos, Alex C.
Trade barriers to the public good : free trade and environmental
protection / Alex C. Michalos.

Includes bibliographical references and index.
ISBN 978-0-7735-3352-3 (bnd)
ISBN 978-0-7735-3380-6 (pbk)

1. Free trade – Environmental aspects – Canada – Case studies.
2. Interprovincial commerce – Environmental aspects – Canada – Case
studies. 3. Manganese – Environmental aspects – Canada – Case studies.
4. Dispute resolution (Law) – Canada. 5. Dispute resolution (Law) –
North America. 6. Free trade – Environmental aspects – North America.
I. Title.

KDZ944.M52 2008   363.7'00971   C2007-907196-1

Typeset by Jay Tee Graphics Ltd. in 10/13 Sabon

To Deborah, with love

Contents

APPENDICES

Acknowledgments

I would like to thank the following people for providing me with information for this project: Bovas Abraham, Christine Allen, Annie Azan, Benjamin Bieber, Susanne Burkhardt, Monica Campbell, Elizabeth Craig, Helen Doyle, Marika Egyed, Ed Finn, Wolfgang Glatzer, Natasha Guillot, Kevin Haley, Jonnette Watson Hamilton, Stephen Hill, Michael Howlett, Sandy Jackson, Karen Kelly, Barbara Kotschwar, Béatrice Kowaliczko, Josée Lalande, Jack Lee, Mark Lee, Bill Leiss, Denyse MacKenzie, Elizabeth May, Bruce McEwen, Donna Mergler, Kathleen Orth, David Pimentel, Deborah Poff, Bob Rae, William Rees, Henri Sader, Jim Stanford, Jenny Stathopoulos, Debra Steger, Don Stewart, Don Voaklander, Todd Weiler, Gary Wilson, Kathe Wishart, and Don Zinger.

André Dimitrijevic arranged to have the entire AIT file on the MMT case photocopied for me, which was in size a stack of paper two feet high and in importance a veritable goldmine of vital information. He also read the chapters on the AIT case, corrected errors, and offered several helpful comments.

Christopher Kukucha gave me detailed comments on every chapter, which enabled me to see connections and omissions that I had totally missed and certainly improved the whole book.

Stephen Hill provided an excellent introduction to the MMT cases in Hill and Leiss (2001) and helped me find many important sources for my own investigation. Then he read the entire manuscript, raised questions I had not asked, challenged me to rethink some arguments, and continued to be a source of good information throughout the process of revising the text.

Scott Sinclair has been a steady and reliable critic of practically all of the recent trade deals. He provided valuable comments on several chapters, and I learned a great deal about a number of agreements from his published work.

Joselito Arocena, Randall Brazzoni, John Crooks, David Gourley, Ahmed Hussein, Frank Rossi, and Sam Walters helped me understand many of the issues involving physical science and motor vehicle technology in chapter 4.

Gail Curry and Charles Hogg helped me access archival materials from a variety of sources on the web, and Sandy Jackson, Nathalie Kin, and Josée Lalande kindly searched through historical records at the Royal Society of Canada.

Lesley Andrassy improved the prose considerably and spotted additional errors requiring remedial action. Finally, my old friend Philip J. Cercone contributed wisdom and enthusiasm when both were needed. Without his help this book would not be appearing here and now.

Of course none of these people should be held responsible for the final product, because I do not always recognize good advice when I get it and sometimes recognition is not sufficient to get me to act appropriately anyhow.

TRADE BARRIERS TO THE PUBLIC GOOD

1

Introduction

Negotiations for the North American Free Trade Agreement (NAFTA) officially began in February 1991, and on 1 January 1994 the agreement came
into force. In Canada, at least, the most important achievement of the
agreement according to those responsible for drafting it involved the so-
called dispute settlement provisions. We were told that those provisions
would help restrain the overwhelming power of the United States and
create "a level playing field" for the three North American countries.
Recalling those claims, I considered writing a book that would answer the
following question: How have the dispute settlement provisions performed? A little research and reflection rapidly revealed that the question
was much too broad to yield a worthwhile investigation and answer. So I
decided to restrict my question to a single case involving the investor-state
provisions of NAFTA Chapter 11. After examining the list of cases decided
under those provisions (Sinclair 2007), I concluded that the most interesting of the completed cases involved the gasoline fuel additive generally
referred to as MMT (methylcyclopentadienyl manganese tricarbonyl). This
case was the first investor-state complaint litigated under the Chapter 11
rules.

After some months of digging up the story about this dispute, I began to
suspect that it might be a dead issue. Then I ran across a preposterous quotation in a scholarly journal article published fairly recently that significantly boosted my research energy level: "To date, Canadian automobiles
have accumulated more than 1 trillion km using gasoline treated with MMT
without any documented problems relating to vehicle exhaust emission systems or to air quality" (Bhuie and Roy 2001, 1288–9). The fact that such a
claim could pass peer review unscathed revealed a genuine need for the
book I was planning to write. As I will show, many problems were docu-

mented. Then other people challenged those documents. Each side assembled its own experts and scientific research, and experts on each side were found wanting by experts on the other side, as well as by relatively unbiased third parties. The array of claims and counterclaims is truly bewildering, and there is still no end in sight.

Sometime after discovering the Bhuie and Roy article, I stumbled upon another remarkable assessment of the importance of the NAFTA MMT case, which provided a further boost to my spirits. According to Jackson and Sanger (1998, 38):

> Ethyl Corp. probably wouldn't want to take credit, but its law-suit over
> the banning of MMT probably did more than anything else to spur
> public opposition to expanded investor-protection rights as set out in
> the MAI [Multilateral Agreement on Investment]. The idea that the
> maker of a toxic substance could sue any government that banned its
> use is so bizarre that hypothetical examples could have been dismissed
> as the ravings of the lunatic fringe. But Ethyl Corp. provided a real-life
> example. It illustrated the nature of "investment," of "expropriation"
> and of the kind of private dispute resolution that would shut out the
> Canadian public.

As I will show in considerable detail, plenty of very complicated and controversial issues were connected to MMT, only a few of which were even touched on in the NAFTA case. Nevertheless, that case became relatively famous, though usually misunderstood and misjudged.

About seven months after the NAFTA case was initiated, another case involving MMT was initiated under the Canadian Agreement on Internal Trade (AIT). The AIT is an intergovernmental agreement signed by the First Ministers of Canada in July 1994. It came into force on 1 July 1995. The two cases proceeded simultaneously for about ten months until they were both settled in June 1998. Because the AIT case proceeded to a final decision on the merits of the case while the NAFTA case was settled early without a final decision on its merits, the AIT case was much more interesting and required considerably more attention to obtain an adequate assessment. It took me about four years to write this book, and for most of that period I was unable to decide which side was right regarding MMT or the legislation concerning it. Finally, I decided that the opponents of the product and the proponents of the legislation were right. While those decisions were of fundamental importance for this book, neither one constitutes its thesis, suggested somewhat ironically in its title, which is that the pursuit of commercial trade over every other value can destroy opportunities for achieving the broader public good. In support of that thesis, a careful examination of the NAFTA and AIT cases concerning MMT reveals how the investment dispute settlement procedures serve as the instruments of destruction. With my two Science for Peace volumes on the commercial trade in arms (Michalos 1989) and foreign currency speculation (Michalos 1997c), and my book on a pragmatic approach to business ethics (Michalos 1995), this is the fourth volume in which I have defended that basic thesis.

Public Citizen (2001, 5) asserted that "Canada moved to rescind its environmental and public health measure regulating a gasoline additive [MMT] developed by Ethyl even before the final NAFTA tribunal ruling in an effort to avoid a large damage reward." Clarke and Barlow (1998, 37), Shrybman (1999, 133), Soloway (1999, 83), Luz (2000–01, 67), Hoberg (2002, 187), Vaughan (2003, 67) and Public Citizen (2004c, 2) expressed similar views. Furthermore, Public Citizen claimed that the resolution of this case had four dangerous implications. First, the NAFTA tribunal's view that the importing restrictions placed on MMT may have constituted expropriation according to Article 1110 effectively gave U.S. firms the opportunity to sue governments under NAFTA rules for alleged regulatory takings, although such suits would not be allowed under U.S. domestic law. Second, the case illustrated that governments could be intimidated by the threat of a NAFTA suit and withdraw possibly worthwhile legislation. Third, the case showed that a government's commitment to the so-called Precautionary Principle could be overridden by its fear of a NAFTA trade challenge. Fourth, "Ethyl's NAFTA lawsuit succeeded in reversing Canada's ban on MMT" and "encouraged other corporations to ... challenge government policies" in Canada more than in any other NAFTA country (Public Citizen 2001, 9–10).

This book will present evidence that strongly suggests, if it does not prove, that Canada rescinded the *Manganese-based Fuel Additives Act (MMT Act)* more in response to the determination of the AIT panel than "in an effort to avoid a large damage award" following the NAFTA tribunal's ruling, and that it was likely that the same determination "succeeded in reversing Canada's ban on MMT." The federal government's strategy for eliminating MMT from unleaded gasoline in Canada was to prevent it from crossing any borders, between Canada and the United States and between any two provinces in Canada. The final determination of the AIT panel effectively destroyed that government's strategy by insisting that interprovincial trade in the additive could not be prevented. So there was no point in continuing the NAFTA fight, since the panel's decision implied that Ethyl could manufacture the additive in any province and sell it throughout the country. In other words, in the circumstances in which the MMT Act was contested, losing the AIT case was sufficient for the failure of the federal government's strategy of eliminating MMT from the Canadian market, while winning the NAFTA case would not have been sufficient to eliminate MMT from the Canadian market. In short, losing the AIT case, not fear of losing the NAFTA case, led to the abandonment of the MMT Act.

Although it is true, as Lee (2000) explained, that AIT Article 1809 was included in the agreement precisely to prevent the use of any AIT panel decisions as the basis for claims made under any other agreement (e.g., CUSTA, NAFTA, WTO), anyone can see the clear implications of such decisions and take appropriate defensive action. Article 1809 says:

> 1. Nothing in this Agreement is intended to provide nor shall be construed to provide, directly or indirectly, to any national, enterprise, state or other person any right, claim or remedy under any international agreement.
> 2. In the event that one of Canada's trading partners alleges that, contrary to the intention stated in paragraph 1, on the basis of this Agreement, a national, state or other person has been provided with a right, claim or remedy under any international agreement ... the Committee [on Internal Trade] shall ... take the necessary action which includes, among other things, amending or removing, as appropriate, the obligation under this Agreement that gives rise to the allegation, or rebalancing the benefits under this agreement.
> 3. Where, notwithstanding any action the Committee make take under paragraph 2, the trading partner proceeds to an international panel and is successful in establishing a right under an international agreement based on a provision of this Agreement, that provision is to that extent of no force or effect, unless the provision expressly states that it shall continue to exist notwithstanding the panel ruling. (AIT 2002)

Since any government representatives worthy of the name would be smart enough to "read the handwriting on the wall" and not risk being beaten by an international panel operating with the same discretionary authority and biases as a national panel, there is little chance that such a government would ever have to engage in a battle over some alleged "right" claimed in an international forum on the basis of a decision of a national panel in a national forum. The MMT case demonstrates how AIT panel decisions may make those of an international panel redundant and why the former may be at least as dangerous as the latter to the public good. Lee (2000) and Sinclair (1994) asserted that one aim of AIT proponents was to facilitate the implementation of international agreements like the NAFTA and the WTO in areas arguably under provincial jurisdiction. The material reviewed here illustrates such facilitation in an area clearly under federal jurisdiction.

After reviewing all the documents relevant to the NAFTA and AIT cases, as well as the parliamentary documents relevant to the *MMT Act*, I realized that the most important story to be told was not about the relatively greater importance of the AIT case compared to the NAFTA case but about something that is equally neglected: the difference between the focus of the legal cases (see chapters 11–16) and the legislative history of the *MMT Act* (see chapters 5–8). A careful analysis of that history and those cases reveals that, as slow and sometimes ponderous and wandering as the legislative process is, it does a better job than the NAFTA and AIT dispute settlement processes of protecting the interests of the broader public over narrower private interests. What comes out most clearly when all the documents are reviewed is that when attention was focused on the *MMT Act*, the broadly construed benefits and costs of its passage for all Canadians were exhaustively examined. Practically everyone (or at least their delegated representatives) who had an interest in the outcome of the debate had an opportunity to be heard. However, once the NAFTA and AIT cases got under way, the focus of attention shifted radically from what was best for all Canadians, all things considered, to what was consistent with the NAFTA and AIT rules as interpreted by the respective tribunal and panel established to adjudicate each case. What is consistent with those rules is what is commercially most advantageous from the point of view of preventing any reduction in trade, which is a relatively second-best alternative to maximizing trade. Thus, although broad public policy regarding MMT is being made in both arenas, in parliament and in the dispute settlement venues, in the latter case policy is guided by relatively narrow commercial interests and in the former it is guided by broader public interests. If one's primary interest is commercial, then one automatically gains something when the battle shifts from parliament to trade dispute settlement. Whichever side seems most advantageous for commercial trade wins. Advantages to other things are safely laid aside, perhaps given lip service but not anything that might have teeth.

If this treatise helps Canadians to see the great differences in making public policy through legislative decision-making rather than arbitrators' decision-making in the NAFTA and AIT venues, and the great danger to democracy in substituting the latter for the former, it will have served an important public purpose. If it helps people find their way to a more balanced set of trade rules, that will also be worthwhile. I think David Schneiderman hit the nail on the head when he wrote:

> The MMT story reveals yet another instrument by which corporate power can discipline the democratic state. The AIT – in addition to NAFTA, the bilateral investment treaty regime, and the World Trade Organization – helps to complete the web of agreements that limit the capacity of democratically elected legislatures to act on behalf of the public good. Nor should we expect arbitration or dispute panels constituted under these agreements to adopt interpretations of these agreements favourable to legislative intervention and contrary to the prevailing orthodoxy of limited government. Freeing the state from these overreaching legal restraints should now be a matter of the highest democratic priority. (Schneiderman 1999, 4)

Structurally, this book proceeds from relatively more general and uncontroversial to more particular and controversial issues. In chapter 2 I explain the philosophic, moral, and logical foundations of the investigation. This book is primarily about public policy-making and secondarily about business ethics. Because the field of ethics is generally broader than that of public policy-making, the chapter dealing with ethics comes first. Chapter 3 sketches some logical relationships among concepts that are central to contemporary public policy-making, namely, globalization, democracy, and federalism. Some of the empirical consequences of two agents and products of globalization, the NAFTA and the Canada-United States Trade Agreement (CUSTA), on Canada, the U.S., and Mexico are described. The nature of Canada's particular brand of federalism is also outlined, with special emphasis on the evolution of legal authority and responsibility for trade and environmental policy and regulation since confederation.

In chapter 4 the performance of certain components of motor vehicles is described, because this has an important role to play in our story. In particular, brief accounts are given of spark plugs, on-board diagnostic systems, and catalytic converters and their relation to chemical emissions produced by gasoline-fuelled engines. MMT and its corporate owners and manufacturers are also described.

In chapter 5 I review the salient parts of the regulatory history of MMT in the United States, outlining the variety of tests run and the supporting data obtained by various concerned companies and researchers, the EPA regulatory rules and administrative procedures, and contributions of the u.s. Court of Appeals. Chapter 6 provides an overview of the diverse ideas, theories, policies, and proposals about harmonization that formed an important part of the historical context in which the MMT cases were played out.

In chapter 7 I critically evaluate a report presented to the House of Commons Standing Committee on Environment and Sustainable Development regarding the proposed *MMT Act*. It was prepared by the Motor Vehicle Manufacturers Association (MVMA) and the Association of International Automobile Manufacturers of Canada (AIAMC). Chapter 8 gives an assessment of the *Interim* and *Minority* reports of the Senate Standing Committee on Energy, Environment and Natural Resources hearings on the *MMT Act*. Generally speaking, the weight of evidence in chapters 7 and 8 favours the proponents of the *MMT Act*.

Chapter 9 reviews some of the philosophical and broader socioeconomic roots and issues surrounding commercial arbitration, in preparation for the more detailed discussions of the dispute settlement procedures of the NAFTA and AIT in chapter 10.

Chapters 11 and 12 focus on the NAFTA case and chapters 13–16 deal with the AIT case. For the NAFTA case, I present the Ethyl Corporation's claims against the Government of Canada (11) and then the government's response and the tribunal's determinations (12), including my evaluations. For the AIT case, I present the Government of Alberta's claims against the Government of Canada (13), the claims of the Governments of Québec and Saskatchewan (14), the federal government's response (15), and then the panel's determinations (16), again with my evaluations.

Claims and counterclaims were sometimes made by lawyers for the various parties (corporations or governments) in the disputes, and sometimes by officeholders in the parties (e.g., members of parliament, corporate managers). In every case, I have tried to provide some sort of job title for each person making a claim, although often the context is sufficiently clear for me to say, for example, "Ethyl claimed that ..." or "Canada claimed that ..." Because many of the documents on which my story is based are not readily available to the average reader, I have provided some fairly substantial quotations. Besides enabling the reader to assess my descriptions and evaluations of issues, the quotations provide insight into the thinking and motives of the human agents driving the whole story. I have tried to keep my opinions to a bare minimum while explaining the positions of the disputants in chapters 11–15, but could not resist an occasional comment. My main critical work regarding the two cases is in chapters 7, 8, 12, and 16. Chapter 17 concludes the book.

For readers interested in a historical overview of all the activities related to the NAFTA and AIT cases, the U.S. EPA cases, and the parliamentary debates over the *MMT Act* in its two incarnations, appendix 2 has a fairly detailed chronology pieced together from many different sources. When different dates were given by different sources, I recorded the one that seemed most likely to be accurate given all the other information available.

2

Philosophical Foundations and Method

This chapter explains the broad philosophic perspective and the narrower moral perspective from which this treatise is written. It then outlines the critical methods employed in the analyses. Although I was tempted to suggest that readers who are primarily interested in public policy issues might skip this chapter, after reading the 1999 statement of the *Government of Canada Regulatory Policy*, I think that would not be a good idea. Much of the content of this chapter is directly relevant to satisfying the conditions specified in that document.

This book is written from the point of view of a pragmatist and moral consequentialist. Insofar as moral consequentialism may be regarded as a type of moral theory resulting from the application of a pragmatic approach to morality or ethics (terms that are regarded here as synonyms), consequentialist moral theory is a species of the more general philosophy of pragmatism.

The defining characteristic of any sort of pragmatic philosophy and of moral consequentialism is the emphasis on evaluating actions and beliefs on the basis of their consequences. For example, if one asked whether, all things considered, it was reasonable or morally right for the government of Canada to enact the MMT *Act*, a pragmatist or moral consequentialist would search for an answer by examining the consequences of that legislation. Unfortunately, there is no generally accepted rule book to tell pragmatists in general and moral consequentialists in particular which consequences to consider or exactly how they should be considered. So, at best, these two theories provide necessary but insufficient guides to action. As different criteria are prescribed by different people for the selection of consequences to be considered in any particular assessment, different kinds of actions and beliefs may be accepted or rejected.

Practically all pragmatists would accept the notion that an action is rational or reasonable if and only if the consequences of its performance produce benefits that are equal to or greater than its costs. It is irrational if it produces greater costs than benefits. More precisely, one might say that an action is constructive insofar as its benefits exceed its costs, barely sustainable insofar as its benefits just balance its costs, and destructive insofar as its costs exceed its benefits. Actions that are rational in the sense just described could plausibly be regarded as efficient, and I do so regard them. By extension, then, rational or reasonable beliefs are those such that action in accordance with them would be rational, reasonable, or efficient. As explained in Michalos (1978), this pragmatic approach to rational, reasonable, or efficient action applies to actions regarded as means, ends, or combinations of both, as well as to decision processes and the decisions produced by them. I first sketched an overview of the conceptual links between efficiency and morality in Michalos (1972).

The apparently plausible definitions of rational, constructive, sustainable and destructive actions hide at least two huge assumptions. First, they assume that rational or efficient action need not lead to the maximization of utility or anything else. This is important, because all explications of rationality in terms of the maximization of something must fail, since the prescription to maximize this or that cannot be satisfactorily specified, as I explained in Michalos (1973, 1978) following Simon (1945, 1957) and March and Simon (1958). I also explained why Simon's (1957) notion of "satisficing" behaviour, which produced results that were "just good enough," although not maximally beneficial for an actor, would be an equally unacceptable explication of rationality. Although Simon (1957) seems to have originally crafted the term as a descriptor of actual behaviour, he also regarded satisficing behaviour as rational. That was a mistake, since it leads to the implausible conclusion that no matter what action science or common sense tells us is strange, stupid, or horrendous, we would be obliged to regard it as rational provided that the actor regards it as satisfactory or satisfactorily suited to his or her levels of aspiration. The brief definition of rational action presented in the previous paragraph was designed to be a compromise between maximizing and satisficing. It seems to be consistent with Simon's (1978, 8) remark that "Parsimony recommends that we prefer the postulate that men are reasonable to the postulate that they are supremely rational when either one of the two assumptions will do our work of inference as well as the other."

The second huge assumption hidden in the apparently plausible definitions concerns at least nineteen questions that would have to be answered to operationalize the definitions. In particular, and briefly, to know whether one's action is rational or efficient according to the definition offered above, one would have to have acceptable answers to the following questions:

1. *Recipient population*: Who should be included as a recipient of benefits and/or burdened with costs? Aristotle (1925, 1140a) thought that "the mark of a man of practical wisdom [is] to be able to deliberate well about what is good and expedient for himself," and many today would accept that view. However, such egoism is not universal, not self-evidently required, and, from a logical point of view, only one of perhaps an infinite number of possibilities. After all, one might say that a given actor should consider only his or her own well-being, that plus a loved one, those plus friends, plus neighbours, fellow citizens, and so on until everyone affected by the actor's action is included. In the MMT cases, the parties to the dispute clearly focused on different recipient populations, with the interests of Ethyl Corporation, producers and refiners in Alberta, Saskatchewan, and Québec, and citizens of Canada, respectively, being of primary concern to the lawyers and representatives (hereafter, agents) of Ethyl, those provinces, and Canada.

2. *Spatial coordinates*: Across what amount of space should one look? From the actor's own home and backyard to the whole world? Depending on the nature of the action involved, a wider or narrower space may be appropriate. In the MMT cases, Ethyl's agents were immediately concerned with the whole of Canada, but always had one eye on what the cases could mean for the company's future performance in the United States and the rest of the world; the provincial agents had the luxury of mandates largely circumscribed by provincial boundaries; and Canada's agents had both national and international responsibilities.

3. *Temporal coordinates*: Across what length of time should one look? From now into the future? People sometimes talk about a long or short view being more or less appropriate for a given action, but such notions have to be constructed from a medium (time) that is infinitely divisible. In the MMT cases, Ethyl's agents were content to look backwards to what they regarded as twenty years of trouble-free usage of their product in Canada; the provincial agents seemed especially concerned with the immediate future and the fate of local industries; and Canada's agents were forced to take a very long view because practically every medical authority in North America warned them of the uncertainties regarding long-term, low-level exposure to manganese.

4. *Population composition*: How should the affected individuals be characterized, if at all, in terms of sex, age, education, ethnic background,

income, etc.? For some actions one or another characterization might be highly relevant while others are irrelevant. In the MMT cases, Ethyl's agents were relatively oblivious to any particular population aggregations; the provincial agents made specific claims about workers in the refining industry; and Canada's agents were particularly concerned with fairness to owners or buyers of new motor vehicles whose warranties might not cover MMT-damaged catalytic converters or on-board diagnostic systems, as well as to infants whose relatively undeveloped bodies might be unable to resist damage from exposure to emissions from vehicles using gasoline with MMT.

5. *Domains of life composition*: What domains of life should be examined? For some actions it might be appropriate to look for an impact on recipients' health, job, family life, housing, or physical environment, while for others not. In the MMT cases, Ethyl's agents focused on the legal commitments made by Canada in the NAFTA and AIT, and on motor vehicle performance, with special attention to tail-pipe emissions from vehicles with and without MMT; provincial agents were concerned with the legal commitments made in the AIT, and with the existence or nonexistence of jobs, but not with working conditions that might be affected by manganese or MMT; and Canada's agents were concerned with health, job availability, and job content, motor vehicle performance, the physical environment (especially smog management), and keeping commitments made in the NAFTA and AIT. Although all parties focused on the legal domain and even on the same documents from that domain, different parties emphasized different articles and clauses of the documents, and sometimes interpreted the same articles and clauses in different ways.

6. *Objective versus subjective indicators*: Should one ask recipients how they feel or what they think (subjective indicators) about how they or others are affected by an actor's action, or is it enough to merely observe their behaviour or other things that may be affected (objective indicators); e.g., what people feel or think about being unemployed versus unemployment rates. Supposing one grants that both kinds of indicators are important, how should one decide exactly which kind to use for which domain? In the MMT cases, Ethyl's agents never showed any interest in what consumers might have thought or felt about the use of MMT. Ethyl and the petroleum producers and refiners totally rejected the federal Minister of the Environment's challenge to allow consumers to choose gasoline with or without MMT by making both available in service stations. The provincial agents seemed to be equally indifferent to consumer preferences, and completely convinced that what was acceptable to the sellers was acceptable to the buyers. Even though the motor vehicle manufacturers and dealers, who

represented the primary link in the chain leading to consumers, were insisting that they had serious problems with and did not want MMT in gasoline, the other side remained unmoved. In stark contrast, Canada's agents bent over backwards to hear from all interested stakeholders and to examine whatever relatively objective data happened to exist.

7. *Input versus output indicators*: Should one measure only what one invests in an action, what comes of the investment, or both? Were it not true that some people explicitly recommend assessments entirely focused on results or outputs, while others are consumed with keeping inputs to a bare minimum regardless of outputs, one might think it is pointless to even raise this question. In the MMT cases, Ethyl's and provincial agents frequently mentioned that if MMT were not used to increase the octane level of gasoline, it would be increased by increased processing of increased amounts of fuel stocks, which would be counter-productive from the point of view of energy conservation. Canada's agents thought that other additives, like ethanol, provided a more reasonable strategy, with reduced inputs of petroleum fuel stocks leading to increased octane levels and reduced CO_2 emissions.

8. *Benefits and costs*: Talking about benefits and costs is another way of talking about values. Michalos (1981b) presents a systematic review of theories of value connected to a theoretical discussion of costs and benefits in Michalos (1978). Here I only ask what particular benefits and costs should be counted. In the MMT cases, the agents for all parties assumed that costs and benefits counted in dollars could not be neglected. The trouble was the variety of estimates of dollar benefits and costs to diverse recipients, and the lack of agreement on which were most accurate. The agents for Ethyl, the petroleum producers and refiners, and the provinces had several different estimates of the costs of abandoning MMT that were typically lower than the same costs calculated by the agents for Canada. Besides, the latter had some wonderful figures concerning the dollar benefits of switching from MMT to ethanol. Proponents of MMT also counted benefits in terms of estimated reduced oxides of nitrogen emissions, while opponents challenged those benefits and produced estimates of reduced hydrocarbon emissions. Proponents counted reviews of the apparently negligible health impacts of MMT as important benefits, while opponents counted the absence of good information about long-term, low-dose impacts as an indicator of the risk of significant costs.

While these specific issues related to the MMT cases provide concrete illustrations of the importance of thinking outside the monetary box usually posited for discussions of benefit-cost analyses (Howarth and

Monahan 1996), a more general argument can be made for insisting on the insufficiency of monetary accounting in the determination of rational or efficient action: Suppose a person's willingness to pay for something is regarded as a measure of its value to that person. One's willingness to pay is partly a function of one's ability to pay. Because one's ability to pay for what one needs to live (e.g., extraordinary medical treatment), and what one deserves as a matter of right or fair treatment (e.g., equal treatment in law courts) are not necessarily connected, neither are the commercial or market value of what one needs to live and what one deserves as a matter of right or fair treatment. That is, the market value of things one needs to live and things one deserves does not measure the real value of such things. Therefore, it would be a mistake to regard a person's willingness to pay for something as a measure of its real value to that person, and any comprehensive assessment of the real value of things for purposes of determining rational or efficient action must include benefits and costs beyond their commercial value. (A more detailed discussion of this argument may be found in Michalos 2003b.) Insofar as this argument is sound, it shows that even subtle analyses of non-user values (e.g., option values, bequest values, prestige values, educational values) that are based on the assumption that one's willingness to pay for something is a fair measure of its real value are defective (Frey 2001).

9. *Discount rates*: How much should one discount costs and benefits delivered some time in the future, compared to those delivered today? In the MMT cases, agents for Ethyl and the provinces acted as if what might happen to people in twenty or thirty years was simply beyond their concern, while Canada's agents had to try to take account of those eventualities in their deliberations. Nobody tried to quantify the relevant discount rates, but implicitly one side practically wrote off any benefits and costs to people in the long term while the other side tried to include them somehow.

10. *Measurement scales*: Usually the same and different things can be measured in different ways. How should one choose the best scale or measuring device? Having decided, for example, that it is important to know how recipients feel about the benefits or costs coming to them as a result of one's decision, how should one decide how to measure how they feel? How large does the number of potential recipients have to be before it is appropriate to consider sampling rather than full census measurement? Regarding results of relatively objective scientific tests, how many positive results are required to balance negative results (Michalos 1971)? These issues were not explicitly addressed in the MMT cases. Although agents for Ethyl and the provinces seemed to think that enough research had been conducted to

allow an unbiased, expert group like the Royal Society of Canada to reach a definitive conclusion on the main scientific issues, agents for Canada disagreed. As far as the latter were concerned, additional review of available evidence would produce the same controversial conclusions that previous reviews had produced.

11. *Distributions*: How should central tendencies and variations be measured in diverse fields? Are distributions always important? What rules should one follow in deciding whether simple means, medians, or modes are sufficient, or whether variations must be measured? When economists pose the false dilemma of balancing efficiency against equity or equality (Okun 1975; Hart and Dymond 2002, 165–6), they are usually talking about weighing the importance of some sort of a maximization measure against some sort of distribution measure. A critique of this mistake may be found in Michalos (1972). In the MMT cases, evaluations of the reliability and validity of models and results concerning observed emissions and estimated future emissions from motor vehicles of different designs, in different states of repair, with different test conditions and different fuel mixtures were significantly affected by measured central tendencies and variations based on relatively few cases that were not well suited to standard statistical estimation procedures.

12. *Interaction effects*: How should one measure causal interactions in any particular array of phenomena? We know, for example, that people's levels of reported satisfaction are partly determined by perceived gaps between what they have versus what some significant others have, what they want and what they think they deserve (Michalos 1985). How are such contingencies to be accommodated in one's calculations about people's reports about how they feel about things? In the MMT cases, it was impossible for anyone to predict exactly what environmental problems would be caused from any estimated levels of motor vehicle emissions of diverse chemicals and particles because different emissions create different kinds of problems depending on the atmospheric conditions receiving the emissions. How should these be accommodated when one measures the impact of emissions on air pollution or human health?

13. *Probabilities*: Since one's life is lived on the edge of largely unobserved and unobservable events, usually one's actions must be based on probabilistic assessments of those events. One must first assign some meaning to the concept of probability. Supposing one adopts a logical, empirical, or psychological interpretation of the idea of probability, a variety of distinct theories remain regarding the measurement of numerical values of probability and still more theories of the proper way to use probability

values in those cases in which one is able to calculate them (Michalos 1969). In the MMT cases, although all parties occasionally talked about "the balance of probabilities," nobody ever suggested that relevant probabilities might be rigorously quantified and applied, much less how.

14. *Confidence levels*: Since one often lacks complete certainty regarding the truth of claims, what level of confidence should one require to accept any particular claim? By convention, social scientists usually assume that it is appropriate to accept a claim as true if the chance of error is 5 per cent, but everyone knows that 5 per cent may be too small or too large depending on the particular consequences of being wrong. It may be acceptable if the issue is a matter of watering the flowers or waiting for rain, but not if the issue is a matter of airplanes dropping out of the sky. In the MMT cases, no explicit references were made to acceptable confidence levels for any particular claim, but there were several heated exchanges about the levels of certainty or uncertainty required before one may appropriately invoke the Precautionary Principle, i.e., the principle of taking action in the absence of scientific certainty regarding particular risks. In fact, no generally accepted threshold level of uncertainty regarding risks of any particular size is available to demonstrate the reasonableness of invoking the Precautionary Principle.

15. *Research procedures*: Since one's data are as good as one's search and research procedures, what adequacy criteria should be used to assess procedures? Again, depending on the issues and actions involved, there may be many or few generally accepted research procedures to be used to obtain reliable and valid information. The history of science is a history of searches for and controversies over more appropriate research methods for exploring increasingly complex issues. What is worse, there are no general adequacy criteria for making appropriate choices of methods for all kinds of problems, from all kinds of disciplines. In the MMT cases, references to U.S. Environmental Protection Agency (EPA) mandated procedures regarding emissions were made by all parties, but the EPA did not specify health-related procedures until 1999, long after the NAFTA and AIT cases were concluded.

16. *Research personnel*: How should one choose one's experts, if indeed experts are to be chosen at all? How should experts be taught, by whom and under what conditions? In the MMT cases, agents for motor vehicle and equipment manufacturers emphasized that they did not believe that the scientists for Ethyl or the petroleum producers and refiners knew enough, and certainly not as much as the manufacturers knew, about the construction and functioning of catalytic converters and on-board diagnostic

computers. From the point of view of the manufacturers, people with training and experience in their industry were the only ones with the right credentials, while those on the other side often implied that the chemistry of fuel additives was largely beyond comprehension by the vehicle and equipment manufacturers. One of the most remarkable signs of the mistrust that agents for motor vehicle manufacturers had for those on the other side was provided by a list of references in an SAE Technical Paper Series (Benson and Dana 2002) in which the researchers' sponsors were given for each article cited. For examples, the references ran "(Ethyl) Brown ...; (General Motors) Benson ...; (Ethyl) Meffert ...; (Ford) Hubbard ..." (12).

17. *Aggregation function*: How should all the diverse elements of the assessment be aggregated? Our simple formulae assume some common measure or scale of benefits and costs whose values admit of the basic arithmetical functions of addition, subtraction, multiplication, and division, but this is clearly not the case. The operationalization of our formulae for determining rationality and efficiency requires multiperson and multiattribute decision-making on a monumental scale, a scale vastly more complicated than any considered by March and Simon in all their critiques of the so-called synoptic model of decision-making. In the MMT cases, apart from the difficulties already mentioned regarding the need to make a decision "on the balance of probabilities," no attention was paid to aggregation functions. The absence of consideration of such issues was especially noticeable in the various brief "Terms of Reference" prepared by the Canadian Petroleum Producers Institute regarding a review of available evidence by an expert panel of the Royal Society of Canada.

18. *Assessment assessor*: Who should decide (audit) whether the assessment is adequate or appropriate? Should we expect to find and/or be able to train people to be experts in the assessment of the rationality or efficiency of actors and actions? Must we have ideal observers or will ordinary human beings operating with ordinary procedures be sufficient for our needs? This question was not raised in the MMT cases.

19. *Assessment criteria*: What criteria should be used to assess (audit) the adequacy of the assessment, the adequacy of the procedures used for the audit, and the adequacy of the answers to all the previous eighteen questions? This question was also not raised, but raising it reveals the threat of an infinite regress, a circular argument, or an arbitrary end to one's analysis. Suppose, for example, someone decides that for the question regarding the reasonableness of enacting the *MMT Act*, the appropriate recipient population is everyone living in Canada. An auditor should ask whether that is a reasonable selection. Then, using our synoptic model, to

answer that question the auditor would be faced with a whole new round of questions requiring answers. Alternatively, the auditor might just stipulatively define (Michalos 1969) that recipient population as appropriate, effectively certifying its appropriateness in a circular fashion, or just admit that all analyses must end somewhere and that the selection of that particular recipient population was essentially arbitrary. Clearly, none of these options is very attractive, but the very nature of foundational work means that such a point must be reached. That was at least part of what Wittgenstein was getting at near the end of his *Tractatus Logico-Philosophicus* (1961, 6.54) when he said that his reader had to "so to speak, throw away the ladder, after he has climbed up on it."

With so many questions to be answered, it is not surprising that even pragmatists who share the same general approach to determining the rationality or efficiency of particular actions or of holding particular beliefs might reach very different conclusions about the same cases. In such cases, in order to reach agreement, those who answer different questions in different ways will have to negotiate a common set of assumptions or ground rules, which may or may not be possible depending on the cases and the appraisers. Clearly, given the array of different positions held by different parties to the MMT cases, the chances were slim to nil that sufficient levels of agreement could have been reached for each side to allow that the other side was behaving reasonably or efficiently. On the contrary, each side regarded (and may still regard) the other side as self-serving and unreasonable.

Leaving aside the difficult political problems of reconciling the very different views that different people may have about the variety of questions requiring answers to operationalize our formulae for rationality and efficiency, individual decision-makers and actors are still left with immense problems. If one could solve all the problems except those regarding aggregation, one might employ a *cost-effectiveness strategy* or a *cost-benefit dominance* strategy, which are less demanding in terms of measurement issues. In Michalos (1970b) I discussed these strategies and other ways in which some of the problems could be reduced, leaving many unanswered questions. Almost thirty years later in Michalos (1997a) I admitted that I still did not have a nice solution for the problems raised in my earlier work. Alas, a nice solution is still beyond me. Lindblom (1959, 1979) was right about our limited capacity leaving us little more than room to muddle through in relatively small increments that Simon would have regarded as good enough. Nevertheless, I remain committed to the view that the synoptic model outlined above is the most appropriate model to use in explicating the ideas of rational or efficient action. All things considered, and granting our limited ability to consider all the things one would like to consider, the closer one gets to operationalizing that model, the more I am inclined to believe one's claims to rational or efficient action. Regarding its application to the MMT cases, again granting our limited capacity to consider everything one might like to consider, the synoptic model provided an excellent heuristic device to reveal the variety of fundamental disagreements among the parties to the disputes. Indeed, if one accepts that our capacity is practically always limited in matters of public policy-making, the most one can hope for from any model is that it will serve as a good heuristic device for calling our attention to important issues. Cosbey (2004, 16) recommended a "list of sustainable development constituents and determinants" serving a similar purpose. Following a brief account of the "theory of computational complexity," Simon (1978, 12–13) wrote:

> computational difficulties, and the need to approximate, are not just a minor annoying feature of our world to be dealt with by manufacturing larger computers or breeding smarter people. Complexity is deep in the nature of things, and discovering tolerable approximation procedures and heuristics that permit huge spaces to be searched very selectively lies at the heart of intelligence, whether human or artificial ... Many of the central issues of our time are questions of how we use limited information and limited computational capacity to deal with enormous problems whose shape we barely grasp ... When problems become interrelated, as energy and pollution problems have become, there is the constant danger that attention directed to a single facet of the web will spawn solutions that disregard vital consequences for the other facets.

One of the most important benefits of accepting the pragmatic approach to rational or efficient action as sketched above is the ease with which one may move from a model of such action to a model of morally good action from a consequentialist point of view. Historically, moral consequentialism may be traced back fairly directly to Jeremy Bentham's ideas about a "felicific calculus" that would allow decision makers to calculate the net pleasure or pain connected to every action for everyone affected by that action, with public policy choices made to get the greatest net pleasure or least net pain for the greatest number of people (Bentham 1789). Since pleasure and pain are usually relatively transient experiences, something more durable would have better suited Bentham's purposes. If happiness is regarded as a relatively long-lasting positive experience and/or attitude (Tatarkiewicz

1976; Veenhoven 1984), then that would distinguish it from transient plea-
surable mood states and would justify moving from Bentham's greatest
pleasure principle to Mill's greatest happiness for the greatest number principle (Mill 1861).

For economists, utility theory is the apparent heir of Bentham and Mill
(Mitchell 1918). Utility theory is formally elegant and has been an enor-
mously fruitful source of research programs in individual and group
decision-making related to commercial markets, social and political relations, bargaining, conflict resolution, gaming, and scarce resource allocation in practically all areas. Unfortunately, utility theory (as many, if not
most, other theories) is much better on paper and in classroom exercises
than it is in practice, especially in public policy-making. What is worse,
utility theory begins with revealed preferences, which are the mere tips of
socially, psychologically, and pragmatically constructed icebergs of more or
less coherent systems of knowledge, opinions, attitudes, desires, needs, and
values (Michalos 2003a). The main reason for constructing multiple discrepancies theory (Michalos 1985) was to provide an empirically supported theoretical foundation for all those subjects resting on the rather
shallow foundation of utility theory. However, for present purposes, the
defects of utility theory as a psycho-social theory of perceived well-being
are not its biggest problem. Its biggest problem is that it merely provides
information about the subjective states of people, although we know that
people's objectively measurable circumstances are also important features
of the quality of their lives. Because, morally speaking, one ought to be as
concerned about the relatively objective circumstances of people's lives as
with how people feel about their lives and circumstances, the basic principle of one's moral consequentialism ought to include more than the latter.
For reasons reviewed earlier in this chapter, one's basic principle ought to
avoid any maximization requirements.

In the light of these considerations, I propose the following basic principle for my version of moral consequentialism. *One ought to try to act
such that one's actions tend to improve the quality of life of all those
affected by one's actions.* It should be apparent that the operationalization
of this principle suffers from the very same problems troubling the
operationalization of our formulae for rational or efficient action. As the
basic principle of a moral theory it has its own array of problems (Michalos
2001). However, one of the nineteen questions raised about those formulae
admits of a straightforward and, I think, uncontroversial answer. The
recipient population required for any acceptable operationalization of our
basic moral principle must be *all those affected* by an actor's actions. Inso-

far as one's actions have an impact on anyone, one is morally obliged to take that impact into consideration when assessing the moral goodness or evil of one's actions. To deny that is to allow actors to simply disregard the impact that their actions might have on other people, effectively treating such people as morally irrelevant, unworthy of moral consideration or, as the philosopher Immanuel Kant (1788, 1797) might have said, as mere means rather than as ends in themselves.

As formulated here, my basic moral principle is intended to reflect Aristotle's insight that every human action is characterizable in terms of an intention or motive, some physical behaviour or content, and some consequences. Because each of the three aspects of an action might tend to improve or destroy the quality of life, every action implies at least eight possible states of affairs. In Michalos (1992) some complications resulting from the eight different states of affairs were examined in detail. Here it is enough to note that my basic moral principle, as articulated, does not require the maximization of anything and it does not require that one's efforts produce success. It does require something like a good faith effort or, perhaps, due diligence in the pursuit of the specified task. It does not require that the quality of every affected person's life should be improved, much less equally improved. Coase (1960, 35) was certainly right when he wrote that "nothing could be more 'anti-social' than to oppose any action which causes any harm to anyone." An action designed to improve the quality of life of everyone affected by it might in fact make some people worse off and others better off, but it would still be consistent with our basic principle. While I would not go as far as Kant went in insisting that the only purely good thing from a moral point of view is a good will (intention, motive), it does seem fair to weigh actors' intentions at least as heavily as their actual accomplishments when one is making a moral appraisal of their actions. It seems fair because normally one has more control of one's intentions or motives than one has of the consequences of one's actions.

I use the phrase "quality of life" to capture the relatively objective circumstances of people's lives as well as people's feelings and beliefs about their lives. When people use the phrase *quality of life*, they sometimes intend to contrast it with quantities or numbers of something. There are, then, two quite different sorts of things that one might want to refer to when using this phrase. First, one might want to refer to sorts of things rather than to mere numbers of things. For example, one might want to know not merely how many people were exposed to harmful smog last year and for how long, but also what sorts of people they were, male or female, young or old, rich or poor, and so on. When the term *quality* in the phrase *quality of life* is used in this sense, one may say that it and the phrase in which it occurs is intended to be primarily *descriptive*. Second, however, one might want to refer to the value or worth of things by using the term *quality* in the phrase *quality of life*. For example, in the MMT cases decision-makers had to think about trade-offs between the value of jobs and incomes of workers in the refining industry and the value of the health of infants and older people who might be exposed to airborne manganese particles. Presumably the exchanges would involve monetary and some other values. When the term *quality* in the phrase *quality of life* is used in this sense, one may say that it and the phrase in which it occurs is intended to be primarily *evaluative*.

Both senses of the phrase are important. It is important to be able to describe human existence in a fairly reliable and valid fashion, and it is important to be able to evaluate human existence in the same way. The philosopher Plato is still celebrated for raising the evaluative question at least 2,300 years ago when he asked: What is a good life for an individual person and what is a good society? But it is often forgotten that he also raised the descriptive question: What is the nature of an individual's or a society's life?

Pragmatism in general and moral consequentialism in particular seem to me to be tailor-made for public-policy making. The main difference between the analyses and obligations of a moral consequentialist and those of a maker of public policy lies in the specification of appropriate recipient populations. The mandate of a public policy-maker may reach only as far as the village boundary, or the city limits, or the county, province, or country. In general, the gap between what is morally required on consequentialist grounds and what is required on the grounds of one's particular mandate or role decreases as the size of one's mandated recipient population increases. If there were a rigorous way to measure the size of such gaps, it might be used as a measure of at least one aspect of some moral dilemmas.

If a public policy-maker were lucky, all of his or her official actions would affect only those included within the boundaries of his or her official mandate. So, his or her official and moral obligations would be coextensive, at least regarding whose interests had to be considered. Obviously, most policy-makers are not so lucky, and sometimes choices must be made between serving the common interest or public good as officially mandated and serving the human community as mandated by the fundamental principle of moral consequentialism.

The phrase "public good" is used in the title of this book because it has a fairly precise and narrow sense in economic terms and a fairly imprecise and broad sense in political terms, and both senses capture something important for our purposes. Regarding the narrow sense, there is a substantial body of literature on the theory of public goods. Such goods are supposed to be distinguishable from private goods on the basis of either of two characteristics, namely, jointness and nonexclusiveness (Olson 1965). To say that a good is characterized by *jointness* is roughly to say that using it does not imply using it up. To say that a good is characterized by *nonexclusiveness* is roughly to say that nonpurchasers cannot be excluded from using it. Information is an example of a public good displaying the character of jointness, and clean air is an example of a public good displaying nonexclusiveness. The fundamental problem concerning the provision of public goods is often referred to as the *free-rider problem*. Because, without taking special measures, no one in a society can be excluded from public goods displaying nonexclusiveness, (hypothetically self-serving) citizens may be tempted to try to pass the costs of such goods on to everyone else. So, for example, because all Canadians will enjoy the benefits of good government whether or not any particular Canadian pays the price of becoming well-informed about political issues and candidates, and takes the time to vote, this or that particular citizen might take a free ride on the rest of us, assuming that enough of the rest of us will pay the price to ensure the desired benefits are obtained. Solutions to the free-rider problem may take the form of coercion (e.g., forcing people to pay taxes for pollution abatement) or rational and/or moral suasion.

Regarding the broader sense of "public good," in a very useful review Pal and Maxwell (2004, 3) wrote:

Some sort of equivalent to the notion of the "public interest" is as old as political philosophy itself. For example, Aristotle referred to the idea of the "common interest"; Aquinas to the "common good"; Locke to the "public good of the people"; Hume to the "public good"; Madison to the "public", "common" or "general good"; Rousseau to the "common good" ... In all these cases, the public interest or common good was equated in some fashion to morality, justice and the best ends of the state or of political society. Even someone as resolutely devoted to individual liberty as John Stuart Mill was prepared to concede the existence of common welfare or general or societal interest. Indeed, so ubiquitous is the notion of a public or common interest, that is has spawned a range of synonyms which seek to capture the same rough idea that there is a common good that embraces an entire community and that is distinct from individual, sectional, or regional interests:

"common vision", "shared vision", "shared purpose", "common goals", "social contract", "core values", "general welfare". In one sense the concept of a public interest is indispensable to a modern democracy, which presumes that public policy is to be undertaken in the interests of the entire community (or at least a substantial majority), not one section of that community.

Nevertheless, despite its importance and apparent centrality to our thinking about public policy, the concept of the public interest is notoriously slippery. Virtually every treatment in the literature – even those that are squarely supportive of the idea – begins with the caveat that the public interest is susceptible to many different interpretations and approaches ... [and] they have very different consequences for how one perceives the policy process and appropriate outcomes of that process.

Pal and Maxwell's review of "interpretations and approaches" led them to propose a Public Interest Accountability Framework that could be used by "all regulatory authorities" as a heuristic device for raising and answering questions central to the determination of the public interest as they conceptualize it. The main point of introducing the long quotation from those authors was to illustrate the broader sense of "public good" that is necessarily implied by that phrase. As I use the phrase, the public good that is usually referred to by the various roughly equivalent phrases listed above typically designates a subset of what I described as the quality of life of all those affected by anyone's action. Thus, insofar as actions undertaken in the interest of trade become barriers to the achievement of the public good for any community, they are also barriers to the improvement of the quality of life of all those affected. Therefore, such actions would be morally wrong and ought to be condemned and resisted (cf. Swenarchuk 1998, 4).

Howarth and Monahan (1996) reject economic cost-benefit analysis in favour of a "sustainability criterion" for making climate policy on the grounds that the operationalization problems can be adequately solved for the latter approach but not for the former. Briefly:

The sustainability criterion may be taken to imply that it is morally wrong to impose catastrophic risks on members of unborn generations if reducing those risks would not significantly diminish the quality of life of existing persons. Under this interpretation, a case can be established for significant greenhouse gas emissions abatement given current knowledge of mitigation costs and the risks of climate change. (188)

While their analysis of the "steep information requirements" of merely *economic* cost-benefit analysis is certainly accurate and their search for a less demanding model is worthwhile, I think the information requirements of the sustainability criterion would be at least as demanding as those of the other model if a thorough review of those requirements were made. Like the Public Interest Accountability Framework, the sustainability criterion could serve a useful purpose as a heuristic device, but it would not provide as much guidance as the synoptic model outlined above.

Having sketched the philosophical foundations of this work, I now turn to methods. Traditionally, the structure of a philosophical treatise was designed along the following lines. One would begin by stating some thesis to be proved. In our case, for example, the thesis to be proved might be the proposition that, all things considered, it was reasonable for the government of Canada to enact the *MMT Act*. Then one would list every possible argument against one's thesis and show that each argument was defective for one reason or another. Following this attempt to give the other side its due, one would list every possible argument for believing one's thesis to be true. Then one would review every possible criticism of these supporting reasons and show that all the possible criticisms are also defective. This is the structure of a kind of narrow benefit-cost analysis, in contrast to the broad or synoptic benefit-cost analysis described earlier. It is a pragmatic defence of one's thesis insofar as it involves the examination of the consequences of accepting the thesis. If one could successfully do everything called for in it, then one certainly would establish one's thesis according to the specifications of the traditional model. In the following chapters dealing with the details of arguments for and against the *MMT Act*, it will be apparent that my analyses are guided by aspects of both the narrow and the broad models of pragmatic assessment.

Over many years, I have shed a lot of ink on variously defined concepts of the "weight of evidence" and the "balance of probabilities" (e.g., Michalos 1971, 1973, 1978, 1980b, 1992), and these relatively troublesome notions will appear later in our story. One fairly easy way to understand and link them was suggested by Reichenbach (1949) in discussions of the assessment of scientific theories. As he explained it, one can think of a theory as an instrument for generating predictions, some of which will be successful and others not. After deriving and testing several predictions from a theory, it is possible to interpret the percentage of successful predictions as the probability of the theory being true. In other words, the ratio of successful to total predictions made from a theory may be used as a measure of the theory's empirical support, a measure that Reichenbach called the *weight of evidence* for the theory. Quite generally, then, one may apply this relatively simple notion to the assessment of arguments for and against any theory, hypothesis, hunch, belief, or claim. In our case, the notion will be applied to arguments for and against the *MMT Act*. Rather than undertaking the very onerous task of trying to distinguish the relative weight of each argument, I will simply assess each one as sound or unsound, or probably so. Blunt as this instrument may sound, it will become obvious that it would be perilous to try to do more with the material available to us.

Generally speaking, the difference between having beliefs that are merely opinions and beliefs that may justifiably be regarded as knowledge is that the latter sort of beliefs must be not only true but accepted for good reasons. Good reasons may be regarded as good arguments. A good argument, which logicians call a *sound* argument, must satisfy three conditions. It must have (i) a valid logical form or structure; (ii) all true premises; and (iii) no methodological flaws. Any argument failing to satisfy one or more of these conditions is a bad or *unsound* argument. Regarding the first condition, because most of the arguments involving issues of public policy require some assessment of what is probably the case or what probably happened or probably will happen, usually the relevant valid logical form is nondemonstrative (inductive) rather than demonstrative (deductive) (Michalos 1969). The distinguishing feature of good nondemonstrative arguments is that their conclusions are at best more or less acceptable given their premises, while the conclusions of good demonstrative arguments are certainly true given their premises. Regarding the second condition, because one is often uncertain of the truth of some premises, one often simply assumes their truth and proceeds to examine the argument from the point of view of the third condition, or one grants that the uncertain premises are probably true or more or less acceptable. If one assumes that the premises are at best more or less acceptable, then the argument as a whole can be at best a good nondemonstrative argument. Finally, regarding the third condition, there are easily several dozen ways in which an argument may suffer from a methodological flaw (Michalos 1970a). For examples, methodological flaws may take the form of defective definitions of key terms (e.g., definitions that are ambiguous, vague, too broad, too narrow, circular or question-begging, self-contradictory, empirically false, operationally meaningless), question-begging premises, oversimplified premises, special pleading, appeals to pseudo or even imaginary authorities, irrelevant appeals (e.g., attacking motives or people instead of propositions, attacking arguments of straw), constructing false dilemmas, faulty analogies, citing misleading percentages or totals, and attributing false causes.

These are the most general philosophical and methodological foundations upon which this treatise is erected. Although there is no logically tidy progression from these foundations to the next level of political and economic foundations, from those to the NAFTA and AIT documents, and so on through the detailed accounts of motor vehicle mechanics, EPA, NAFTA, and AIT cases, there is at least an attempt to move from the most general to the most specific issues across the body of the book. Characteristically, one's most general philosophical and methodological claims cannot be as well supported as the lower level claims following from them. All analyses must end somewhere, and mine end with some pretty primitive notions about rationality and morality.

3

Globalization, Democracy, and Federalism

This chapter outlines some logical relationships among concepts of globalization, democracy, and federalism, and describes some of the empirical consequences of two agents and products of globalization, the NAFTA and the Canada-U.S. Free Trade Agreement (CUSTA), on Canada, the United States, and Mexico. The nature of Canada's particular brand of federalism is also sketched, with special emphasis on the way in which legal authority and responsibility for trade and environmental policy and regulation have evolved since confederation.

Globalization may be described as an interactive mixture of economic, political, and cultural phenomena, with causal arrows proceeding in different directions according to different analysts (Newman 2000). From the point of view of neo-classical economists, the process of globalization is the natural and predictable product of the growth of capitalism, caused by transnational corporations expanding their trade, investment, and production systems across many countries, usually supported by binational and international treaties (Griffin and Khan 1992; Waters 1995). As trade, investment, and production systems expand, supposedly so do employment, real wealth, and productivity, leading to improvements in the quality of people's lives. Since barriers to trade are apparently barriers to such expansion, they should be eliminated. Hence, proponents of the neo-classical model are strong advocates of wide-open, global markets. "Though the speed and sequencing of liberalization will have to be determined by each country in the light of its particular circumstances," an OECD (1997, 18) document asserts, "policies should be geared to the ultimate objective of full integration into the global financial system."

Some theorists regard the vision of a wide-open global market as inherently incoherent and dysfunctional. For example, Gill (1996, 217–18) wrote:

the neoliberal vision of a globalized market utopia (associated with the ideology of business civilization) is both theoretically and in practice unachievable – and not only because certain types of business enterprise (e.g., large-scale, monopolistic or oligopolistic firms) seek systematically to restrict market competition rather than to promote it. The pure commodification of society that this type of globalization implies is fundamentally contradictory; it implies the atomization and perhaps annihilation of the social and cultural basis upon which the entire edifice of market institutions stands and depends upon for its existence.

Others take a more modest line, only asserting that the theoretical and empirical support for the neo-classical model is relatively thin. For example, Rodrik (1999) summarized his excellent review of the performance of the model as follows:

there is no convincing evidence that openness, in the sense of low barriers to trade and capital flows, systematically produces these consequences. In practice, the links between openness and economic growth tend to be weak, and to be contingent on the presence of complementary policies and institutions ... [especially] institutions of conflict management – legally guaranteed civil liberties and political freedoms, social partnerships, and social insurance ... In the absence of these complements to a strategy of external liberalization, openness will not yield much. At worst, it will cause instability, widening inequalities, and social conflict ... Neither history nor recent evidence provides support for a straightforward association between the level of trade barriers and long-term growth. (137–43; Helliwell 2002, 33 and Cosbey 2004, 48, agree)

Regarding export-led growth, Rodrik (1999) claimed:

In general, there is little reason to believe that one dollar of exports will contribute to an economy more than a dollar of any other kind of activity, nor to believe that one dollar of DFI [Direct Foreign Investment] will contribute more than a dollar of any other kind of investment ... the evidence that exports and DFI per se generate economic growth, or that they produce significant positive spillovers, is scanty. Furthermore, the belief that exports can increase the overall level of employment in an economy over the longer term is a mercantilist fallacy, which, taken to its logical conclusion, leads to a preference for trade surpluses ... The evidence is clear: although countries that grow fast tend to experience rising export-GDP ratios, the reverse is not true in general ... What seems to happen is that efficient producers are more likely to enter export markets ... there is no evidence that firms with a continuous export record experience an increasing productivity advantage over firms that never export. (24–36)

Five years before Rodrik published the preceding remarks, Albo (1994, 170) described the counter-productive nature of the "preference for trade surpluses": "Each country reduces domestic demand and adopts an export-oriented strategy of dumping its surplus production, for which there are fewer consumers in its national economy given the decrease in workers' living standards and productivity gains all going to the capitalists, in the world market. This has created a global demand crisis and the growth of surplus capacity across the business cycle."

Criticizing the export-led growth strategy from the point of view of its ecological unsustainability, Rees (1994, 29, 42–3) wrote:

Mainstream economic theory assumes a world "in which carrying capacity is infinitely expandable." Inter-regional trade is said to relieve local constraints on growth, eliminating concerns about ecological carrying capacity. By contrast, I argue that any perceived increase in carrying capacity is illusion ... The free exchange of ecological goods and services allows the population of any given region to grow beyond its local carrying capacity unknowingly and with apparent impunity ... At the same time, the expanding network of trade-dependent regions may be drawing down "surplus" natural capital stocks everywhere ... Trade, therefore, only appears to increase carrying capacity. In fact, by encouraging all regions to exceed local limits, by reducing the perceived risk attached to local natural capital depletion, and by simultaneously exposing local surpluses to global demand, uncontrolled trade accelerates natural capital depletion, reducing carrying capacity and increasing the risk to everyone.

Since binational and international treaties can only be negotiated among nations or countries, and are often negotiated with the aim of increasing trade, some analysts see globalization as primarily the product of political processes, usually supported by those whose economic interests are likely to be improved with increases in international trade (Polanyi 1957). As fundamental economic and political changes occur within and across particular cultures, the latter may be expected to be complementary and hospitable to some changes, contradictory and hostile to others, and probably neutral to still others.

McBride (2001) claimed that Canada's three national policies of the governments of John A. Macdonald (1878–91), William Lyon Mackenzie King (1935–48) and Pierre Elliott Trudeau (1968–79) "all sought to facilitate economic development in the context of a relatively trade-dependent economy integrated into world markets" (46), but the claim was equally true of the governments of Brian Mulroney (1984–93) and Jean Chrétien (1993–2004), as revealed in their notorious trade deals. Insofar as Canada's "embrace of globalization ... was not structurally determined" and "can be explained quite satisfactorily by reference to domestic political factors, reinforced as they were by international pressures," it follows "that Canada, like other states, retains a distinct capacity to manage its continuing encounter with globalization" (McBride 2001, 18). A similar line is taken by Cox (1987, 253) and Clarkson (2002a, 12–13).

Granting these governmental commitments to policies of export-led economic growth, it may still be allowed that the commitments were the product of pressures from certain Canadian businesspeople demanding government support for their strategies of market expansion through increased international trade. Following Merrett (1996), McBride (2001, 71) asserted: "Business in Canada wanted a free-trade agreement before Ottawa launched the free-trade initiative. Indeed, a delegation from the BCNI [Business Council on National Issues (Michalos 1997)] broached the free-trade idea with U.S. officials as early as 1982 and began to promote the idea in Canada publicly from 1983 ... the BCNI had a major impact, working on its own and through the government in maintaining a 'united front' in the business community in support of the deal."

For members of the BCNI a free-trade agreement with the United States promised the benefits of a defensive weapon against U.S. protectionism, the opportunity to realize additional economies of scale as their markets expanded to the relatively huge population south of the border, the opportunity to discipline labour with threats of capital flight, practically irreversible neo-liberal policy changes favouring deregulation, privatization of some state enterprises and commercialization of others, rejection of industrial development strategies outside the neo-liberal paradigm and severe constraints on governments' capacity to extract concessions from investors in the interests of any sort of industrial and/or regional development strategy (Royal Commission on the Economic Union and Development Prospects for Canada 1985; Doern and Tomlin 1992; Clarkson 2002a).

According to Robinson (2003, 197), the most important benefit of the NAFTA and other international trade agreements for their proponents is "the creation of new international private property rights, backed by trade sanctions." All these apparent benefits to trade agreement proponents such as the members of the BCNI seemed to be costs to Canadians who suffered from reduced employment insurance and reduced state expenditures on health, education, and welfare, especially women, children, and members of rural and remote communities (McBride 2001, 82–100).

Regarding the role of the NAFTA in particular in locking in neo-liberal policy changes, in an often-cited primer on this deal, one of Ethyl's lawyers wrote: "The NAFTA represents the supremacy of a classical liberal conception of the state with its imposition of significant restraints upon the role of government. All international trade agreements entail some self-imposed limitation on government authority, for example governments regularly agree not to increase their tariff rates. However, the NAFTA appears to approach an extreme. It does this by the extensiveness of its obligations which attempt to lock-in one perspective of governmental role for all successive North American governments" (Appleton 1994, 207).

In McBride's view, "the entire neo-liberal globalization project" suffers from a "legitimacy deficit." He believes, following Max Weber, that:

> legitimacy in modern societies is derived principally from the operation of legal-rational rules and procedures. Decisions and rules are viewed as legitimate, and are therefore obeyed and accepted, based on the nature of the procedures used in making them. To confer legitimacy the procedures must be seen as binding on both rulers and ruled and as carrying no necessary implications in terms of outcomes. The international organizations responsible for implementing neo-liberal globalization lack legitimacy in this sense. They are remote, secretive and technocratic. Outcomes are written into the text of the agreements they administer. Their membership consists of national states that are only presumed to be speaking for their societies. The extension of an aura of democratic control from the national level to the international level is problematic.
>
> Indeed, the contents of the agreements that international organizations administer increasingly diminish national states' autonomy. This exposes the emptiness of democratic control – more and more aspects of decision-making are excluded from the purview of national (and democratic) politics. This leaves the concepts of state and, behind it, popular sovereignty, increasingly threadbare. Sovereignty, for many

states, seems confined to the formal legal right to withdraw from the international economic agreements that have diminished state (and democratic) capacity. (McBride 2001, 150–1)

While these remarks are focused on international organizations and trade deals, they can be usefully applied to the AIT as well. Here one discovers that the troublesome "remote, secretive and technocratic" features of the trade deals are the product of the distance between the procedures and priorities acceded to by national states in trade deals and the procedures and priorities preferred by most people living in those states, not of the distance between national states and their international masters. The "emptiness of democratic control" that was constructed by duly elected representatives of the people of Canada was never explicitly demanded by those people. The "increasingly threadbare" popular sovereignty that Canadians have in the presence of the AIT is confined to whatever is acceptable to five-membered panels of unelected elites whose decisions will be constrained by a set of rules biased in favour of trade. No wonder that the rules are not granted legitimacy. It would be more remarkable and distressing if such rules were met with widespread and joyous compliance.

"The provision that regulations should not be more trade-restrictive than necessary opens the door to a variety of challenges to national systems of regulations. The text privileges trade above other legitimate policy goals. For example, the least trade-restrictive health or environmental regulations may not be the best regulations as viewed from health or environmental value systems" (McBride 2001, 116).

McBride (2001, 156) recommends deals whose priorities are much broader in contrast to trade deals that privilege trade above everything else. Instead of the insecurity-generating neo-liberal paradigm of free trade, he recommends a "human security paradigm":

At its core, human security implies that the well-being of people –
expressed through employment, social welfare, political democracy,
health, culture and education – should be the prime objective of political life ... Since the logic of neo-liberal globalization is to provide
security and risk-avoidance – for investors only – one major difference
between neo-liberalism and an alternative paradigm centres around
"who" will be secure and protected from risk.

The promise of security and greater equality was at the core of the
full-employment and welfare state policies of the postwar era. No
evidence existed that significant numbers of people rejected those goals

... They are certainly goals that cannot be met through the free market, which by its very nature must produce uneven, irregular results and thus insecurity and greater inequality. This means in turn that markets will have to be regulated and controlled to produce security/ equality outcomes rather than efficiency/flexibility outcomes. Strong government at the nation-state level is an absolute essential if such regulatory measures are to be set in place. (McBride 2001, 159–60)

Similarly, Panitch (1996, 109) claimed that "The first requirement of a strategy to counter globalization must be to seek the transformation of the material and ideological capacities of states so that they can serve to realize popular, egalitarian, and democratic goals and purposes."

The "human security paradigm" is similar to that in the *Alternatives for the Americas* (Alliance for Responsible Trade et al. 1999), and its emphasis on broad-based democratic decision-making with a broad array of legitimate priorities is consistent with the pragmatic moral consequentialist model recommended here. Insofar as the efficiency and flexibility posited by neo-liberals is constrained by their insistence on policies that are the least trade restrictive and by their failure to include everyone affected by those policies in their preferred recipient population, their notion of "efficiency" should always be put in scare quotes. Their notion is certainly not efficient for most people and not acceptable from a moral point of view.

To mark the NAFTA's tenth anniversary, a group of researchers from the three parties to the deal, calling themselves the Hemispheric Social Alliance's Monitoring and Alternatives Committee, evaluated its overall impact on people in Canada, Mexico, and the United States (Hansen-Kuhn and Hellinger 2003). Their general conclusion was:

the impact of NAFTA on most of the people in all three countries has been devastating. The agreement has destroyed more jobs than it has created, depressed wages, worsened poverty and inequality, eroded social programs, undermined democracy, enfeebled governments, and greatly increased the rights and powers of corporations, investors, and property holders.

NAFTA has also been used to weaken Canada's sovereignty and promote its economic assimilation by the United States. It has led to greater pressure on Canada and Mexico to conform to U.S. foreign policy objectives. Most alarmingly, the three governments are bent on extending this failed model to other countries in Central and South

America and the Caribbean in the proposed Free Trade of the Americas (FTAA). (Hansen-Kuhn and Hellinger 2003, 1)

A group at the Carnegie Endowment for International Peace undertook a similar exercise and released its report in the same year (Audley, Papademetriou, Polaski and Vaughan 2003). Consistent with our purposes and language, the authors wrote that they "set out to determine how the quality of life in North America, particularly in Mexico, has fared as a result of trade liberalization in North America" (5). Although they paid relatively more attention to Mexico than to Canada and the United States, their general conclusion was:

> At ten years, the long-term effects of NAFTA on employment, wages, and incomes in the countries of North America cannot yet be judged. However, short- and medium-term impacts can now be assessed on the basis of substantial, accumulating data.
>
> The most important result of the NAFTA experience, and the most surprising when compared with predictions of political advocates and opponents, is that the trade agreement has produced disappointingly small net gains in employment in the countries of North America ... the strong productivity growth in the United States and somewhat weaker growth in Mexico and Canada may have had the unwelcome side effect of reducing the pace of job creation in the three countries, as workers produced more and fewer jobs were created ... during the NAFTA period, productivity growth has not translated into wage growth, as it did in earlier periods in Mexico. Mexican wages are also diverging from, rather than converging toward, U.S. wages, as trade theory would suggest ... In all three countries, the evolution of wages and household incomes since NAFTA took effect has been toward greater inequality, with most gains going to the upper 20 percent of households and higher-skilled workers. (Polaski 2003, 31–4)

Below I provide some details of the *primarily economic* findings from both reports, including statistics for some years prior to the CUSTA (1989) and NAFTA (1994). I emphasize the phrase "primarily economic" because all economic statistics have social and political implications, which are ignored in the summarized material below but are discussed in the sources cited and briefly here later in this chapter. Not surprisingly, given the slightly different focus of each report and the absence of a specific set of guidelines to ensure that each report covered the same material, a wide variety of statistics were produced and different researchers made different judgments about the overall meaning of the numbers. Causal relations among the numbers are seldom examined in these reports and they would be difficult to unravel. For example, considering the creation and elimination of jobs, one must first disentangle jobs created or eliminated specifically by international trade (exports and imports), and then, within the class of trade-related changes, one must decide which are directly related to the NAFTA versus other trade deals or other trade in general, which result primarily from monetary exchange rate changes (in particular, devaluations in the peso and Canadian dollar), and which result from technological changes, to mention only a few important variables. A fine review of additional variables may be found in Clarkson (2002a, 188–202).

CANADA

1 From 1989 to 2002:
   - Exports from Canada to the USA rose by 221%, and imports rose by 162%.
   - The Gross Domestic Product (GDP) per capita average annual growth rate was 1.9% in the eight years prior to CUFTA, and 1.6% in the 1989–2002 period.
   - Average real wages grew at an annual rate of 0.4%.
2 From 1993 to 2002:
   - The total hourly output for the manufacturing sector increased by 14.5%.
   - The total labour costs decreased by 13%.
3 From 1985 to 2002:
   - There were 6,437 takeovers of Canadian by American corporations, out of a total of 10,052 takeovers.
   - 96.6% of the new foreign direct investment (FDI) in Canada was for takeovers and 3.4% for the creation of new businesses.
4 The average hourly labour productivity rate was 1.6% in the 1981–88 period, 0.6% in 1989–93, and 2.1% in 1994–2002.
5 The Canadian manufacturing productivity level was 83% of the U.S. level in 1988 and 65% in 2000.
6 In 1989 U.S. FDI accounted for 12% of the Canadian GDP, compared to 20% in 2001.
7 Between 30% and 40% of Canadian investment abroad is "foreign investment by foreign corporations located in Canada."

8 Personal disposable income increased on average 3% per year in 1973–81, 1.1% in 1981–89, and decreased on average 0.3% in 1989–99.

9 In the 1984–99 period, the share of the nation's total wealth owned by the poorest 40% of Canadians dropped from 1.8% to 1.1%, while the share owned by the richest 10% rose from 51.8% to 55.7%.

10 Since 1989, Canada's trade inside the NAFTA area has increased from 30% to 60% of GDP.

11 About 1% of Canada's exports go to and 3.6% of its imports come from Mexico.

12 From 1989 to 2001:
   • the share of unemployed workers getting unemployment insurance benefits dropped from 87% to 36%.
   • the U.S. share of Canadian merchandise exports rose from 73% to 85%.
   • the U.S. share of Canadian merchandise imports rose from 70% to 73%.
   • U.S. FDI in Canada increased from 12% to 20% of Canadian GDP.
   • Canadian FDI in the U.S. increased from 10% to 18% of Canadian GDP.

13 In the 1989–2001 period, total Canadian farm debt rose from c$22.5 billion to $44.2 billion.

14 In 1992 total non-defence program spending by all levels of government in Canada was 15.2% higher than that in the U.S., compared to 5.7% in 2001.

MEXICO

1 From 1993–2002:
   • Total exports from Mexico to the rest of the world grew by 300%, from U.S.$51.9 million to U.S.$160.7 million.
   • Manufactured goods represented 87.4% and petroleum represented 9% of total exports.
   • Mexico imported 8.8 million metric tons of grains and oilseeds at the beginning of the period, compared to 20 million metric tons at the end.
   • The share of employment in the agricultural sector dropped from 25.7% at the beginning to 17.3% at the end.

- About 7.8 million hectares of forest were cleared in Mexico, largely as a result of demands for more farm land and fuel for subsistence farmers.

2 From 1994 to 2002:
- Mexico accumulated a trade deficit with the rest of the world of U.S.$43.7 billion and a current account deficit of U.S.$121.4 billion.
- Mexico had a U.S.$3.7 billion trade deficit with Canada, compared to a surplus of U.S.$667 million in the nine years prior to NAFTA.
- Maquiladora manufacturers bought about 3% of their component inputs within Mexico.
- Direct foreign investment in Mexico increased from an annual average of U.S.$3.9 billion to U.S.$13.4 billion.
- The average annual GDP per capita growth was 0.96%.
- There was a net job loss of 9.4%.
- Productivity in non-maquiladora manufacturing increased by 53.6%, while total labour costs fell by 36%.
- Prices for a basic basket of food increased 257%, while prices paid to agricultural producers increased 185%.
- Agricultural employment dropped from 8.1 million at the beginning of the period to 6.8 million at the end.
- Wages for manufacturing workers in maquiladora and non-maquiladora firms were higher at the beginning than at the end of the period.
- The share of the national income going to the top 10% of earners increased while that going to the other 90% decreased or stayed the same.
- Mexican exports to the U.S. increased from U.S.$2.5 billion to U.S.$5.1 billion, while U.S. exports to Mexico increased nearly four-fold to U.S.$6.8 billion.

3 From 1993 to 2001, hourly compensation costs of production workers in manufacturing in Mexico decreased from 14.5% to 11.5% of those in the U.S.

4 From 1994 to 2003:
- The number of jobs in non-maquiladora manufacturing dropped from 1.4 million at the beginning of the period to 1.3 million at the end.
- There was a net increase of 550,000 in the number of jobs in maquiladora manufacturing.

5 In 1996, the inputs used by non-maquiladora manufacturers contained 37% national content, compared to 91% in 1983.

6 On average, farmers in the United States get about U.S.$120 of government assistance per hectare, compared to U.S.$45 for Mexican farmers.

7 On average, the productivity of an agricultural worker in the United States is 18 times greater than such a worker in Mexico.

8 In 2002, 89% of Mexican exports went to the United States and 1.7% went to Canada, while 63% of Mexican imports came from the United States and 4.2% came from Canada.

9 In the 1992 to 2002 period, U.S. exports to Mexico of wheat, maize, fresh vegetables and fruit increased 182%, 240%, 80%, and 90%, respectively.

10 The 182% increase in wheat exports to Mexico represented about a 1% increase in U.S. wheat production.

UNITED STATES OF AMERICA

1 From 1990 to 2000:
   • On average, labour productivity increased by 25% while real wage growth increased by 8%.
   • The richest 5% of Americans increased their share of total U.S. family income by 3%, while the poorest 20% lost about 4% of their share.
   • Income inequality increased by 3.5%.

2 In 1993, the United States had a trade surplus with Mexico of U.S.$1.7 billion, compared to a deficit of U.S.$25 billion in 2000.

3 In 1993, the U.S. had a trade deficit with Canada of U.S.$10.8 billion, which increased to U.S.$44.9 billion (partly as a result of devaluing the Canadian dollar).

4 U.S. net farm income in 2002 was 16% lower than its average for the 1990–95 period.

5 U.S. total farm business debt rose every year from 1993 to 2003, for a total increase of almost 50%.

6 About one-third of total U.S. trade is with NAFTA partners.
   (Foster and Dillon 2003, 84–97; Jackson 2003, 3–4, 14; Polaski 2003, 15–36; Picard 2003, 19–45; Cruz and Schwentesius 2003, 54–9; Vaughan 2003, 62–9; Ranney 2003, 26, 68–72; Public Citizen 2004a, 3–4; Public Citizen 2004b, 3)

The best way to assess the difficulty of reaching an overall judgment of the economic impact of the trade deals for each country individually and for the three countries taken together is to try to determine whether each item in the list should be counted as positive or negative for each country and for the area as a whole. Without labouring the point, my own assessment is that each country suffered more economic losses than gains, with Mexico losing the most, followed by the United States, and then Canada. The nature of the data leaves plenty of room for doubts and discussion, but on the whole I agree with the authors of the two summary reports and, more importantly, on the whole they agree with each other. However, some important differences should be recorded.

Broadly speaking, the report of the Carnegie Endowment is more cautious than that of the Hemispheric Social Alliance. While the authors of the former report emphasize the need to have language in trade deals like the NAFTA that will prevent unnecessary harms, the authors of the latter report condemn the NAFTA for including provisions that practically guarantee such harms. For example, in the Carnegie report one finds remarks such as the following:

> The experience of NAFTA shows that trade pacts will shift the composition of jobs, with some winners and some losers, but cannot be expected to create a net gain in jobs in economies that are at full employment, such as the United States and Canada. In developing economies with surplus labor, such as Mexico, the NAFTA experience demonstrates that trade pacts cannot be counted on to produce much, if any, net employment growth in the absence of other targeted policies. Policies to maximize employment gains from trade would include measures to promote supplier and support industries as well as terms in the trade agreement that reward rather than discourage the use of domestic inputs in the production of exported goods. (Polaski 2003, 32)

Contrast that with the following comments from the Alliance report:

> Mexico exports a lot but what it exports is not very Mexican, both in terms of its owners and its components. This could be the most profoundly negative macroeconomic impact of NAFTA: the disintegration of productive linkages and the de-nationalization of the productive structure ... The rules of origin agreed to in NAFTA do not favor increases in domestic content of exports, since they only require North American regional, not national content ... Under these rules, intra-firm or consortium integration is facilitated, helping large consortia to integrate their own productive chains. These rules do not favor the integration of

the Mexican economy into the global dynamic ... In reality, the large transnational firms promoted free-trade agreements to facilitate their own intra-firm integration without having to comply with various requirements or standards set by each country's legislators ... In addition, NAFTA and the FTAA negotiations serve to ratify those rules, practically prohibiting demanding performance requirements or rules of conduct for foreign investors. Under these conditions, the state cannot establish policies to ensure that foreign investment plays a positive role in national development and the population's welfare. Under the NAFTA rules on trade and investment, conditions are created so that companies maximize their profits, but without the requirement of any quid pro quo in terms of contributing to the country's development. (Picard 2003, 28–30)

Ten years earlier, before the NAFTA came into force, Drache (1993, 84–5) wrote: "the key to having higher levels of economic and social well-being is to shape the traded-goods sector and organize the internal market rather than drive a wedge between the two. This is an inherently different approach to trade than that espoused by trade liberalization ... Countries are unlikely to do well internationally if they do not exercise greater control over their basic internal market."

Drache was only one of several contributors from Canada, the United States, and Mexico to a collection of essays that were generally critical of the NAFTA and CUSTA, i.e., Grinspun and Cameron (1993). Re-reading those essays in the light of the reports from Carnegie and the Alliance, one cannot help being struck by the accuracy of their analyses and predictions.

Since the prevention of performance requirements for investors was a fundamental aim of all proponents of the CUSTA and since those same people managed to have the NAFTA rules against performance requirements expanded and strengthened (Michalos 1995), anyone familiar with the historical record of disputes over the texts of the agreements will recognize that the hazards that Polaski cautions developing countries to avoid are probably the most prized parts of the deals according to their proponents. Therefore, besides cautioning negotiators of new deals against such harmful provisions, one ought to be condemning them and calling for their elimination.

Lest anyone suspect that Polaski and I are exaggerating, here is the first half of the NAFTA article 1106 on performance requirements:

1. No Party may impose or enforce any of the following requirements, or enforce any commitment or undertaking, in connection with the

establishment, acquisition, management, conduct or operation of an investment of an investor of a Party or of a non-Party in its territory:

(a) to export a given level or percentage of goods or services;

(b) to achieve a given level or percentage of domestic content;

(c) to purchase, use or accord a preference to goods produced or services provided in its territory, or to purchase goods or services from persons in its territory;

(d) to relate in any way the volume or value of imports to the volume or value of exports or to the amount of foreign exchange inflows associated with such investment;

(e) to restrict sales of goods and services in its territory that such investment produces or provides by relating such sales in any way to the volume or value of its exports or foreign exchange earnings;

(f) to transfer technology, a production process or other proprietary knowledge to a person in its territory, except when the requirement is imposed or the commitment or undertaking is enforced by a court, administrative tribunal or competition authority to remedy an alleged violation of competition laws or to act in a manner not inconsistent with other provisions of this Agreement; or

(g) to act as the exclusive supplier of the goods it produces or services it provides to a specific region or world market. (NAFTA 2002)

A priori, could any reasonable person have imagined that the regime specified in these clauses would produce anything in Mexico but what it did produce? In the light of Article 1106, one may sympathize with Grinspun and Kreklewich (1994, 56) when they asserted that "The main objective of 'free trade' arrangements is to protect the interests of corporate capital; they are protectionist, rather than liberalizing, institutional arrangements." A similar line was taken in Michalos (1995, 226–31).

According to Grinspun and Kreklewich, the trade deals are "conditioning frameworks" that "promote and consolidate neoliberal restructuring" by restricting policy choices through the institutionalization of binding "international constraints and obligations incurred to another country, to foreign corporations, foreign investors, or to a multilateral agency. Failure to comply with the policy package would place the country in conflict with international forces" (35–6).

Clarkson (2002a, 52) claimed that the trade deals "can be used to constitutionalize a domestic ideological position" and that they create "supraconstitutional" norms "because they control government behaviour even though they are not part of the Canadian constitution." Clarkson's discussion of the "eight features considered characteristic of a constitution" and the way those features are captured in the trade deals is exceptionally thorough.

McBride (2003) invented the term "quiet constitutionalism" to emphasize that "conditioning frameworks" effectively produce constitutional change "without overtly engaging in constitutional reform" (cf., "new constitutionalism" in Gill 1992, 1996, 1997). After recalling C.B. Macpherson's (1965, 1977) arguments concerning the contingent relationship between liberalism and democracy in liberal democracies, McBride claimed that:

> in the name of creating a liberalized global economy, the democratic elements of liberal democratic systems are being reduced and confined to a much narrower range of human activity ... Instead of providing opportunities for democratic choice, quiet constitutional change imposes liberal rules of behaviour on governments and other actors and denies them the ability to make choices that lie outside of that value framework ... Neoliberal globalization ... has modified significantly the doctrine of parliamentary supremacy and, through it, the potential reach of democratic governance. It is true that Parliament could pass legislation withdrawing from these agreements and exercise its international legal sovereignty in doing so. Short of that, however, its reach is circumscribed and constrained in ways that would hardly have been imagined even two decades earlier. (255–69)

Newman (2000) revealed the complex conceptual and practical relationships among "the ideology of globalization," capitalism, liberalism, and democracy, beginning with the observation that proponents of globalization confuse "economic liberalization with political liberalization," fully expecting that the latter naturally flows from the former. In a manner reminiscent of Macpherson (1973), he demonstrated that such an expectation is unwarranted and that in fundamental ways the causal arrow travels in the opposite direction:

> It would be easier to believe that globalization will foster democracy if globalizing capitalism were itself inherently democratic. If that were true, we could take for granted the creation of a genuinely participatory public culture wherever the capitalist firm put down roots. Alas, it is simply not true ... In whatever form it takes, the capitalist enterprise is private property; thus, in contrast with political democracy, it is not

membership in the enterprise but ownership that is the source of control ... no matter how often consumers vote with their pocketbooks, they remain outside the loop of capitalist decision making ... Nor does sensitivity to consumer demand translate into democratic accountability. *Private enterprise does not exist to serve a public purpose* ... The ideology of globalization obscures but can never overcome the hard fact that modern capitalism, at a minimum, requires a supportive legal regime, so that property rights are protected and contracts enforced. But while capitalism has always needed the protection and encouragement of the state, it has had a markedly ambivalent relationship with democracy for the simple reason that the democratic state affords access to power to societal interests antagonistic to capital. While by no means hostile to market capitalism, the modern democratic state typically has legislated standards for health and safety in the workplace, consumer protection, environmental quality, employment equity, and other domains that limit the discretion of private entrepreneurs and impose additional costs on them. The democratic state has also strengthened the hand of labor by recognizing a right of collective bargaining. It was modern democracy, moreover, that gave birth to the redistributive welfare state of the post-World War II era. (18)

Rodrik (1999) is not a political scientist, but he expressed related concerns about the impact of globalization on democratic accountability. In his view:

The internationalization of production and investment raises a fundamental question of accountability: to whom will national economic policymakers be accountable? The implicit answer provided by the globalization model is that they will be accountable to foreign investors, country fund managers in London and New York, and a relatively small group of domestic exporters. In the globalized economy, these are the groups that determine whether an economy is judged a success or not, and whether it will prosper ... The fundamental dilemma of accountability in today's world economy is that it is domestic voters who choose national governments – and appropriately so – and not global markets. International markets, particularly financial ones, do not always get things right with respect to economic efficiency. They are even less likely to get things right with regard to societal outcomes suitable to each nation's aspirations ... It is national governments that are held responsible for producing outcomes that are consonant with national aspirations. If governments can no longer be responsive to these aspirations, they can no longer be accountable to their electorates. (150–2)

In Michalos (1997c) I explained the failures of the so-called "efficient market hypothesis" for international financial markets, and the travesty as well as the danger of grounding public socio-economic and fiscal policy on such a patently false empirical claim. Here it is only necessary to examine the issues of accountability and quiet constitutionalism insofar as they touch upon federal-provincial relations, especially concerning three things: Canada as an economic union, trade, and environmental policy. One should know something, in fairly general terms, about the constitutional and legislative provisions assuring that someone or some governmental agency is finally responsible and legally held accountable for matters concerning the Canadian economic union, trade, and environmental policy. Quiet constitutionalism concerns the relatively surreptitious transformation of some of these provisions in the absence of appropriate democratic safeguards. In large measure, my overview of the historical and legal issues is greatly indebted to the splendid analysis provided by Monahan (2006).

Monahan (2006, 10–11) began by introducing a quite general "federal principle" constructed by Wheare (1963, 11), according to which federalism is "the method of dividing powers so that the general and regional governments are each within a sphere coordinate and independent." A federal principle thus defined may be thought of as serving what Robinson (2003, 230) called the "substantive constitutional objective," namely, that "territorially concentrated subnational political communities should be able to define their own priorities, and the appropriate policies for realizing them, in matters of vital interest to them insofar as this is consistent with the flourishing of the national political community."

The *British North America Act, 1867* (*BNA Act*, called the *Constitution Act, 1867* in the first section of the *Constitution Act, 1982*) created a federalist system roughly consistent with Wheare's principle, serving Robinson's objective. Although the long introductory sentence to section 91 of the *BNA Act* refers to "Classes of Subjects ... assigned exclusively to the Legislatures of the Provinces" and to matters that are "(notwithstanding anything in this Act) the exclusive Legislative Authority of the Parliament of Canada," and section 92 is entitled "Subjects of exclusive Provincial Legislation":

Today, in most areas of policy, there is a significant regulatory presence of both the federal and provincial levels of government. In fact, one recent survey of federal and provincial legislation and regulation [Stevenson 2000] found that the only exclusive federal areas were military defence, veterans' affairs, the postal service, and monetary policy; in all other areas of federal law and regulation, the provinces had laws or regulations dealing with the same subjects or issues. Conversely, the only exclusive provincial areas were municipal institutions, elementary and secondary education, and some areas of law related to property and other non-criminal matters. In this sense, it is entirely misleading to conceive of the federal and provincial classes of subjects as being mutually exclusive watertight compartments. (Monahan 2006, 105)

Procedurally, as apparently originally planned, to determine what level of government held supreme authority over some existing or proposed law, it was first necessary to appropriately classify the law into one or another of the listed areas or "heads of power" in sections 91 and 92. This was not as straightforward a task as it might appear. On the basis of the opening sentence of section 91, the Parliament of Canada seems to be given supreme authority "to make Laws for the Peace, Order, and good Government of Canada" over all matters not "assigned exclusively to the Legislatures of the Provinces." That is, the so-called POGG clause seems to limit the authority of the legislatures to the sixteen areas listed in section 92 while granting parliament authority over the twenty-nine areas listed in section 91 plus any others that might arise in the future. However, section 92(13) assigns supreme authority over "Property and Civil Rights in the Province" to legislatures and, insofar as practically any law may be construed as affecting civil rights, section 92(13) may be regarded as granting legislatures authority over the sixteen areas listed in section 92 and the twenty-nine areas listed in section 91 plus any others that might arise in the future provided that the matters affect rights "in the Province." Thus, the interpretation of these important clauses was bound to lead to litigation in search of clarification regarding which level of government had legislative authority over any particular law.

The Supreme Court of Canada was created in 1875 by the *Supreme Court Act*, but until 1949 the Judicial Committee of the Privy Council (JCPC) served as the "highest legal authority" for matters concerning the *BNA Act*. Typically the JCPC resisted applying the expansive logic of the previous paragraph to give the provinces authority over the twenty-nine areas listed in section 91. Not unreasonably, the committee regarded its task as merely that of providing legal interpretations of laws written by selected representatives of the people: "It was for the legislature and not the courts, the JCPC reminded its readers on many occasions, to evaluate the wisdom of an enactment. For the JCPC any open assessment of the relative importance of a particular statute, or of its necessity to the economic and political life of the nation, was anathema. The Board therefore attempted to fashion a series of tests that could be applied without reference to such factors" (Monahan 2006, 233).

The tests included, but were not limited to, such things as trying to avoid conflicts by treating the diverse areas mentioned in sections 91 and 92 as relatively "watertight compartments," trying to determine the fundamental purpose, aim or "pith and substance" of acts (regardless of effects), examining acts from different perspectives or aspects (the "aspect doctrine"), and giving federal laws precedence when "compliance with one law would involve breach of the other" (the "doctrine of federal paramountcy"). As one might have expected, in practice it was impossible for the JCPC to avoid making decisions about Canada's constitution that did not have significant political implications. In fact, Monahan claimed:

> The JCPC took a document whose clear intention was to create a centralized federation and interpreted it as allocating many of the most important areas of legislative jurisdiction to the provinces. Furthermore, the scheme of federalism created by the JCPC turned out in many respects to be unworkable ... One of the largest challenges facing both levels of government in Canada since [the latter's development as a moderately progressive welfare state in] 1945 has been to devise mechanisms that will permit them to escape or to bypass the unworkable and impractical constitutional framework created by the JCPC. (Monahan 2006, 232)

Reviewing the powers listed in sections 91, 92, and 121, Monahan was able to make a compelling case for his claim that: "One of the principal motivations behind political union in British North America had been the desire to create a political unit that was sufficiently large and stable to permit expansion westward and the creation of a transcontinental economy ... The 1867 Act was carefully designed to ensure that the federal government would have all the tools necessary to undertake this westward expansion, including the financing and construction of the necessary transportation infrastructure" (Monahan 2006, 108).

The section 91 list of areas relevant to the proposed expansion includes:

> The Public Debt and Property ... The Regulation of Trade and Commerce ... The raising of Money by any Mode or System of Taxation ...

The borrowing of Money on the Public Credit ... Militia, Military and Naval Service, and Defence ... The fixing of and providing for the Salaries and Allowances of Civil and other Officers of the Government of Canada ... Navigation and Shipping ... Currency and Coinage ... Banking, Incorporation of Banks, and the Issue of Paper Money ... Savings Banks ... Bills of Exchange and Promissory Notes ... Interest ... Legal Tender ... Bankruptcy and Insolvency ... Indians, and Lands reserved for Indians ... The Criminal Law (*BNA Act, 1867*, as reprinted in Monahan 2006)

Added to all these resources, section 92(10) says:

In each Province the Legislature may exclusively make Laws in relation to ... Local Works and Undertakings other than such as are of the following classes:
(a) Lines of Steam or other Ships, Railways, Canals, Telegraphs, and other Works and Undertakings connecting the Province with any other or others of the Provinces, or extending beyond the Limits of the Province;
(b) Lines of Steam Ships between the Province and any British or Foreign Country;
(c) Such Works as, although wholly situate [sic] within the Province, are before or after their Execution declared by the Parliament of Canada to be for the general Advantage of Canada or for the Advantage of Two or more of the Provinces. (*BNA Act, 1867*, as reprinted in Monahan 2006)

And section 121 requires that "All Articles of the Growth, Produce, or Manufacture of any one of the Provinces shall, from and after the Union, be admitted free into each of the other Provinces" (*BNA Act, 1867*, as reprinted in Monahan 2006).

Considering all these provisions together, it cannot be doubted that at least one central aim of the authors of the *BNA Act* was to guarantee that the new country would have all the legal tools necessary for rapid and sustainable economic development. Whatever Canada was supposed to be politically or socially, it was supposed to be a strong economic union extending from sea to sea to sea. Supposing this is so, it is a proposition difficult to reconcile with the fact that sometimes the JCPC and the Supreme Court seemed to regard section 91(2) as taking precedence over 121, and sometimes the reverse, as I will show. This may have added support to proponents of the AIT.

Section 91(2) gives the Parliament of Canada "exclusive Legislative Authority" over "The Regulation of Trade and Commerce." Insofar as the pith and substance of an international treaty concerns trade, one would suppose that 91(2) would provide the Parliament of Canada with the head of power for such agreements. With some complications arising from diverse judgments rendered by different judges in different cases, that supposition is warranted.

In *Citizens' Insurance Co. v. Parsons* (1881), the JCPC decided that sections 91(2) and 92(13) had to be read together so that the trade and commerce power was divided into two branches. The first branch took a specific, categorical approach, granting parliament power over international and interprovincial trade, and granting each province power over trade within its own territory. The second branch took a fairly general approach requiring an assessment of the economic impact of any proposed law or activity, and granting parliament power over any "trade affecting the whole dominion" (Monahan 2006, 244–7). The first branch has been used more often than the second, and the following cases seem to be most important for our purposes.

In *Reference Re Validity of s.5(a) of Dairy Industry Act (Can.)* (1949), the Supreme Court of Canada decided that "it was open to Parliament to attempt to protect the dairy industry within Canada and within particular provinces by banning imports of or interprovincial trade in margarine" (Monahan 2006, 280). That is, the protection of the economic viability of an industry located in some province against assaults originating in a foreign country or in another province was a legitimate activity of parliament under section 91(2).

In *R. v. Dominion Stores Ltd.* (1980), the court decided that parliament could compel companies to use standardized grade names for certain agricultural products that were traded internationally and interprovincially, but it could not compel their use for the same products traded locally under 91(2). However, producers who believed it would be advantageous to adopt any particular standardized grade names on a voluntary basis for products only traded locally were free to do so (Monahan 2006, 280–1).

With the *Motor Vehicle Safety Act, S.C. 1993*, parliament established national safety standards that had to be met by every vehicle traded across international or interprovincial borders. Vehicles meeting the standards are certified with national safety marks. Although parliament did not have the power under 91(2) to require producers of vehicles intended only for a local, provincial market to meet the same standards, such power is effectively in the hands of consumers who usually prefer more over less safe vehicles. Since "over 90 percent of all motor vehicles manufactured in Canada cross either a provincial or an international border," the standards of the *Motor Vehicle Safety Act* are applied to the vast majority of vehicles manufactured here. In fact, producers of any products that might be sold across provincial or national borders, gain some advantage in meeting design specifications acceptable in the broadest potential market (Monahan 2006, 283–5).

Taking the results of *Citizen's Insurance Co. v. Parsons*, the *Dairy Industry Act, R. v. Dominion Stores Ltd*, and the *Motor Vehicle Safety Act* together, it seems that parliament's power under section 91(2) takes precedence over section 121. So, the *MMT Act*, which prohibited trading MMT across provincial borders, could have been successfully defended under 91(2) in spite of 121. That is, without the AIT, the *MMT Act* could have had a very different fate.

For our purposes, the most important case involving the second branch of section 91(2) was *General Motors of Canada Ltd. v. City National Leasing* (1989). In that case, Chief Justice Dickson constructed a "preliminary checklist" of five criteria that could be used to determine whether any proposed legislation would be warranted under the general trade and commerce power of parliament. Each of the criteria is apparently to be regarded as indicative or suggestive, rather than absolutely necessary. Briefly, legislation would be warranted under the second branch of 91(2) if it were (1) part of a regulatory scheme, (2) administered by a regulatory agency, (3) applicable to "trade as a whole rather than with a particular industry," (4) constitutionally beyond the legislative authority of provinces, and (5) potentially inoperable if a single province was not covered by it (Monahan 2006, 294). Depending on how one defines "industry," the *MMT Act* did deal with one or possibly a few industries (e.g., petroleum and refining), which would imply that it did not pass the test of applying to "trade as a whole." Since the exact status of the five tests in that "checklist" is unclear, it is unclear how the *Act* might have fared on this score, without the AIT.

In support of the Canadian economic union, in *Manitoba (A.G.) v. Manitoba Egg and Poultry Assn.* (1971), the Supreme Court reaffirmed the prohibition indicated in section 121, namely, that provinces may not restrict the free flow of goods from other provinces. Two decades later, in *Morguard Investments Ltd. v. De Savoye* (1990) and *Hunt v. T & N PLC* (1993), the court "expressly stated that Parliament has the legislative authority to enact legislation designed to enhance the functioning of the economic union" (Monahan 2006, 304). In particular, in the two last-named cases the court insisted that the results of court proceedings in any province must be recognized in all other provinces, and documents must be shared. The first of the three cases mentioned pretty clearly indicates that in the court's view, section 121 may take precedence over 91(2). Had the court consistently maintained this view, the case for the AIT would have been significantly weakened.

Granting the clear intention of the authors of the BNA Act, as interpreted by the JCPC and the Supreme Court, to create a single economic union on the basis of sections 91(2), 92(10), and 121, there is still a subtle difference between provisions designed to prevent the free flow of goods and services across provinces and provisions designed to harmonize regulations in every province. The former kinds of provisions are often described as instruments of *negative integration*, while the latter are instruments of *positive integration*. Positive integration may require the identification of a single standard or regulation that is acceptable to all provinces (and perhaps the federal government) or different standards or regulations that all provinces are willing to accept as equivalent. The difference between these two types of integration is especially important for issues over which parliament and the provincial legislatures share jurisdiction. Regarding the doctrine of paramountcy, for example, Monahan (2006, 309–10) wrote: "to the extent that a federal law prohibiting barriers to internal trade was found to be in conflict with a provincial law creating such barriers, the provincial law would be rendered inoperative or unenforceable. At the same time, the federal legislation could not in itself prescribe a single harmonized standard to replace any provincial legislation that was rendered inoperative. The harmonization, or positive integration, of provincial measures affecting internal trade would still require voluntary legislative or regulatory action on the part of the provinces."

Since no province had a law requiring the use of MMT, the necessary condition of applying the doctrine of paramountcy (i.e., a clear conflict between the demands of a federal and a provincial law) was not fulfilled in the MMT case. So that doctrine would not have had any contribution to make toward bringing the provinces around to some sort of harmonized position with the federal government.

Section 132 of the BNA Act says: "The Parliament and Government of Canada shall have all Powers necessary or proper for performing the Obligations of Canada or of any Province thereof, as Part of the British Empire, towards Foreign Countries, arising under Treaties between the Empire and such Foreign Countries" (BNA Act, 1867, as reprinted in Monahan 2006).

Because the section explicitly referred to "Treaties between the Empire and ... Foreign Countries," some clarification was required regarding the head of power for treaties involving not the Empire but the Dominion or the provinces. In *Canada (A.G.) v. Ontario (A.G.) (Labour Conventions)* A.C. 326 (1937), the JCPC decided that the head of power for any particular treaty should be determined according to the pith and substance of that treaty, under sections 91(2) or 92(13) as appropriate. Although that decision apparently implied that the federal government might not be able to guarantee the implementation of treaty obligations falling under provincial jurisdiction, Monahan (2006, 300) was certainly right when he wrote that "as the experience of the past decade has demonstrated, the *Labour Conventions* case has certainly not precluded Canada from negotiating comprehensive trade agreements, including the WTO, FTA, and the NAFTA."

When treaties create obligations for the federal government that are inconsistent with provincial laws, parliament must pass special implementing legislation in support of the treaties, e.g., the *North American Free Trade Agreement Implementation Act, S.C. 1993, c.44*. Regarding objections that might be raised about certain provisions of the treaties, the implementing legislation, or their implications, on the grounds of "quiet constitutionalism," the following comment from Monahan (2006, 301) is instructive: "The most powerful argument in favour of a federal power to implement international trade agreements is that such treaties are mainly concerned with international trade, which is clearly a matter subject to the jurisdiction of Parliament. Although the treaties do have an effect on matters falling within provincial jurisdiction, such incidental effects do not detract from the validity of a statute whose main purpose, or pith and substance, is international trade."

The question is: How much "quiet constitutional" change can be tolerated before one must admit that a treaty or its implementing legislation is politically unacceptable? "Pith and substance" is not measurable like salt and pepper, and even documents with a majority of provisions dealing overtly with trade may have aspects that are qualitatively devastating for the public good or simply for the majority of people affected by the provisions. Unfortunately, given the complexity and intangibility of "pith and substance," there may be no way to find a definitive answer to this question.

Although the specific BNA *Act* sections and the supporting JCPC and Supreme Court judgments we have just reviewed seem to provide sufficient authority to parliament in matters concerning the regulation of trade, the introductory POGG clause of section 91 has also been used as a head of power in this area. Because it is possible to read the long sentence introducing the specific provisions of section 91 in different ways, there was a fairly early demand for judicial interpretations. In *Ontario (A.G.) v. Canada (A.G.) (Local Prohibition Reference) A.C. 348 (P.C.)* (1896), the JCPC decided that the POGG clause should only be used as a residual power for those cases to which no particular provision in section 91 or 92 applied. In *Reference Re Board of Commerce Act, 1919 (Can.), 1 A.C. 191 (P.C.)* (1922), it was decided that the clause should be applied only in emergencies, loosely described as "special circumstances, such as those of a great war," and in *Toronto Electric Commissioners v. Snider,* A.C. *396 (P.C.)* (1925), such emergencies became those presenting "some extraordinary peril to the national life of Canada, as a whole" (Monahan 2006, 241).

In *Ontario (A.G.) v. Canada Temperance Federation,* A.C. *193 (P.C.)* (1946), the JCPC abandoned its insistence on emergency circumstances and asserted that the POGG clause would be applicable in any case which "must from its inherent nature be the concern of the Dominion as a whole." Examples of matters that the Supreme Court regarded as having "inherent national concern" include aeronautics (*Johannesson v. West St. Paul (Rural Municipality), 1 S.C.R. 292* (1952)); the national capital region (*Munro v. Canada (National Capital Commission), S.C.R. 663* (1966)); seabed minerals off the coast of British Columbia (*Reference Re Offshore Mineral Rights (British Columbia), S.C.R. 792* (1967)); marine pollution (*R. v. Crown Zellerbach Canada Ltd., 1 S.C.R. 401* (1988)); the environment (*Friends of the Oldman River Society v. Canada (Minister of Transport), 1 S.C.R. 3* (1992)); and nuclear energy (*Ontario Hydro v. Ontario (Labour Relations Board), 3 S.C.R. 327* (1993)) (Monahan 2006, 261–271). Monahan (2006, 254) claimed that the POGG clause could now be used to support federal legislation, in four types of circumstances, namely, those involving emergencies, issues of "inherent national concern," issues not captured by any of the special provisions of sections 91 and 92, and "matters that are of interprovincial concern." Baier (2003) claimed that the Supreme Court has tried to avoid appealing to the "inherent national concern" justification because of its bias toward centralization. In Monahan's view, it would be difficult for anyone to substantiate a claim that a "national emergency" exists unless it meets one of the conditions specified in the *Emergencies Act,* R.S.C. 1985. That is, the situation would have to be such that it:

"(1) seriously endangers the lives, health or safety of Canadians and is of such proportions or nature as to exceed the capacity or authority of a province to deal with it, or

(2) seriously threatens the ability of the Government of Canada to preserve the sovereignty, security and territorial integrity of Canada" (Monahan 2006, 257).

What's more, anyone making such a claim must lay it "before parliament for debate and confirmation," following "prior consultation with the province(s) concerned."

Perhaps even more importantly for our purposes, as demonstrated by passage of the *Clarity Act* (i.e., *An Act to give effect to the requirement for clarity as set out in the opinion of the Supreme Court of Canada in the Quebec Secession Reference, S.C. 2000, c.26*), Monahan (2006, 259) asserts: "It has also been settled that Parliament can enact legislation to pre-empt or avoid an emergency, and does not have to WAIT until the emergency has actually commenced before taking action."

As explained below, although the federal government could not have sustained its claim that an emergency situation existed that called for passage of the MMT *Act*, it might have been able to sustain a claim that passage of the *Act* would effectively "pre-empt or avoid an emergency." Since MMT was used across the country, its use apparently would have qualified as a matter of "inherent national concern." In my opinion, it is precisely because the MMT cases involved a matter of "inherent national concern" and the potential avoidance of an emergency situation endangering life, health, and safety that trade tribunals or panels were the wrong bodies, with the wrong decision procedures and rules, to have had the last words on what should have been the appropriate national public policy position about the use of MMT.

The last head of power that might be applicable to issues involving MMT or the MMT *Act* concerns criminal law. Section 91(27) of the BNA *Act* gives the parliament of Canada authority over "The Criminal Law, except the Constitution of Courts of Criminal Jurisdiction, but including the Procedure in Criminal Matters," and section 92(14) gives the legislatures of the provinces authority over "The Administration of Justice in the Province, including the non-renewable natural resources, forestry resources and electrical energy" (BNA *Act 1867*, as reprinted in Monahan 2006). The range of issues covered by this head of power has been expanded by judgments made in several important Supreme Court cases, and today the criminal law power provides the broadest array of areas that might be supported by federal legislation. I believe the evidence that will be reviewed in detail as we work through the NAFTA and AIT cases clearly reveals that the MMT *Act* could easily have been supported under the criminal law power.

In *Reference Re Validity of s.5(a) of Dairy Industry Act (Canada), S.C.R. 1 (Margarine Reference)* (1949), the Supreme Court decided that three conditions had to be satisfied for proposed legislation to be warranted under the criminal law head of power, namely, (1) some activity must be prohibited; (2) there must be a penalty for violation of the prohibition; and (3) the public purpose for which the law is enacted must involve criminal activity, i.e., activity that might undermine "public peace, order, security, health, [or] morality" (Monahan 2006, 334, quoting Rand). The idea of a criminal public purpose was sharpened in *RJR-MacDonald Inc. v. Canada (A.G.), 3 S.C.R. 199* (1995) to a purpose aimed at the prevention of activities that would have "an 'evil' or injurious effect upon the public" (Monahan 2006, 337, quoting La Forest).

In *Labatt Breweries of Canada Ltd. v. Canada (A.G.), 1 S.C.R. 914* (1980), the court held that the criminal law power could support federal laws prohibiting "trade practices contrary to the interest of the community such as misleading, false or deceptive advertising and misbranding," i.e., consumer protection (Monahan 2006, 343, quoting La Forest). In *R. v. Wetmore, 2 S.C.R. 284* (1983), the court said that the same power could be used to support laws protecting the "'physical health and safety of the public' as well as the 'moral health' of the public" (Monahan 2006, 338, quoting Laskin). Finally, in *R. v. Hydro-Quebec, 3 S.C.R. 213* (1997), "All nine members of the Court agreed that the 'protection of the environment' should be added to the list of criminal public purposes identified by Rand J. in the *Margarine Reference* as capable of supporting the enactment of criminal legislation" (Monahan 2006, 339).

Besides unanimously affirming that the protection of the environment could be supported by the criminal law head of power, two other aspects of this case are important for our purposes. The first was recorded in Monahan's footnote 17, i.e., "the fact that the relevant legislative provisions applied to emissions [of polychlorinated biphenyls (PCBs)] that, while harmful to the environment, may not have been harmful to human health, did not constitute a basis for overturning the legislation."

This is important because it seems to establish the principle that the pollution of the environment, regardless of its impact on human health, may be prevented on the basis of the criminal law power. How much pollution would be required to justify legal action in the form of legislation or prosecution is not clearly indicated, but these issues may have been or may yet be addressed elsewhere.

The second important aspect of *R. v. Hydro-Quebec* for our purposes concerns the extension of the force of the criminal law power. Prior to this case, it had been assumed that the criminal law power could be used to support prohibitions, but not regulations. So, writing for the minority of the court in this case, Chief Justice Lamer claimed that sections 34–35 of the *Canadian Environmental Protection Act, 1988* (CEPA), which were central to the case and failed to mention any prohibition, could not be supported by the criminal law power (Leiss 2001, 198). Although Leiss claimed that "All nine justices agreed in effect that Parliament can only prohibit, not regulate" (198), the court's five to four majority decision affirmed precisely the opposite proposition. Here is Monahan's summary:

> the relevant statutory provisions [of CEPA] contain no requirements or prohibitions but merely authorize the enactment of regulations prescribing requirements respecting the release of toxic substances into the environment. In this sense, La Forest J.'s reference to the statute and the regulations as being concerned with the enactment of "prohibitions" seems wholly at odds with the plain and obvious wording of the relevant provisions. Thus, the majority judgment in *Hydro-Quebec* appears to extend the reach of the criminal law power such that it seems capable of supporting the enactment of legislation that is predominantly regulatory in nature. On this basis, the criminal law power may well be used to prescribe packaging and labeling standards for foods or other products. (Monahan 2006, 340; Valiante 2002, 7, has a similar view of the regulatory extension made in this case)

CEPA will appear later in our story, along with a slightly different vocabulary and set of rules constructed for the AIT that allow the federal government to make regulations (prohibitions in the *Hydro-Quebec* case language) on its own, but require consultations with the provinces and territories to set new standards (regulations in the *Hydro-Quebec* case language) for traded goods or services. In the view of the federal government, the *MMT Act* contained a prohibition (regulation in AIT language) against buying and selling MMT across international or provincial borders, while Ethyl and the provinces claimed the *Act* set a new standard (in AIT language; regulation in the *Hydro-Quebec* case language). As explained below, I believe the CEPA did not have any useful application in the MMT cases. As far as Leiss is concerned, "the scope of the federal power in environmental management is pretty much useless," "the original CEPA has done almost nothing to achieve better environmental protection in Canada" and "All of these problems are rooted in the fact that CEPA simply repackaged the basic thrust of its predecessor legislation [i.e., the *Environmental*

Contaminants Act, 1975] without changing it, despite the fact that its predecessor was widely acknowledged to be unworkable, even by officials at Environment Canada" (Leiss 2002, 198, 202).

With fewer than three dozen "CEPA-toxic" substances reaching the stage of regulation since 1988 and over 23,000 substances remaining to be examined, it is difficult to disagree with Leiss's harsh judgment of CEPA. However, without attempting to resolve in any way issues around the limits of "federal power in environmental management," some observers think the problem is one of an absence of will on the part of the federal government, rather than an absence of constitutional prerogative. For example, Harrison (2003, 319) claimed that the federal government has traditionally been reluctant "to test the limits of its authority" and that "Time and time again the Supreme Court has adopted a more generous reading of federal environmental jurisdiction than asserted by the federal government itself."

Summarizing her view, she said that there is:

a need to reconsider the common assumption in the literature on Canadian federalism that governments invariably seek to expand their jurisdictional grasp. In fact, intergovernmental competition for jurisdiction over the environment has been the exception to the rule over the past four decades. Depending on the potential political costs and benefits, federal and provincial politicians can be expected to perceive some fields of jurisdiction as worth fighting for, and others to be surrendered without a fight. The environmental case also raises questions about the unqualified value often attributed to intergovernmental co-operation. Intergovernmental harmony for the most part has prevailed in the environmental field because federal and provincial governments typically have had compatible objectives – the federal government's being to avoid political blame from the business community as a result of environmental regulation, and the provinces' being to defend their authority to exploit natural resources. In other words, intergovernmental relations have been most co-operative when federal and provincial governments have been *least* committed to environmental protection. Finally, while one should be careful to acknowledge that that lack of commitment was not created by the federal system, federalism may nonetheless exacerbate governments' disincentives to protect the environment by providing a convenient opportunity for the federal government in particular to pass the buck to the provinces. (Harrison 2003, 343; see also Harrison 1996)

Valiante (2002, 19–20) shared Harrison's view of the federal government as a reluctant defender of the environment:

Canadian courts have repeatedly vindicated a central role for the federal government in environmental protection, interpreting the constitution generously and forcing federal compliance with its statutory and regulatory commitments. These decisions have opened the door to more comprehensive legislation, including CEPA and CEAA [the *Canadian Environmental Assessment Act 1992*]. However, at the same time as it is being empowered to act boldly, the federal government is bent on sharing authority with the provinces and territories through harmonization efforts and delegation of administration, with industry through voluntary initiatives, with First Nations through self-government and land claims agreements, and with the public through greater participation guarantees. As well, there is a desire, quite self-serving, by governments and industry to avoid litigation, whether prosecution or judicial review, on the grounds that it creates uncertainty and costs. It is hoped that these trends will not cancel each other out but that strong legal tools will be available and used when appropriate to achieve environmental protection.

Assuming that Harrison and Valiante were right about the federal government's reluctance to take a strong leadership role in protecting the environment, the fate of the MMT Act in the hands of an AIT panel and a NAFTA tribunal could only have reinforced that government's reticence. The environmental ministers who boldly brought the *Act* into being from conception to Royal Assent were not reluctant warriors. Opponents of the *Act* certainly regarded them as overzealous, but I doubt that anyone examining the record would accuse them of reticence. The federal government's defensive teams in both cases were also aggressive, though this would probably have been expected. More's the pity, then, that the initiatives of all those people were not rewarded with success. However these cases are stored in whatever institutional memories governments maintain, they are not likely to be favourable to future initiatives along the same lines.

Perhaps this is enough of an overview of the most relevant constitutional provisions and court cases dealing with the economic union, trade, and environmental policy. We began the chapter with an overview of globalization and then proceeded to a review of its economic impact as revealed through the relatively narrow lens provided by summary reports of the consequences of adopting the NAFTA and CUSTA. An examination of what has happened to the residents and economic, social and political institutions of North America under the NAFTA and CUSTA is not only valuable to those residents, but may be instructive for people in other countries living under other relatively globalized regimes, as well as those contemplating adopting the FTAA or its successors, the Security and Prosperity Partnership of North America (SPP) and the Trade, Investment, and Labour Mobility (TILMA) agreements among provinces (Dobbin 2007; Gould 2007; Grinspun and Shamsie 2007). In general, it seems that there were more costs than benefits for most residents of the three North American countries.

In the second half of the chapter our focus was narrowed further to see what provisions the Canadian *Constitution Act, 1867* and subsequent court cases provided for the creation and maintenance of an economic union, trade, and environmental policy. Clearly, our brief overview of these issues has revealed a powerful set of provisions based on the original visions of those who wrote the *BNA Act* and on judicial and judicious interpretations in a wide variety of cases, by many thoughtful experts over many years. In later chapters it will be shown that very little of this accumulated wealth of knowledge was brought to bear in either the NAFTA or the AIT cases.

I agree with Monahan's (2006, 310) view that "the choice of an enforcement mechanism is a policy choice [of parliament] rather than a constitutional requirement." It cannot be doubted that parliament accepted the dispute resolution provisions of the NAFTA, CUSTA and AIT, including the use of tribunals and panels, as well as its own implementing legislation for those agreements. There is also a consensus among experts that the agreements and implementing legislation are constitutionally valid (Monahan 2006, 301–2; Senate 1988, 20). Nevertheless, it is reasonable and morally right to examine the actual operation of those dispute resolution provisions with a view to determining whether or not they have produced decisions that are consistent with the great body of work that has already been accomplished. With respect to the MMT cases, I hope to show that they are not, and that what has been lost is worth recapturing. Clarkson (2002a, 59) claimed that chapter 11 is the most controversial part of the NAFTA because it allows "firms to overturn the outcomes of national political debates on the desirable regulatory regime to secure the health and safety of the citizenry." The dispute settlement provisions of the AIT are equally objectionable insofar as they allow a province to accomplish the same feat for the nation as a whole.

Robinson (2003, 228) claimed that international trade agreements have altered the Canadian federal system in two important ways:

[First] the regulation of the Canadian economy now involves three powerful tiers – the supranational (e.g., the NAFTA arbitration tribunals), the federal, and provincial. GATT and other international treaties meant that such a supranational tier has long existed, but the power and importance of that top tier is now much greater than ever before ... [second] under the neo-liberal principles currently defined and enforced by this three-tiered regulatory system, no government has the same capacity to regulate the behaviour of corporations and market forces that both the federal and the larger provincial governments possessed in Canada under the more closed, Keynesian model of regulation. Nor does either have the same capacity to redistribute the gains from economic growth to prevent the exacerbation of economic inequalities."

Although Robinson believed that the two-tiered system is gone forever, he also thought that as the costs of the neo-liberal system increase along with the increasingly large numbers of marginalized people, the supranational regulatory tier would be redefined in ways that will give regulators at all three levels more control over the behaviour of transnational corporations, and with it, the capacity to capture and redistribute resources so as to ensure that everyone is adequately protected from the fluctuations of the global market economy, and everyone shares in the wealth and opportunities that it creates. This will require reductions in the scope of the new international private property rights created by the FCAS [Free Capital Agreements], and the addition of strong international social dimensions. (Robinson 2003, 228–9)

Robinson's vision of a three-tiered governance system is clearly consistent with the "human security paradigm" of McBride and the Hemispheric Social Alliance. It would be a system much more capable of meeting the "substantive constitutional objective" specified earlier.

4

Motor Vehicle Technology

Because the MMT cases involve a variety of claims and counter-claims about the normal and abnormal performance of certain components of motor vehicles, some relatively unbiased explanations of their design and function should be provided before entering into controversial matters. Broadly speaking, the alleged risks posed by the use of MMT involve issues related to (1) the variety and levels of chemical emissions following combustion of the product; (2) the product's negative impact on spark plugs, on-board diagnostic systems, and catalytic converters; and (3) the neurological disorders that are known to be related to high levels of inhalation of manganese particles. This chapter very briefly covers the first two issues.

The most frequently cited authority concerning the components of particular interest to us is *Automotive Electric/Electronic Systems* (Adler 1995). This overview follows that book, supplemented occasionally by some other neutral texts like the Province of British Columbia's (1997) Student Study Guide for *AirCare: Vehicle Emissions Inspections and Maintenance* and DuPuy (2000). British Columbia had the first vehicle emissions inspection program in Canada, introduced in 1992 (VanNijnatten 2002, 155).

The engines in most of the cars sold in North America are powered by burning a mixture of air and fuel, mainly gasoline. Gasoline is a mixture of hydrocarbons with diverse numbers of carbon atoms in their molecular structure. Even gasolines with the same octane number may have different compositions. The octane number of gasoline measures its capacity to resist spark or combustion knock. Knocks may be caused by fuel spontaneously igniting (auto-ignition) in an engine as a result of high temperatures and pressure. The combustion creates a powerful "pressure wave" that pounds the cylinder wall and head with a pinging sound. "Besides sound, spark knock can result in pitting or erosion of the combustion chamber, damage to spark plug electrodes, and possible structural damage to the engine" (Asik and Anglin 1997, 176–7).

In a "four-stroke spark-ignition engine," the process of converting the energy in fuel into kinetic energy begins with the descent of a piston in a cylinder. The descent of the piston draws an air-fuel mixture into a combustion chamber in which the mixture is then compressed as the piston ascends. When the compressed mixture is ignited by a spark from a spark plug, heat is created in the combustion process, which raises the pressure in the cylinder and forces the piston down on the crankshaft. Work energy or power is produced as the crankshaft turns. Following each combustion stroke, exhaust gases are released from the cylinder and a new air-fuel mixture is sucked in. "In automotive engines this exchange of gases is generally regulated according to the four-stroke principle, with two crankshaft revolutions being required for each complete cycle" (Adler 1995, 4).

The air-fuel mixture plays a crucial role in combustion and properties of air-fuel ratios play a crucial role in the MMT cases. According to DuPuy (2000, 44):

> The air-fuel ratio is the proportion by weight of air and gasoline that the carburetor or injection system mixes as needed for engine combustion. This ratio is important, since there are limits to how rich (more fuel) or lean (less fuel) it can be and remain combustible. The mixtures with which an engine can operate without stalling range from 8 to 1 to 18.5 to 1 ... These ratios are usually stated this way: 8 parts of air by weight combined with 1 part of gasoline by weight (8:1) which is the richest mixture that an engine can tolerate and still fire regularly; 18.5 parts of air mixed with 1 part of gasoline (18.5:1) which is the leanest. Richer or leaner air-fuel ratios cause the engine to misfire badly or not run at all. Air-fuel ratios are calculated by weight rather than volume. If it requires 14.7 pounds or kilograms of air to burn one pound or kilogram of gasoline, the air-fuel ratio is 14.7 to 1 ... The ideal mixture or ratio at which all the fuel combines with all of the oxygen in the air and burns completely is called the **stoichiometric ratio** – a chemically perfect combination. In theory, this ratio is an air-fuel mixture of 14.7 to 1. In reality, the exact ratio at which perfect mixture and combustion occurs depends on the molecular structure of gasoline, which varies somewhat. The stoichiometric ratio is a compromise between maximum power and maximum economy. Late model computerized vehicles are designed to regulate the air-fuel ratio at stoichiometric.

Excess air in the air-fuel mixture is measured by its deviation from the ideal mixture using the formula λ (lambda) equals the actual inducted air mass divided by the theoretical air requirement. Thus, when the numerator and denominator of this fraction are the same, then λ=1, meaning the air-fuel mixture is perfect. When the mixture is running rich, then λ<1, meaning there is too much fuel for the amount of air available. When the mixture is running lean, then λ>1, meaning there is too much air for the amount of fuel available (Adler 1995, 18). For the best fuel economy, λ should range from 15:1 to 16:1, while the maximum power output is delivered when λ ranges from 12.5:1 to 13.5:1. Unfortunately:

> No single air-fuel ratio provides the best fuel economy and the maximum power output at the same time ... If the goal is to get the most power from an engine, all the oxygen in the mixture must burn because the power output of any engine is limited by the amount of air it can pull in. For the oxygen to combine completely with the available fuel, there should be extra fuel available. This makes the air-fuel ratio richer, with the result that some fuel does not burn.
>
> To get the best fuel economy and the lowest emissions, the gasoline must burn as completely as possible in the combustion chamber. This means combustion with the least amount of leftover waste material, or emissions, provides the greatest economy. The intake system must provide more air to make sure that enough oxygen is available to combine with the gasoline. This results in a leaner air-fuel mixture than the ideal. (DuPuy 2000, 45)

Generally, the smoother the entrance of the air-fuel mixture into the cylinder, the more thorough is its combustion. If it enters in uneven bursts, the pressure in the cylinder increases unevenly and may produce misfires and combustion knock. By employing different designs for diverse components of engines, spark plugs, air and fuel injection systems, fuels, additives, and electronic monitoring systems, it is possible to obtain greater thermal efficiency without engine knock. However, greater thermal efficiency creates higher temperatures in the combustion chamber, which in turn tends to create greater emissions of some harmful pollutants. Exactly which pollutants, with what sort of distribution?

To answer these questions, note first that gasoline is a hydrocarbon (HC) compound made up of hydrogen (H) and carbon (C). If the combustion process were complete, no pollutants would be emitted in an engine's exhaust gases. But it is practically impossible to get a complete process. Nevertheless, setting aside carbon dioxide as a special case concerning indirect effects of greenhouse gases, only about 1 per cent of the total emitted gases is supposed to be harmful to the environment or humans (Adler 1995, 16). One must read such percentages with considerable caution because different sources give different estimates of the relative amounts of exhaust gases, sometimes under the same and sometimes under different experimental conditions. Estimates vary with the specific combination of chemical additives and fuel stocks used, the mechanical apparatus, heat and combustion levels, and the duration, replication, and verification of tests. After examining several sources, I cobbled together the following fairly representative list from the Province of British Columbia 1997, SG1.2– SG1.6, 15.1–15.14; DuPuy 2000, 4–5; and Adler 1995, 16–17:

1. Nitrogen (N_2) makes up 71% to 78% of exhaust gases. It is the most abundant element in the atmosphere and it is not toxic. Ordinary air is about 78% nitrogen, 21% oxygen (O_2), and 1% other gases.

2. Carbon dioxide (CO_2) makes up from 13.5% to 16.5% of exhaust gases. It is formed during respiration and organic decomposition, as well as during combustion, and is one of several so-called greenhouse gases that are raising the earth's temperature by trapping ultraviolet radiation. Generally, the more thorough the combustion, the greater the share of CO_2.

3. Carbon monoxide (CO), making up from 0.1% to 0.5%, is an odourless, colourless, tasteless, and highly toxic gas formed as a result of the inadequate supply of oxygen leading to incomplete combustion.

4. Oxides of nitrogen (NO_x), making up from 0.05% to 0.1%, include nitric oxide (NO) (about 0.01% of the total gases emitted), nitrogen dioxide (NO_2), nitrous oxide (N_2O), and nitrogen trioxide (N_2O_3). They are all toxic substances, formed when oxygen combines with nitrogen at combustion temperatures of at least 2500°C. When combined with volatile organic compounds (VOC), hot, stagnant air masses, and sunlight, they produce the dangerously irritating pollutant ground level ozone, which is the main ingredient of smog.

5. Hydrocarbon (HC), making up less than 0.005%, which is just unburned fuel.

6. Oxygen (O_2), making up from 0.1% to 1%.

7. Water (H_2O), approximately 6% to 7%.

8. Particulate matter (PM) or soot/carbon of diverse sizes; e.g., matter less than or equal to 10 microns ($PM \leq 10$), or less than or equal to 2.5 microns ($PM \leq 2.5$).

9. Traces of sulphur dioxide (SO_2), hydrogen, and aldehydes.

Anyone familiar with nineteenth-century literature and biography will recall vivid descriptions of the streets of major urban centres polluted with the excrement of hundreds of horses carrying individuals and pulling wagons and carriages. For people living in such circumstances, one of the main benefits of horseless carriages was the elimination of horses' pollutants. If anyone had warned those people that in the future their streets would be awash in an array of exhaust gases flowing out of the tailpipes of horseless carriages that were at least as dangerous if not as disgusting as what was flowing out of the tail-end of horses, the history of motor vehicles might have been quite different.

In North America, it was not until the passage of the U.S. Clean Air Act in 1970 and the establishment of the U.S. Environmental Protection Agency (EPA) that a serious national effort was initiated to get exhaust gases under control. Since then, the severity of legislation concerning allowable pollutants has continuously increased in that country and Canada. We will not review this legislation here, but it is important to remember that government has played and will continue to play a key role in controlling motor vehicle pollutants. It is also important for Canadians to recognize the extent to which they have been and will continue to be relatively free riders on the initiatives of the EPA, rather casually and informally from 1970 until 1992.

As I explain more thoroughly in chapter 6, in February 1992 Transport Canada and the motor vehicle manufacturers signed a *Memorandum of Understanding* committing them to harmonizing Canadian emission standards with those of the United States, and in July 1997 the Canadian Motor Vehicle Safety Regulations were officially changed to harmonize national emission standards for HC, CO, and NO_x with those of the United States. The regulations even included the U.S. requirement to have sophisticated on-board diagnostic monitoring systems (OBDs) installed in all new vehicles. While some Canadians may believe that such dependence on our neighbour borders on parasitism, it is entirely reasonable, considering that Canada has about 8 per cent of the North American motor vehicle market and that about 88 per cent of the vehicles made in Canada are sold in the United States (SSCEENR 2/4, 1997b, 13; CPPI Technical Task Force 1995, 3). Besides, given the relative aggressiveness of the EPA on air quality issues compared to the relatively passive approach of any relevant federal agency in Canada, Canadians are better off harmonizing our regulations than making up our own. (This claim will be supported in detail below in a fuller discussion of issues around harmonization.) In Canada we have peculiar jurisdictional responsibilities. While Transport Canada regulates emission technology, Environment Canada regulates fuel formulation. However, the strength of these two departments is not the same. Transport Canada can make regulations for the whole country, but Environment Canada can only set standards which become effective only if provincial governments agree (SSCEENR 2/6, 1997e, 18–20; SSCEENR 2/19, 1997g, 14; see also detailed discussion in chapter 5). As VanNijnatten (2002, 152) explained: "the provinces actually establish air quality standards for air pollutants within their boundaries. The federal government sets science-based guidelines for ambient levels (in the surrounding atmosphere) of 'criteria' air pollutants (ozone, SO_2, NO_2, volatile organic compounds or VOCs, CO_2), but these are non-binding. The provinces do tend to fashion their policies in a manner consistent with the national objectives, however."

Regarding emission technology, the three components we have yet to describe are spark plugs, catalytic converters, and OBDs. Because of the extraordinary demands made on them, spark plugs come in a great variety of shapes using a variety of materials. One end of the plug has a high-voltage connector attached to an ignition cable, which is in turn connected to an ignition coil, which is connected to a vehicle's battery. The purpose of the coil is to step up the 12 volt battery voltage to the 10,000 to 25,000 volts needed to produce an arc across the spark plug gap. When an operator turns the key to start the vehicle, a charge is sent from the battery to the high-voltage connector, which proceeds down a centre electrode to the bottom of the plug and then arcs across the small air gap to a ground electrode. That arc between the centre and ground electrodes is the spark that ignites the air-fuel mixture, and the size of the arc is a function of the plug's materials, the original voltage, and the distance between the electrodes.

The demands on a plug's materials are severe. It must be able to sustain voltages as high as 30,000 volts without uncontrolled arcing, and pressures up to 100 bar. (A bar is a unit of pressure equal to 10^5 newtons per square metre, and a single newton is a force strong enough to accelerate a kilogram of mass one metre per second, per second.) The plug's insulator must be able to tolerate thermal shocks, with temperatures rising as high as 1000°C when the air-fuel mixture burns and then rapidly cooling when the next mixture of relatively cool air-fuel is inducted into the chamber. Over time, ignition sparks literally burn away bits of electrodes (erosion) and diverse chemical deposits form (corrosion) that alone and in combination cause misfiring and engine knocking. Older engines sometimes leak oil into the combustion chamber, which also leads to "deposits of soot, ash and oil carbon on the spark plug and may lead to shunts" (Adler 1995, 182–96). A shunt occurs when, instead of a charge causing a spark across the air gap between the centre and ground electrodes, it grounds itself by travelling down the shell of the plug, again producing a misfire and increased pollutants.

Catalytic converters were introduced in the United States in 1975 to accommodate EPA exhaust emission standards for HC, CO and NO_x. We need not review the levels of permitted exhaust gases since 1975, but there has been and will continue to be a demand for fewer and fewer emissions leading eventually to Zero Emission Vehicles (ZEV) (Province of British Columbia 1995). According to the Province of British Columbia (1997, 7.5), although "the catalytic converter became an almost universal device beginning in 1975 ... In Canada ... there were calls from industry to resist adopting catalyst-forcing emission levels, citing fuel economy benefits to be derived from less stringent regulations ... The less stringent emission standards continued in Canada through the 1987 model year...[but] there was never any positive proof supplied that indicated that the fuel economy of a Canadian-recalibrated [system] was superior to its U.S. counterpart with a 3-way system."

Of the many converters, those of interest to us are three-way catalytic converters (TWCs) which convert the three exhaust gases, HC, CO, and NO_x to H_2O, CO_2, N_2, and O_2. Two different chemical processes are involved in TWCs: oxidation and reduction. Through oxidation, which is just combustion, HC and CO are converted to H_2O and CO_2. Through reduction, O_2 is removed from NO_x, converting the latter into N_2 and O_2.

TWCs are designed to allow exhaust gases from engines to flow through them on their way to being emitted through a vehicle's tailpipe. The TWC has two chambers, each with a ceramic or aluminum oxide substrate in the shape of a honeycomb that is covered with thin layers of inactive or inert metals called "noble metals." HC and CO are oxidized by passing them over platinum, palladium, or cerium, while NO_x is reduced by passing over rhodium. Since oxygen is required for the oxidation process, the rhodium bed chamber is the first in line in a TWC and oxygen produced in the reduction process supplements additional oxygen injected into the second chamber for the oxidation process.

A catalyst begins to work at 50 per cent effectiveness when its temperature reaches about 250°C and becomes fully effective from about 400°C to 800°C. "In the range from 800°C to 1000°C, thermal aging is significantly aggravated ... [and] Above 1000°C, thermal aging increases severely, up to the almost total ineffectiveness of the catalytic converter" (Adler 1995, 25). These figures suggest that to bring a TWC relatively rapidly to its optimum operating temperature, installing it close to the engine would offer some advantage, but to prevent it from excessive thermal aging, installing it farther away from the engine would offer some advantage. Nevertheless, wherever a TWC is located, engine misfires can cause its temperature to increase to over 1400°C, which is enough to destroy it.

One of the most interesting, useful, and important things about the functioning of TWCs is their ability to reduce exhaust gas emissions of HC, CO, and NO_x at the same time. The earliest versions of catalytic converters used only the oxidation process, which converted HC and CO but left NO_x unchanged. Following that, a second converter using the reduction process was connected in series to the oxidation converter, achieving the conversion of all three gases, but relatively expensively compared to TWCs. Thus, TWCs have become the preferred type of converter.

Figure 4.1, taken from a 1989 edition of the *Automotive Electric/Electronic Systems* handbook, displays the problem that TWCs have to solve and the nature of the solution. The left half of the figure shows the distribution curves for the three engine exhaust gases before they flow through the converter and the right half shows the distribution of the same curves after they flow through the converter. In both halves, the horizontal axis measures deviations from ideal air-fuel mixtures, with the perfect mixture ($\lambda=1$) at the vertical axis in the centre of the figure, rich mixtures ($\lambda<1$) to the left, and lean mixtures ($\lambda>1$) to the right. Immediately below the λ values in both halves, air-fuel ratios (A/F ratios) are recorded, with the ideal ratio (14.7:1) at the vertical axis, rich mixtures as low as 13.2:1 to the left, and lean mixtures as high as 16.2:1 to the right. The vertical axis is not labelled in figure 1 in Bosch, but it represents various levels of HC, CO, and NO_x emissions. For our purposes, the relative shapes of the curves are what is important.

The curves on the left side of the left half of the figure indicate the engineering problem to be solved. As the air-fuel mixture becomes richer (i.e., from the perfect 14.7:1 to 13.2:1), the HC and CO curves ascend but the NO_x curve descends. That means that while an engine's power and HC and CO exhaust emissions are increasing, its NO_x exhaust emissions are decreasing. The curves on the left side of the right half of the figure show the engineered solution effected by TWCs. The right half of the figure shows that as the air-fuel mixture becomes richer, the HC and CO curves still ascend but the NO_x curve is perfectly flat. However, even more important, note that in the right half of the figure, the closer all three curves come to the ideal air-fuel ratio of 14.7:1 (where $\lambda=1$), the lower each curve is on the vertical axis. That means that a TWC can minimize the emissions of all three exhaust gas pollutants by maintaining an air-fuel ratio of approximately 14.7 to 1. The heavy black vertical band in the figure indicates the very narrow range in which the air-fuel mixture is allowed to vary, roughly within 1 per cent of

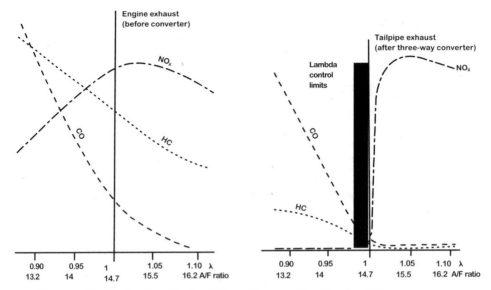

Figure 4.1 Pre-Catalyst/Post-Catalyst Exhaust Concentrations (Bosch, 1989)

the ideal $\lambda=1$. Also, as indicated by the Province of British Columbia (1997, 17.11): "When high CO readings are observed, a three-way catalyst vehicle will have almost no NO_x emissions. Conversely, if the CO readings are around zero, NO_x emissions may be very high. Since the NO_x conversion efficiency of a three way catalyst more or less switches from 100% on the rich side to 0% on the lean side, an excursion into lean operation will be accompanied by a huge change in NO_x results. Since the HC and CO curves are relatively flat around the stoichiometric point, there will be little, if any, noticeable change in either of these readings."

In addition, an excursion into rich operation from a slightly leaner operation will be accompanied by a huge change in NO_x results, this time a huge decrease rather than a huge increase.

Apparently, then, TWCs are quite remarkable devices. The trick is to control the diverse components of the engine and emission systems (including the TWCs) to make sure that the air-fuel ratio is as close to 14.7 to 1 as possible. That is the job of the Powertrain Control Module, acting on signals from OBDs. The California Air Resources Board (CARB) demanded the first OBD systems to be introduced in automobiles in the 1988 model year. Called OBD I systems, they consisted of on-board computers that would monitor "critical emissions-related components" and warn drivers of any malfunctions. The main problem with OBD I technology was that different manufacturers used different diagnostic codes which "caused some confu-

sion within the repair and service sectors of the automotive industry."
Thus, following some consultations with the public and manufacturers, a
new generation of OBDs called OBD II were developed for 1994 and later
models. "The USEPA adopted the OBD II strategies into the US Clean Air Act
of 1990. As Canada harmonized its emissions standards with the US since
the 1988 model year, OBD II is a reality for the Canadian fleet. In Canada,
the phasing in of OBD II means that 40% of all 1994 model year vehicles,
80% of all 1995 model year vehicles and all 1996 model year vehicles will
be equipped with OBD II" (Province of British Columbia 1997, 2).

Generally speaking, OBDs work by receiving voltage signals from strategically placed sensors, decoding and storing them for periodic inspection or
immediately sending out signals to various management systems to make
required changes in certain functions. For example, by placing oxygen sensors in front of and behind TWCs, and comparing the concentration of the
various gases (based on voltage signals) as they enter and leave a TWC, an
OBD II system may test the efficiency of a converter and command adjustments to the air-fuel mixture. According to a report submitted to the House
Standing Committee on Environment and Sustainable Development, "OBD
II systems mandated by CARB and EPA" as early as 1995 monitored "over
100 subsystems," including "catalyst deterioration, spark plug misfire,
evaporative system, oxygen sensors, electronic input, electronic output,
EGR [exhaust gas recirculation] system, fuel system [and] secondary air"
(MVMA/AIAMC 1995, 39).

The last bit of basic science we need concerns the chemical compound at
the centre of our story. MMT is a fuel additive that has been used in Canada
since 1976 to increase the octane rating of unleaded gasoline and reduce
engine-knocking. Chemically, it is an organometallic compound with a
molecular formula of $C_9H_7MmO_3$ and molecular weight of 218.1, 25.2 per
cent of which is manganese. In appearance, "it is a flammable orange liquid
with a faint herbaceous odor" (Midwest Research Institute 1987, 4). Its
half-life in the atmosphere is about 15 seconds (Wood and Egyed 1994, 1).
On average, until 2004, about 9 milligrams per litre (mg/l) were added to
unleaded gasoline in Canadian refineries, although the Canadian General
Standards Board allows 18 mg/l. In 1995 the Canadian Petroleum Products
Institute (CPPI) Technical Task Force reported that "While all refineries use
MMT, its use rate is not predictable by geographic location, by refinery, or
by time of year" (1).

MMT is sold in Canada by Ethyl Canada Inc., a corporation incorporated
in Ontario with a head office in Mississauga, Ontario. Ethyl Canada Inc. is
owned by a single shareholder, Ethyl Corporation, an American corpora-

tion incorporated in the State of Virginia with a head office in Richmond. Ethyl Corporation purchases raw materials to make MMT and supplies these materials to an independent Albemarle Corporation in Virginia, which processes them to make MMT. Ethyl Corporation then sells the finished product to Ethyl Canada Inc. in a concentrated form, either directly or indirectly through its wholly owned subsidiary, Ethyl Petroleum Additives Inc. Upon importing the concentrated product, Ethyl Canada Inc. processes it in a blending facility in Corunna, Ontario, and sells the finished MMT to petroleum refiners across the country. It is important to emphasize that MMT is only manufactured in the United States. Only blending occurs at the Corunna facility. By December 1995 MMT was used in about 95 per cent of the unleaded gasoline sold in Canada and was approved for use in forty-nine American states (Appleton, 1997a, 5; 1997b, 2; AIT Hearings, 1998a, 121).

In 2004 most major oil companies in Canada voluntarily discontinued the use of MMT in unleaded gasoline (Finn, 2004). On the basis of my own enquiries to companies and an e-mail dated 1 October 2004 from Bruce McEwen, Oil, Gas and Energy Branch, Environment Canada, it was determined that use of the product was suspended on 1 January 2004 by Shell Canada; 1 April 2004 by Petro-Canada; 15 April 2004 by Imperial Oil; 1 May 2004 by Suncor Energy Products Inc.; and 15 July 2004 by Ultramar.

Answering my question "Could you tell me why it [MMT] was finally removed?" (20 September 2004), Petro-Canada's Customer Service representative replied the very next day that "Petro-Canada's number one priority is our customers. We appreciate there are conflicting views about the continued use of MMT and have therefore temporarily suspended the use of MMT at our manufacturing facilities as of April 1st, 2004."

Although I did not put the question to other companies, McEwen's letter included some relevant quotations from newspapers and industry journals. For example, an article in *Inside Fuels and Vehicles* (18 March 2004) said: "An official with one of the two oil companies suspending use of MMT (Shell and Imperial), said: 'The data [on MMT's effects on emissions control systems] is compelling enough to make us concerned.'" An article from *Octane Week* (12 April 2004) said: "At least two major refiners are voluntarily suspending MMT use until the Canadian government finishes an independent third-party review of the additive ... Petro-Canada confirmed that it is one of the companies suspending MMT use until the review is complete."

Regarding the usage suspensions and the proposed third-party study of MMT, Ethyl Corporation's website (at Afton Chemicals) reported on 8 March 2004:

the Government of Canada recently released its "Proposed Framework for an Independent Third Party Review of New Information on the Effects of MMT on Vehicle Emissions." In their proposal, the Canadian Government provided no timetable for the commencement or completion of the review. Ethyl welcomes the independent third-party review of MMT, which we believe, when properly designed, conducted and interpreted, will reaffirm that MMT is compatible with modern emission control devices.

Ethyl Corporation has been informed by our two largest customers in Canada of their intention to suspend the use of the gasoline additive MMT pending the results of the Government of Canada-sponsored independent third party review. While this suspension will have a negative impact on our Canadian business, Ethyl's management believes that the suspension is not likely to have a material adverse effect upon the overall financial performance of the Company. MMT is one of the most extensively tested fuel additives in history. While we are disappointed with the decision of our customers, we believe the MMT is an environmentally beneficial product that has proven its effectiveness in real-world use. (Accessed 10 January 2005)

Responding to my question about whether "any progress had been made" on the third-party review (10 January 2005 e-mail), Don Stewart, Strategic Advisor, Transportation Systems Branch, Environment Canada, told me that "We are finalizing terms of reference for the review. They should be distributed to stakeholders in the next few weeks. Our hope is to have a contract in place later this winter so the review can begin before the spring" (11 January 2005 e-mail).

The original proposal that was put on the Environment Canada website may be found at http://www.ec.gc.ca/transport/mmt2003/draftProposal _e.htm. The following items illustrate the relatively narrow limits of the expected review:

The third-party review process would not be expected to make policy recommendations. The findings of the third-party review process would provide a technical basis to support a determination by the Government of Canada as to whether there may be a need for any government action on this issue ... the third party must have a formalized set of procedural guidelines and a proven track record to ensure that the expert panel can operate in a manner that is independent,

objective, unbiased and free of conflicts of interest, real or perceived ...
the third party would not address issues related to:
- the possible effects of MMT on emissions from refineries;
- tailpipe emissions of manganese-containing substances, except any
  contribution to tailpipe emissions of total particulates;
- health effects resulting from any emissions of manganese-containing
  substances from the tailpipe or from any effect of MMT on emissions
  of criteria pollutants; or
- potential regulatory or non-regulatory measures by the government,
  including any related cost analyses ...

[the third-party would address the questions]

i.   Does the use of MMT in gasoline affect emissions (increasing or
     decreasing them) from any specific models of vehicles under
     operating conditions that may be reasonably expected to occur in
     Canada? In the affirmative, can it be concluded that there is a
     consistent effect across all vehicles, specific groups of vehicles or
     emission control technologies?

ii. Would the use of MMT in gasoline adversely affect the introduction
     of any vehicle combustion or engine technology or emission control
     equipment that has been developed to the point where it would oth-
     erwise be expected to be in general use in North America within a
     reasonable time? (Website address above, accessed 10 January
     2005)

As we saw earlier in this chapter and will see in most of the following
chapters, the four items that will not be addressed and the two questions
that will be addressed by the third party are very problematic. One can
appreciate Environment Canada's strategy of addressing a limited number
of issues sequentially, assuming that some issues may or may not require
research depending on results obtained from this first round. The focus on
any effects on emissions is also wise. According to Juanós i Timoneda
(1997, 289), "the regulation of MMT should focus (regardless of, or in addition to, other health and welfare considerations) on the increased emission
of particulate matter caused by MMT's combustion products," because of
the increasing evidence concerning the dangers of such emissions. I can
only wish them well.

5

EPA Regulations, Company Tests, Appeals, and Judgments

This chapter reviews the salient parts of the regulatory history of MMT in the United States, sketching the variety of tests run and the supporting data obtained by various concerned companies and researchers, the EPA regulatory rules and administrative procedures, and the contributions of the U.S. Court of Appeals. Several features of this history had a significant impact on the NAFTA and AIT cases, and will continue to have an impact on the commercial prospects of MMT.

The *U.S. Clean Air Act*, section 211 (f)(1) prohibits the introduction of new fuels and fuel additives unless they are "substantially similar" to fuels or additives that were used in the certification of light-duty motor vehicles of any model in 1975 or later. However, it is possible under section 211 (f)(4) to obtain a waiver for the section 211 (f) prohibition if a manufacturer can show that the fuel or additive "will not cause or contribute to a failure of any emission control device or system ... to achieve compliance by the vehicle with the emission standards" (Court 1995, 2). Sections 211 (a)–(c) introduce broader potential barriers to the sale of fuels and additives. Section 211 (a) says that the sale of fuels or additives may be prohibited by the EPA administrator unless they are registered under section 211 (b). The latter section says that manufacturers may be required:

"to conduct tests to determine potential public health effects of such fuel or additive" and to furnish information regarding the fuel additive's effect on "the emission control performance of any vehicle ... or the extent to which such emissions affect the public health or welfare" ... [section 211] (b)(2)(A),(B). Under section 211 (c), the Administrator may "control or prohibit" the manufacture or sale of any fuel additive, if she determines that "any emission product of such ... fuel additive causes, or contributes, to air pollution which may reasonably be anticipated to endanger the public health or welfare" or "impair to a significant degree the performance of any emission control device or system which is in general use." [Section 211] (c)(1)(A),(B) (Court 1995, 4)

Information requirements to obtain a waiver under section 211 (f)(4) were posted by the EPA in 1978 and, according to Chief Judge Edwards, whose account I am following throughout this section, those requirements "do not mention a public health criterion or any testing procedures for determining public health effects. Before the waiver decision at issue in this case [argued 13 January 1995], the Agency had considered twenty-three applications for waivers under section 211 (f)(4), and it never previously relied on public health effects in denying a waiver" (Court 1995, 5–6).

Ethyl Corporation filed its first application for a waiver for MMT under section 211 (f)(4) on 17 March 1978; it was denied on the grounds that the product had "a statistically significant adverse HC emissions effect." Ethyl's second application was filed on 26 May 1981; it failed because the company "failed to demonstrate that the requested level of MMT in unleaded gasoline would not cause or contribute to the failure of vehicles to comply with emission standards." A third application was submitted on 9 May 1990 but withdrawn on 1 November 1990 because "the EPA had generated some data at an Ann Arbor, Michigan test facility that contradicted Ethyl's data; Ethyl subsequently demonstrated that contaminated fuel caused the Ann Arbor test results." On 12 July 1991 Ethyl made its fourth application for a waiver; it was denied on 8 January 1992 because of data provided to the EPA by Ford Motor Company showing that "MMT-induced HC emissions increases are potentially far greater than those reported by Ethyl" (Court 1995, 6–7).

Ethyl filed a petition for review of the EPA's fourth denial in the U.S. Court of Appeals for the District of Columbia on 13 February 1992 and, at the same time, gave the EPA new test data contradicting Ford's data. The EPA was impressed enough by what it saw to ask the Court of Appeals to remand Ethyl's petition back to the EPA so the latter could reconsider its fourth denial. The court granted the EPA's request on 6 April 1993 and sent its mandate to the agency on 3 June 1993, giving the latter 180 days (to 30 November 1993) to decide what to do about Ethyl's fourth application. After more negotiations between Ethyl Corporation and the EPA, Ethyl resubmitted its fourth application on 30 November 1993. That automatically began another 180-day review period, which was extended to 13 July 1994, at which time the EPA again denied Ethyl's resubmitted fourth application. That, of course, led Ethyl to another petition for review by the Court of Appeals which, as we will see shortly, finally brought the company success (Court 1995, 7–8; FR 1994, 42,229–30).

Around the early 1990s, people at the EPA began to worry about the "possible adverse health effects of ... airborne manganese resulting from MMT use". In particular, knowing the "severe neurotoxic effects of high-level exposure to manganese in humans," they were concerned about the absence of good information about people's exposure to low levels of inhalation of manganese tetroxide (Mn_3O_4, also called hausmannite) over long periods and what effects such exposure might have. Manganese tetroxide is the main emission product from the combustion of MMT, along with traces of manganic oxide (Mn_2O_3) and from 0.05 to 0.1 per cent unburned MMT (Midwest Research Institute 1987, 5).

Everyone knew that "manganese will accumulate in people" (Kraucher 1993, 5). Walter M. Kraucher was Manager for Advanced Environmental and Fuels Engineering, Ford Motor Company. Earlier research had shown neurobehavioural effects (e.g., tremor, reduced hand steadiness), reproductive effects (e.g., fewer children born to manganese-exposed workers), sexual dysfunction, and respiratory tract illnesses. "The evidence for the neurobehavioral effects of low-level Mn exposure by inhalation was compelling and consistent across several well-conducted studies," and there was no reported threshold of exposure for such effects. On 12–15 March 1991, with the National Institute of Environmental Health, the agency held a conference on issues related to "manganese health risk assessment." By the time of the remand of Ethyl's fourth waiver application (November 1993), the EPA Office of Research and Development (ORD) revised its reference concentration (RfC) for inhaled manganese and manganese compounds from the 1984 figure of 1.0 µg Mn/m^3 (i.e., one microgram (10^{-6} or one-millionth of a gram) of manganese per cubic metre) and the 1990 figure of 0.4 µg Mn/m^3 to 0.05 µg Mn/m^3 (Wood and Egyed 1994, ii).

An inhalation reference concentration is defined as an estimate (*with uncertainty spanning perhaps an order of magnitude*) of a continuous inhalation exposure to the human population (including sensitive subgroups) that is likely to be without appreciable risk of deleterious non-cancer health effects during a lifetime. The methodology for establishing an RfC accounts for uncertainties and gaps in the health data base through the assignment of uncertainty factors. (FR 1994, 422,30; emphasis added)

It is important to emphasize the italicized phrase in the preceding quotation and to realize that a scientifically reasonable estimated RFC number of x might lie anywhere in the range from $1/10$ of x to 10 times x. If you imagine standing on an ordinary weighing scale that registers your 150 pound weight at anywhere from 15 pounds to 1,500 pounds, you get some feeling for the kind of uncertainty involved in RFC estimates. The range of uncertainty regarding the RFC value of 0.05 μm Mn/m^3 runs from 0.005 μm Mn/m^3 to .5 μm Mn/m^3. The last sentence in the quotation tells us that in order to compensate for "uncertainties and gaps in the health" information currently available, measures of uncertainty ("uncertainty factors") are estimated. In fact, a variety of procedures and formulae for estimating such uncertainties are described in the *Federal Register* document followed in this summary (FR 1994, 42,240–45).

The EPA's current (i.e., at 25 August 2007) RFC for inhaled manganese has not changed since it came into effect on 1 December 1993 (http://www.epa.gov/iris/subst/0373.htm). The Health Canada RFC is 0.11 μg Mn/m^3 and the World Health Organization's is 0.15 μg Mn/m^3. Tellingly, the main studies cited in support of all these RFCs are those from Roels et al. (1987, 1992), although as we will see in chapter 11 quite a bit has happened since then. However, before becoming overly stressed about the problems of discovering the most appropriate RFC figure, one should remember a remark of Tony Clarke, Assistant Deputy Minister for Environment Canada, to the Senate Standing Committee: "in the environmental field today, we are dealing with trace amounts of things in the environment that accumulate over time. It does not matter whether it is one drop or two or three. Using dioxins as an example, one part in a billion will ensure that there will be reproductive effects in certain forms of wild life ... My point is that quantity is not always important; it is trace amounts and the accumulation in the human systems that are of concern" (SSCEENR 2/4, 1997a, 10).

Similarly, more recently Zayed (2001, 430) reminded us that "Risk assessment for Mn toxicity cannot be done only on the basis of cross-sectional evaluations because of Mn being a neurotoxic substance with a cumulative mechanism of action. Therefore, an estimated 'safe exposure level' derived from cross-sectional analysis cannot be appropriate to protect a population with a prolonged period of exposure. This is clearly important for the general population that may be exposed for an entire life-time. The risk assessment and the establishment of RFC should be based on cumulative exposure indices, that better reflect the long term exposure situation."

As explained above, while section 211 (f)(4) of the *Clean Air Act* focuses on emission control systems, sections 211 (a)–(c) introduce broader considerations of "public health and welfare." From the EPA's point of view, satisfaction of each section was necessary and their joint satisfaction was sufficient to warrant granting a waiver. Unfortunately, the court did not see it that way. Among other things, the EPA argued that because section 211 (f)(4) said that "The Administrator ... *may* waive the prohibitions" (emphasis added), there was no obligation to waive them. Congress apparently intended to give the administrator some "discretionary authority." The court's view was that the force of "may" in that clause applied only to that clause, meaning that the administrator had the discretionary authority to grant or not grant the waiver but, if nothing at all was done, at the end of 180 days the waiver would be automatically granted (Court 1995, 11–12).

The following passages summarize the court's position with respect to the two parts of section 211:

> The language of section 211 (c)(1) demonstrates that Congress crafted a very definite scheme in which the Administrator was to consider certain criteria before taking certain actions. Specifically, she considers emission effects of fuel additives before granting waivers under section 211 (f)(4), and emissions effects as well as public health effects before prohibiting or controlling the manufacture or sale of fuel additives under section 211 (c)(1). The language of section 211 (c)(1) only underscores our conclusion that Congress did not delegate to the Agency the authority to consider other factors "in the public interest" such as public health when acting under section 211 (f)(4) ... we see no need to imply authority under section 211 (f)(4) to consider public health when Congress explicitly directed the Administrator to consider public health in 211 (c)(1) proceedings ... Should the Administrator wish to consider whether the emission products of MMT "may reasonably be anticipated to endanger the public health" ... she may initiate proceedings under section 211 (c)(1). (Court 1995, 16–21)

While the court's interpretation of the relevant parts of section 211 seem to be very narrow so far, when it addressed the claim of the American Automobile Manufacturers Association (the intervenor) that the statute explicitly talked about "any emission" failure (Ford made the same claim in Kraucher 1993, 2), the court's interpretation became fairly broad:

In determining that Ethyl met the emissions criterion, the Administrator noted that the applicant bears "the burden of establishing that its fuel will not cause or contribute to the failure of any vehicle to meet emission standards," however, "if interpreted literally ... this burden of proof imposed by the Act would be virtually impossible for an applicant to meet, as it requires the proof of a negative proposition: that no vehicle will fail to meet emission standards to which it has been certified" ... thus, the Agency allowed "reliable statistical sampling and fleet testing protocols" to be used to demonstrate that the additive will not cause emissions failures ... The Agency analyzes emission effects "using statistical tests to determine if the fuel additive will cause a 'significant' number of vehicles to fail emissions tests" ... The Administrator also examined "Ethyl's data on the use of the additive with newer technology vehicles under more stringent criteria," requiring that "the additive cause no statistically significant increase in emissions," and found that the EPA could not "discern any 'real' emissions increase at all – that is, no increase that [it could] not reasonably attribute to sampling error" ... The Administrator's analysis of the data submitted by Ethyl was careful and searching; AAMA did not come close to proving that the Administrator's analysis of the data was arbitrary and capricious. (Court 1995, 22–4)

The last quoted sentence above refers to one of two criteria that the court had indicated it would use to decide whether it should "reverse the Agency's action," namely, "arbitrary and capricious" analysis of data by the agency. The other criterion was based on the "Agency's action" that was judged to be "in excess of statutory jurisdiction, authority, or limitations, or short of statutory right," which was in fact the criterion actually employed (Court 1995, 22). According to the EPA's interpretation:

Although the discretion of the Administrator to consider other factors in making a waiver decision is broad, it is not unfettered. To assure that any decision based on factors other than emission standard failures is not arbitrary and is based on a proper record, the applicant and other interested persons should be afforded proper notice of any additional factors to be considered by the Administrator and an opportunity to comment or submit information concerning those factors. Any decision based on the discretionary authority of the Administrator to consider other factors should include an explanation of the factors which were considered and the relation of those factors to the decision. Moreover, any policy adopted as part of a decision to deny a waiver on a discretionary basis should be applied consistently to all similarly situated applicants. (FR 1994, 42,234)

Speaking of consistency, as remarked above, the court remembered that there had been twenty-two previous waiver applications and the question of public health effects had not been raised.

At the end of its written decision, the court addressed the "auto manufacturers' concerns about the effect of MMT on OBD systems" saying that "The EPA explained that it was 'currently reviewing' the recent submission [by Ford] and that 'if after further investigation EPA concludes that the concerns expressed by the vehicle manufacturers are warranted, EPA intends to initiate an appropriate rulemaking under section 211 (c)'" (Court 1995, 24).

The court then granted Ethyl's petition for review and instructed "the EPA to grant Ethyl's request for a waiver," emphasizing that this decision did "not have any bearing on the Administrator's authority to initiate appropriate proceedings under section 211 (c) to satisfy any Agency concerns relating to matters of public health" (Court 1995, 25).

Finally, although the court did not accept the EPA's two-step waiver process, there was no mention of the EPA's other assumption that the statute did not allow trading off emission effects. In the EPA's view, "The waiver applicant bears the burden of demonstrating that a fuel will neither cause nor contribute to an emission standard failure for any regulated pollutant. Balancing of the emission effects of a fuel for one pollutant against those for other pollutant(s) is not permissible under the statutory language. For example, an applicant would not meet its burden of proof if its testing of a fuel shows that it causes or contributes to an emission standard failure for CO, even though testing shows decreases in emissions of HC and NO_x" (FR 1994, 42,232).

This assumption had important consequences for auto manufacturers. Testifying before the Senate Standing Committee on Energy, the Environment and Natural Resources, for example, Glenn Brickshaw from Honda Canada said:

As auto manufacturers, we know that we could reduce NO_x. It is very simple for us to do that. If you understand the balancing act that is done, you try to run a vehicle at the very fine tight control point. You have three regulated pollutants to worry about and it is a trade-off between those three: NO_x on one side and hydrocarbons and carbon monoxide on the other. You cannot optimize all three other than at the point right in the middle. If you shift that point to get oxides of nitrogen lower, hydrocarbons and carbon monoxide go up ... We could reduce the NO_x by shifting the point. But we create hydrocarbons, carbon monoxide and more CO_2 because we burn more fuel. It is simple. We could do it, but you are asking us to do something that we cannot do because the regulations say that you must keep all three of those emissions below certain levels. (SSCEENR 2/4, 1997b, 39)

What sorts of tests were required by the EPA, and what was provided by Ethyl Corporation and the motor vehicle manufacturers?

The EPA distinguishes two types of emission testing, back-to-back and durability testing. Regarding the first type, the agency says "Back-to-back emission testing involves testing a vehicle on a base fuel (i.e., a gasoline which meets specifications for certification fuel or is representative of a typically available commercial gasoline), then testing that same vehicle on the fuel for which the waiver is requested. The difference in emission levels is attributed to the waiver fuel" (FR 1994, 42,233).

Regarding the second type:

Unlike materials traditionally allowed in unleaded gasoline, metallics, such as MMT, produce non-gaseous combustion products, some of which may be deposited in the parts of the vehicle that come in contact with the combustion products of the burned fuel. These areas of the vehicle include the combustion chamber, the catalyst, the oxygen sensor, and all parts of the exhaust system. Since these materials build up over time, it has been traditionally accepted that the emissions effects of such additives occur over time as miles are accumulated, and that the method of deposition suggests that the effects are permanent. If the fuel is predicted to have such a long-term deteriorative effect, durability testing over the useful life of the vehicle, in addition to back-to-back testing, is appropriate ... Durability testing over the useful life of the vehicle has involved testing two identical sets of vehicles ... one set using the base fuel and the other using the waiver fuel. Each vehicle is tested for emissions at 5,000 mile intervals. This is essentially the same testing pattern which has been required for certification of a new motor vehicle under Sec. 206 of the Act. (FR 1994, 42,233)

For light-duty vehicles of year model 1993 or earlier, "useful life" meant 50,000 miles or five years, whichever came first. For 1994 and later models, it meant 100,000 miles or ten years. Following its explanations of the two types of testing, the EPA wrote: "The Agency believes that its present statistical tests and criteria do not give adequate weight to the requirement in Section 211 (f)(4) that an applicant demonstrates that a fuel will not 'contribute' to an emission standard failure ... The Agency expects to initiate a rulemaking in the near future which will propose more appropriate criteria and statistical methodologies for reviewing waiver applications and will afford formal notice to future applicants of the Agency's intention to adopt revised criteria and methodologies" (FR 1994, 42,233–34).

In 1988 Ethyl Corporation tested forty-eight light-duty vehicles with the aim of demonstrating that MMT would not "cause or contribute" to the failure of any vehicle's emissions control systems. The vehicles were selected to be fairly representative of those in use in the United States in 1988: six Buick Centurys (2.5 litre); six Buick Centurys (2.8 litre); six Buick Centurys (3.8 litre); six Chevrolet Cavaliers (2.0 litre); six Ford Escorts (1.9 litre); six Ford Tauruses (3.0 litre); six Ford Crown Victorias (5.0 litre); and six Dodge Dynastys (3.0 litre). They were driven according to a standardized routine called the Alternative Mileage Accumulation Cycle (AMA). As the EPA described it:

A driving cycle is a description of how to drive a vehicle to accumulate mileage, including such things as what percentage of driving should be done at what speed and what the overall average speed should be ... A driving cycle is used so that test vehicles accumulate mileage in a manner that is supposedly representative of in-use vehicles. The emissions of a test vehicle that has accumulated mileage according to a driving cycle representative of in-use vehicles are more likely to be representative of in-use vehicles' emissions. There are actually three alternative cycles associated with the AMA; however, the average speeds of the three alternatives are very similar, ranging from 29.9 mph to 30.72 mph. (FR 1994, 42,234)

Using two different laboratories and tests specified by the EPA in 1978, emissions from every vehicle were examined following the durability guidelines mentioned above "at 5,000-mile intervals up to 75,000 miles in the case of most vehicles and up to 100,000 miles in the case of several." Exhaust emissions were measured for levels of the regulated pollutants HC, NO_x, and CO, and measures were also made of some vehicles for "evaporative HC, particulate and manganese emissions, materials compatibility, driveability and catalyst durability" (FR 1994, 42,234).

On the basis of all its tests, Ethyl reported that:

Its analysis indicated that, on average, MMT at the requested concentration would result in a 0.018 gpm increase in HC emissions and decreases in NO$_x$ and CO emissions. The analysis further indicated that, when EPA's previously used tests are applied, the increase in HC emissions would not cause or contribute to vehicles' failure to meet the current HC emission standard. The results of Ethyl's testing for materials compatibility, driveability and catalyst durability also indicated that MMT would have no significant adverse effects on vehicles' ability to meet current emission standards under average driving conditions. On that basis, Ethyl claimed that it had made its statutorily required showing. (FR 1994, 42,234)

To prove that MMT did not damage catalyst efficiency, Ethyl performed and reported the results of back pressure tests on several vehicles "after accumulation of 75,000 miles": "Back pressure tests are used to determine if significant plugging has occurred in a vehicle's catalyst. The total pressure ahead of a catalyst is back pressure. This pressure is a measure of constriction in flow through the exhaust system caused by flow of the exhaust through the emissions control system and the noise-reducing components of the vehicle. If plugging has occurred in a vehicle, the total pressure ahead of its catalyst, the back pressure, should be greater than expected (e.g., greater than a matching control vehicle)" (FR 1994, 42,234).

Back pressure tests were performed on pairs of vehicles, one using MMT-fuel and the other using clear fuel. Two Ford Crown Victorias were run at higher speeds than those used in the 48-vehicle test program; two Corvettes were driven "at extremely high speeds (100 mph) for 25,000 miles"; and four Chevrolet Corsicas were run for 100,000 miles. "Slave engine" tests were also run on half of Ethyl's fleet. "'Slave engine' testing is the testing of vehicle components on a single engine which is not in a vehicle. In this case, catalyst efficiencies between control and MMT vehicles were investigated using exhaust gases from this single engine which were routed through the removed catalysts. This would likely result in a more accurate analysis of catalyst efficiency, since one possible confounding factor, vehicle to vehicle variability, would be eliminated" (FR 1994, 42,235).

On the basis of this additional testing, Ethyl reported that "Catalyst efficiencies of the MMT vehicles were not significantly different when compared to the clear fuel vehicles" (FR 1994, 42,234-5).

Impressive as Ethyl's testing programs were, its results were not entirely consistent with those of the Ford Motor Company, which also ran a signifi-

cant set of tests. Unfortunately, the tests run by both companies were sufficiently different to make strict comparisons of results impossible.

Ford tested eight vehicles, representing two model groups using its "newest technology" and running for 105,000 miles. The two models selected
for testing were likely to reveal problems if any models were. The Ford
Explorer was especially vulnerable because of "significantly higher operating temperatures and loads than those of passenger cars," while the Ford
Escort was vulnerable because it had "close-coupled catalysts" (i.e., catalysts installed relatively close to the engines) designed to "meet tighter
emissions standards."

Although Ford and Ethyl tested their fleets with clear fuel versus fuel
with 1/32 grams MMT per gallon of gasoline, the tests run by the two companies differed in at least three ways:

(1) Ford used an ordinary fuel with a fairly standard assortment of additives, while Ethyl used "a very high quality test fuel" without additives.
Parenthetically, the EPA wrote "Although used for actual emissions
testing purposes, Ethyl's fuel would not be allowed for mileage accumulation when certifying vehicles since it is not representative of in-use
fuel" (FR 1994, 42,235).

(2) Ford accumulated mileage using higher average speeds and higher percentages of high speeds than those used in Ethyl's AMA cycle described
above.

(3) Ford tested emissions at five intervals (from 5,000 to 105,000 miles)
using six tests at each one, while Ethyl tested emissions at fifteen intervals (every 5,000 miles to 75,000 miles) with two tests at each one.

At the end of the testing, "Ford's test vehicles showed an elevation of HC
emissions with MMT that was substantially greater than the 0.018 gpm
reported by Ethyl from its test program" (FR 1994, 42,235).

Around the same time, Toyota ran tests on a single vehicle that accumulated 30,000 miles with a fuel containing MMT and then 30,000 more miles
with an MMT-free fuel. After the first 30,000 miles, the catalyst and oxygen
sensor in the vehicle were replaced by new ones, allowing comparison of
the components in the two different fuel environments. Toyota's driving
cycle used higher speeds than Ethyl's, and its fuels contained more lead and
phosphorus than Ethyl's.

Toyota referred to this test procedure as the "Toyota 9-Laps" and
presented evidence which it said suggested that the catalyst degradation

seen by vehicles using the Toyota 9-Lap test was very similar to in-use catalysts tested by Toyota. Hence, Toyota suggested, these "adjustments" made in creating the Toyota 9-Lap make the testing of a vehicle more consistent with what would happen in actual in-use driving. Toyota's data indicated an HC level after the first 30,000 miles of vehicle use (on MMT fuel) about 0.1 gpm higher than the same vehicle with a new catalyst and oxygen sensor. Toyota also submitted data indicating that the efficiency at which the catalyst was operating for the MMT-exposed components was less than that for the non-MMT exposed components. (FR 1994, 42,235)

Undaunted by the EPA's fourth rejection of its waiver application on 8 January 1992, Ethyl filed a petition for review in the U.S. Court of Appeals on 13 February 1992 and continued testing its product in diverse circumstances and on diverse vehicles. The company submitted results of new tests made on six 1991 Escorts, using the relatively high-speed driving cycle that Ford used on its 1991 Escorts and its standard AMA cycle, with half the vehicles using MMT-free fuel and half using fuel containing MMT. The catalysts and oxygen sensors were changed between the Ford cycle and the AMA cycle. Then it tested six 1988 Escorts that were used in its original test program, only with new catalysts and oxygen sensors, using the Ford cycle and accumulating from 75,000 to 100,000 miles. Next it tested six 1988 Buicks from its original program, accumulating from 100,000 to 115,000 miles with the Ford cycle, but without replacing any parts. Finally, it accumulated "from 45,000 to 100,000 miles beyond break-in with and without MMT, using the Ford cycle" on four Crown Victorias, six Buick Regals, and four Mustangs:

> Based on its inspection and analysis of the new Ethyl data, the Agency ultimately concluded that Ethyl's program had demonstrated driving cycle does not contribute significantly to MMT-induced increases in hydrocarbon emissions. However, in addition to addressing the issue of driving cycle, the Ethyl data appeared to confirm the finding by Ford that 1991 Escorts experienced a much higher MMT-induced HC increase than that observed in other models tested ... The Agency was concerned that these data could indicate that certain engine and emissions control system configurations were more vulnerable to an MMT-induced emissions increase irrespective of driving cycle. (FR 1994, 42,235–6)

In fairness to the industries involved and to ensure that any future tests performed were adequate to address the outstanding questions about MMT, in October 1992 the EPA sponsored a workshop in which its proposed test program was reviewed. The two questions to be answered were:

"(1) Whether other vehicles utilizing fuels containing MMT are likely to experience increases in hydrocarbon emissions similar to those observed in 1991 Ford Escorts; and

(2) whether fuels containing MMT have significant adverse effects on emissions from vehicles utilizing the technologies most likely to be employed to meet future standards" (FR 1994, 42,236).

Using the proposed test program, Ethyl backed up its rejected fourth application for a waiver with a report based on the accumulated mileage on 1992 models of "four Crown Victorias to 100,000 test miles, six Buick Regals to 65,000 test miles and four Ford Mustangs to 45,000 test miles" as well as 1993 models of "six Toyota Camrys to 85,000 test miles, six Oldsmobile Achievas to 65,000 test miles, six Dodge Shadows to 55,000 test miles, six TLEV Ford Escorts to 85,000 test miles, six Honda Civics to 80,000 test miles and four 49-state Ford Escorts to 30,000 test miles, with and without MMT" (FR 1994, 42,236).

The driving cycles averaged 45 mph for the 1993 vehicles, 55 mph for the 1992 Mustangs and for the first 45,000 miles of the 1992 Crown Victorias and Regals, and then 45 mph for the latter two models after 45,000 miles. Nothing more is said in the *Federal Register* about the nature of the fuel blend beyond "with and without MMT," but we know that the blend can make a difference.

The EPA put Ethyl's report in the public docket, invited a response, and received a flood of written comments on it "from a wide variety of interests, including refiners, automakers, emission control manufacturers, states' committees, environmental and public interest groups and private citizens" (FR 1994, 42,236). In the EPA's summary, objections to EPA's granting a waiver for MMT were based on the following charges:

(1) Use of MMT will lead to increases in HC emissions.

(2) Because "newer technology vehicles" will likely install catalytic converters relatively close to engines (i.e., close-coupling) to reach higher temperatures faster, MMT-fuel will lead to more manganese deposits.

(3) Increased manganese deposits in converters would plug their honeycomb surfaces leading to decreases in their efficiency.

Ford Motor Company (Kraucher 1993) had additional objections, which I have tried to integrate into my entire text rather than simply list here. However, the company objected to what it regarded as Ethyl's vague reporting about maintenance provided to various vehicle components (how many, which, and why) and about specific blends of fuels used in their tests (Kraucher 1993, 6, 8). A similar array of objections to the auto manufacturers' most recent studies (Benson and Dana 2002) may be found in the Ethyl-sponsored critical review (Roos, Hollrah, Guinther, and Cunningham 2002).

In response to the objections, Ethyl claimed that "assertions that it must 'conclusively' demonstrate the absence of negative effects is not required by the section 211 (f) (4) standard" of the *Clean Air Act*. Ford Motor Company made this assertion in Kraucher (1993, 1). It added that EPA's workshop test program indicated that 65,000 test miles "would be sufficient for purposes of gauging the effect of MMT on emissions," although tests on three of the eight vehicles run beyond 65,000 miles revealed no differences in emissions. In addition, the 1993 Honda Civic has a close-coupled catalyst of the most extreme sort (i.e., the converter is connected to the exhaust manifold), but "the differences in hydrocarbon emissions between clear and MMT-fueled 1993 TLEV Honda Civics was minimal." Besides, "Ethyl tested two 1988 models and three 1993 models equipped with close-coupled catalysts without showing any significant adverse effects on catalysts" (FR 1994, 42,236).

In response to Toyota's submission of data and photographs apparently showing that "exhaust emissions of hydrocarbons and carbon monoxide are higher from catalyst/oxygen systems collected in Canada [where MMT was used] than comparable catalyst/oxygen systems from U.S. vehicles," Ethyl said that "without a detailed vehicle history, there is no basis to conclude that MMT had an effect on the catalyst/oxygen system data" (FR 1994, 42,236–7).

In response to Chrysler's submission of data and studies by Johnson Matthey Incorporated apparently showing that in vehicles driven in Canada "large quantities of manganese oxides" were deposited on top of the precious metals in catalysts, decreasing converter efficiency, Ethyl said that it had "already provided extensive data showing that the Additive does not adversely affect any of these emission system components" (FR 1994, 42,237). The question of where the manganese oxide deposits might have come from was not raised or answered, but Ethyl's main point was that the company's own tests had shown manganese deposits had no significant adverse effects on converter efficiency. So it did not matter whether additional manganese deposits were found.

In support of Ethyl's report, "Nineteen small refiners including the National Petroleum Refiners Association all recommended approval." They agreed with Ethyl's claim that if MMT were banned as an octane enhancer, refinery emissions of aromatics and benzene would increase, as well as capital and operating costs to achieve higher octane numbers, and the amounts of gasoline extracted from every barrel of refined crude oil would decrease (FR 1994, 42,237).

Considering these contradictory claims, based on different evidence obtained from different procedures, what should the EPA have done? At a minimum they should have examined all the claims and the supporting evidence very carefully. In fact, that seems to be exactly what they did do. They examined the "body of all available and appropriate long-term emissions data on High-Tech 3000 [the commercial name for MMT]," where "Appropriate data are considered to be those collected with Federal Test Procedure (FTP) testing using an experimental design with a control group and no obvious sources of bias. The data referred to here include eight 1988 models tested by Ethyl, two 1991 models tested by Ford, and nine 1992 and 1993 models tested by Ethyl" (FR 1994, 42,237).

Some sort of standard test for the difference between the means of two sets of numbers was apparently applied using standard confidence levels of 90% and 95%. (The footnotes in the text reveal that a more subtle analysis was made, but the subtleties can be neglected without misleading anyone.) Given the relatively small number of cases (19) to be compared, a statistically significant difference in the means for the measured HC and CO emissions from the control and experimental vehicles would only show up at the 90% confidence level if 13 of 19 model groups failed the test and would only show up at the 95% confidence level if 14 of the 19 vehicles failed. In other words, at least 13 (68%) pairs of vehicles (with a matching control and experimental vehicle in each pair) would have to have mean HC or CO emissions levels far enough apart to judge that it was not a chance event before the EPA would say that something (MMT in our case) in the experimental group "causes or contributes" to the observed differences in emissions between the two groups.

Clearly, then, the EPA's standard allowed for plenty of counter instances to their final judgment, a fact that was very troubling to Ford manufacturers (Kraucher 1993, 3–5). Imagine a doctor pronouncing a drug dangerous to use *only if* at least 68 per cent of the people who used it dropped dead, or an engineer pronouncing an airplane model unsafe *only if* it crashed at least 68% of the time! From Ethyl's point of view, it was no doubt comforting to know that only 4 pairs of vehicles (4/19 = 21%) had differences in mean emission levels for HC and only 5 pairs of vehicles (5/19 = 26%) had differences in mean emission levels for CO large enough to be attributed to something other than chance sampling error. Even more satisfying to Ethyl would have been that "None of the nine [1992 and 1993] models failed the 'cause or contribute' test (i.e., at least 68% failures) for hydrocarbons and only one failed for carbon monoxide" (FR 1994, 42,237). From the vehicle and component parts manufacturers' point of view, the same facts would have been less comforting.

To its credit, granting that it had "some concerns regarding the appropriateness of these criteria and tests for current conditions" and reflecting on all its evidence, the EPA concluded that "Ethyl's additive passes the most critical of the historical tests with a comfortable margin." The agency was not going to slip in a new standard at the last minute, but made it clear that it "considers its existing tests and the criteria that they implement to be obsolete under current conditions." Curiously, the most critical points about their tests were made in a long footnote:

> The tests are extremely conservative in that they place most of the burden of proof on the Agency rather than on the applicant. The "cause or contribute" test is failed by an engine family only under circumstances where emissions from the family are so high that an additive-caused increase in some pollutant pushes more than ten percent of the vehicle fleet into violation of the standard. Moreover, the final sign test that is applied to the model-specific results is failed by the additive only when it may be concluded with high confidence that more than half of the models in the represented population would fail the model-specific test. In practical situations with relatively small samples, this sign test permits a high percentage of the models in the sample to fail before the additive is declared to have failed the test. These tests, then, may permit the granting of waivers in the face of substantively significant emissions increments attributable to an additive – increments that would tend to offset the benefits from an increasingly stringent regulatory program aimed at bringing the nation's most serious air quality problems under control. (FR 1994, 42,237–8)

In the light of its concerns about the older tests, the EPA employed a new "more stringent" test. According to the new criterion, an additive passes the test only if it causes "no statistically significant increase in emissions." The new "approximate randomization test" was applied to "the full mileage range of HC emissions data from Ethyl's tests of 1992 and 1993 vehicles" and revealed no emissions increases that one "may not reasonably attribute to sampling error rather than to an additive effect on HC in the sampled vehicle population" (FR 1994, 42,238). Curiously again, in a footnote to the last quoted sentence, the EPA added that "It is important to note that the original Ethyl test fleet of 1988 model year vehicles that are now older than those representing the newest Ethyl data set did not fare as well and, as mentioned previously, do demonstrate statistically significant increases in HC emissions" (FR 1994, 42,238). I find it puzzling that information regarded as "important" should be inserted in a footnote. Apparently nothing was done about it, although it would have reminded Ethyl that the EPA could have chosen to be more aggressive. For present purposes, it is enough to remember that Ethyl's results on its 1988 fleet of vehicles could not be matched using the EPA's more stringent tests, but its results on its 1992 and 1993 fleet could be matched.

Finally, considering all the available evidence, on 30 November 1994 the EPA administrator said: "Ethyl has satisfied its burden under Clean Air Act 211 (f) (4) to establish that use of HiTec 3000 at the specified concentration will not cause or contribute to a failure of any emission control device or system (over the useful life of any vehicle in which such device or system is used) to achieve compliance by the vehicle with the emission standards with respect to which it has been certified" (FR 1994, 42,238).

Unfortunately for Ethyl, satisfaction of that "burden" did not relieve it of other burdens. Amendments to the *Clean Air Act*, effective 27 May 1994, "established new health effects testing requirements for the registration of designated" fuels and fuel additives, including MMT. A three-tier system was constructed that allows the EPA to require different procedures and tests to be undertaken to address different perceived gaps in the agency's information about certain products. A letter to Ethyl's Counsel, F. William Brownell, from EPA Counsel, Tim Backstrom, dated 24 November 1994, stated that the EPA intended "to require special testing under the Alternative Tier 2." A year later, in a letter dated 9 November 1995, Backstrom reminded Brownell that it was EPA's "understanding that Ethyl has agreed to assume responsibility for coordinating any Alternative Tier 2 testing requirements with other responsible parties, specifically registrants of unleaded gasoline products who have amended (or will amend) their composition statements to permit use of MMT in their products." Nearly four years later a letter dated 25 January 1999 was sent to Donald R. Lynam, Vice President for Air Conservation, Ethyl Corporation, officially notifying him "of a test program which the Environmental Protection Agency (EPA) proposes to require for … (MMT)." Lynam was informed that:

The Alternative Tier 2 testing requirements proposed by this letter are intended to be the first stage in a two-stage Alternative Tier 2 test program. The purpose of this notification is to afford you an opportunity to comment on this first stage. EPA will notify you separately of any additional Alternative Tier 2 testing to be included in the second stage, and will afford you a separate opportunity to comment on such testing when it is proposed. EPA intends to evaluate the results produced in the first stage of testing, as well as any other information which may be submitted to or obtained by EPA in the meantime, in determining the specific nature and scope of any second stage of Alternative Tier 2 testing. A new assessment of the risks associated with MMT use was presented in a revised risk assessment in 1994 and ... These evaluations concluded that: ... it is impossible to state whether projected population exposures would lie above or below a presumed threshold level on the actual concentration-response curve for Mn neurotoxicity. This gap between expected exposure levels and the lowest concentrations obtained by modeling the concentration-response relationship ... makes it impossible to make any assertion regarding the likelihood of a health risk at projected exposure levels. However, this conclusion should not be interpreted to imply that, therefore, no health risk is expected to exist at exposure levels exceeding the inhalation reference concentration (RfC). (Oge 1999, 1–4)

The proposed testing program included not only extremely detailed studies focused on "the development of a physiologically-based pharmacokinetic (PBPK) model capable of accurately predicting the disposition of manganese in target tissues of interest following exposure to different manganese compounds" on male and female rats of different ages, and on non-human primates, but also studies of the emission of various species of manganese particles (e.g., manganese oxides, manganese phosphates, manganese sulfates) from the combustion of fuel containing MMT, requiring estimated times of from 30 to 51 months to complete different studies. About the emission studies, Oge (1999, 5–6) wrote:

there are important unresolved questions regarding the relative proportions of the various manganese species present in vehicle exhaust. For example, although Ethyl concludes in its submission that "manganese from the use of MMT is emitted primarily as manganese phosphate", it appears that in some cases, the amount of phosphorous needed to produce the manganese phosphate may not be available in sufficient concentrations from potential phosphorus sources (i.e., crankcase oil). Furthermore, the Ethyl report clearly shows that other manganese species, i.e., manganese oxides and manganese sulfates, are likely present. Thus, the Agency believes it would be helpful to evaluate whether various untested driving scenarios (e.g., other vehicle types and other driving cycles more representative of urban driving), result in significant differences in the proportional contribution to total manganese of manganese species other than manganese phosphate.

As detailed as the new emissions studies would be, Oge emphasized (in a footnote) that they would have no bearing on the EPA's decision of 30 November 1994. In particular, she wrote: "Because these speciation tests will not include any control vehicles utilizing fuels without MMT and because of general uncertainty surrounding the effects of the mileage accumulation driving cycle on emission control system durability, EPA has determined that this study cannot be construed as identifying or measuring the gaseous emission products of MMT, the effect of MMT on gaseous emissions, or the effects of the emission products of MMT on the performance of emission control devices or systems" (Oge 1999, 25–6).

The final notification was sent to Ethyl by a certified letter on 19 May 2000 (FR 2000, 44,776). In case it was not already clear, the passages from the original notification letter reveal that while the EPA encourages and welcomes studies from all interested parties, it also sets its own research agenda and insists on having it implemented. Regarding the variety of possible impacts of manganese from combusted MMT on living and nonliving things, it is fair to say that it will still be some years before we have closure on many of the outstanding issues. "EPA recognizes that unforeseen problems or emergency situations can create unavoidable delays in any large testing program, especially when new technologies are being employed" (Oge 1999, 9). (See also EPA (1999) for a detailed discussion of Ethyl Corporation's petitions for reconsideration of three new EPA regulations, and reasons for EPA's denial of each.)

6

Harmonization

This chapter outlines the variety of ways in which diverse ideas, theories, policies, and proposals about harmonization formed an important part of the historical context in which the MMT cases were played out. It proceeds from relatively general and global issues to specific issues related to harmonization agreements among the key players in our story.

In the *Republic* (c. 360 BCE), Plato enquired into the nature of the good life for an individual and for a society. He noticed, first, that a society in which individuals were constantly in conflict with each other would be relatively less attractive to inhabit as well as relatively weak in competition against societies in which individuals lived in harmony. Then, reasoning by analogy, he argued that an individual whose reason and passions were in harmony would be relatively happier (at peace, content, satisfied) with himself or herself as well as relatively stronger than those who were at war with themselves. Reflecting that old model of harmony, today one might say that people are happy when their heads and hearts are together, or that people who have it all together are happy.

In the light of these ancient observations and contemporary common sense, the idea of having a coherent, harmonious body of public policies is difficult to resist. The idea of having a coherent, harmonious set of regulations and standards regarding trade and environmental matters in particular is an equally attractive corollary. Thus, advocates of increased trade, environmental protection, and public health and safety often share common interests in the pursuit of the construction of similar if not identical regulatory measures. In a thought-provoking book examining the diverse impacts that such advocates and their implemented policies were predicted to have, actually had up to 1995, and may be expected to have in the future, Vogel (1995) described two opposite possibilities called the

"Delaware effect" and the "California effect." Among American states, Delaware is notorious for having relatively weak requirements for corporate charters, and California is notorious for having relatively strong environmental regulations. When states or countries compete for investment by adopting increasingly weak policies of environmental protection, one may describe the phenomenon as a "race to the bottom" or a Delaware effect. When they compete by adopting increasingly strong policies, there is a "race to the top," or a California effect. In a nutshell, Vogel's thesis was that:

> trade liberalization can just as easily be achieved by forcing nations with lower standards to raise them as by forcing nations with higher standards to lower them. While both have in fact occurred, the former has been more common than the latter. To the extent that trade liberalization has affected the level of consumer and environmental protection, it has more often strengthened than weakened it. There is, however, nothing automatic about this process. The impact of trade liberalization on regulatory standards is primarily dependent on the preferences of wealthy, powerful states and the degree of economic integration among them and their trading partners ... The stronger the commitment of nations to coordinate their regulatory policies, the more powerful is the California effect. (Vogel 1995, 5–8)

Although Vogel's thesis was defended by a careful examination of the provisions and impacts of five treaties (i.e., the Single European Act, Treaty of Rome, CUSTA, NAFTA and GATT), he remarked on the long tradition of "using trade restrictions to advance environmental objectives." For example, in the United States, legislation was introduced in 1905 preventing "the importation of pests injurious to crops, forests, or 'shade trees'"; in 1906 sponges from the Gulf of Mexico could not be imported if they "had been gathered by methods which harmed the sponge beds"; imported "plumes and feathers from specified wild birds" were banned in 1913; and imported "salmon caught in ways that violated American fishing regulations" were banned in 1926 (Vogel 1995, 8–9). As documented in chapter 15, the same tradition exists in Canada and the MMT Act fits squarely within that tradition.

Reviewing the statistical time series, Vogel noticed that since the 1960s, "international trade as a proportion of GNP has significantly increased in every industrial nation" while "environmental and consumer regulations have become progressively stricter." Also, "All industrial nations and a number of industrializing ones now devote substantially more resources both in absolute and relative terms to environmental and consumer protection than they did in 1970" (Vogel 1995, 254).

In contrast to "automotive safety, emission, and fuel economy standards" that were strengthened throughout that period, he noticed that "real wages, fringe benefits, and employment security for American automobile workers declined, in part due to increased international competition" (Vogel 1995, 257). The difference between the two cases appeared to be the relatively lower costs of compliance with the new regulatory standards.

Regarding the harmonization of standards for motor vehicle emissions, Vogel's analysis is particularly relevant to our story. Opponents of the MMT *Act* felt that motor vehicle manufacturers' interest (e.g., see chapter 14) in having MMT-free gasoline widely available in Canada was a consequence of their interest in reducing production costs by using the same emission control equipment on vehicles sold in Canada and in the much larger market of the United States. When the countries in the European Union decided "to harmonize emission requirements for automobiles in the late 1980s":

[the] "standards the EU selected were the ones preferred by Europe's most export-oriented producers – namely, the German manufacturers of medium and large cars. These standards not only made it easier for German manufacturers to sell their vehicles throughout the EU, but because these standards were similar to those of one of their major export markets, they made it easier for the Germans to produce vehicles for sale in the United States as well … It was precisely the firms supplying the largest, wealthiest automobile market in Europe who took the lead in pressuring the EU to adopt the product standards already set by the world's largest, richest market, the United States. They made common cause with German environmentalists to demand adoption of "US 83" standards by the EU. Significantly, half of German automobile sales in the United States are in California … The expansion of trade between the United States and Canada following the Free Trade Agreement prompted Canada in 1993 to establish automobile emission requirements similar to those imposed on vehicles sold in America three years earlier. (Vogel 1995, 250–62)

One of the peculiar twists of the MMT story, as will be explained in detail in chapter 14, is that while the kinds of motor vehicles sold in Canada, and eventually the emission standards, were identical to those in the much larger market south of our border (consistent with Vogel's account), use of the fuel additive in non-leaded gasoline was largely voluntarily abandoned by all the major oil companies in the United States but not in Canada (until 2004), although the same companies or their subsidiaries operate in both countries. Assuming that Vogel was right in supposing that relative compliance costs largely determine what companies do, it would appear that these companies did not reintroduce MMT into the U.S. market after it became legal to do so (November 1995) but maintained it in the Canadian market, at least until early in 2004, because it was more profitable for them to maintain those positions in each market. This is consistent with Bernstein's observation that "corporations tend to address specific issues based on how policies directly affect their profits" (Bernstein 2002, 16).

Bernstein (2002) reviewed some of the same literature and history as Vogel from a more recent view point and produced a more subtle account of the dynamics involved in trade and environmental policy changes. In his view, since the 1992 UN Conference on Environment and Development (UNCED, Earth Summit) there has been an international "convergence" around a particular set of assumptions and norms that he called "liberal environmentalism." According to this doctrine, international trade and development policies may be harmonized with environmental polices to create a win-win situation all around:"Liberal environmentalism accepts the liberalization of trade and finance as consistent with, and even necessary for, international environmental protection. It also promotes market and other economic mechanisms (such as tradable pollution permit schemes or the privatization of the commons) over "command-and-control" methods (standards, bans, quotas, and so on) as the preferred method of environmental management" (Bernstein 2002, 7).

As explained in chapter 16, the AIT panel seemed to be operating from a liberal environmentalist perspective when it criticized the Government of Canada for not exploring options such as tradable pollution permits instead of passing the MMT Act.

Following Chatterjee and Finger (1994), Bernstein (2002, 234) claimed that "the type of environmentalism promoted at UNCED left unexamined the industrial processes and unsustainable economic models that caused the current environmental crises." According to those authors, "UNCED has promoted business and industry, rehabilitated nation states as relevant agents, and eroded the Green movement ... UNCED has boosted precisely the type of industrial development that is destructive for the environment, the planet, and its inhabitants. We see how, as a result of UNCED, the rich will get richer, the poor poorer, while more and more of the planet is destroyed in the process" (Chatterjee and Finger 1994, 3).

Bernstein did not believe that "power and material interest" theories (such as that proposed by Vogel) were able to predict policy preferences with much success. Alternatively, he proposed a "socio-evolutionary explanation" for such preferences:

> This explanation begins not with actors or state power and interests (as do liberal and realist explanations), nor with economic structures and class interests (as do Gramscians) but with systemic social structure ... The main argument is that the *social* fitness of proposals for new norms with extant social structure better explains why some norms are selected, while others fall by the wayside ... The explanation argues that three factors determine the selection of new norms: *the perceived legitimacy of the source of the new ideas; fitness with extant international social structure; and fitness with key actors' identities at various levels of social structure* ... Since social structure and state identities and interests are mutually constitutive, this explanation does not exclude material interests or power as important factors in the selection process. Rather, by using extant social structure as a starting point of analysis it endogenizes an important source of interests, and thus offers a more efficient explanation ... certain kinds of knowledge and policy responses are privileged not because of their inherent truth or even effectiveness, but because the institutionalization of liberal environmentalism grants them legitimacy. (Bernstein 2002, 20–1)

Thus, Bernstein's socio-evolutionary explanation for the international attractiveness of environmental policies that are consistent (i.e., harmonize) with liberal environmentalism is similar to Kuhn's (1957, 1977) explanation of scientific revolutions based on the abandonment of old and the adoption of new paradigms. Like Kuhn's notion of a paradigm, Bernstein's notion of social structure is not easy to discern. Nevertheless, these relatively robust though somewhat opaque notions do seem to provide plausible starting points for a more subtle explanation of why certain ideas are perceived to be better than others regardless of the lack of supporting empirical evidence. What recommends them is their logical coherence with other received views, assumptions, norms, and practices. Several studies have shown that market-friendly environmental policies are not especially effective in achieving environmental policy goals, e.g., OECD

1994; UNCSD 1996; Braadbaart 1998; Reitan 1998. However, market-friendly environmental policies are well-suited (well-adapted in Darwinian terms) to the general market-friendly worldview (or paradigm) characterizing public policy-making in most industrialized countries in the latter quarter of the twentieth century and today (Bernstein and Cashore 2002).

While the idea of harmonization is attractive in abstract philosophical terms, liberal environmentalism generally harmonizes well with the dominant worldview of the most powerful people in industrialized countries at this period of history. Real harmonization of regulations and technology has been and can yet be profitable certainly for producers and possibly for consumers (if producers share their reduced costs with consumers). But policy and standard harmonization does present some troublesome issues regarding federal and provincial jurisdictions here in Canada. Chapter 3 examined the constitutional roots of Canadian federalism, including the fundamental interests in obtaining the benefits of a broad economic union covering all the provinces and territories as well as the benefits of allowing the provinces and territories to have some privileged status regarding legislation concerned with relatively local or regional matters. Unfortunately, the pursuit of harmonization initiatives designed to further the former interest may undermine the latter. There are, therefore, legitimate limits to the harmonization of public policies in a federal state. As Lenihan (1995, 112–13) wrote:

> To the extent that strengthening the economic union comes at the expense of provincial (or territorial) autonomy, each party can be expected to support harmonization only to the extent that it judges the benefits to its citizens to outweigh the price it must pay in terms of its autonomy.
>
> This judgment will be based in part on ideology. A government sympathetic to *laissez-faire* economics will be more easily persuaded of the benefits of harmonization than one that leans to intervention. But ideology is only part of the picture. Whatever its political stripe, every provincial government is by definition a committed federalist. The existence of each rests on the view that, in Canada, provincial governments are essential to the protection and promotion of local interests.

Perhaps more succinctly than any other author, Lenihan presented the theoretic argument against all barriers to complete economic integration, and immediately revealed its defect:

The argument goes something like this: The commitment to economic union is a commitment to eliminate trade barriers. Anything that impedes or affects the free flow of goods, services, labor, or capital is a barrier. Divergent regulations and standards distort the natural patterns of economic activity; hence, they are barriers that should be eliminated.

This way of defining trade barriers stacks the deck in favor of those who prefer economic integration to respect for diversity. Right from the start, it cedes the theoretical high ground to one basic value, efficiency, thereby making it the overarching norm against which all exceptions must be explained. Attempts by provincial leaders to resist this set of assumptions are judged to be motivated by parochialism.

The obvious rejoinder is that there are many aspects of life in a federalist, liberal society such as Canada in which the market plays a key role but which, for all that, are shaped as much, and often more, by other overarching norms – for example, respect for social equality or provincial autonomy – whose logic and rationale are quite different. In reality, in a country such as Canada, the legitimate political interests and objectives of the state and the economic interests of private actors in the marketplace overlap at many points ... Federalism ... [permits] some degree of fragmentation of the economic space, in order to protect regional diversity: this, in fact, is the inescapable price of federalism. (Lenihan 1995, 115–16. Similar critiques may be found in Schwanen 1995; Trebilcock and Behboodi 1995; Swinton 1995; and Breton 1995)

Howse (1990, 171) covered some of the same ground, and raised the question "Why should the economic efficiency concerns that dictate global cooperation necessarily trump provincial autonomy concerns, including social regulation and the protection of under-developed communities and regions?"

Because of the basic principle of my moral consequentialism (see chapter 1), it might be expected that I would object to Lenihan's critique and Howse's question on the grounds of the characterization of the "basic value" of the thoroughgoing economic integrationists as "efficiency." As indicated earlier, the range of benefits and costs typically captured by their concept of efficiency is extremely narrow compared to that required by the version of moral consequentialism adopted here. While it would beg the question to claim that either the narrow or robust concept is in some neutral sense correct, the alleged "theoretical high ground" of the integrationist enthusiasts is, after all, fairly low. This is particularly important if one takes the extra step usually taken by economists, namely, identifying efficient action with rational action (Hodgson 2001). There is nothing particularly rational about neglecting all values except financial ones in one's daily decision-making or using language that misleadingly implies that it is rational in the ordinary sense of this term to do so (McMurtry 1999, 2002).

Apart from my objection to the narrow notion of efficiency assumed by these authors, the concept of provincial autonomy would also be unable to bear the weight of a supreme principle for moral consequentialism. From the point of view of pursuing and obtaining public policies and programs designed to get something like the greatest good for the greatest number, one cannot simply rely on a particular geographical or jurisdictional division of labour to provide an automatic solution for the variety of issues facing Canadians in particular and human beings in general. Morally appropriate reflection from a consequentialist point of view requires consideration of all those affected by one's policies and programs, and different recipient populations may have their benefits and costs assessed in accordance with different policies and programs.

The Canadian Council of Ministers of the Environment (CCME) is the established forum for provinces, territories, and the federal government to promote cooperation on and coordination of interjurisdictional issues related to the environment and resource development. At the end of a national conference on Resources for Tomorrow in 1961, a suggestion was made to initiate a Canadian Council of Resource Ministers, which was finally incorporated on 26 February 1964. In 1972 the name was changed to the Canadian Council of Resource and Environment Ministers, and in 1989 it was changed again to the Canadian Council of Ministers of the Environment. Each name change was accompanied by some mandate and by-law changes, but for our purposes, the most important new provisions came in 1991. The relevant sections from By-law No.1991-1 to 1991-3 are as follows:

> [The purpose and objects of the corporation became] (a) to establish and maintain an intergovernmental forum for discussion and joint action on environmental issues of national, international, and global concern; (b) to harmonize the development and implementation of environmental legislation, policies, procedures and programs; and (c) to develop nationally consistent environmental objectives, standards and scientific data bases and complementary strategies, accords and agreements ...[and a significantly new decision procedure was introduced,

which is] consensus-based decision-making: CCME set a precedent by incorporating and entrenching the concept of consensus into its constitution. Consensus is defined in 1.01 (d) as "the absence of dissent and includes the process of narrowing an issue until there is no dissent." (CCME 2002c, 1–3)

The CCME's fourteen ministers meet twice a year to review the work of the Environmental Planning and Protection Committee, which consists of senior staff from each jurisdiction. Among other things, through extensive consultations and negotiations, the CCME has established Canada-wide standards for ambient air quality regarding particulate matter; emission standards for mercury, benzene, dioxin, furan, and nitrogen oxide; clean-up standards for sites contaminated with petroleum hydrocarbons in soil; Canadian Water Quality Guidelines; the National Packaging Protocol; a Policy on the Management of Toxic Substances; a national classification system for contaminated sites; guidance manuals for assessment and remediation; and, in 1990, the *Statement of Interjurisdictional Cooperation on Environmental Matters*. Most relevant to our purposes, this *Statement* says that the governments agree "To work together through a strengthened Canadian Council of Ministers of the Environment (CCME) to contribute to the achievement of:

- the harmonization of environmental legislation, policies and programs and of their implementation ...
- the continued development of nationally consistent environmental standards and objectives to achieve a high level of environmental quality." (CCME 1990, 3)

Harrison (2002, 135) noted that "adoption of a Canada-wide standard by the CCME is typically several steps removed from voluntary programs or regulations being adopted by individual jurisdictions." More importantly, regarding the CCME's accountability for its performance on standard-setting, she wrote:

With respect to accountability, it is striking that the CCME has offered no consistent philosophy for setting Canada-wide standards. The CCME promises only that some combination of health and environmental risks, technological feasibility, and socio-economic costs of control will be considered in setting Canada-wide standards. Indeed, the CCME acknowledges that the manner in which these factors are weighed will vary from standard to standard. In the absence of either more explicit principles for standard-setting or more complete explanation of the basis for particular standards, it will be difficult for Canadians to hold the CCME or any of its member governments accountable for the Canada-wide standards they set. To be fair, though, the discretionary enabling statutes historically adopted by Canadian parliamentary governments also typically decline to offer a principled basis for standard-setting. (Harrison 2002, 137–8)

On 29 January 1998 the *Canada-Wide Accord on Environmental Harmonization* (CCME 2002a, 1–3) came into force, with Quebec the only province withholding its support. Although the AIT case involving the *MMT Act* was initiated before the accord came into force, the spirit of the latter agreement was entirely consistent with the mandate of the CCME and the 1990 agreement cited above. The vision statement of the accord is "Governments working in partnership to achieve the highest level of environmental quality for all Canadians." The objective of harmonization is to be reached "using a cooperative approach, to develop and implement consistent environmental measures in all jurisdictions, including policies, standards, objectives, legislation and regulations" (CCME 2002b, 1). In Hogg's (1997, 29–32) terms, "Canada-wide standards are to be set, not by federal law alone, but by consensus among the three levels of government." It is unclear whether the accord provides mere "statements of policy goals" or legally binding commitments, although Valiante (2002, 9) claimed that it has "no effect on constitutional powers."

In Clarkson's view, which Harrison (2002) and VanNijnatten and Lambright (2002) share, the accord was viewed by many environmentalists "as the opening shot in a competitive race to the bottom." "Over 90 environmental groups issued a joint statement urging the federal government to reject the Accord, depicting it as an 'abandonment of the federal role' in environmental protection" (Harrison 2002, 131). Clarkson claimed that:

Environmentalists remained committed to an activist federal state where intergovernmental competition would produce higher, rather than lower, levels of regulatory protection. In their view, the checks and balances of shared jurisdiction led to positive results. By the same token, a shift of responsibilities to the provinces increased the risks of "regulatory capture" by powerful local resource industries and encouraged jurisdictions to compete for business by weakening their environmental laws. Activists deplored the democratic deficit created when the

CCME made public policy through a version of executive federalism unaccountable to either federal or provincial voters. The resulting policy framework reflected the preferences of industry rather than those of citizen-based ENGOs [Environmental Non-Governmental Organizations]. (Clarkson 2002a, 340–1)

Because the accord "allowed for variable and inconsistent implementation, including voluntary rather than mandatory approaches," variable "ambient environmental standards," and "departures from uniform discharge standards," and "gave each participating government an effective veto over environmental initiatives" through its "consensual decision making," environmentalists had some cause for concern (Clarkson 2002a, 340). Trebilcock and Behboodi (1995, 76) claimed that "The EU experience with respect to positive integration measures suggests that a consensus rule is likely to substantially impede progress in negotiations over harmonized or minimum regulatory standards."

Those who supported the accord "emphasized the benefits of promoting consistency of standards and approaches between the provinces and federal government, cost savings from elimination of duplication, and opportunities to identify and fill gaps by working together" (Harrison 2002, 132).

Although there were certainly good reasons for the fears of opponents and the hopes of proponents, I have not seen any comprehensive assessment of the overall consequences of the adoption of the accord or of Quebec's non-adoption up to now (August 2007). Harrison (2002, 135) quoted from a two-year review by the CCME following adoption of the accord, which said, "There is general recognition that the two years since the Accord was signed have led to progress in agreements among jurisdictions, but little impact on the environment." Harrison (2002) and VanNijnatten (2002) provided good foundations for a thorough assessment, including analyses of the great diversity among provincial standards and commitments to environmental policies. As we will see, the accord and the CCME had roles to play in the MMT cases, but they were relatively minor supporting roles.

Although the NAFTA does not require or in any way commit the parties to the harmonization of environmental standards and regulations, the AIT does, in general and specific terms that, unfortunately, do not provide clear guidelines for legislators, litigators, or adjudicators. Lenihan (1995, 107) correctly commented that "the commitment to harmonization, made in a number of chapters, is usually very general. The task of negotiating and implementing the details is typically postponed to further discussions."

Because some of the fundamental provisions of the AIT regarding harmonization were central to the MMT case, a detailed examination of those provisions as they applied to and were interpreted by the specific parties to the
case follows in chapters 13–16. Here I only outline the main provisions as
they appeared to experts assessing them prior to and independently of the
MMT case. The most thorough reviews were published in Trebilcock and
Schwanen (1995) and Doern and MacDonald (1999).

Easson (1995) gives the most succinct summary:

> the Agreement on Internal Trade identifies the harmonization of stan-
> dards and regulations as one of the principal mechanisms for reducing
> or eliminating barriers to interprovincial trade (Articles 101(3)(c) and
> 405) … the agreement uses a number of different terms to convey the
> concept of harmonization. Parties are required to "reconcile" relevant
> standards and regulations to provide for free movement (Article
> 101(3)(c)); reconciliation is to be achieved by "harmonization, mutual
> recognition or other means" (Article 405(1)), and by "cooperation" to
> remove obstacles caused by differences in regulatory measures (Article
> 405(2)); elsewhere throughout the agreement, the terms *reconciliation,
> harmonization, mutual recognition* and *other means*, are variously
> employed …
>
> *Harmonization* is defined, in Article 200 … as "making identical or
> minimizing the differences between standards or related measures of
> similar scope." *Mutual recognition* is defined, in the same article, as the
> "acceptance by a Party of a person, good, service or investment that
> conforms with an equivalent standard or standards-related measure of
> another Party" … However, the agreement's provision for the use of
> "other means" to achieve the desired objective seems to undermine to
> some extent the significance of the distinction between the terms. The
> key concept, and the objective to be pursued, appears to be that of
> "reconciliation" (Articles 101(3)(c), 405(1), 606, 708, 807, 1007,
> 1105, 1408). Harmonization, mutual recognition, and other means are
> simply ways of achieving that objective, and, as a general rule, the par-
> ties to the agreement are free to adopt the most appropriate method or
> technique to that end (Article 405). (Easson 1995, 122–3. Appendix 3
> has the complete text of the Articles cited in this quotation.)

Absent from Easson's list is Article 1508, which requires parties to
"endeavour to harmonize environmental measures" and plays a very
important role in our story. (See appendix 3 for the full text.) Also missing

are definitions and difficult questions about what counts as a standard, standard-related measure, and regulation, according to the AIT. Doern and MacDonald (1999, 135–6) captured the general problems with these notions very well in the following:

> Standards can be seen as just another kind of rule or regulation (delegated legislation), but they are also seen ... as a separate realm ... In the context of free-trade federalism, they raise issues of preferred framework regulatory principles such as mutual recognition, harmonization, and performance-based regulations and standards whose origins are increasingly found in international-trade and related agreements, but which play out differently in domestic politics ... Article 405 enshrines the principle of reconciliation, which the parties agree to support. However, reconciliation, given the need to leave room for legitimate objectives, is deemed to mean many things. It can mean "mutual recognition", where the requirements of the provinces are equivalent in purpose and effect. It can also mean harmonization, which itself is seen to be a broad concept ranging from compatibility to full convergence ... [In negotiating the AIT] the federal government sought harmonization with international standards and with harmonization obligations in international-trade agreements. Within the country, the federal government also tended to see harmonization through the creation of national standards ... the provinces were not well disposed to these views, and in particular saw harmonization as a reciprocal arrangement between affected provinces.

Although Easson noted the difference in the AIT's definitions of "harmonization" and "mutual recognition," he thought that the distinction between the two notions was "without consequence," apparently because the various articles cited above seemed to use the terms practically interchangeably. Doern and MacDonald (1999, 107) refer to "mutual recognition" as the "drivers licence" model; i.e., the mutual agreement among provinces to recognize the validity of driver's licences obtained in other provinces.

Easson was impressed by the language of Article 807.1 ensuring that parties could not be obliged by anything in the AIT to lower consumer protection standards in the interests of reconciliation, and Article 1508.2 prohibiting parties from lowering environmental protection standards in the interests of harmonization (Easson 1995, 143). Trebilcock and Behboodi (1995, 66, 73) make the same points. (NAFTA Article 1114.2

seems to be close to but noticeably weaker than AIT Article 1508.2.) As I show in chapter 16, in the MMT case, one of the strongest arguments offered by the government of Canada was based precisely on the prohibition contained in Article 1508.2, but the AIT panel simply ignored it. While significant issues of consumer protection were also involved in the case, no appeal was made to Article 807.1, though nothing in Chapter 8 or Chapter 15 of the AIT precludes drawing on provisions of both Chapters.

Another important feature of the AIT, according to Easson, is the absence of any "particular instrument of harmonization." Again, in his words,

> The essential nature of harmonization in the Canadian agreement ... is the amendment or adaptation of provincial/national laws and practices to achieve an agreed objective ... the Agreement on Internal Trade makes no explicit provision for either the preparation or the adoption of any legislative instrument, be it called a directive, a decision, or something else. Its principal body, the Committee on Internal Trade, has no formal authority to adopt harmonization measures, and the Secretariat does not appear to have the resources to draft proposals. It seems to have been left to the parties themselves to "establish mechanisms" to cooperate on matters relating to standards (Annex 405.1(13)) ... the Agreement on Internal Trade imposes the obligation to harmonize in a somewhat half-hearted manner. (Easson 1995, 144–6)

These observations are especially relevant to the MMT case because the panel claimed that Article 1508.1 required parties to use procedures crafted by the CCME, and that the Government of Canada failed to live up to its obligation to do so. Following the interpretations of Easson and others regarding Article 1508.1, I will argue that the panel was wrong on both counts (chapter 16).

More than three years before the introduction of the *MMT Act* on 20 February 1992, Transport Canada, the Motor Vehicle Manufacturers Association (MVMA) and the Association of International Automobile Manufacturers of Canada (AIAMC) signed a *Memorandum of Understanding* in which the parties agreed to certain principles of harmonization with regulations in the United States. Among other things, it was agreed that:

> [all 1994 and 1995] model year gasoline-fuelled, light-duty vehicle models marketed and sold in Canada shall comply with the same exhaust emission standards applicable to the same 1994 [and 1995]

model year gasoline-fuelled, light-duty vehicle models marketed and sold in 49 states in the U.S.A.... [such] vehicles shall demonstrate compliance with the applicable emission standards ... set out in ... Chapter IV of the Motor Vehicle Safety Test Methods, dated October 1, 1985 ... [and] shall be covered by a manufacturer's emissions component warranty and non-compliance recall provisions ... [as] in 49 states in the U.S.A. ... The manufacturer will supply to Transport Canada in a timely fashion, all relevant and sufficient data regarding certification, production and sales forecasts, updates, end of model year final sales figures, and recall activities relating to and representing ... [such] vehicles ... This Memorandum of Understanding shall remain in effect until both parties mutually agree that such an understanding is no longer desirable. (*Memorandum of Understanding*, 1–2)

These provisions are notable because they indicate that as early as February 1992 Transport Canada and the auto makers were committed to harmonizing emission standards with those in the United States, and that the manufacturers agreed to give Canadian consumers the same warranty protection given to American consumers and to give Transport Canada timely data including data on recall activities. For our purposes, the addendum to the memorandum is even more important, because it reveals that the manufacturers were already protecting themselves against problems arising from fuel compositions peculiar to Canada:

Manufacturers agree to warrant all emission components in Canada for which they offer warranties in the U.S. The Memorandum recognizes that durability of certain emission control components could be adversely affected by Canadian fuel composition. Therefore, for these components, the duration or component life covered by the Canadian warranty may differ from that offered on comparable U.S. models.

In addition, manufacturers agree to recall and repair (field fix) in Canada all models recalled and repaired in the U.S. Manufacturers are *not required* to recall models in Canada for component failures attributable to unique Canadian fuel composition unless such recalls are also initiated in the U.S. (*Memorandum of Understanding*, 3)

According to the last paragraph, the manufacturers agree to "recall and repair" in Canada whatever they would "recall and repair" in the United States. They will even "recall and repair" component failures "attributable to unique Canadian fuel composition" provided that "such recalls are also initiated in the U.S." But how could a problem be "initiated in the U.S." that was "attributable to unique Canadian fuel composition" and what is a "unique Canadian fuel composition"? Since the main difference between most of the unleaded gasoline sold in Canada and the U.S. was that the former had and the latter did not have MMT, the phrase "unique Canadian fuel" is probably a euphemism for "fuel containing MMT."

A letter dated 12 October 1994 was sent from Mark Nantais, President of the MVMA and T. Robert Clapp, Vice-President, External Relations of the Canadian Petroleum Products Institute (CPPI), to Micheline Desjardins, Assistant Deputy Minister for Transport Canada, and Tony Clarke, Assistant Deputy Minister for Environment Canada, informing the latter that the CPPI and MVMA had agreed to a "concise position on harmonization" that they believed "will guide us in the years to come as we deal with the complex fuel/engine, and emission control technology issues" (Nantais and Clapp 1994, 1).

The MVMA was incorporated in 1926 as the Canadian Auto Manufacturers and Exporters, went through several name changes and became the Canadian Vehicle Manufacturers' Association (CVMA) in 1996. It represents twenty-one manufacturers inside and outside Canada. The CPPI was created in 1989 as "an association of Canadian companies involved in the refining, distribution, and/or marketing of petroleum products" (http://www.cppi.ca/cppi.htm).

Most of the "position on harmonization" is taken verbatim from the conclusion of a "consensus statement" prepared by federal government officials for the Joint Government-Industry Committee on Transportation Fuels and Motor Vehicle Control Technologies, as requested by the committee on 17 August 1993. The key points of the agreement are as follows:

Canada will continue to adopt the same emission standards and test procedures nationally that apply to the U.S. Federal standards to benefit from the availability of leading emission control technology.

Fuel supplied to Canadian consumers must be fully compatible with all emissions control equipment installed on new vehicles to ensure the proper operation of vehicles to meet consumer demands and to meet U.S. Federal emission standards.

Therefore, fuels commercially available in Canada must not adversely affect the ability of a vehicle to comply with vehicle emission certification standards[1], in-use emission standards[1], or the performance of the emission control technology for its useful life[1].

It is recognized that fuel parameters have an effect on actual in-use emissions. Therefore, *changes in fuel quality, beyond that needed for compliance with national vehicle emission standards – U.S. Federal, may be considered for controlling actual in-use emission performance*[2] from in-use vehicles to deal with local or regional environmental needs or for a national requirement to reduce the exposure *to a fuel component determined to be toxic. A decision to adopt such measures shall be made on the same basis as for any other mitigation strategy.*

(1) Emission certification standards, in-use emission standards, and useful life are those referenced in the latest applicable U.S. Federal Register.

(2) Actual in-use emission performance: Actual day-to-day emissions using commercially available fuel. Intent of "emission certification standards" is to control these emissions. (Nantais and Clapp 1994, 2; emphasis added)

The italicized parts of the agreement are especially important for the disagreements that arose immediately after two events: On October 12 (the same day as the letter on harmonization) the Minister of the Environment, Sheila Copps, told a Canadian Press reporter that if the oil industry did not voluntarily remove MMT before August 1995, she would introduce legislation requiring its removal; then, in a letter dated 14 October 1994, the MVMA sent a letter to the CPPI informing the member companies that:

If your company is unwilling to eliminate MMT from gasoline, we may pursue a number of options including recommending to our customers that they purchase gasoline only from those companies which have indicated to us that they will be supplying MMT-free fuels, *or consider making necessary changes to our warranty programmes.* We are not prepared to offer Canadians inferior vehicle emissions technology than that which is provided across the U.S., nor can we afford to assume the significant additional warranty costs caused by the inclusion of MMT in Canadian gasolines. (Canada 1998, 18)

Goodbye harmony, hello hostility. The MVMA could and did (MVMA/ AIAMC 1995, 4,16; SSCEENR 2/4, 1997b, 34) point to the first italicized part in the harmonization agreement and insist that the CPPI member companies had agreed to provide fuels "fully compatible with all emissions control equipment":

The theme of harmonization and the resultant availability of the best available technology and cost-effective control systems for the Canadian market has a high level of acceptance after considerable debate in the early 1980s. Even the petroleum producers have acknowledged this in their signing of the 1995 MOU. It is time for them to implement their stated intentions. The legislation being discussed here today [*MMT Act*] would be unnecessary had they respected their harmonization commitment. (MVMA/AIAMC 1995, 18)

Members of the CPPI could and did (SSCEENR 2/4, 1997b, 34, 37; SSCEENR 2/4, 1997d, 3) point to the other two italicized parts and insist that MMT was beneficial in controlling an indirectly "toxic" emission substance, NO_x, and that the heavy-handed tactics of the minister were not consistent with usual practice. So, each side could and did, with some justification, accuse the other side of negotiating in bad faith. Leaving that issue aside, one must wonder about the practical wisdom of those in the MVMA who sent a threatening letter to the CPPI only two days after both sides had agreed to harmonize their efforts to improve "domestic and international air quality." Had I been working for the CPPI, I would have expected that the spirit of the harmonization agreement implied at least a few months of good faith initiatives for collective action.

7

MVMA and AIAMC Report to the House Standing Committee on Environment and Sustainable Development

On 19 May 1995 the Minister of the Environment, Sheila Copps, introduced Bill C-94 (later Bill C-29), the MMT *Act*, to the House of Commons for first reading. The most important provisions of the Act are in the following sections:

4. No person shall engage in interprovincial trade in or import for a commercial purpose a controlled substance except under an authorization referred to in section 5.

5. (1) The Minister may authorize any person to engage in interprovincial trade in or to import for a commercial purpose a controlled substance if the Minister is satisfied

(a) that the controlled substance is not unleaded gasoline; and
(b) that the controlled substance will not be added to unleaded gasoline.

(2) The Minister may attach to the authorization any condition respecting the controlled substance, the use that may be made of it, the term of the authorization and its renewal and any other condition that the Minister considers appropriate.

At the end of the *Act* there is a schedule (list) of controlled substances containing a single item, MMT.

The House Standing Committee on Environment and Sustainable Development held hearings on the bill on October 18, 19, 24, 26, 1995 and, among other things, received a substantial report from the MVMA and AIAMC (MVMA/AIAMC 1995).

This chapter reviews and critically evaluates the contents of that report, several aspects of which reappear in the NAFTA and AIT cases.

The report did an excellent job of summarizing their industry's problems with MMT, beginning with a provocative overview statement:

MMT, an octane enhancing gasoline additive is touted by its maker to reduce virtually all motor vehicle exhaust emissions, to be totally compatible with advanced emission control systems, and to be essentially without adverse effects. These assertions are being vigorously opposed by the world's motor vehicle manufacturers. Faced with incessant demands for lower and lower emissions, these manufacturers would be strong proponents of and the first to applaud an additive with the claimed benefits if such was the case. The strange dichotomy which apparently exists is based on testing and Canadian in-use experience over many years which indicate characteristics and effects differing significantly from those claimed. (1)

A list of eighteen "benefits" that Ethyl was supposed to have claimed for MMT was offered. No particular sources were cited. The report just suggested that its authors made "a review of technical papers dealing with MMT and its effects, including many by Ethyl." The claims appear to have been taken from sources such as Society of Automotive Engineers International (SAE) papers (which go through some sort of reviewing process), the U.S. *Federal Register*, material in the EPA's public dockets, material submitted to the House Committee, and probably some face to face meetings with representatives of Ethyl and/or the CPPI. In his remarks to the Senate Standing Committee meeting two years later, Nantais said:

Amongst ... information [given to the Committee] are 25 technical papers prepared by the Society of Automotive Engineers. These span the years from 1975 to 1994 and have been prepared by engineers from independent research companies, automotive engineers, as well as Ethyl Corporation. As you will note from the summaries that have been provided with the papers, a large majority demonstrate that MMT damages automobile emission control systems. Interestingly, the only papers which claim any beneficial effects of MMT were prepared by Ethyl Corporation itself. Even so, four out of seven of Ethyl's own papers made reference to some evidence of problems in areas like catalyst plugging, increased emissions and increased particulates due to MMT. (SSCEENR 2/4, 1997b, 8)

I do not know exactly what papers were included in the collection referred to by Nantais, but good lists of relevant technical publications from both sides may be found in Benson and Dana (2002) and Roos, Hollrah, Guinther, and Cunningham (2002).

The following is a summary of the main arguments from the MVMA and AIAMC report and an evaluation of each:

1 Ethyl accepts its own controlled experiments with limited numbers of vehicles, conditions, mileage, and so on, but it rejects reports of uncontrolled in-use data, e.g., warranty data (6).

Evaluation. This is an oversimplification. As indicated below (8), Ethyl has used in-use data from several sources when it supports their position, e.g., warranty claims data provided by vehicle manufacturers showing that there are relatively more problems with OBD systems in Nova Scotia than in Ontario, and many problems with such systems in the United States, although no MMT is used there. Roos also described "in-use testing sponsored by Ethyl Corporation. Recently, a set of four OBD vehicles belonging to salesmen were tracked in Ontario and periodically evaluated. After more than two years, no OBD fault codes were found and all vehicles displayed low emissions." (SSCEENR 2/5, 1997d, 8)

2 Although many very specific emissions testing protocols have been developed through consultations between industry and government, "In a number of areas ... Ethyl did not adhere to the rigorous requirements which regulators demand of manufacturers for emissions certification ... Examples from the 1988 model Ethyl test fleet program include ... use of an atypical gasoline without detergents ... use of 1,000 miles test as a start point [instead of the standard] 4,000 ... unscheduled maintenance of major fuel system components ... [incomplete] maintenance data ... less demanding [driving cycle]" (6–7).

Evaluation. As indicated earlier, the EPA was fairly scrupulous in using only some of the data provided by Ethyl and auto makers. It seems to me that too often both sides in the dispute, as well as the EPA, were not particularly clear about exactly what blend of gasoline was used. For example, testifying before the Senate Standing Committee, J.W. Roos, Manager Fuels, Research and Development for Ethyl Corporation, described the fuels used in "the most extensive testing ever performed" by saying merely that "For each pair of vehicles, one car used base fuel and one used MMT fuel" (SSCEENR 2/5, 1997d, 3). Both sides complained about unscheduled maintenance by the other side, sometimes unreasonably so. For example, Ethyl complained about manufacturers replacing or fixing broken equipment in order to continue a test even though the maintenance was fully documented and would have been exactly the sort that a consumer would have had if the problem occurred outside a test.

3 There is insufficient "comprehensive post-program inspection, test and evaluation of important emissions control components" (7).

Evaluation Very little post-program information is reported by anyone; so this may be another defect shared by both sides.

4 The extreme variations in reported emissions test values "mock the absolute and unequivocal certainty with which Ethyl draws and presents conclusions" (7).

Evaluation. As shown in chapter 8, a very similar charge was made by Abraham and Lawless, correctly I think.

5 Ethyl's reports about how MMT survived the EPA's "cause or contribute" criterion misleadingly suggest that there were no impaired emission components, no HC emissions increases, and no more Canadian than American warranty claims for spark plugs, catalysts and oxygen sensors, although all of these problems occurred (7).

Evaluation. This is fairly accurate, and all of these problems are mentioned here in chapter 5.

6 Ethyl includes OBD II systems among the components that were supposed to have been unharmed according to the EPA "cause or contribute" criterion, but the EPA specifically withheld a final judgment about those systems (7–8).

Evaluation. This was confirmed earlier in chapter 5 with quotations from the *Federal Register.*

7 Contrary to Ethyl's claims, use of MMT contributes to the problem that "Manganese oxides ... coat the engine combustion chamber and the entire vehicle exhaust system including the catalyst and oxygen sensors ... The oxide coating builds throughout a vehicle's life but its growth is highly dependent on manganese concentration in the fuel, vehicle fuel consumption, and on exhaust temperatures which in turn are generally a function of vehicle service and catalyst proximity to the engine" (9).

Evaluation. All sides agree that about 80 per cent of the residue resulting from the combustion of MMT remains inside the engine and emissions system (CPPI Technical Task Force 1995, 1–2, 13). What Ethyl objects to is the claim that its product does any damage. Since manganese oxides can be found plugging honeycomb passages and storing oxygen, these charges against the product seem to be well-founded.

8 Ethyl claims that MMT does not contribute to spark plug misfire or to the fact that spark plug warranty claims in Canada are from one and a half to six times higher than those in the United States. However, there is a long history of technical papers describing spark plug problems caused by MMT. Most importantly, "Ethyl also points to the fact that spark plug replacement rates are much higher in Atlantic Canada than in British Columbia despite higher annual average MMT concentrations in the western province. This ignores the fact that MMT-free unleaded gasolines are available in B.C. and also that the ratio of B.C. spark plug warranty claims to those of the geographically and climatically similar Northwestern states is higher than is found in a comparable comparison for the Atlantic region. Driving speeds and patterns found on both coasts appear to accentuate the frequency of complaints" (9–10).

Evaluation. As suggested earlier and again below, although they are not the only sorts of deposits that can cause shunting and misfiring, deposits of manganese oxides on plugs can certainly lead to such problems. Without knowing the proportion of MMT-free gasoline sold in British Columbia, it is impossible to determine how much difference this might make to differences in warranty claims. The argument beginning with "the ratio of B.C." seems to be suggesting that if spark plug warranty claims in British Columbia (where MMT is used) are greater than those in, say, Washington (where MMT is not used), then it does not matter that warranty claims in Atlantic Canada are higher than those in British Columbia. Presumably, it is not supposed to matter because the northwestern U.S. states are "geographically and climatically similar" to British Columbia while the Atlantic provinces are significantly different. So, the northwestern states are a better comparison group than the Atlantic provinces, and when one compares spark plug warranty claims between British Columbia and that of states in the better comparison group *versus* British Columbia and that of provinces in the weaker comparison group, one finds that relatively more claims are made in British Columbia than in Washington. The additional claims are then attributed to MMT, as the distinctive feature in British Columbian gasoline.

If I understand argument of the Northwestern states correctly, I believe it is a relevant response to Ethyl's Atlantic provinces argument. The latter asserts that if MMT is used on the east and west coasts, and there are many more warranty claims on the east coast, then MMT cannot be the cause of the complaints on both coasts. Why would the same cause produce such different effects on each coast? If significantly less MMT were used on the west coast than on the east coast, that might explain the difference, but the argument of Northwestern states does not explain the difference. Chapter 8 includes testimony from Doug Bethune claiming that the average use of MMT in British Columbia is nearly twice as high as its use in the Atlantic provinces, a claim that I have not been able to confirm or disconfirm. Nor does it help matters to say that on both coasts "driving speeds and patterns ... accentuate the frequency of complaints."

9 Ethyl claims that use of MMT will contribute to lower emissions of HC, CO, NO$_x$, benzene, and other toxic emissions, but (1) the majority of technical papers over the past twenty years have found statistically significant increases of HC emissions when MMT is used; (2) the most recent testing by Ethyl showed mixed results for HC and CO; (3) "Ethyl has ignored a large portion of the real world fleet of vehicles (trucks)"; (4) trucks are probably "more susceptible to MMT effects because of the more severe duty cycle they normally operate under and their higher fuel usage"; (5) tests have not been done on the most advanced technology, and (6) Ethyl reports average emissions but auto makers must be "responsible for each pollutant on each and every model" (10–11).

Evaluation. Taking the claims one at a time, although I have not made a careful count of all the papers addressing HC emissions, my impression is that the auto makers' judgment on point (1) is accurate. Regarding point (2), earlier we reviewed the mixed results from the tests following the fourth waiver application. Examining the types of vehicles listed earlier in all the tests by Ethyl and the auto makers, the only truck mentioned is the Ford Explorer, which was tested by Ford. So the third point (3) is true. Compared to the performance of light-duty vehicles and their components, trucks have been neglected. Point (4) sounds plausible, but I do not know whether there is good evidence to support it. The paper by Benson and Dana (2002) was based on an analysis of data from 20 out of 40 vehicles. The 40 vehicles included 8 light-duty trucks, 4 General Motors S10 Blazers, and 4 Daimler Chrysler Caravans (Alliance of Automobile Manufacturers 2002s, 6). Information on the performance of the trucks is not reported in the paper and as far as I can tell from the main report, the trucks do not fare especially poorly compared to some of the other vehicles. Point (5) is difficult to quarrel with because, as indicated in testimony before the House Standing Committee, the technology is continuously developing (HSCESD 10/24, 1995b, 22). Perhaps this was part of the reason for the EPA withholding its judgment about the impact of MMT on OBD II equipment. Point (6) is an oversimplification because, as we saw above, the EPA does allow for some sampling of models and some failures of some tests. In fact, that was one of the things the automakers found objectionable above in 5.

10 Considering claims regarding reduced emissions of NO_x resulting from the use of MMT, the authors of the report say that (1) Ethyl's test results from 1988 and 1992–93 model fleets differ from Ford's test results; (2) "All of these other test programs found only marginal and statistically not significant NO_x differences between MMT and clear fuels"; (3) manufacturers often get lower reductions of NO_x with "clear fuels required for emissions certification" than with fuel containing MMT; (4) two vehicle models had extraordinary MMT effects and these outliers skewed the averages offered by Ethyl; (5) Ethyl claimed that their 1988 fleet represented 53.3 per cent of U.S. passenger car sales, but only 29 per cent of Canadian sales; (6) "It is doubtful that any of the 1988 engine family/emission system combinations are truly representative of current models. Five of the eight engines are no longer available in 1996 passenger car models"; (7) three of the eight systems tested in the 1992–93 fleet are also not available in 1996 models; and (8) "The two Transitional Low Emissions Vehicles (TLEV's) in this fleet are likely the most representative of 1996 and future technologies and ... [they] showed no statistically significant evidence of the claimed NO_x reduction according to the University of Waterloo study which noted that this is also the case for 75% of the vehicles in each of the Ethyl fleets" (11).

Evaluation. We saw earlier that claim (1) is true, but the test procedures were too different to know what to make of the differences in results. I am not sure about "all" the other programs (claim (2)), but the points made in 11 suggest that Ethyl's claims about MMT's advantages for NO_x reduction are exaggerated. (See also chapter 8, *Minority Opinion* argument 6.) The results reported in points(4) and (8) regarding the University of Waterloo study are true (more on this in chapter 8). Point (3) is examined in detail in 12, and does not receive a clear pass. I suppose the auto makers are strategically placed to have the most accurate motor vehicle sales data (5), as well as data on engine family/emission system combinations ((6) and (7)).

11 Ethyl's estimated increases in the "annual tonnage of motor vehicle NO_x emissions in Canada" that would result from eliminating MMT from gasoline are exaggerated and inaccurate because (1) projections are based on outdated 1988 emissions control systems (cf. 10, points (6) and (7)); (2) projections were made from a model ("Mobile 5c") that "inflates tonnage estimates"; (3) "Ethyl assumed that NO_x differentials between clear and MMT-fueled vehicles continues to increase to 195,000 miles" although tests on the 1992–93 fleet revealed that "NO_x emission trends for both fuels were essentially parallel above 10,000 miles, Ethyl's 1994 Thunderbird tests ... displayed convergence rather than divergence at higher distances [and] Ford's testing ... indicated marginally higher NO_x emissions and deterioration for MMT-fueled vehicles"; (4) it was assumed that "future emission systems will deteriorate at high absolute rates" although the historical record reveals steady improvements in deterioration rates; (5) advantages of OBD II systems were ignored, as well as (6) those of "inspection and maintenance programs" (12, 38); (7) new regulations for "lower sulphur limits for gasolines" will be introduced since it has been "demonstrated" that lower sulphur levels "reduce the levels of all three regulated emissions (HC, CO, NO_x) and particulates (15); and (8) as soon as problems are detected, vehicle "recall action would be required to restore lower-emissions" (37).

Evaluation. Point (1) is easily established on the basis of what we already know about the testing program. I cannot confirm or disconfirm point (2), but point (3) may be confirmed by examining the data, and points (4) to (8) are most likely true, if only because nobody would know how to estimate alternative deterioration rates resulting from currently unknown as well as relatively new technologies, monitoring programs, and recall procedures.

12 Because routine durability tests of engine/emission systems conducted by auto manufacturers to obtain EPA certification often reveal lower levels of system deterioration using MMT-free fuels than the levels revealed in Ethyl's tests using fuels with MMT, all reductions in deterioration levels in the presence of MMT cannot be attributed to the additive. In the report's own words,

> Auto manufacturers are regularly required to demonstrate the durability of their engine/emission systems. Durability tests (formerly 50,000 miles and currently 100,000 miles) are a necessary part of the comprehensive testing protocol to achieve EPA certification ... The nature of these tests [sic] are similar to those conducted by Ethyl for their MMT waiver application and the ... Ford tests ... The deterioration factors

established in these durability tests using approved test fuels *without* MMT vary considerably but are often found to be lower than those reported in Ethyl's tests on vehicles using MMT fuel. Since the durability tests must be conducted with MMT-free fuel it is obvious that the favorable NO_x deterioration rates which are the basis for Ethyl's NO_x benefit claims are not unique to MMT usage. This is further supported by EPA testing of in-use vehicles for their emissions factors program. (34)

Evaluation. Assuming that the data are accurately described in these passages and available for inspection in an EPA public docket, the basic argument is similar in form to one frequently used by Ethyl against the auto manufacturers, e.g., argument 7 (chapter 8) regarding the first question in the *Minority Opinion* of the Senate Standing Committee. Simply put, the argument is that if many things can cause something to occur, then one cannot be sure which thing is the cause in any particular case without controlling for all the other possible causes. In the present case, we are given only two possible causes to consider, namely, fuel with and without MMT. Since, as we saw in chapter 5, EPA test protocols require fuels representative of those in use (which include an array of additives), while Ethyl's tests sometimes use fuels without any additives and sometimes with a special blend of additives (with or without MMT), there is no way for us to know exactly what other variables may have been present in the fuels used in the routine durability tests or the tests used for comparison. So, plausible as the argument appears to be, it does have a troublesome loose end.

13 Criticizing Ethyl's tests described in Roos et al. (1992), the report states that (1) Ethyl "created their own monitor index" which "was never described anywhere in the paper"; (2) "Ethyl chose to plot their monitor index on a log scale" which "will tend to minimize the effect of contamination"; (3) "Ethyl's laboratory test setup does not represent a relevant operating condition for an analysis of Ford's catalyst monitors" because it runs at relatively high velocities that "will tend to mask the real world oxygen storage effect of manganese"; (4) "Ethyl tested catalyst cores using new oxygen sensors, NOT sensors aged on MMT fuels"; and (5) "Because of all of Ethyl's test differences, the catalyst monitor relationship they developed would not provide the sensitivity in the hydrocarbon efficiency 'threshold area' specified by EPA to qualify as a catalyst monitor usable in the OBD II system" (40–1).

Evaluation. The first point is easily confirmed by examining the paper, but not the next two or the last. The fourth point seems ill-founded. Two other sentences follow the quotation above: "The lab setup is NOT representative of the way oxygen storage would be measured in a vehicle, as a complete system. Aged oxygen sensors are slower than new sensors, and sensors aged on MMT fuel exhibit a rich bias (fuel metering system)" (41).

It is unclear to me how one could precisely measure the oxygen storage capacity of a catalyst using oxygen sensors that were fouled in any way, from any cause. According to Leavitt (1996), an article in *Automotive News* (8 April 1996) by Chuck Ruth, General Product Manager at Robert Bosch Corporation, claimed that "about 66 percent of all vehicle emissions test failures result from worn-out O_2 sensors," although "an analysis of 9036 AirCare repair data forms from 1988 and newer vehicles showed that 25 percent of O_2 sensors required replacement or service." From these two facts he concluded that "The actual percentage of sensors requiring replacement probably lies between these two values." For our purposes, the most important implication of Leavitt's remarks is that defects in O_2 sensors often lead to erroneous assessments of catalysts' performance. Thus, to avoid such errors, performance tests on catalysts that are based on O_2 sensors must have sensors that are known to be functioning properly, i.e., sensors fouled by MMT would be inappropriate.

My evaluation of these thirteen arguments tends to confirm eight (4–11), disconfirm one (1) and leave four indeterminate (2, 3, 12, and 13). In Reichenbach's terms this would give the MVMA/AIAMC case a success ratio of about 62 per cent, i.e., the weight of evidence is more favourable than not for their case.

After challenging Ethyl's claims regarding the alleged benefits of MMT, the MVMA/AIAMC report went on the offensive. A review of the arguments follows:

1 It was asserted that of the four broad strategies for addressing all the problems concerning fuels and additives, the harmonization strategy was clearly superior to the others. The four strategies were (a) "harmonize the entire control strategy, including fuel specifications"; (b) "accommodate unique Canadian fuel characteristics in design," which was judged to be "unrealistic in terms of its costs and impossible as the resources required for its accomplishment (facilities, personnel, etc.) do not exist"; (c) "compromise (Canadian conditions don't warrant best available technology," which it was supposed "would be rejected by most Canadians as inappropriate and wasteful of the efforts and costs associated with the devel-

opment and production of today's advanced emissions control systems";
and (d) "live with the differences (essentially the approach adopted in
the late 1970s/early 1980s)," which was regarded as "no longer an acceptable approach with the far more stringent emissions standards of the late
1990s, the extended warranty periods, impairment of sophisticated
on-board-diagnostic systems, high consumer expectations, and the unacceptability of perpetuating only the appearance of serious emissions control" (MVMA/AIAMC 1995, 17–18).

Evaluation. Although the four options are not mutually exclusive and
may not be exhaustive, they do seem to be realistic and not just cooked up
to make a point. Given the relatively small Canadian share of the North
American market, (b) would be unnecessarily costly, and it is almost certain
that (c) would not be acceptable to most Canadians. Option (d)'s reference
to the "impairment of sophisticated on-board-diagnostic systems" is
question-begging, but the points about "extended warranty periods" and
"high consumer expectations" are accurate. The Canadian government's
and relevant industries' commitment to a broad policy of harmonization of
standards with the United States and to using the EPA's enabling legislation,
testing, review, and adjudication procedures since the agreement of 12
October 1994 were even stronger arguments in support of option (a). So I
think the auto manufacturers are right about this one.

2 "Current Canadian expectations regarding motor vehicle emissions control ... are incompatible with current Canadian" gasolines insofar as "proposals to match California are being heard with increasing intensity and
frequency," but it is impossible to satisfy California's standards without
adopting California's MMT-free, reformulated fuels. There is, the auto manufacturers believed, an "unrealistic reliance on [a] hardware solution to
very complex problems" (19).

Evaluation. We were not told exactly how many or what percentage of
Canadians had the designated expectations, or given any evidence for the
claim. Still, we have already seen that the EPA and California (through
CARB) have taken serious remedial actions to deal with the state's exhaust
pollution problems, including the requirement of MMT-free, reformulated
gasoline. So it might reasonably be expected that Californian standards
and requirements would eventually become Canadian standards and
requirements, i.e., Vogel's "California effect."

3 "Numerous scientific papers" were published "in the late 1970s"
showing

increases in both engine-out and tail pipe emissions of HC with MMT
but with little or no discernible effect on CO and NO_x. Numerous papers
also noted small increases in catalyst conversion efficiencies but of an
insufficient magnitude to offset the higher engine-out HC. Also frequently discussed was the coating and physical plugging of catalysts
with Mn_3O_4 ... Other conditions reported in these late 1970s papers
evaluating MMT included spark plug fouling, catalyst efficiency deterioration, effects on oxygen sensors and certification difficulties. (20)

Evaluation. References to some of the early papers may be found in
Benson and Dana (2002) and Roos, Hollrah, Guinther, and Cunningham
(2002). Even a report produced by Ethyl in May 1959 included the assertion that "AK-33X (research code for MMT) can drastically reduce spark
plug life in severe duty service" (MVMA/AIAMC 1995, 24). While the papers
do cite the results indicated in the auto manufacturers' report, the variety
and uncertainty of test conditions, as well as of the precise nature of the
particular hardware and fuel mixtures used, makes it difficult to assess the
value of those results as indicators of problems for the vehicles, component
parts, and fuel mixtures of the 1990s and later. It is probably wise to regard
the studies' results as suggestive but inconclusive warning signs.

4 The United States *Federal Register* (FR 1994) has several caveats regarding the weakness and obsolescence of their tests of MMT on the 1988 and
1992/1993 vehicle model year test fleets (27–8).
Evaluation. The article cited is thoroughly reviewed in chapter 5. While
the EPA was dissatisfied with its tests and called for the development of new
protocols and tests, the agency administrator thought it would be unfair to
change the rules in the middle of an on-going adjudication process. However, the developmental work and testing are continued.

5 "In contrast to Ethyl's claim that air toxic emissions (primarily Benzene)
will be reduced when MMT is introduced, Ford's October 3, 1991 submission to EPA reported higher toxic emissions (formaldehyde, 1.3-butadiene,
toluene, etc.) from vehicles operating on MMT fuel. Ethyl has not offered
any new test data on the toxic emissions from this additive to refute the
Ford data" (30).
Evaluation. I have not been able to confirm or disconfirm this.

Summarizing my evaluation of these five arguments, I believe three are
sound (1, 2, and 4), and two are indeterminate. Considering these results,

combined with those obtained earlier, I find more support for accepting than for rejecting the MMT *Act*. The House Standing Committee on Environment and Sustainable Development assessed the case in the same way. Accordingly, on 26 October 1995 the committee agreed to recommend to the House of Commons acceptance of Bill C-94 without any changes. Unfortunately, parliament was prorogued shortly afterward (2 February 1996) and the bill died on the order paper. However, it was reintroduced by Minister Marchi in the next session (March 1996) as Bill C-29.

8

Interim Report and *Minority Opinion* of the Senate Standing Committee on Energy, the Environment, and Natural Resources

This chapter reviews and critically assesses the arguments presented for and against the *MMT Act* in the reports of the Senate Standing Committee. On 4 February 1997 the Senate of Canada passed a motion asking the Senate Standing Committee on Energy, the Environment and Natural Resources to prepare "an interim report before submitting its final report on Bill C-29 [formerly C-94]" that would answer the following three questions: (1) Is MMT-based petroleum the cause of OBD malfunctioning? (2) Does MMT in gas cause a health hazard to Canadians? (3) Does MMT in gas cause direct damage to the environment? (SSCEENR 3/4,1997k, 1)

On 4 March 1997, the committee tabled its *Interim Report Concerning Bill C-29* (SSCEENR 3/4,1997k). The committee had oral testimony from fifty-eight witnesses, as well as the opportunity to question them, and also received forty-six written submissions. The *Interim Report* began with a one-page summary of the history of Ethyl Corporation's attempts to get a waiver from the U.S. EPA for MMT, briefly covering the ground reviewed in chapter 5. It then proceeded to address the three questions, first (2), then (3), and finally (1).

Regarding question (2) about MMT as a potential health hazard, the majority perceived two main health-related concerns, namely, (a) "the health impact of the manganese emitted from vehicles as a result of the combustion of MMT" and (b) "the potential for increased emissions of smog-forming pollutants if OBD-II systems are compromised by the use of MMT" (SSCEENR 3/4, 1997k, 3). After it was noted that Health Canada had been "assessing this issue [(a)] since 1978," testimony of D. Krewski, Health Canada, (06/02/97) was quoted, indicating that "The main conclusion of this assessment was that the manganese emissions from MMT are unlikely to pose a risk to health for any sub-group of the population" (SSCEENR 3/4, 1997k, 4).

Immediately following that testimony, the authors of the *Interim Report* remarked that some witnesses before the committee were still very concerned. In particular, the representative from the Learning Disabilities Association of Canada, B. McElgunn, recalled the history of lead in gasoline and asserted that the Association did "not believe that adequate data have been collected on the toxic effects of low level, long-term exposure to manganese ... [and that] More than forty organizations and scientists in the U.S. and Canada oppose the use of MMT in gasoline because of concerns about health effects" (SSCEENR 3/4, 1997k, 4).

In response to the comment about the history of lead, the *Report* included the following quotation from Krewski:

> Much of the opposition to MMT on health grounds is based on the fear that manganese from MMT will prove to be like lead from gasoline in the 1970s and 1980s. However, there are several critical differences between them. Lead is toxic at all concentrations while manganese is an essential element required in small amounts by cells in the body. Lead is toxic by ingestion as well as by inhalation, while manganese is not toxic when ingested even in quite large amounts. Much of the lead exposure by young children occurred as a secondary result of contamination of dirt and dust, which was ingested in sufficient amounts to raise blood levels in this age group. Finally, lead was added to gasoline in amounts about 16 times higher than the amount of manganese additive, leading to higher airborne lead and higher ground deposition. *Nonetheless, considering the seriousness of the end point, it is not inappropriate to invoke the precautionary principle in the consideration of regulatory options to limit exposure to this substance* ... (06/02/97). (SSCEENR 3/4, 1997k, 5; emphasis added)

The *Interim Report* went on to quote from a 1995 report of the Teaching Health Units, Metro Toronto and the Toronto Department of Public Health, which also expressed concerns about our lack of information regarding the impact of the predominant combustion product from MMT, manganese tetroxide, on public health. Still, the majority group concluded that, "Despite some lingering concerns about the effects of long-term, low-level exposure to Mn, there appears to be sufficient data to conclude that the emission of manganese resulting from the combustion of MMT in gasoline does not pose a public health problem" (SSCEENR 3/4, 1997k, 6).

The committee then turned to the question (3) on the environmental impact of MMT. In the *Interim Report's* view, the question raised a health concern because of "the debate over how the presence or absence of MMT in fuel will affect the environment by altering vehicle emissions of CO (carbon monoxide), HC (hydrocarbons), and NO_x (nitrogen oxides). Indirectly, this is a health issue since increases, especially in NO_x and HC, contribute to an increase in urban smog, and hence affect the health of those with respiratory problems such as allergies and asthma ... If MMT use is proven to cause increases in emissions of HC, CO and NO_x, it could pose a public health risk" (SSCEENR 3/4, 1997k, 6).

The following testimony from J.W. Roos, Ethyl Corporation, was then quoted: "MMT provides significant emission benefits, lowering a vehicle's average NO_x emissions by 15 to 20 per cent compared to vehicles not using the additive. Analysis performed by Environment Canada shows that changes in fuel formulation caused by MMT removal could result in the increase in air toxins such as benzene, acetaldehyde and formaldehyde. These are all toxic or proven cancer-causing chemicals. MMT removal would result in a 15 to 20 per cent increase in NO_x emissions ... (05/02/97)" (SSCEENR 3/4, 1997k, 7).

The majority of members noted that "Canadian refiners share this opinion," but that the U.S. EPA had a "somewhat lower" estimate of an NO_x reduction benefit of "8 per cent of the standard" while Environment Canada's "own research" produced a figure of 5 per cent. Most importantly, "Environment Canada also noted that this benefit had to be weighed against the benefits to be gained by properly functioning pollution control equipment. The Committee was told that: ' ... if there is a NO_x benefit and you are in a policy decision then the question which must be asked is: Are there trade-offs here? ... The rationale here is one is protecting pollution control equipment and ensuring that it works well. Obviously, if it does, then that benefit must be greater than this potential NO_x increase.' (F. Vena, Environment Canada, 04/02/97)" (SSCEENR 3/4, 1997k, 7).

There did appear to be "trade-offs" because, according to other testimony by Vena, the EPA reported that there would be a "hydrocarbon increase with manganese fuels" although according to David Wilson, President of Ethyl Canada, the EPA reported that "increases in hydrocarbon emissions observed in the entire fleet of 1992 and 1993 vehicles tested by Ethyl ... are not statistically significant" (SSCEENR 3/4, 1997k, 8; see chapter 5). Yves Landry, President and CEO of Chrysler Canada and President of the CVMA, told the committee that: "In 1985, Environment Canada ordered an independent study to determine the impact of MMT on vehicle emissions. The study was conducted by a multi-party working group representing the petroleum and automobile industries, the government and the Ethyl company, under the direction of the Committee on Standardization of Forms of the Canadian General Standards Board. The study ended in 1986.

The main finding of the study was to recognize that MMT increased exhaust emissions of hydrocarbons. As a direct consequence of this finding, since 1986 Transport Canada has been monitoring standards on exhaust systems of new vehicles through vehicles using MMT-free fuel" (SSCEENR, 2/4, 1997b, 2).

So the committee concluded that "The evidence relating to the impact of MMT use on emissions of hydrocarbons and carbon monoxide, and consequently on the Canadian environment, is contradictory and therefore, inconclusive" (SSCEENR 3/4, 1997k, 8).

Finally, the *Interim Report* focused on question (1) on the impact of MMT-based gasoline on OBD malfunctioning. The following summary remarks clearly reveal the majority group's quandary:

> This, more than any other question is at the heart of debate about MMT. It is also the question to which the Committee received the most diametrically opposed views. There is very little middle ground on this issue. One side states categorically that it has volumes of data proving that MMT is responsible for damaging the OBD-II systems. The other side states just as vehemently, and cites a similar volume of evidence that MMT does not impair the functioning of OBD-II systems ... it is impossible for the Committee to answer the question raised in the motion from the Senate regarding OBD-II because the evidence is so contradictory ... the technical information and the interpretation of test results were highly contradictory. (SSCEENR 3/4, 1997k, 8–9)

Testimony from the presidents of Ford, General Motors, Honda, Nissan, the MVMA, AIAMC, and the Car Dealers Association was quoted on one side and testimony from Ethyl Corporation, the CPPI, and the refining industries on the other side. Reports from the U.S. EPA and additional testimony from Environment Canada indicated considerable uncertainty about the available evidence (SSCEENR 3/4, 1997k, 8–11).

Granting all the uncertainty, the committee quoted the testimony of Tony Clarke, Environment Canada, 04/02/97: "The government decided to be prudent and to err on the side of caution, the environment and human health. This is an excellent example of the precautionary principle which this government signed on to at Rio, with Agenda 21, back in 1992" (SSCEENR 3/4, 1997k, 11).

Following that, the majority concluded that "There is evidence supplied by 21 car manufacturers who are unanimous in their opinion that MMT has a negative effect on OBD-II systems. There is evidence supplied by one corporation, the manufacturer of MMT, which believes that MMT does not have a negative effect on OBD-II systems. *Based on the preponderance of evidence the government was justified in invoking the precautionary principle and introducing Bill C-29 as the prudent, responsible course of action*" (SSCEENR 3/4, 1997k, 11; emphasis added).

As explained in chapters 5 and 7, my evaluation of the evidence given to the EPA and the report of the MVMA and AIAMC to the House Standing Committee generally supported an affirmative answer to questions 1 and 3.

On 4 March 1997, four members of the Senate Standing Committee on Energy, the Environment and Natural Resources filed a minority report to the *Interim Report* of the majority of the committee (SSCEENR 3/4, 1997l). The four senators were John Buchanan (Nova Scotia), Ron Ghitter (Alberta), Ethel Cochrane (Newfoundland), and Noël A. Kinsella (Fredericton-York-Sunbury). The authors of *The Minority Opinion* claimed that "The Interim Report was written before the transcripts of the testimony of the Minister of Environment were available for a careful and considered review of the evidence he supplied. A minority of members disagree with the content and the conclusions of that report. We therefore present this minority opinion" (SSCEENR 3/4, 1997l, 1).

The *Opinion* is divided into three sections, each dealing with the minority's views about one of the questions that the Senate put to its committee. I will present and evaluate the minority's views about each question in turn. Because the *Opinion* contains the final considered views of those who disagreed with the official position of the committee, a fair assessment of the work of the committee requires a careful consideration of these views. Some material covered earlier is repeated, but only enough to guarantee that nothing regarded as important by the minority in the committee is neglected here. Most of the arguments presented in the *Opinion* are or appear to be unsound, but this does not relieve us of the burden of giving them a fair hearing, without which that fact could not be established.

QUESTION 1: IS MMT-BASED PETROLEUM THE CAUSE OF OBD MALFUNCTIONING?

1 "Environment Canada admitted that it had not, nor had any other department of government conducted itself, nor contracted an objective

third party to conduct independent testing on MMT and its effects, if any, on OBD systems" (SSCEENR 3/4, 1997l, 2).

Evaluation. This is probably the single most frequently raised objection to the federal government's management of the MMT file by those opposed to the *MMT Act* (see, for example, Hill and Leiss 2001). However, it is not extraordinary for any government office or regulator to depend on information or evidence produced by or for those governed or regulated. This is fairly standard practice for everything from personal and corporate income tax reports to demonstrations of drug efficacy and environmental impact statements. Also, just as governments accept the assessments of third party auditors of tax statements, they often accept the assessments of third party assessors of research reports offered by producers in support of their products. The assessment by Abraham and Lawless (1995) of the McCann Report is a good example of an independent third party assessment contracted by government.

2 Although it was "suggested by Environment Canada Official Frank Vena that: 'In essence, what we have seen is that in a limited number of tests that data is [sic] still inconclusive. We don't have a lot of data on which to say a definitive yea or nay.' The basis, however inclusive, of the government's rationale for Bill C-29 is the claim of the auto manufacturers that MMT damages automobiles' OBD systems – the equipment which monitors pollution leaving the vehicle" (SSCEENR 3/4, 1997l, 2).

Evaluation. This is an oversimplification. Besides the "claim of the auto manufacturers," claims were made by the manufacturers of OBD systems, by car dealers, by the Canadian Automobile Association, by Ethyl Corporation about its own tests, by third party assessors contracted by government and industry, by the U.S. EPA and by the U.S. Court of Appeals.

3 It was reported to the committee by Environment Canada in December 1996 that "'The automotive industry is so convinced of the detrimental effects of MMT that they are conducting a $10 million test program in the U.S. in order to obtain definitive evidence to support their position.' The Government is not interested in knowing the results of this 'definitive' study before proceeding with Bill C-29. This is irresponsible" (SSCEENR 3/4, 1997l, 2).

Susan Whelan (MP, Essex-Windsor) also reported that to the House (PD9/25, 1996a, 21).

Evaluation. Given the first two objections of *The Minority Opinion*, the authors would hardly give any credence to yet another study by the auto manufacturers. So the value of this objection from their point of view is unclear. The study referred to began in 1996 and cost U.S.$8 million; and many of the results are reported in Alliance of Automobile Manufacturers (2002a, 2002b) and Benson and Dana (2002). The *Backgrounder* on the website with the two parts of the MMT *Program* says:

> A total of 56 vehicles from 6 automobile manufacturers underwent mileage accumulation of up to 100,000 miles (160,000 km) and were emissions tested at specific intervals during the program. A total of about 3.65 million miles (5.84 million kilometres) were driven during the six-year evaluation ...
>
> The study results showed that MMT impaired catalyst and emission control performance and caused low emission vehicles to fail hydrocarbon (HC) emission standards.
>
> The study also showed that, compared to low-emission vehicles driven on clear gasoline, MMT-fueled low-emission vehicles had these significant impacts at 100,000 miles (160,000 km):
>
> 31% higher HC emissions
> 24% higher oxides of nitrogen (NO_x) emissions
> 14% higher carbon monoxide (CO) emissions
> 2% higher emissions of carbon dioxide (CO_2), a greenhouse gas
> 2% lower on-road fuel economy. (1)

Roos, Hollrah, Guinther, and Cunningham (2002) severely criticized the Benson and Dana (2002) paper, as well as the more detailed longer reports. Nevertheless, they claimed that the study was good enough to prove that "All vehicles tested in the study met the emission standards for all pollutants that apply to the test vehicles in-use and analysis of the data show MMT had no effect on fuel economy. What is especially noteworthy about the present study is that the compatibility of MMT has now been demonstrated in a program commissioned by the automobile industry using the most advanced vehicles currently available operated under extremely severe conditions as part of the test protocol" (Roos, Hollrah, Guinther, and Cunningham 2002, 1).

After carefully studying the disagreements presented in these publications from 2002, I concluded that opponents and proponents of the MMT *Act* would still be unwilling to change their positions about what ought to be done, and therefore a detailed review of this material would serve no useful purpose for our story. At a minimum this supports the view of those, such as the Canadian government and the minority voice on the AIT panel (see chapter 16), who believed and said that the two industrial giants involved in the dispute would never agree on the scientific evidence, making more studies relatively useless for obtaining scientific closure on the issues in dispute.

4 Environment Canada should have been but was not impressed by the position taken by the U.S. EPA.

> The conclusion of the U.S. Environmental Protection Agency on the scientific evidence presented to it, by both Ethyl and the auto manufacturers, is recorded in the United States Federal Register, Volume 58, N.235, Thursday, December 9, 1993, p.64761.
>
> "... the EPA Administrator has determined that Ethyl has demonstrated as required (under the Clean Air Act) that use of HiTEC 3000 (MMT) at the specified concentration will not cause or contribute to a failure of any emission control device or system (over the useful life of any vehicle in which such device or system is used) to achieve compliance by the vehicle with the emission standards with respect to which it has been certified." (SSCEENR 3/4, 1997l, 2)

Evaluation. As indicated in chapter 5, the EPA reached this conclusion with some uncertainty and a clear intention to continue monitoring the situation with regard to possible adverse effects on OBD II systems and health.

5 Requests by officials from the governments of Nova Scotia and Alberta to have MMT evaluated through a process agreed upon by the CCME were simply ignored or denied by the federal government. "Mr. John Donner, Executive Director, Environmental Affairs, Department of Energy, Government of Alberta added that: 'In both April of 1996 and April of 1995, Minister Ty Lund expressed concern about MMT, and specifically requested that this go through the CCME process. At the officials [sic] level, I do know we were informed that the bill would proceed. There was no opportunity to discuss its merits. It was presented as a *fait accompli.* It would be introduced and there was nothing we could do to discuss it or investigate it or change it'" (SSCEENR 3/4, 1997l, 2–3).

Evaluation. The role of the CCME in all the decisions made regarding MMT and the *MMT Act* is discussed in detail in chapter 13. The AIT panel agreed with the complainants' claims that the federal government did not make sufficient use of the CCME process. In chapter 16 I explain why I disagree with the panel and complainants on this score. Here it is enough to say that the historical record of opportunities to "discuss it or investigate it or change it" proves that Donner's belief that they did not exist was false. After all, Bill C-29's predecessor, C-94, was introduced in the House of Commons on 19 May 1995 and both bills were subject to scrutiny in the House, in House and Senate committees, in the press, in the Ontario Court (General Division) injunction case, and even in the initial stages of the NAFTA and AIT cases before Bill C-29 came into force two years later on 24 June 1997.

6 The minority members' *Opinion* asserted that:

Ethyl Canada, the manufacturer of MMT, presented the Committee with data indicating that MMT is compatible with the latest in OBD technology and that it serves to improve air quality by reducing automobiles' emissions of nitrogen oxides (NO_x), a key component of urban smog, by significant amounts ... Ethyl Corporation conducted what has been termed [by the EPA] "the most extensive series of tests ever undertaken on a gasoline additive." The testing program was designed with the assistance of the EPA and U.S. auto makers to evaluate and document the effect of MMT on automobile emissions monitoring systems. Over 120 vehicles representing a broad cross-section of automobiles driven in North America, including vehicles that meet California's low emission requirements and those equipped with the latest OBD technology were used and accumulated over 16 million kilometres for the test. For each pair of vehicles, one car used a base fuel while its twin used the base fuel plus MMT. This provided a direct comparison for evaluating the effect of MMT on OBD system's components and for rigorous statistical analysis of the data. (SSCEENR 3/4, 1997l, 3–4)

Evaluation. The minority members did not tell us why they believed these industry-sponsored tests were more credible than the industry-sponsored tests coming from the other side. Nor did Hill and Leiss (2001, 93), who asserted that "direct emissions data showed that MMT did not affect hydrocarbon or carbon monoxide emissions and actually reduced NO_x emissions." However, the Government of Canada hired B. Abraham and J.F. Lawless from the University of Waterloo's Institute for Improvement in Quality and Productivity to examine the evidence for Ethyl's claim that MMT reduces NO_x emissions. The Government of Nova Scotia was apparently convinced by that evidence (SSCEENR 2/11, 1996, 3). Environment Canada had already questioned Ethyl's results on the grounds that they were based on "an extremely well maintained test fleet" of vehicles rather than on ordinary vehicles in various states of maintenance and repair. The report from these two independent researchers was dated 18 October 1995. Among other things they reported that "the NO_x reduction due to MMT is not statistically significant" (Clarke 1997, 23). In the Government of Canada's words, Abraham and Lawless concluded that "there is a substantial uncertainty surrounding estimates of NO_x emissions based on the Ethyl test fleet data" (Canada 1998, 27).

Three years earlier, the Chair of the House Standing Committee on Environment and Sustainable Development read the following passages from the Abraham and Lawless report into the official record:

> The McCann report (1995) in our opinion considerably overestimates reductions in NO_x emissions due to MMT. Indeed, no conclusion about such emissions over the period 1995–2010 can be reached on the basis of the Ethyl Corporation data. Reasons for this are as follows: (i) the Ethyl Corporation's experiments have not been shown to be representative of field vehicle use, and the scientific rigour of the experiments is uncertain. (ii) the test fleets included only a small number of models, but demonstrated very large model to model variations in emissions. This suggests that projections of Canada-wide emissions should employ different emission rates for different types of vehicles. (iii) the MOBILE5C program used for prediction of total emissions requires emission rates up to 195,000 miles, whereas test fleet cars were driven only to somewhere between 50,000 and 100,000 miles. There is no statistical basis to support extrapolation of test results much beyond the test mileages. (HSCESD10/24, 1995b, 36)

Asked by the chair to comment on the passages, Alison Pollack, Principal, ENVIRON International Corporation, said: "Statistics is not an exact science. I guess that's the simplest way to say it. I am not sure if the Waterloo statisticians were provided with exactly the same database I was looking at. That's unclear, since I haven't seen the report. I am not sure exactly what questions they were asked to answer. Even if we had the same database and were asked identical questions, as I said, statistics is not an exact science. There isn't only one right way to look at a set of numbers" (HSCESD10/24, 1995b, 37).

Christopher Hicks, Vice President of Ethyl Canada and Ethyl Corporation, then remarked that "I know Environment Canada has done a study that says the NO_x reduction is only 5%, but whether it's only 5% or 20% or something in between, depending on how the statisticians massage the numbers, everyone agrees that the removal of MMT will make emissions go up" (HSCESD10/24, 1995b, 37).

According to Beth Phinney, Liberal MP for Hamilton Mountain, commenting a month later: "In 1992 a report was prepared for Ethyl Canada. It indicated that if the additive were banned Canadian refineries would emit 40 to 50 tonnes more of nitrogen oxide per annum and 34 to 43 more kilotonnes of carbon dioxide. Those amounts represent 0.0025 per cent of our yearly emissions of nitrogen oxide and 0.01 per cent of our carbon dioxide emissions. Such slight increases are clearly minuscule" (PD11/9, 1995g, 3).

Thus, we have claims by apparently reputable experts indicating that (a) MMT reduces NO_x emissions in varying amounts; (b) that it makes no statistically significant difference to such emissions (i.e., the alleged measurable reductions attributed to MMT could have been the result of mere chance variation); (c) that statistical analysis is useless because, after all, "it is not an exact science"; (d) that "everyone agrees that the removal of MMT will make emissions go up"; and (e) that the increased emissions would be "clearly minuscule" anyhow. No wonder that later on AIT panelists were reluctant to wade into the scientific debate! But more to the point, what are we to make of this?

Let me say first that the different views of the impact of MMT on nitrogen oxide emissions could be multiplied for other chemicals and other aspects of the case, as indicated in chapter 4. Second, it is certainly not true that "everyone agrees the removal of MMT will make those emissions go up." To say that the measured changes may be the result of chance, as Abraham and Lawless said, is a statistically precise way to say that we do not know whether MMT has the effect attributed to it. Third, statistical science is far from the "anything goes grab bag" suggested by Pollack. Statistical procedures, including formulae for extrapolating unobserved from observed figures, typically include necessary conditions to be met to achieve measurable levels of reliability and validity. Abraham and Lawless told us that the conditions were not met in the McCann report and that, therefore, the report's conclusions about the effects of MMT were not warranted. That means that there may not be even "minuscule" effects.

During the Senate Committee hearings sixteen months after the House Committee hearings, Senator William Romkey asked Wilson about the Waterloo study, and got the following response:

We became aware of the Waterloo study at the October House committee hearings when that report was tabled. We had not seen it before. We immediately asked one of our consultants, Environ – whose representative incidentally has asked to appear before this committee and I am sure she would be delighted to talk in more detail about the University of Waterloo study – to review that study. She immediately found that the data that they had been supplied was [sic] incomplete. She sent them the complete data. They did further analysis. We wanted to have our consultant, Environ, get together with the University of Waterloo to discuss the technical aspects of their evaluation. An attempt was made to meet with the two authors. This started, I believe, around February of 1996. Eventually, after many phone calls, our consultant was informed that they could not meet with her until they got approval from General Motors, who had contracted the study. General Motors, to the best of our knowledge, must never have released the University of Waterloo to sit down with our consultant to discuss these differences. Again, it is stonewalling. We want to sit down and discuss these differences. They would not come forward. General Motors would not allow their consultant to sit down with us. (SSCEENR 2/5, 1997d, 21–2)

Because of the importance of the Waterloo evaluation, I sent an e-mail to Professor Abraham on 7 October 2002, asking him, among other things, whether he had found new evidence indicating that MMT helps reduce NO_x emissions to a statistically significant degree. We exchanged a couple of notes and, in the last (25 April 2003), he said that his client did not want him to release any more information. I thanked him and left it at that. So, we cannot confirm or disconfirm any "further analysis" on more complete data and, if so, what that analysis showed. However, although Wilson said that "further analysis" was done by the University of Waterloo experts, he did not say that their original assessment of the evidence changed. It is unlikely that Wilson would have failed to mention such a change if he had any knowledge of it, if the change was favourable to his case.

As if the five different claims just reviewed about MMT's impact on NO_x emissions were not trouble enough, an additional twist, about which all of the above-mentioned parties were apparently unaware, is that in certain circumstances "increased levels of NO_x may actually decrease ozone levels" and, therefore, smog (VanNijnatten and Lambright 2002, 270). An article by Dewar (1997), the source of this important fact, reported on a lecture by the Canadian atmospheric chemist, Dr Harold Schiff:

Schiff began to speak about how geography affects the chemistry of the air we breathe. He started by describing what everyone in the room thought they knew – how ozone is made when hydrocarbons and nitrogen oxides interact with sunlight. The general theory is that if the hydrocarbons increase, then the amount of ozone increases. "But, if we increase the nitrogen oxides," he said, "the amount of ozone might increase or decrease. This is due to the ambivalent role it plays in the photochemistry of ozone." Like the two-faced Hindu god Shiva, in one kind of ratio to hydrocarbons, nitrogen oxides create ozone. In another ratio, they destroy it.

Schiff noted, as [an] EPA report had done, that there is not much ground-level ozone in the centre of Los Angeles. Why? There is too much nitrogen oxide, a product of all combustion, and too little in the way of hydrocarbons. (The San Fernando Valley is right next door. Its suburban lawns and farms produce significant hydrocarbons. In the valley, the ratio of hydrocarbons to nitrogen oxides shifts: voila, the valley is drenched in ozone.) Such subtleties, said Schiff, are why one needs to have good emission inventories that include natural as well as manmade sources. (Dewar 1997, 57)

Thus, if one's aim is to reduce smog, the presence of more or less NO_x might be helpful or harmful, depending on what else is present in the area. So, the alleged automatic benefits of less NO_x in any particular place should be regarded as just that, alleged, not guaranteed.

7 Although "Environment Canada officials stated that they had sufficient evidence from the auto manufacturers to make a determination that MMT causes OBD malfunctioning," the minority members did not believe they had seen such evidence and, perhaps more importantly, they thought that:

... it is clear that Environment Canada officials are not privy to all pertinent information pertaining to this matter. Environment Canada officials appearing before the Committee had not received and were not aware of a copy of General Motors Service Bulletin #57–65–71, dated November 1995. This particular GM Bulletin was issued only days after the hearings finished in the House of Commons and it goes to the heart of the assertion by the auto manufacturers that MMT is the cause of OBD malfunction. The GM Bulletin is a list of several causes of OBD malfunction. Reasons for OBD malfunctions include, but are not limited to: low fuel levels; failure to properly secure the gas cap after refueling; electronic interference caused by routine equipment such as cellular phones, stereo systems and anti-theft alarms; excessive vibrations; environmental conditions such as winter, flooding, altitude; and mud on portions of the wheels. (SSCEENR 3/4, 1997l, 3; see also Roos's testimony at SSCEENR 2/5, 1997d, 4–5)

Evaluation. This material is quoted again in the AIT Hearings 1998, 168–70, although the quotation is a bit scrambled there. There are at least two ways to interpret the argument in the quotation, one unsound and the other probably sound, but possibly troublesome. In the first case, the argument would rest on the premise that "If OBDs malfunction when MMT is not present then any malfunction attributed to MMT when it is present is not justifiable." If that premise were accepted as true, then one would have to accept the following clearly false claim as well: "If people die when they have not been poisoned then any death attributed to poison when it is present is not justifiable." The case against MMT is not that its presence is, in general, a necessary condition of malfunction or that there are no other necessary or sufficient conditions of malfunction. Rather, the claim is that, regardless of the existence of other necessary or sufficient conditions of malfunction, MMT functions as a necessary or sufficient condition in diverse contexts. For example, we know that cerium is used in some catalytic converters and that it has the capacity to store oxygen (DuPuy 2000, 379). As well, we know that manganese deposits in converters will also store oxygen (Hubbard, Hepburn, and Gandhi 1993; Kraucher 1994). Thus, in the presence of MMT, a converter's oxygen sensors might be misled by the storing of oxygen by manganese deposits, by cerium or by a combination of both. It would be a mistake to blame MMT when it is not in the fuel, but it would also be a mistake to exonerate MMT when it is in the fuel and might well be a contributing factor.

Another possible argument based on the information in the quotation above would be that if many things, including possibly MMT, can cause OBD systems to malfunction, then, in the absence of experiments controlling for all the other things, OBD malfunctioning cannot or should not be attributed to MMT. (Jean-François Jobin, Acting Internal Trade Representative for the Government of Québec, made a similar argument featuring sulfur as a possible contaminant in AIT Hearings 1998a, 217–18.) We know that many of the people calling for more research and testing of MMT believe that no or too few appropriately controlled experiments have been conducted, while those on the other side believe that enough have been conducted.

I characterized the preferred alternative as "probably sound, but possibly troublesome" because of all the ink that has been shed by philosophers of science over what is called "Duhem's thesis" (see Michalos 1980a, and Harding 1976). Briefly, Pierre Duhem (1906) argued that because isolated hypotheses cannot be tested and a single test cannot determine whether a particular hypothesis or the experimental test conditions are defective, there can be no crucial experiments of any hypothesis. We cannot analyze Duhem's thesis here. It is mentioned because serious people defended it long before anyone ever articulated "the precautionary principle"; for such people, there could never be enough appropriately controlled experiments. Such a high level of epistemic scruples would be devastating for public policy-making as well as for ordinary scientific research. Reading the critiques that the various players in our drama offer against each other's arguments, one begins to suspect that both sides are selective Duhemians, usually believing that just enough experiments have been conducted to show that their side is right but never enough to show that the other side is right.

8 Six pages later in the *Opinion*, the minority members accuse the auto makers of "presenting conflicting stories as to the causes of the OBD difficulties in Canada and the United States. In Canada, we were told that MMT is the root cause of their OBD problems. However, in the U.S. where MMT only became available in December 1995, they have blamed individually and in combination: high altitude, temperature, sulfur, poor fuel quality, fuel vaporization, road conditions, customer driving habits, and extreme environmental conditions. Rationalizations given us by witnesses from General Motors and Toyota were unsatisfactory" (SSCEENR 3/4, 1997l, 9).

Evaluation. This is not necessarily anomalous. From the vehicle manufacturers' point of view, several things, alone or in combination, had an adverse effect on OBD systems. Since MMT was not used in the United States, mentioning it in complaints there would have been pointless. Since they heard similar reports from several manufacturers, it is unclear why they singled out the witnesses from General Motors and Toyota. For example, Ernst Lieb, President of Mercedes-Benz Canada told the committee that "Mercedes-Benz introduced advanced emission control technology in 1994 which continuously monitors the systems and alerts vehicle operators to a malfunction within the system which requires vehicle servicing. However, we have determined that MMT causes deposits within the emission control system leading to premature elumination [sic] of the indicator lights. In Western Europe, our passenger cars are equipped with similar exhaust emission technology, and in these markets we do not experience emission-control-related consumer complaints due to MMT deposits" (SSCEENR 2/4, 1997b, 30).

Ikuo Shimizu, President of Honda Canada, said "We are selling the same system in the United States, Japan and our major markets. As Mr. Lieb said, basically we have no experience in other market areas. In the last year in the United States, for instance, we sold almost 800,000 cars with the system and we have not had a problem. It is a situation unique to Canada" (SSCEENR 2/4, 1997b, 37).

9 As an example of an "unsatisfactory" rationalization, the minority group cited the testimony of Roger Thomas of General Motors of Canada. Thomas said, "We have had some minor teething problems, and I do stress the word 'minor' with the functioning of OBD systems in the United States." But the group said:

> this statement appears to be incongruent with what is actually occurring in the United States ... in 1995 ... the EPA Administrator stated:
> " ... manufacturers have expressed and demonstrated difficulty in complying with every aspect of the OBD-II requirements, and such difficulty appears likely to continue into the 1996 and 1997 model years" [U.S. Federal Register, 15244, 23 March 1995].
> As stated previously, the car companies have divulged similar problems in California where MMT is not in use. Recently, they have complained about false dashboard lights and petitioned the state for regulatory relief from OBD-II requirements ... Deficiencies across a full product line for both the 1996 and 1997 model years hardly constitute "minor teething problems". Rather, the auto companies documented their difficulties sufficiently to be successful in their campaign for regulatory relief from the State of California. (SSCEENR 3/4, 1997l, 9–10)

Evaluation. Regarding the "problems in California," the Minister of Environment, Sergio Marchi, told the Committee:

> I also read testimony where Ethyl claimed before your committee that, somehow, the systems in California were running into problems, and they queried how they can be running into problems if California is MMT-free. I am saying that that claim made by Ethyl is, in fact, incorrect. We have a report we wish to leave with you, if you wish, dated October of 1996 from the State of California, indicating that OBD-II

systems have proven to be very effective in detecting emissions related to the problems in use. Furthermore, the same California report indicates that several manufacturers have acknowledged that the systems have been a tremendous help in improving the overall vehicle quality.

As well, Ethyl made the claim that California gave the auto companies the option of either having these systems or not. Again, that is factually incorrect. We have a second report from the State of California dated August of 1996 which confirms that it is not a question. It clearly says that there is no waiver of compliance for automobile companies to have OBD-II. (SSCEENR 2/20, 1997h, 14)

Assuming Marchi's documents were as he described them, the minority group's charges (9) were apparently false.

10 The minority members believed there was still more evidence about which the Minister of the Environment was unaware:

Additionally, that the Minister of the Environment, during his appearance before the Committee, was unaware of what Ford Company executives had stated on December 12, 1996 before the California Air Resources Board (CARB) is of equal if not greater cause for concern. Ford Motor Company officials asked to have a delay on the satisfactory implementation of OBD systems until the car model year 2004 because of problems with OBD malfunctioning. Mr John Trajnowski, speaking for Ford Motor Company, said: " ... it's essential the (CARB) board revise the OBD II regulation to allow up to two monitoring deficiencies per vehicle without fines through the 2003 model year and one deficiency per vehicle without fines thereafter". The key point is that MMT is not used in California's reformulated gasoline. Therefore, the OBD malfunctions in California could not possibly be related to MMT use. (SSCEENR 3/4, 1997l, 3)

Evaluation. The "key point" referred to in this quotation seems to direct us back to the argument in item 7.

11 Addressing the issue of alleged caveats connected to the EPA's final determination, the minority *Opinion* said: "Several witnesses including the Minister of the Environment, and indeed several Senators on the Committee, suggested that the EPA's conclusion was flawed, lenient or based on a mere technicality. However, a closer examination of the facts suggests the

opposite. The EPA received and reviewed hundreds of comments and studies in coming to this evaluation, including numerous submissions from the auto companies. In arriving at this conclusion, the EPA rejected every one of the auto makers' claims that MMT harms OBD systems" (SSCEENR 3/4, 1997l, 4).

Evaluation. On the contrary, the record shows that the EPA did not reject "every one of the auto makers' claims that MMT harms OBD systems." Rather, as indicated in chapter 5, the court quoted the EPA's remark that it was reviewing Ford's submission about the possible direct effect of MMT on OBD systems and its possible indirect effect on health.

12 The *Opinion* also asserted that "the American Automobile Manufacturers Association's (AAMA) arguments against the EPA's waiver decision were soundly rejected by the United States Court of Appeals for the District of Columbia Circuit. The Court held that: ' ... [t]he Administrator's analysis of the data submitted by Ethyl was careful and searching; the AAMA did not come close to proving that the Administrator's analysis of the data was arbitrary and capricious'" (SSCEENR 3/4, 1997l, 4).

Evaluation. The AAMA could hardly have "come close to proving that the Administrator's analysis of the data was arbitrary and capricious" because the AAMA never even suggested, let alone tried to prove, that it was either arbitrary or capricious. As indicated in chapter 5, the court had the option of basing its decision on that criterion but used its other criterion instead.

13 According to the *Opinion*, the court addressed the question of "the purported leniency of the EPA's analysis" by saying that "the EPA had imposed new, 'stringent criteria,' requiring that 'the additive cause no statistically significant increase in emissions.' Applying these stringent criteria, the Court upheld the EPA's inability to 'discern any real emissions increase at all – that is, no increase that [it could] not reasonably attribute to sampling error'" (SSCEENR 3/4, 1997l, 4).

Evaluation. As explained in chapter 5, the court's decision had nothing to do with the EPA's "new 'stringent criterion'." Rather, it was based on the judge's belief that the EPA did not have the statutory right or authority to insist on the requirements of Section 211 (c) (1) in a case proceeding under Section 211 (f) (4) of the *Clean Air Act.*

14 The authors of the *Opinion* said it was "important to note that the courts did not force the EPA to grant Ethyl a waiver for MMT. Rather, it was the EPA's own independent, voluntary determination that MMT 'does not

cause or contribute' to the failure of emissions systems which obligated it to grant the waiver" (SSCEENR 3/4, 1997l, 4–5).

Evaluation. Not exactly. As reviewed in chapter 5, the EPA regarded satisfaction of each Section, 211 (f) (4) and 211 (c) (1), as necessary, and their joint satisfaction as sufficient to warrant granting a waiver. That is why the agency was unwilling to grant a waiver in spite of its determination that Section 211 (f) (4) had been satisfied according to its 1988 criteria. Because Ethyl Corporation did not share this view, it appealed to the Court of Appeals which, fortunately for Ethyl, also did not share this view. Thus, in reaching its judgment against the EPA, the court did "force the EPA to grant a waiver for MMT" against its own judgment of its obligation.

15 In the view of the authors of the *Opinion*, it was "Equally significant ... that under section 211 (c) (1) of the Clean Air Act, the EPA has the power to prohibit the use of any fuel or fuel additive even if it is already approved and in use. The EPA, therefore, has the power to remove MMT from the American market at any time had it credible evidence that MMT harmed the operation of emissions monitoring equipment or resulted in air pollution which adversely affected public health. No such action has been taken by the EPA" (SSCEENR 3/4, 1997l, 5).

Evaluation. This is true. As indicated in chapter 5, following the court judgment, the EPA set out to determine whether a case could be made against MMT under Section 211 (c) (1). At the time the *Opinion* was written and since, no such case had or has been brought forward by the EPA.

16 A test by Ethyl of "six 1995 Toyota Camrys purchased and driven by salespeople in Ontario" with gasoline containing MMT did not reveal any problems "in the functioning of OBD systems or in meeting the 1998 emission standards." The results of the test were described as "anecdotal in that no comparison is made to similar conditions on MMT-free gasoline" (SSCEENR 3/4, 1997l, 5).

Evaluation. We do not have enough information about the test, the procedures, or the results to give this any weight.

17 ORTECH Corporation and Protect Air Inc. undertook a study for the Canadian Petroleum Products Institute in 1996, investigating the impact of MMT on "1994 to 1996 model vehicles equipped with the latest emissions technology. The test vehicles had an aggregate mileage of 11.4 million kilometres accumulated by their owners under Canadian driving conditions" (SSCEENR 3/4, 1997l, 5). Jim Pantelidis, Executive Vice-President of Petro-

Canada, described the aims and results of the ORTECH study for the Senate Committee as follows:

> The objectives of our study were to determine if any emission problems could be detected and also to determine if the vehicles' computers were noting any failures of the emission control systems.
>
> The results indicated that the vehicles' emission control performance was excellent. All the vehicles tested were well within the Ontario test standard, which covers hydrocarbon, carbon monoxide and nitrogen oxide emissions.
>
> In addition, tests of the vehicles' on-board diagnostic systems showed problem-free performance in 184 of 185 vehicles. One vehicle had an indication of a problem related to a faulty spark plug, but there was no evidence to suggest the failure was related to MMT.
>
> As with any sample survey of this nature, we did not expect to get conclusive evidence solving the issue, but we did expect to get sufficient information to either validate claims about MMT's impact on vehicle systems or at least give some indication of a trend. We found a very high level of performance of vehicle systems integrated with fuel containing MMT. (SSCEENR 2/4, 1997a, 20)

Evaluation. The *Opinion* said results of this study were "buttressing Ethyl's scientific evidence" but it did not say how or provide any other information. Since ORTECH is not a member of the CPPI, its conclusions were probably regarded as additional independent supporting evidence, although it was clearly evidence from an industry-sponsored source of the sort regarded as objectionable in arguments 1 and 2 above. When Michael O'Brien, Executive Vice President of the Sunoco Group, Suncor Inc., mentioned the ORTECH research, he was not very informative about its elements (SSCEENR 2/19, 1997g, 42), so it is difficult to give it much weight. We do not know which models were driven, in what way, under what conditions, with what speeds, what maintenance, what fuel mixtures, and what sort of standardization of inspection and evaluation of test conditions and components. In short, we do not have precisely the sort of information that Ethyl and members of the CPPI routinely demand of any studies produced by the other side.

18 In November 1994 the CPPI proposed that the Royal Society of Canada should appoint an independent expert panel "to determine if the presence of the additive in motor gasoline has an impact on the operation

of vehicle emission components (OBD II) and an impact on tailpipe NO_x emissions." According to the *Opinion*, "'Terms of Reference' were negotiated between Béatrice Kowaliczko, Executive Director of the Royal Society of Canada (RSC) and Kerry Mattila, Vice-President of Operations, CPPI ... The Royal Society was asked to submit its report within three months. If that process had been accepted by members of the Motor Vehicle Manufacturers Association (MVMA), or embraced by the then Minister of the Environment, the study would have been completed approximately two years ago [from March 1997]. It is not reasonable that such a balanced approach to a contentious issue was given such short shrift" (SSCEENR 3/4, 1997l, 5–6).

Evaluation. A search of the Royal Society archives and correspondence with Béatrice Kowaliczko, John Meisel (President of the Society at that time), Lawrence Mysak (President of Academy III of the Society at that time) and Stephen Hill revealed:

(i)   A memo from Frank Vena and Chandra Prakash, Industrial Sectors Branch of Environment Canada, to Copps, dated 24 October 1994, indicating, among other things, that "The CPPI is expected to ask for an independent panel to assess the effects of MMT on control technologies and emissions (preliminary indications from the MVMA is [sic] that they are opposed to the idea)."

(ii) A letter from Claude Brouillard, President of the CPPI, to Mark Nantais, President of the MVMA, dated 26 October 1994, proposing "an independent scientific panel of five members ... agreeable to the interested parties ... to render its conclusions quickly based on the information available to it ... [with costs] shared by the CPPI, MVMA and Ethyl." The aim of the panel would be to "objectively assess the technical concerns associated with MMT in Canadian gasoline and their potential impact on air quality, *and balance this impact with the positive gains in NO_x reduction provided by MMT*" (emphasis added).

(iii) A letter from the CPPI and its eleven members to Maureen Kempston-Darkes, President of General Motors of Canada, dated 26 October 1994, replying to her letter of 14 October 1994, which was sent to "certain gasoline manufacturers in Canada." The CPPI letter asserts that "if an independent scientific panel concludes that MMT in Canadian gasoline impairs the effectiveness of emission control equipment on new cars and that any harmful effects of MMT exceed the environmental benefits MMT provides in urban smog reduction," then "the

CPPI is willing to voluntarily commence an expeditious removal of MMT from gasoline by October 1, 1995."

(iv)   A *News Release* from the CPPI, dated 27 October 1994, announcing that the CPPI "told the federal government and Canadian auto makers today that it is willing to commence removal of the octane-enhancer MMT from gasoline by October 1, 1995, if an independent scientific panel concludes that using MMT in gasoline harms air quality ... Brouillard ... says the panel could be set up within two months and asked to render its decision quickly based on existing information."

(v)   A note from Kowaliczko to the RSC Executive Committee, dated 7 November 1994, informing the committee of her planned luncheon with Mattila "regarding the possibility for the Society to be the organization which would set up the panel and produce the report," and asking for members' "reactions" and "suggestions of names for the panel, suggestions of potential difficulties, etc."

(vi)   A letter from Kowaliczko to Mattila, dated 18 November 1994, informing him that the Executive Committee of the Society "thinks that it is a delicate file and would like to have a clear statement of the terms of reference and of what is to be expected from the Royal Society of Canada. At this point we understand that the Society will play the role of a referee and will hear both parties and then produce a report. Is this what you want?

I was also asked to clarify with you whether the Automobile Association is participating in the funding of the project: the Society feels that it can undertake the study only if the MVMA is involved.

In the meantime I am enclosing some details and financial projections"(1).

The estimated cost of a five-member committee was put at $50,000.

(vii) A "letter of transmittal and proposed Terms of Reference for our panel" from Mattila to Kowaliczko, dated 28 November 1994. Responding to Kowaliczko's suggestion that the society would "play the role of a referee," Mattila said, "It should be apparent that we are not expecting this Panel to be an arbiter or referee. We do expect the Panel to review and assess the available scientific test data on MMT and render an independent opinion. As you are aware, timeliness is important on this issue, so a prompt launch is necessary." Responding to her remark that "the Society feels that it can undertake the study only if the MVMA is involved," he said, "While it is obviously desirable to engage MVMA as partners, we are fully prepared to proceed without them. I am told that *the scientific studies conducted by*

MVMA *members are on the public record with the* US *Environmental Protection Agency*" (emphasis added). The terms of reference indicate that the task of the panel would be "to review and assess the existing scientific information" with the aim of determining whether "MMT in motor gasoline has any significant impact on the operation of vehicle emission control components in the OBD-II systems and if use of the additive results in significant reductions in tailpipe NO_x emissions." The panel was to be "formed as quickly as possible (i.e., early December) and ... submit its final report within 3 months".

(viii) A letter from Nantais to Copps, dated 17 February 1995, reaffirming points made in an earlier letter to her (31 January 1995) and rejecting a research "program as described in the CPPI proposal" because it "would only serve to further delay the introduction of MMT-free gasoline in Canada."

(ix) A letter from Adrian Bradford of the AIAMC to Copps, also dated 17 February 1995, responding to her letter of 16 February 1995, saying that the "AIAMC cannot support the ... (CPPI) proposal for continued use and field testing of ... MMT ... in Canadian vehicles" for "a number of reasons." The three reasons mentioned were the AIAMC's belief that (a) tests on the impact of MMT at "the 9 mg/litre level proposed by CPPI" would not "produce results significantly different from those shown to date by individual manufacturers' tests"; (b) there was not enough time to complete all the tests required by 1 September 1995, a deadline that the manufacturers set for getting new equipment into 1996 models (although the letter noted that "the first 1996 models of AIAMC members are being introduced this spring"); and (c) "five vehicle manufacturers' field tests, showing the adverse effects of MMT, and made fully available to CPPI members, have confirmed that elimination of MMT is warranted." The letter also unhappily noted "the absence of any reference to AIAMC in the CPPI proposal, even though two of the five manufacturers' field testing programs, confirming the adverse effects of MMT, were those of AIAMC members." Although these two letters from 17 February 1995 do not explicitly mention a Royal Society panel, it seems likely that they are addressing such an investigation.

The first thing to notice about this eighteenth complaint is that even if there had been a balanced approach and it had been "given short shrift," it would not follow that the decision procedures actually employed were not equally balanced or were otherwise defective, or that the decisions produced by those procedures were somehow wrong or defective. The minority members' preference for a different procedure does not destroy the integrity of those that were used.

Given the degree of commitment to their positions by the motor vehicle and equipment manufacturers and dealers on the one hand, and Ethyl and the petroleum companies on the other, one would have thought that everyone on both sides would have jumped at an opportunity to get an authoritative, objective, and quick decision, which everyone on both sides would have been convinced would favour its side. Each side risked public embarrassment at least and some loss of business at most if the expert review revealed emission control equipment that failed to properly control emissions or alleged pollution abatement additives that failed to abate harmful pollutants, but these risks should have appeared small to both sides.

Putting myself in the shoes of the manufacturers' strategists, I suppose they would have shared their opponents' view that the federal government was convinced by their lobbying and prepared to bring in legislation in support of their position. So there was no point in putting their position at risk by undertaking any new initiatives. All they had to do was wait and events would unfold in their favour. As it turned out, that is what happened, until the NAFTA and AIT cases came along.

Whatever the strategy of the MVMA and AIAMC, it is by no means clear that the Royal Society of Canada would have participated in the proposal. Indeed, the proposal itself is far from clear. It would not have been extraordinary for a person or group to talk to someone at the Royal Society about a possible study that never occurred. Nor would it have been extraordinary for someone to imagine that the Royal Society could establish a panel and solve a complicated and controversial scientific problem within three months. However, anyone familiar with the panel work of the Royal Society would find it highly unrealistic to suppose that three months would be sufficient for such a task. Speaking particularly of the MMT issue, I doubt that three months would have been enough time to assemble all the relevant studies and information and to produce a reliable and valid decision. Although the three-month figure was unrealistic, it was frequently presented as plausible to the Senate Standing Committee (see SSCEENR 2/19, 1997g, 44, 54; SSCEENR 2/20, 1997h, 7).

Ignoring the proposed time-frame and examining Kowaliczko's suggestions in her November 18 letter and Mattila's responses in his November 28 letter, one finds some discrepancies. While she envisioned a procedure in which both sides would make their case to a panel of independent expert referees, he seemed to envision a procedure in which members of the panel would find and evaluate existing scientific reports. She emphasized the necessity of having the MVMA's participation, but he suggested that they could proceed without the MVMA because the latter's "scientific studies" were "on the public record with the US Environmental Protection Agency." Since the EPA had announced its view a year earlier (30 November 1993) that the evidence it had reviewed revealed that MMT does not contribute to the failure of emission control systems (given the EPA standards), it is not surprising that the CPPI would have been comfortable having the society panel review that evidence again. In the presence of all the caveats around the EPA assessment (chapter 5), the MVMA might have been equally comfortable with a review of that evidence. After all, members of the MVMA knew that officials at Environment Canada had access to at least as much evidence as the EPA had and had decided that the *MMT Act* was warranted. Furthermore, we just saw Bradford's complaint that the AIAMC shared its supporting data with the CPPI and it was ignored. Hill and Leiss (2001, 90) claimed that "the full data set used to substantiate the car manufacturers' claims on emission control impacts had not been made available to the CPPI and certainly not to the public." While that is true for the public (though not the public's official representatives), it is probably not true for the CPPI. In any case, it is clear that the Royal Society regarded the MVMA participation as necessary, but not sufficient, for the panel to go ahead.

Setting aside all of these issues, I think that the biggest barrier to a Royal Society panel was the vagueness of the test being proposed. An examination of a couple of proposals will illustrate the difficulty of determining exactly what is being proposed. Hill and Leiss (2001) mentioned the proposals several times and regarded the failure of the proponents of the *MMT Act* to accept any of them as a mark against these proponents. These authors went so far as to say that the proposals were not accepted because "the federal cabinet had decided to capitulate to the unbearable pressure from the vehicle manufacturers" (93). In the CPPI letter of 26 October 1994 to Kempston-Darkes, the proposal is worded as follows: "the CPPI is willing to voluntarily commence an expeditious removal of MMT from gasoline by October 1, 1995, *if an independent scientific panel concludes that MMT in Canadian gasoline impairs the effectiveness of emission control equipment on new cars and that any harmful effects of MMT exceed the environmental benefits MMT provides in urban smog reduction*" (CPPI 1994, 2, emphasis added).

The difficulty arises in understanding and operationalizing the italicized condition. We know that some very difficult judgment calls are to be made as to what counts as appropriate test conditions for determining whether or not fuel containing MMT harms emission control equipment. But exactly how is one to measure and balance "any harmful effects of MMT" against "the environmental benefits MMT provides in urban smog reduction," and what could one do if one discovered that the use of MMT decreases nitrogen oxides in some places, under some conditions, for some people, but increases hydrocarbons and carbon monoxide in other places, under different conditions, for other people? Does anyone think that a panel of scientists could or should decide what to do in the presence of such complexities? Such issues are essentially political and require properly constructed political decision procedures and fora to address them.

In the letter of November 28 from Mattila to Kowaliczko, it is proposed that the panel should decide whether "MMT in motor gasoline has any significant impact on the operation of vehicle emission control components in the OBD-II systems and if use of the additive results in significant reductions in tailpipe NO_x emissions." There is no mention of "harms to air quality" or of the difficult problems involved in balancing harms against benefits.

A page headed "Canadian Petroleum Products Institute MMT Proposal," enclosed with a letter dated 1 February 1995 from Claude F. Brouillard, President of the CPPI, to the Honourable Sheila Copps (Brouillard 1995a), includes this sentence: "If, at the conclusion of the agreed upon test period, there is conclusive evidence that the yearly cost of warranty issues, which can be directly attributed to MMT, exceeds the cost of removal of MMT from 9Mg/litre to 0 Mg/litre, then the CPPI will support the removal of MMT" (Brouillard 1995a).

Exactly how one would measure all those costs is not indicated, but two weeks later (February 15), in another letter to Copps, a revised proposal is attached without that line (Brouillard 1995b). While there is nothing inherently wrong with suggesting and revising proposals for a scientific panel, it does suggest that there is both more and less to such proposals than immediately meets the eye. Because the details are often unclear and apparently negotiable, it is difficult to make much out of any particular proposal in whole or in part.

19 The authors of the *Opinion* thought:

> [it was plainly] inconsistent that Health Canada recently commissioned an independent panel of international experts, assembled by the Royal Society of Canada, to consider the quality of the risk assessment of asbestos contained in a report by France's Institut national de la santé et de la recherche médicale (INSERM) and not commission a panel on MMT. It is

unacceptable that in two recent instances senior federal Ministers and the Prime Minister himself have expressed support for the RSC panel process but have not acted on the MMT controversy in a similar, balanced fashion ... On February 10th, 1997, in the House of Commons, Prime Minister Chrétien expressed complete satisfaction with the RSC process and commended his Ministers for engaging such a well respected and reputable organization in a complex technical matter with both health and trade implications. (SSCEENR 3/4, 1997l, 5–6)

Evaluation. The question of whether or not the federal government was consistent in its treatment of the asbestos and MMT cases turns on the degree of similarity between the two cases. With Leiss (2001), I certainly agree that Royal Society panels can play a significant role in adjudicating controversial scientific issues. In the light of the massive study of the Alliance of Automobile Manufacturers, and its report (Benson and Dana 2002) and the critique of its report (Roos, Hollrah, Guinther and Cunningham 2002) in the SAE Technical Paper Series, I doubt that such a panel could have been useful in this instance, especially given the proposed time constraints and the impossibility of gathering new data within those constraints.

20 Regarding Ethyl's tests, the minority members claimed that "contrary to the auto makers' assertions, the test vehicles' OBD systems showed problem free performance in 184 of 185 vehicles. One vehicle had a problem related to a faulty spark plug but there was no evidence to suggest that its failure was due to MMT. The test vehicles' emissions control performance was also excellent. The entire fleet was well within the Ontario test standard for emissions which covers hydo-carbon, carbon monoxide, and nitrogen oxides" (SSCEENR 3/4, 1997l, 6).

Evaluation. These claims came from the ORTECH study that is described and evaluated in 17.

21 "In contrast to Ethyl Canada's data," the *Minority Opinion* said, "the very limited information submitted by the government and the auto makers to support their allegations against MMT must be questioned – for several reasons." Taking each in turn, it was asserted first that "both the government and the auto manufacturers have refused to allow Senators full access to the data used to justify their claim that MMT harms OBD systems" (SSCEENR 3/4, 1997l, 6). Chuck Strahl (MP, Fraser Valley East) made a similar point regarding Members of the House (PD10/22, 1996e, 2).

Evaluation. I have not been able to determine exactly what data the senators saw. It is not unusual for some strategically placed government officials and regulatory agencies such as the EPA to have access to some private and/or proprietary information that is not available to everyone. However, during the House Committee hearings, Julian Reed, Liberal MP from Halton-Peel, asked Rick Colcomb, Director of Engineering and Future Product Planning for GM of Canada, about data being "made publicly available." Colcomb replied:

> I'm not quite sure what "make public" means. As you know, we sat down with all the interested government parties and reviewed the data in some detail. We also had a lengthy session with the petroleum producers, where we shared all data, including the warranty data. We broke out in separate sessions, where, for instance, General Motors said, here's our warranty data, because we don't want to share our dirty laundry with our partners here. So we did in fact share that [sic] data. Again, it's very sophisticated. The CPPI group put together a panel of experts. We're of the view that it's very hard to find experts outside the industry. EPA is having the same issue in trying to put together a test program that's outside the auto industry, when the expertise is inside the auto industry.
>
> You might note that the only person on that CPPI panel that we'd consider an expert, Steve Carter, who has actually done engine emission control systems and is an expert in the field, has concluded as a witness to Environment Canada that he supports our conclusions, based on the science involved in the emission systems.
>
> So I would submit to you that we have shared the data. (HSCESD 10/24, 1995b, 12–13)

The CPPI Technical Task Force referred to by Colcomb met in January 1995, nine months before his remarks above were made, and its work is discussed in more detail in chapter 15. The senators would certainly have had access to at least as much information as I have had, which is a considerable amount. The problem is not in the absence but in the inconsistency of available information.

22 It was then asserted that "these two parties are presently involved in a court case to prevent the public from having access to these data" (SSCEENR 3/4, 1997l, 6).

Evaluation. I have not been able to confirm or disconfirm this.

23 "In light of the fact that no regulatory body or court anywhere has ever accepted the auto makers' allegations against MMT," the minority said, "there is good reason to doubt the validity of these claims and to question why the Government of Canada has so readily accepted them" (SSCEENR 3/4, 1997l, 6).

Evaluation. As we saw in chapter 5, the EPA did accept some of "the auto makers' allegations against MMT" as well as some of Ethyl's own data that confirmed some of the auto makers' claims.

24 The minority also found it incredible that relatively neutral observers and others could not be persuaded of the majority opinion. "Given that over twenty auto companies have publicly stated that MMT damages emissions systems, one would have expected them to easily provide information to convince the EPA, US Courts, the petroleum industry, and this Committee of their position" (SSCEENR 3/4, 1997l, 6).

Evaluation. Presumably, the minority members forgot that the majority of the committee, therefore, effectively, the Committee, was convinced and had indirectly supported the auto companies' position when it endorsed the MMT Act. Regarding the EPA, see chapter 5.

25 Two pages later in the *Opinion*, it was asserted that:

> Testing data provided to the government from Toyota ... cast doubt on the claim that all twenty auto companies have found that MMT negatively affects the functioning of OBD systems. In fact Toyota found MMT has no effect on catalyst monitors. As reported in an internal Transport Canada briefing note of July 19, 1994 to Mr. D. Hrobelsky, Chief, Energy and Emissions, Transport Canada, a witness before the Committee:
>
>> "Toyota has monitored the OBD-II codes on 24 Canadian and 10 US 1994 model year vehicles to determine whether MMT had significantly impacted the capability of the catalyst monitoring function in Canada. Toyota did not find any evidence that false detections made by the catalyst monitoring system occurred as a result of using MMT. Although the monitoring process did not assess the effects of MMT for the full useful life of the vehicle, Toyota is confident that the test results indicate that their OBD-II system could compensate for any potential MMT effect as more mileage is accumulated."
>
> Toyota Canada has provided no additional test results to Transport Canada which would change their experience with MMT, although they

claimed before the Committee that they had found MMT to cause OBD malfunction. (SSCEENR 3/4, 1997l, 9)

Evaluation. In chapter 5 we saw evidence from the U.S. *Federal Register* indicating that some of Toyota's tests revealed higher HC emissions levels and reduced catalyst efficiency with MMT-fuel versus MMT-free-fuel. When he was asked to explain the discrepancy between the positive view expressed in the briefing note and the negative view expressed in Toyota's presentation to the Senate Standing Committee, Martin Ehmann, Manager of Vehicle Compliance and Technical Operations, Toyota Canada, said:

> The document you are referencing, senator [Colin Kenny], is actually a response to something which happened a long time prior – to be precise, in March 1993. At that time, our initial research was rather limited on that particular engine configuration and environmental technology. We had earlier introduced in 1993 and installed in late 1993, only in a selected few engine families, what we consider to be an OBD-II system.
>
> We approached Transport Canada and explained to them our serious concern. We brought our photos and research and analogies. We were concerned that, perhaps, the MIL [warning] light might be falsely triggered ... Since then, we have also conducted additional research which confirmed that, in fact, it is a serious problem. (SSCEENR 2/4, 1997b, 32–3)

One could, of course, raise the question of exactly what "additional research" was conducted, but that would not alter the fact that Ehmann's testimony indicated that the discrepancy was caused by juxtaposing earlier and later studies, and that Toyota's most recent view was that the later studies were more accurate.

26 After reviewing the offers of successive Ministers of the Environment (Copps and Marchi) to allow gasoline containing MMT to be sold at separate pumps or even separate stations across the country, giving consumers a choice between such gasoline and MMT-free gasoline, the minority members said "it is surprising that such an offer would be made by government. The government policy supposedly underlying this legislation cannot be viewed as consistent with the government's offer to sanction continued use of MMT. This product is now suddenly deemed by the government to be so harmful that immediate legislation is required to eliminate it from the Canadian

marketplace. These contradictory positions cannot logically be reconciled" (SSCEENR 3/4, 1997l, 7).

Evaluation. The last three sentences of the preceding quotation were taken verbatim from Robert Perrin's testimony (AIT Hearings, 1998a, 143–4). Perrin was the Internal Trade Representative for the Government of Saskatchewan. A plausible reason for the federal government's offer of a two pump solution does not seem to me to be so hard to find. (see AIT Hearings 1998c, 274–5.) Half a loaf is better than none. So if enough MMT-free gasoline was available to service newer model vehicles with newer model OBD systems, there would have been no or less harm to the latter systems, lower overall short-run costs to refiners for compliance with the government's overall strategy, and less reason for complaints by vehicle and emissions equipment manufacturers.

27 In the view of the minority members, "Unlike the testing data which withstood the evaluation of the EPA and US courts, the warranty information submitted by the auto makers is not scientific and has not been independently evaluated. Rather, it is anecdotal and cannot be replicated. It is non-testable and largely secret" (SSCEENR 3/4, 1997l, 7).

Evaluation. The "warranty information submitted by the auto makers" came from independent reports of twenty-one different vehicle manufacturers – more than enough replication. Since auto makers described the tests on which they based their claims, it is plainly false to say that the claims made were "non-testable." The fact that the opponents of the MMT *Act* did not believe these claims does not make their basis "not scientific." The very notion of what is or is not scientific is arguably as much a matter of philosophy or meta-science as it is of science itself, and there are no universally accepted criteria of demarcation (Michalos 1980a).

28 The minority members were impressed with the testimony of Doug Bethune, "an automotive technology instructor at the Nova Scotia Community College." In particular, they remarked that "He suggested that OBD sensors do not affect emissions. They only check the oxygen storage capacity of catalytic converters ... The manganese oxide on the spark plug is not a conductor. Oxides are insulators rather than conductors. It is the carbon which causes the fouling of the spark plug ... It is not MMT or the residue that is causing the spark plug fouling; it is carbon" (SSCEENR 3/4, 1997l, 7–8).

Evaluation. As explained in chapter 4, sensors respond to diverse conditions (e.g., the amount of oxygen in the air-fuel mixture) by sending a voltage signal to the OBD computer, which in turn sends a signal to some component of the engine and emissions control system that either activates an adjustment mechanism or records a message that will be read whenever the vehicle is taken in for its routine systems check. If an adjustment mechanism is immediately activated (say, by injecting more or less air or fuel into the mixture), then emissions will be immediately affected. If a record is stored indicating some malfunction, then when a service repair person reads the record, he or she will make the necessary adjustment, again possibly affecting emissions depending on the particular malfunction involved. So it is an oversimplification to say "OBD sensors do not affect emissions." It is also a mistake to suppose that if manganese oxides are not conductors then no shunting of a spark plug charge could occur as a result of deposits of these chemicals on the electrodes or that no misfires could be caused by the deposits. Any deposits that prevent the charge from arcing across the electrodes might contribute to a shunt and/or a misfire (Adler 1995, 188–205).

29 Using Bethune testimony again, the minority members remarked that "the very limited warranty data made public by the auto companies do not support their position." According to Bethune's testimony, " … one would expect to find the greatest number of complaints in Canada where the average concentrations of MMT in fuel were the highest. No such correlation exists. As a matter of fact, average use of MMT in British Columbia is nearly twice as high as in Atlantic Canada. General Motors' own warranty figures show that the incidence per 1,000 vehicles rate for B.C. is nearly four times lower than it is in the Atlantic provinces. Gasoline in Ontario and Quebec has the same average concentration of MMT as gasoline in the Atlantic provinces, but for some strange reason the incidence per 1,000 vehicles in the Atlantic provinces is nearly ten times as high as in Ontario and Quebec" (SSCEENR 2/11, 1996, 10).

Evaluation. The substance of Bethune's argument merits a careful response. I do not have the source of Bethune's figures, but one might expect the *total* use of MMT in British Columbia to be nearly twice as high as in Atlantic Canada because that would reflect the populations of the two areas. If Bethune's phrase "average use" means "average annual use" for each of the two areas, then the statistics would be easily explained. If "average use" means "average use for each automobile" in each of the two areas, then the statistics would not be easily explained. Without knowing what other additives are used in the two areas as well as other variables that both sides in the dispute usually bring to the table to account for unwanted statistics, it is difficult to know what to make of the statistics. Equally troubling is the fact that I have not been able to confirm or disconfirm the statistics.

30 Regarding spark plug misfires, the minority group remarked first that "The US EPA determined that misfires can cause deterioration in catalytic converters due to raw fuel entering the catalyst resulting in failure of emission standards." So the problem was not MMT but raw fuel turning up in the wrong place as a result of engine misfires. Second, and more importantly, the group claimed that:

> GM's own 1994 warranty data, when correlated with the use of MMT in Canada, shows there is no relationship between the use of MMT and spark plug misfires. If the auto makers' claim was true one would expect, as Mr. Bethune suggested, that the frequency of misfires would increase with the use of MMT. Indeed, average use of MMT in Ontario and Quebec was about the same as the Atlantic provinces, but warranty claims for the Atlantic provinces were ten times higher. It appears that there is no relationship between spark plug complaints and the amount of MMT in gasoline. Thus GM's spark plug misfires would not be caused by MMT use. Further, substantial differences in warranty terms and administration make a comparison of Canadian and US warranty claims experience a meaningless exercise in evaluating GM's claim. (SSCEENR 3/4, 1997l, 8)

Evaluation. Either the "comparison of Canadian and US warranty claims experience" is a "meaningless exercise" or it is not. If it is meaningless, then it cannot be used to show that "GM's spark plug misfires would not be caused by MMT use." The minority members claim it is meaningless. So they cannot consistently also claim that it proves the opposite of what the auto makers claim it proves.

31 The minority members claimed that:

> the only testing relied on by the auto makers before the Committee to back up their case that MMT damages OBD systems comes from a one car test Ford conducted in 1994. In that test, Ford thermally degraded the catalysts on the test vehicle to a point that the catalyst monitoring dashboard light illuminated showing a failed catalyst. Ford then commenced mileage accumulation on MMT-based fuel to see if the dashboard light would extinguish due to the presence of MMT. After more

than 40,000 miles of operation, the light remained illuminated. Ford then changed the speed at which the catalyst monitoring check took place and the dashboard light immediately went out and Ford immediately stopped the test. Based on this result, Ford asserted that "severely deteriorated catalysts were erroneously measured by the OBD catalyst monitor system to be 'good' solely as the result of MMT-gasoline being consumed in the vehicle." Replication of the test by Ethyl has shown that the speed at which the vehicle operates for the catalyst monitoring test, and not MMT, caused the light to extinguish. Using a degraded catalyst never exposed to MMT and fuel without MMT, Ethyl exactly replicated the Ford test result (i.e. having the dashboard light extinguish) simply by changing the vehicle's speed during the catalyst monitoring test. (SSCEENR 3/4, 1997l, 8)

Evaluation. The "one car test" referred to, involving a 1994 California Thunderbird is reported in Kraucher (1994). It was certainly not "the only testing relied on by the auto makers." Hubbard, Hepburn, and Gandhi (1993, 1) reported results on catalysts in two Ford Escorts and a Mustang, as well as two bench-tested catalysts showing "that manganese which is deposited onto the catalyst during the combustion of MMT-containing fuel provides for an increased level of catalyst oxygen storage capacity." Similar results with other vehicles were reported in Hurley, Watkins, and Griffis (1989), Williamson, Gandhi, and Weaver (1982), and in chapter 5 with the "Toyota 9-laps" tests. Also, we saw earlier (18) that the AIAMC was unhappy that the CPPI proposal failed to mention that field tests from two AIAMC members were among those from five vehicle manufacturers "confirming the adverse effects of MMT." Presumably, Toyota was one of those AIAMC members.

32 The federal government's attempts to help the auto and petroleum industries reach a negotiated settlement were bound to be unproductive because the "former Environment Minister Sheila Copps prejudiced the negotiations from the outset – the auto industry had no incentive to reach a reasonable settlement on the issue nor accept an independent expert panel review" (SSCEENR 3/4, 1997l, 10).

Evaluation. This sounds like sour grapes. As indicated above, a two-pump solution would have been an acceptable compromise to the federal government and the auto industry. Granting that it would not have been the preferred solution of the petroleum industry, it is unclear why such a compromise would not have been "reasonable."

33 The passage of Bill C-29 "raises the possibility of lost jobs for Canadians ... A memorandum ... dated February 24th,1995, from David Head, Industry Canada to Frank Vena, Environment Canada concludes:

'The sale of MMT represents some 50% of Ethyl Canada's total sales revenue. Loss of this business would result in a loss of a few tens of millions of dollars per year. The Corunna plant employs approximately 40 people ... The loss of 50% of sales revenue is a major loss and could cause the parent company to reevaluate maintaining a Canadian operation'". (SSCEENR 3/4, 1997l, 10)

The same point was made in the House by Madeleine Dalphond-Guiral (MP, Laval Centre, PD9/27, 1996b, 7).

Evaluation. It was fair to speculate on the possible loss of jobs (e.g., see the testimony of Johanne Lorrain, Municipal Councillor, City of Montreal, SSCEENR 2/19, 1997f, 1–8), but the petroleum refining industry clearly testified that plant closures were unlikely. For example, Alain Ferland, President of Ultramar, told the committee, "The refineries will not be closed as a result of an MMT ban. The issue for us is the issue of several million dollars per year, which is a fairly large proportion of our annual profit. I would not be specific in front of my competitors, but it is significant for us. However, we will not close our refinery as a result of the MMT ban" (SSCEENR 2/19, 1997g, 55).

Don Ingram, Vice President, Refined Products for Husky Oil Operations, said, "Our situation is slightly different ... It will be a contributor if we have to close. Currently, it is not anticipated that we will close down if we remove MMT" (SSCEENR 2/19, 1997g, 55).

Jack Donald, President and CEO of Parkland [refining] Industries, said, "We are not sure at the end of the day whether or not our refinery will make the cut, as it is the smallest one in Canada, but we are struggling to stay in the game" (SSCEENR 2/19, 1997g, 56).

And Suncor's O'Brien said, "In our case, the issue is the same as for Mr. Ferland, a few million dollars a year. It is not a knock-out issue" (SSCEENR 2/19, 1997g, 56).

So far as jobs are concerned, acceptance of a two-pump or two-station compromise would certainly have required new investments and created new jobs. As we have seen, the petroleum industry's objection to making such investments, among other things, motivated their struggle against any potential reduction in MMT usage.

On the basis of the thirty-three arguments just reviewed, the minority members concluded that:

> Taking into consideration the entire body of evidence presented to the Committee, it is possible to conclude that MMT does not harm the functioning of OBD systems. It is not possible to conclude the opposite ...
> 1. The auto makers are experiencing significant problems with the functioning of their OBD systems;
> 2. The evidence strongly suggests that OBD malfunctions are unrelated to the use of MMT-based petroleum ...
> Based on our conclusion that the evidence strongly suggests that MMT-based petroleum does not cause OBD systems to malfunction, an independent, third party review of the evidence should be undertaken ... [they also recommended] that the Royal Society of Canada undertake a thorough assessment of all information pertinent to Bill C-29 and report its findings back to the Committee at its earliest opportunity. (SSCEENR 3/4, 1997l, 10–11)

It is unclear to me why they thought the need for a third party review was implied by their conclusion. They had access to the same evidence that was available to the majority and that would have been available to the Royal Society. That evidence included some third party reviews, which the minority group discounted. Why would they not discount the conclusions of the Royal Society if it suited their purpose? When four American scientists "reviewed the Commission's *Interim and Final Report*" [*Lead in the Environment*], they concluded that "We find that the report ignores many important scientific findings, fails to recognize the significance of the accumulated toxicological data, and adopts a policy of placing the burden of proof of adverse effects on Canadian citizens themselves" (Rosen 1986, 1). In response, the Commission rejected "any assertion that the evidence was assessed selectively or in an archaic manner, and that its recommendations constitute a disservice to the people of Canada" (Commission on Lead in the Environment 1986, 341). Clearly, the conclusions of panels of expert scientists are not guaranteed to please everyone, not even other expert scientists in the same field. History buffs may recall that Plutarch, writing in the first century A.D., reported that in the fifth century B.C. Nicias and Alcibiades each produced their own priests and diviners in opposition to and in support of, respectively, Athenians invading Sicily (Plutarch 1998, 198).

On the basis of my evaluation of the thirty-three arguments, I would say that thirty are unsound or probably unsound (1–3, 5–21, and 23–33), two are sound (4 and 15) and one is indeterminate (22). In Reichenbach's terms, the success ratio of the *Minority Opinion's* arguments is about 6 per cent, which makes the weight of evidence overwhelmingly unfavourable to the case those arguments were designed to support.

QUESTION 2: DOES MMT IN GAS CAUSE A HEALTH HAZARD TO CANADIANS?

The minority members began answering this question by reminding us that:

> Health Canada officials concurred with Bill C-29 but were unequivocal in regard to the matter of the alleged health impact of manganese emitted from vehicles as a result of the combustion of MMT. They have done four separate studies on MMT since 1978 and on each occasion Health Canada came to the same conclusion. Before the Committee, Mr. Daniel Krewski, Acting Director, Bureau of Chemical Hazards, Health Canada restated Health Canada's position:
>> "Many of you are aware that in December 1994, Health Canada completed a risk assessment on the health implications of the manganese combustion products of MMT. The main conclusion of this assessment was that the manganese emissions from MMT are unlikely to pose a risk to health for any sub-group of the population."
> (SSCEENR 3/4, 1997l, 11)

Following these summary remarks, the authors of the *Opinion* reiterated direct questions put to Krewski during the hearings, and noted that his answers were entirely consistent with his "main conclusion" just quoted. In particular, they emphasized that he believed:

- manganese was very different from lead;
- "lead was added to gasoline in amounts about 16 times higher than the amount of manganese additive, leading to higher airborne lead and higher ground deposition";
- "the risk to human health from MMT-derived manganese is extremely small"'
- the iron and steel foundries of Hamilton and Windsor are "responsible for about 90 per cent of the airborne manganese" in Canada (a claim that is contradicted in Wood and Egyed 1994, 94);

- only in such industrial settings are concentrations of manganese "great enough to cause toxic effects";
- "levels of manganese in Canadian and American cities are about the same – 0.03 or 0.04 micrograms per cubic metre – despite the difference in MMT use between Canada and the u.s.";
- these levels "are not harmful to Americans or Canadians";
- so far as he knew, Health Canada had not "issued any warnings about Hamilton" regarding its levels of airborne manganese. (SSCEENR 3/4, 1997l, 11–13)

After all this, the minority members concluded, "There appear, at this point, to be sufficient data to conclude that MMT in gasoline does not pose a public health problem. Based on the scientific based testimony of Health Canada we accept that MMT use in Canada poses no danger to Canadians" (SSCEENR 3/4, 1997l, 13–14).

No recommendation followed this conclusion, and the *Opinion* proceeded to the third question.

For officials of Health Canada to assert that "the manganese emissions from MMT are unlikely to pose a risk to health for any sub-group of the population," but to support the passage of Bill C-29 seems anomalous. Did they believe that MMT posed a health risk for some reason other than manganese emissions? They certainly did and they said so. Summarizing his presentation to the Senate Standing Committee, Krewski said:

In conclusion, the Health Canada assessment, based on a conservative assessment of the scientific data, concludes that the health risks associated with manganese emissions resulting from the use of MMT in Canadian gasoline are negligible. However, this assessment did not attempt to look at the effect of MMT on other combustion-related emissions ... Several of these, such as particulate matter ... have been associated with mortality and increased hospitalization in studies on three continents, including several Canadian cities. These results indicate that all possible measures should be taken to reduce air pollution. Any measures, such as this bill, which is ultimately designed to reduce vehicle emissions, should therefore be supported. (SSCEENR 2/6, 1997e, 3–4)

A few minutes later in the meeting, responding to some questions by Senator Whelan, Krewski added:

Can we distinguish between MMT per se and manganese, which is produced as a result of the combustion of MMT? Clearly, MMT itself is highly toxic. Most of the remarks that we made earlier related to manganese emissions and exposures to the Canadian population. In that case, our assessment clearly indicates that the manganese risks are not appreciable for the general population ...

The essential notion here is that for a toxic agent like manganese it is quite likely that there exists a safe or sufficiently low level of exposure for which there would be not a strong likelihood of risk. This is supported by the fact that manganese is present in small quantities in your body naturally.

You also asked about MMT per se. *I want to distinguish clearly between manganese and MMT, because MMT is highly toxic and that was not the main focus of the assessment that we were doing.* (SSCEENR 2/6, 1997e, 7; emphasis added)

In the light of these views about the potential dangers of MMT to human health, it is fair to conclude that the second question considered by the Senate Committee was inadequately conceived insofar as negative answers to it could lead one to conclude, as the minority members of the committee did, that the use of MMT poses no health risks at all. If that were true, then Health Canada's support of Bill C-29 would have been seriously anomalous. It would have been nothing more than a rubber stamping of federal government policy, which is not what Canadians expect and deserve from a Ministry whose mandate it is to protect their health. Health Canada's risk assessment examined the health hazards connected to directly ingesting or inhaling relatively high doses of manganese over relatively short periods of time, but did not examine relatively low doses over long periods of time, or secondary, indirect effects of inhaling other pollutants as a result of the direct effects of manganese deposits on emissions control systems. Nor did it focus on the central product in the debate, MMT itself. Had the second question been formulated more precisely to include a full array of potential hazards and risks, Health Canada's conclusion might have been different (cf. Juanós i Timoneda 1997, 304–5).

QUESTION 3. DOES MMT IN GAS CAUSE DIRECT DAMAGE TO THE ENVIRONMENT?

1 In support of a negative answer to this question, *The Minority Opinion* reminded us that "In their appearance before the Committee, Ethyl

Corporation officials took the position that, rather than increasing harmful emissions, the use of MMT actually reduced NO_x emissions significantly. They put before the Committee their research that appears to indicate that MMT lowers average NO_x emissions by between 15% to 20% compared to vehicles not using MMT" (SSCEENR 3/4, 1997l, 14).

This view was also supported by Peter Underwood, Deputy Minister, Department of the Environment, Government of Nova Scotia, and John Donner, Executive Director, Environmental Affairs, Department of Energy, Government of Alberta.

Evaluation. At the risk of flogging a dead horse, I would like to add one more paragraph on the NO_x matter. As explained earlier, three-way catalytic converters are designed such that as the threshold for the ideal air-fuel mixture ($\lambda=1$) is crossed from the lean side to the rich side, there is a dramatic reduction in NO_x while HC and CO levels are unchanged. Within a 1 per cent increase in the richness of the mixture past $\lambda=1$, however, the HC and CO curves begin to ascend. Thus, to assert merely that the use of MMT decreases NO_x emissions as if that were the whole story and that no harmful emissions increase at the same time is an oversimplification. What is worse, however, is that one might be misled into believing that as the richness of a vehicle's air-fuel mixture increases, its emissions of HC and CO are unaffected; i.e., that the alleged benefits of MMT persist beyond the narrow 1 per cent range. If such benefits are associated with the use of MMT, it is remarkable that none of the basic handbooks that I consulted mentioned them. Even if MMT only has the effect of lowering NO_x emissions within the narrow 1 per cent range without changing emissions of HC and CO, it is still remarkable that none of the basic handbooks mentioned that. It seems to me that the authors of books that so carefully describe a fundamental engineering problem and how it is partially solved with TWCs would have been delighted to report the existence of a "wonder-additive" that significantly assists TWCs. Yet, nothing of the sort was ever reported.

2 As a corollary of the NO_x reduction claim, "The officials from Nova Scotia also said to the Committee that they supported the precautionary principle, although they believed that if the federal government was properly invoking that principle they would ensure that MMT remained in the gasoline – as it is known to decrease NO_x emissions" (SSCEENR 3/4, 1997l, 14; see also David Wilson's testimony at SSCEENR 2/5, 1997d, 3).

Evaluation. Insofar as the corollary is based on an oversimplified premise, it is unjustifiable. Besides, it would be a mistake to apply the precautionary principle on the basis of a single benefit, in the absence of any consideration of costs. As a general rule, the principle should only be applied with a reasonably complete benefit-cost analysis.

Following these brief arguments for answering the third question in the negative, the minority members concluded their report as follows:

> The technical data reviewed by the EPA might lead the members of the Committee to conclude that MMT does not increase hydrocarbons and carbon monoxide. However, until a definitive study is conducted, the question cannot be answered with certainty. Given the preponderance of the evidence on this matter, and at this stage in our examination, it is not apparent that MMT causes direct damage to the environment. It remains that the evidence relating to a negative impact of MMT use on emissions of hydrocarbons, and carbon monoxide, and consequently on the Canadian environment, is contradictory, inconclusive and speculative. (SSCEENR 3/4, 1997l, 15)

Again, the minority group seemed to want to have its cake and eat it too. It believed that the evidence was sufficiently convincing to reject Bill C-29, but still wanted "a definitive study." In effect, what it wanted was its first choice, outright rejection of Bill C-29, or failing that, its second choice, which was delayed implementation until there is scientific certainty sufficient to substantiate its first choice. While I can see the advantages for Ethyl and the petroleum industry in these aims, the advantages for everyone else remain unclear.

CONCLUSION

Careful assessment of the arguments presented in the Senate Standing Committee *Interim Report* and in *The Minority Opinion* reveals more support for than against the MMT *Act*. In the light of the results obtained from the House and Senate Standing Committees, Bill C-29 was successfully defended and passed in the House (2 December 1996) and Senate (4 April 1997), received Royal Assent on 25 April 1997, and came into force sixty days later, on 24 June 1997. Prior to the establishment of the NAFTA and AIT, the use of MMT probably would have ended when the available stocks of the additive ran out sometime after June. However, the two trade agreements provided additional arenas in which opponents of the MMT *Act* could continue their fight. In the remaining chapters I continue to trace the history of that fight by means of a detailed examination of the cases pursued according to the rules of those agreements. As in earlier chapters, I proceed from a consideration of relatively more general, philosophical issues concerning commercial arbitration to more specific issues concerning the dispute settlement provisions of the two agreements and the applications of those provisions to the MMT *Act.*

9

Commercial Arbitration

In this chapter I review some of the philosophical and broader socio-economic roots and issues surrounding commercial arbitration. The dispute settlement procedures of the NAFTA and AIT are discussed in more detail in chapter 10. While the AIT is a domestic agreement, its main dispute resolution provisions were adapted and adopted from models of international commercial arbitration. Moreover, as already indicated, the resolution of the domestic AIT MMT dispute effectively destroyed the Canadian government's case in the international NAFTA MMT dispute. Thus, a deeper and broader analysis of international commercial arbitration seems to be appropriate.

Graham (1987, 96) explained that "in common law countries" there is no "precise definition for 'commercial activity'." Paterson (1987, 116) agreed that this applies to Canada. Thus, where arbitration is concerned, apparently no clear legal line can be drawn between what is merely commercial and what is not. So no clear line regarding commerciality can be drawn between what is and is not properly arbitrable by the NAFTA and AIT dispute settlement rules. For our purposes this is important because, among other things, it implies that it was not and is not sufficient for anyone to claim that since the NAFTA tribunals and AIT panels deal only with commercial issues, it is reasonable and morally right to have disputes adjudicated by special judges, in special venues, using special rules designed for commerce. NAFTA Article 1136.7 makes it clear that, in this agreement, the cart is put squarely before the horse insofar as issues are defined as commercial, because they are subject to the Article rather than the reverse. The Article says: "A claim that is submitted to arbitration under this Section shall be considered to arise out of a commercial relationship or transaction for purposes of Article 1 of the New York Convention and Article 1 of the InterAmerican Convention" (NAFTA 2002).

"Arbitration is as old as mankind," Jakubowski (1982, 175) wrote, and "it is older than State courts." In a relatively brief but very thoughtful philosophical essay, Jakubowski revealed many of the key issues concerning international commercial arbitration and briefly documented the existence of some form of arbitration in Greek, Roman, Islamic, and Byzantine law. He was so impressed with its ubiquity in Western civilization, he thought it was "no exaggeration to say that it is universal as a human institution. It is an intercultural phenomenon. It is a product of a universal human need and desire for an equitable solution of differences inevitably arising from time to time between people by an impartial person having the confidence of and authority from these people (not power over them)" (Jakubowski 1982, 176).

Apparently the "need and desire" even arose in the field of organized crime in the United States. In 1934 the "Big Six" crime leaders divided the country into geographic regions and designated a "High Commission" to "hear and arbitrate disputes arising between local bosses. Each leader reigned absolutely in his territory ... The gang leaders also set up a 'kangaroo court of the underworld,' which would hear only those charges considered serious enough to carry the death penalty against top-echelon gang members. Its decisions were final and could not be appealed" (de Champlain 2004, 18–19).

As one might expect from a universal institution, there is a relatively common core of principles and some variance from the central core depending on the requirements of diverse fields. Regarding the common core, for example, many authors mention the principle *pacta sunt servanda*, usually translated as "agreements and stipulations must be observed," and *amiable composition*, calling for judgments "according to justice and fairness" or according to "natural justice in opposition to law created by the State" (Jakubowski 1982, 177–80; Graham 1987, 101–2). In Jakubowski's view, which seems reasonable enough to me, "the sources of these values and principles are elementary moral principles to be found among various peoples and human groups" (179). Thus I would look for the justification for any alleged basic principles of arbitration in my fundamental principle of moral consequentialism as explained in chapter 2, while others might look for a foundation in some sort of contractarian, theological or Kantian moral theories (Michalos 2001). Some alternative accounts follow.

Jakubowski's view of the supplementary principles appropriate to international commercial arbitration was fairly generous, allowing business considerable autonomy.

> In international trade, arbitration is particularly close to the part of the international trade law which is known as new *lex mercatoria* (law merchant) ... States have adopted the principle of their exclusive jurisdiction to settle disputes between people. They have, however, allowed some exceptions to non-State courts, e.g., to religious courts. One of these exceptions is arbitration. Arbitration is a kind of social jurisdiction, opposed to State jurisdiction. *International commercial arbitration is the jurisdiction of the business circles engaged in international trade* ... When the parties [to an arbitration] have a permanent business relationship, the previous practice which has been established between them can be very useful for the arbitrators. The arbitrators are expected to know and take into consideration – in working out the decision – general commercial usages and usages of the respective branch of trade. (Jakubowski 1982, 178–9; emphasis added)

The italicized sentence is a very strong claim, which Jakubowski seems to have regarded as descriptive and evaluative. That is, he seems to have thought that as a matter of fact "business circles" have some special authority (possibly not supreme authority) over international commercial arbitration and that "business circles" ought (morally speaking) to have such authority. He also claimed that "the arbitration agreement is a kind of agreement on jurisdiction" (182). Thus, in his view:

> The role of the parties in arbitration, in contrast to court proceedings, is extremely great. The will of the parties is the basis for arbitration, the law being a very general framework for the articulation of that will. It can be said, roughly, that in the law are contained the State's permission to arbitrate, very general boundaries for the functioning of the arbitrators and guarantees for the execution of the award.
>
> Without the will of the parties, the competence of the arbitration does not exist. The parties appoint arbitrators. They are entitled to determine the procedure ... Generally speaking, the parties have a much wider sphere of influence in arbitration than in State courts.
>
> One of the characteristic features of arbitration is the closeness of the arbitrator to the parties in the dispute or difference. The arbitrators are judges, but not only judges. They should be their friends too. Gather-

ings of judges and the actual or potential parties such as international congresses and symposia, organized, among others, by the International Council of Commercial Arbitration, are hard to imagine in the case of professional state judges ... Such meetings ... cannot be harmful because of the principle of confidence which is the deepest "subsoil" of arbitration. (Jakubowski 1982, 180)

Although he did not explain "the principle of confidence" mentioned in the final sentence, he did say that "The foundation of arbitration is authority in the sense of acceptance, confidence and appreciation" and that such authority is contingent upon arbitrators' "experience, wisdom, generosity, intelligence, personality and courage," and "in specialized branches of life, e.g., in commercial disputes ... The arbitrator must have a special knowledge and experience" (181).

Regarding the idea that arbitrators should take into consideration "general commercial usages and usages of the respective branch of trade" as if they could provide guidance equal to rules of law, Mann (1984, 197) wrote:

It is difficult to imagine a more dangerous, more undesirable and more ill-founded view which denies any measure of predictability and certainty and confers upon parties to an international commercial contract or their arbitrators powers that no system of law permits and no court could exercise.

It is, therefore, a matter of great satisfaction and import that the House of Lords has made short shrift of what the vast majority of lawyers here and abroad is likely to regard as heretical. Thus, Lord Diplock said that

"the purpose of entering into a contract being to create legal rights and obligations between the parties to it, interpretations of the contract involves determining what are the legal rights and obligations to which the words used in it give rise. *This is not possible except by reference to the system of law by which the legal consequences that follow from the use of those words is to be ascertained.*"

Jakubowski's views of the foundations of international commercial arbitration in general and field-specific moral principles, in the will of parties to agreements and in the probity of arbitrators, form a coherent whole which is consistent with his view of the aim of arbitration. Regarding the latter, he wrote:

My personal experience as arbitrator leads me to ... see the essence of solving disputes in the solution of a concrete difficulty which has arisen between parties to the dispute ... The mission of arbitrators in a given case is not to solve general problems of the society, but to solve the specific conflict.

But, on the other hand, the judgment should not be in conflict with general tendencies in solving such disputes. To respect the legal rules is necessary for State courts. But arbitrators, too, should take into account the potential impact of their award on the segment of trade in question and should, therefore, be in accordance with generally accepted values and principles. In this sense an arbitration case is a link in the chain of life and cannot be treated in isolation ...

It is essential to take into consideration the general impact of arbitral awards on future developments in the contractual practice particularly in the newest stage of the development of international commercial arbitration where the publication of such arbitral awards which are of interest, in view of future cases, is becoming a general practice. (Jakubowski 1982, 184–5)

Insofar as a particular dispute involves merely a "specific conflict" between two parties and does not involve a more "general problem of the society," one might be inclined to agree with Jakubowski's overall views about international commercial arbitration. In the jargon of international commercial arbitration, the assumption that parties to an arbitration enter into a contractual arrangement such that they jointly command supreme, if not entire, authority over its rules of procedure is called the Principle of Autonomy. An extreme statement of the principle would omit the phrase "if not entire," but I doubt that many people would subscribe to that view. The majority of works consulted for this investigation seemed to accept the Principle of Autonomy as formulated above, certainly the majority of proponents of the key trade agreements. Describing the situation in the United States, for example, Hoellering (1987, 18–19) wrote:

In recent cases the Courts have construed the [New York] Convention to allow the broadest possible application to subject matter arbitrability, and the enforceability of "foreign" awards, even if rendered within the United States. The "public policy" exception of the Convention has been interpreted narrowly by the Courts ... The most recent case illustrating this attitude is *Mitsubishi Motors Corp. v. Soler Chrysler-Plymouth, Inc.* In *Mitsubishi* the Supreme Court determined that where a transnational agreement contains a broad arbitration clause, antitrust claims are arbitrable, despite a domestic public policy proscribing future agreements to arbitrate such claims ... In fact, at the heart of the arbitrability question is the broad arbitration clause. The Courts have ruled that inclusion of a broad arbitration clause in the agreement of the parties serves to permit arbitration of any controversy which may arise ... The key to the evolution of judge-made arbitration law in the United States is party autonomy. The Courts have continually ruled that the intent of the parties is paramount, unless some greater public policy overrides their agreement ... Thus, the Courts maintain a non-intervention policy regarding arbitration, both domestic and international.

Because in many cases, such as the NAFTA and AIT arbitration cases over MMT, specific conflicts between two or more parties have clear spillover effects or externalities for many other people, I believe it is a serious mistake to accept this principle and its blanket assumption about the nature of international commercial arbitration. This assumption is at the root of the problem with the dispute resolution procedures of the NAFTA and AIT, as well as those of the CUSTA and WTO. As indicated below, proponents of such procedures routinely list many other reasons for preferring them to litigation in public courts and seldom, if ever, mention the avoidance of externality costs (i.e., costs to people who are not parties to the dispute settlement process). According to critics, from a moral point of view, the contribution made by those procedures to parties' ability to avoid externality costs is probably the most objectionable aspect of the procedures; I certainly agree. Where issues of environmental degradation, public health, and consumer safety are concerned, as they often are in cases of international commercial arbitration, it is unreasonable and unacceptable from a moral consequentialist point of view to assume that there are no externalities or that they are simply irrelevant. Morality aside, from an economic point of view, insofar as such procedures allow sellers to surreptitiously pass their spillover or externality costs on to buyers without including them in the purchase prices of goods and services, the "wisdom of the market" is undermined through the spread of false information in the form of inaccurate price signals. One would think, therefore, that if the institutions of morality and free market capitalism are both undermined by such dispute settlement procedures, there is not only an opportunity but a pressing need for people with quite different political ideologies to make common cause in the interest of the public good.

An alternative, and possibly mutually exclusive, fundamental assumption that may form the basis of systems of international commercial arbitration is called the Principle of Judicial Scrutiny. According to this principle, "the courts have a public right and responsibility as organs of the state to ensure that the process of arbitration operates in all cases according to a uniform, if minimum, standard imposed by law" (Law Commission of New Zealand 1991, 65). Note that under this principle state courts would have a "right and responsibility" to prohibit the kangaroo courts of the Mafia, while under the Principle of Autonomy, they might not. It depends on the exact wording of the latter principle and the precise actions of any particular kangaroo court. When the Principle of Autonomy is backed up by Jakubowski's additional assumption that "business circles" have some special jurisdiction over international commercial arbitration, the mutual incompatibility of the two foundation principles and the possible legitimate exclusion of judicial review of the activities of Mafia courts becomes even more likely.

The authors of the report of the Law Commission of New Zealand were especially sensitive to the issues favouring one or the other of the two foundation principles. They recognized that:

> It is well accepted that there are some matters – such as questions of personal status or disputes about illegal transactions – which may fall outside the permissible scope of private arbitration. The public institutions of the state must resolve such matters and others in which there is also a significant public interest ...
>
> The "jurisdictional theory" [i.e., the theory that international commercial arbitration should be founded on the Principle of Judicial Scrutiny] holds that the real authority of arbitration derives not from the contract between parties, but from the recognition accorded by the state. It argues that the court, representing the state and applying its law, is entitled to insist on certain conditions. These need not be limited to the parties' immediate concerns – for instance there are the interests of the state in maintaining a fair and uniform system of law and order ... Subsequently, intervention has been justified in order to protect weaker contractual parties from the consequences of their contracts ... Most recent arguments have been framed in terms of "procedural fairness" ... But these still presuppose that it is for the state to determine whether, and to what extent, parties should be able to order their private relations. (Law Commission of New Zealand 1991, 60–6)

On the other hand, they very clearly indicated that:

The "contractual theory" [i.e., the theory that international commercial arbitration should be founded on the Principle of Autonomy] by contrast holds that arbitration, having its origins in and depending for its continuity solely on the agreement of the parties, is essentially contractual. (It does not however deny that there are some matters which state institutions must resolve ...) The argument here is that the parties voluntarily agree to submit their disputes to arbitration, to appoint an arbitrator and, most importantly, to accept the arbitral tribunal's award as having binding force. Once authorised by the parties to make the award the tribunal acts as agent of the parties, and the award is binding on them as an agreement made on their behalf by their agent. Thus, according to this theory, the authority of the parties is paramount in all respects, and the only essential function of the court is to enforce as unexecuted contracts those agreements and awards which are not honoured. (Law Commission of New Zealand 1991, 66–7)

According to this commission, "the court may be entitled to demand that some standards of conduct are met" because "the tribunal cannot itself enforce the agreement or the award in the event that a dissatisfied party refuses to comply with one or the other." As we know, that handicap would not apply to some Mafia tribunals, but it would be applicable to NAFTA tribunals and AIT panels. Most importantly, the authors of the report wrote: "Ultimately, if contract principles are to mean anything in this context, the freedom of the parties to select arbitration rather than court processes as the means for resolving their disputes must be respected ... This is a practical as well as conceptual necessity. If a court exercises too great a control over an arbitral proceeding and its outcome, the advantages of arbitration over litigation stand to be undermined ... The balance is thus a delicate one and in modern times has tended to move in favour of effective arbitration, while at the same time attempting to ensure minimum standards of legality, fairness and due process" (Law Commission of New Zealand 1991, 67).

As indicated above and as I support in detail below, I believe that minimum standards of fairness to consumers and others affected by the results of the NAFTA and AIT cases concerning MMT were not met and could have been predicted not to be met. If my assessment is accurate, some serious re-crafting of the dispute settlement rules in both treaties should be undertaken, at a minimum. Leaving that aside, I would like to emphasize the relative strength of the enforcement argument versus the freedom to contract argument mentioned in the two quoted paragraphs above. It seems to me that the freedom to contract would be a relatively vacuous freedom if it were not backed up by some capacity for enforcement. Rather than parties becoming their own enforcers or hiring private enforcers as required, states have traditionally been called upon for such services. Quite reasonably, then, states must be able to establish their own performance criteria for parties and arbitrators to satisfy in exchange for the provision of such services, and state courts typically have the "right and responsibility" for determining whether or not those criteria have been met. Even a staunch defender of the Principle of Autonomy such as Jakubowski granted that "Because of the uncertainty of whether the award will be carried out by the losing party, the guarantees of legislation and the assistance of the State are indispensable for arbitration. Practice has shown the limited effectiveness of social pressure (in international trade – the pressure of business circles and professional organizations of businessmen, e.g., chambers of commerce) as a means of enforcing arbitral awards" (Jakubowski 1982, 178).

Therefore, if states – acting through courts and the rest of the legal apparatus required for well-functioning judicial systems, on behalf of taxpayers – must finally be responsible for ensuring that international commercial arbitration procedures function properly, then those states, in behalf of those taxpayers, must have supreme, though not entire, oversight and ultimate control over those procedures. So, the Principle of Judicial Scrutiny should be granted precedence over the Principle of Autonomy. Insofar as states are assigned the responsibility for enforcing arbitral awards but denied the right to oversee and control the arbitral procedures, those relatively few who enjoy the use of such procedures are allowed to take a free ride on the relatively many taxpayers who pay for states' services. That is both morally and economically objectionable.

As already mentioned, many of the procedural and substantive rules of the CUSTA, NAFTA, AIT, and WTO are similar in form and proceed from similar assumptions, including most notably the Principle of Autonomy. In particular, the United Nations Commission on International Trade Law (UNCITRAL) Arbitration Rules and the UNCITRAL Model Law provided useful templates for the treaty rules. The UNCITRAL was formed by the UN General Assembly in 1966 as a "vehicle by which the United Nations could play a more active role in reducing and removing" obstacles to international trade. The mandate of the commission is to "further the progressive harmonization and unification of the law of international trade." The thirty-six UN member states on the commission are elected by the UN General Assembly for three-year terms and are intended to represent "the world's various geographic regions and its principal economic and legal systems." Among other things, the commission produced the UNCITRAL Arbitration Rules in 1976 (UNCITRAL 2002, 1–3) and the UNCITRAL Model Law on International Commercial Arbitration in 1985 (UNCITRAL 2003, 2004). According to Herrmann (1987, 65):

As is well known, the UNCITRAL Arbitration Rules meet fully the needs of modern arbitration practice; they are of high quality and are universally acceptable in countries and to parties irrespective of their legal or economic systems. The universal character of the rules is particularly beneficial to parties involved over time in a number of arbitrations which they may wish or may be required to hold, for practical or legal reasons, in different locations. Such parties and their counsel will appreciate that they may use the same set of rules in each of the different locations and that they may find in these locations one of the many arbitral institutions willing to provide administrative assistance to them.

In his view, the Model Law provided "an 'emergency kit', a skeleton set of suppletive rules which, taken from the UNCITRAL Arbitration Rules, ensure that an arbitration may get started and proceed effectively until the resolution of the dispute" (67).

In the preface to their fine collection of articles on the applications of the UNCITRAL Rules and Model Law in Canada, Paterson and Thompson (1987) remarked that as late as 1982 neither the Canadian Department of Justice nor the Canadian business community seemed to have much interest in the UN-crafted 1958 New York Convention on the Recognition and Enforcement of Foreign Arbitral Awards (UNCITRAL 2004, 5). As international trade increased and a market clearly emerged for international commercial arbitration, businesses and governments became much more interested. In 1985 the Attorney General of British Columbia struck a task force to study the feasibility of "creating a legal climate in the province of British Columbia suitable for the resolution of international business disputes" (Paterson and Thompson 1987, vii).

When the task force began pursuing its mandate the assumption that only disputes involving Canadian parties could be settled in Canada was quickly discarded; it soon realized the overriding need for an international commercial dispute resolution framework that would be attractive to foreign parties. Furthermore, the establishment of an inviting forum would create a new service industry that would spur local development of relevant legal expertise and administrative support services.

Recognizing the special needs of international dispute resolution, the British Columbia task force decided to develop, alongside existing provincial domestic arbitration laws, a provincial law solely governing the resolution of international commercial disputes. No other jurisdiction like British Columbia had such a law ... On 8th March 1986 the task force presented its report ... [including] the draft International Commercial Arbitration Act based on the UNCITRAL Model Law that formed the basis of the International Commercial Arbitration Act, which became law on 17th June 1986. (Paterson and Thompson 1987, viii)

The British Columbia International Commercial Arbitration Centre opened for business (in both senses) in Vancouver in May 1986. As in every other case where such a centre of activity was created, it was opened in the interest of making a profit for the variety of service providers engaged in commercial arbitration as well as for their clients. The private justice to be delivered was designed to be consistent with the aims of the profit motive for all concerned. As Dezalay and Garth (1996, 6–7) put it in their excellent investigation of the history and status of international commercial arbitration:

Over the past twenty-five to thirty years, international commercial arbitration has become big legal business, the accepted method of resolving international business disputes ... Its success is reflected in the arbitrations of high-profile disputes ... Success is also evident in the tremendous growth since the late 1970s in the numbers of arbitration centers, arbitrators, and arbitrations ... The growth of the market *in arbitration* is also evident in the competition that can be seen among different national approaches and centers. Once the International Chamber of Commerce [ICC] began to gain relatively large numbers of high-profile international commercial arbitrations in the 1970s, a process of competition began, aided by the forum-shopping possibilities of large U.S. multinational law firms able to pick and choose among laws, rules, institutions, and places according to the perceived interests of their clients ... Within Europe, first England in 1979, then France in 1981, Belgium in 1985, the Netherlands in 1986, and Switzerland in 1989 enacted new statutes to reform their arbitration laws to satisfy the business users of international arbitration; and the United States achieved the same result through Supreme Court action in 1985 ... This kind of "regulatory competition" ... to gain the business of arbitration has helped promote a form of arbitration detached from the scrutiny and regulation of the national court systems.

According to these authors, legal practitioners and their clients compete for control of the dispute settlement market. For practitioners, this market in conflict resolution is practically paradigmatically "their business," while for clients, it offers a way to more readily control their own particular lines of business. For example, regarding the cases concerning the use of MMT, insofar as the motor vehicle manufacturers, petroleum companies, refiners, and the Ethyl Corporation could control the procedures for managing the disputes, they could more readily control their markets for motor vehicles, gasoline, and its additives. Thus the dispute settlement procedures were a factor of production as important as labour, material, or financial capital in the ultimate determination of market share in their primary products. In this struggle for control:

> The legal profession seeks to pull private justice into the ordinary legal system. The business response is in effect that, if that is the case, they will bypass the courts and the lawyers of the state altogether by arranging to regulate their conflicts between themselves. They may rely on associations of business, like the chambers of commerce and industry, which permit them to draw on business solidarity or on "moral sanctions" available to business peers.
>
> The merchants could even take the option of producing their own "law", outside of the official legal system ... One way to do so would be to utilize corporate counsel ... Further, while house lawyers may lack credibility in some matters, it is quite easy for leading economic powers to look temporarily toward universities or even toward notables who embody the authority of the justice of the state. Business could in this way develop a private justice outside of the legal system that draws selectively on the same guarantees of legal legitimacy available to the state ... Depending on the context, business could even create its own justice. (Dezalay and Garth 1996, 119)

To the extent that the "private justice" developed by business could appropriate the "legal legitimacy available to the state" without paying the price of public scrutiny and control of its dispute settlement processes, business would be able to take a free ride on the public's perception of its activity as well as on the public purse. If the rules of the game of international commercial arbitration defined by business were granted legitimacy by the general public (which is typically regarded as having no legal standing in dispute settlement cases), the general public would be giving business what it would not give its own courts, namely, freedom from public oversight and control. What's more, if the rules of the game were crafted such that business would be able to obtain payments from the public purse for transgressions that were only defined by those rules, the symbolic free ride would be significantly compounded materially. As explained in chapter 10, critics of the NAFTA continue to challenge the legitimacy of its Chapter 11 rules precisely because they are unwilling to grant them legitimacy and to grant business the free ride that such legitimacy would imply.

Notwithstanding the variety of options available to business, "the construction of large regional markets" through trade agreements like the NAFTA and the even grander WTO, with their own dispute settlement procedures, could radically alter the market for international commercial arbitration.

> These institutions and approaches offer new opportunities for business. Even if it is not at first apparent, these institutions compete with the International Chamber of Commerce and private arbitration. At the same time, new approaches and institutions may facilitate the recomposition of this field of practice closer to the pole of the state ... International commercial arbitration can be transformed or even replaced because it is part of a larger international *market* of commercial or business disputes, and the market is inevitably unstable. Instability ... comes from the fact that arbitration is constantly pulled between two contradictory poles – business and law ... States – and among them supranational entities – and state jurisdictions intervene increasingly on the scene of economic conflicts. And the relatively new entities that intervene tend to be jealous of their authority and anxious to build up their regulatory domain ... As states assume more importance, legal professionals and large enterprises tend to move, almost by definition, closer to the pole of the state, leading to a process of acceleration ... If this line of development continues, the field of transnational business justice will be more closely connected to states and to supranational, statelike entities than it was in the period when the ICC gained its eminence. (Dezalay and Garth 1996, 312–15)

Granting that international commercial arbitration is driven at least as much by the interest in financial gain as by the interest in justice, a wide variety of additional advantages over ordinary court litigation are attributed to it. The following list was assembled from diverse sources and is probably not exhaustive.

1 Perhaps the most frequently mentioned advantage of international commercial arbitration is that it allows parties to avoid the courts of their competitors (Dezalay and Garth 1996, 5, 13). Insofar as this option reduces the pressure on public court systems and reduces taxpayers' burdens, it is an advantage for the public at large as well as for businesses (Law Commission of New Zealand 1991, 59). According to Chibueze (2001, 192), parties' "unwillingness to have their disputes litigated in foreign courts is based on the fear that they will be at a disadvantage due to unfamiliarity with the legal system of the foreign jurisdiction, language barriers, and possible national bias leading to a 'hometown judgment'." Brower and Steven (2001, 196) went even farther:

the fundamental reason that the great majority of modern investment protection treaties have opted for international adjudication is that domestic courts are often in fact, and, just as important, usually are perceived to be, biased against alien investors, especially when those courts must evaluate and pronounce upon acts of their own governments. Further, domestic courts often do not have the legal expertise and experience to free themselves from the confines of their own domestic regimes so as to give proper attention and respect to international law ... An international dispute resolution mechanism best serves Chapter 11 precisely because the NAFTA Parties are trying to build an international investment protection and promotion regime. (See also Lillich and Brower 1993)

Herrmann (1987, 67) noted that:

The discretionary power of the arbitral tribunal and the prevailing rule of party autonomy are prominently embodied in Article 19 of the [UNCITRAL] Model Law and section 19 of the ... British Columbia Act ... The main effect of this 'Magna Carta of Arbitral Procedure' is to exclude the application of the domestic arbitration or civil procedure law, including any local Act or Rules of Court regulating the crucial issues of taking evidence.

Viewing this exclusion as a major advantage does not mean to pass any value judgment on the quality or refinement of the domestic law. It is simply based on the finding that local laws are made primarily, if not exclusively, for domestic requirements and thus tend to be unsuitable for cases with parties from different countries and legal systems.

Despite Herrmann's point about Article 19, and Article 5 of the Model Law, which says that "In matters governed by this Law, no court shall intervene except where so provided in this Law" (UNCITRAL 2003), Articles 6, 8, 9, 11, 13, and 34 contain several provisions for such intervention. For example, Article 6 regarding "Court or other authority for certain functions of arbitration assistance and supervision" says that "The functions referred to in articles 11(3), 11(4), 13(3), 14, 16(3) and 34(2) shall be performed by ... (Each state enacting this model law specifies the court, courts or, where referred to therein, other authority competent to perform these functions)" (UNCITRAL 2003).

Commenting on Article 5 in the Model Law and in the British Columbia Act, Lord Wilberforce (1987, 11–12) expressed "misgivings" about ruling out "any questioning, review or restraint by judicial review or otherwise":

> In the first place we are not so sure that the customer wants total exemption from Court control. He may not have liked the stated case, but to leave the arbitrators totally free is another matter. I have myself received a number of representations from developing countries in favour of having points of law decided by the Courts – at least in some cases. Without this, those countries have no means of knowing what the law or practice is. Conversely, published Court decisions (and remember that arbitral awards are often not published) give a valuable guide; they get into textbooks and journals ... Looking at it more broadly, can we accept that in all cases, arbitrators are to be free to decide vital and difficult points of law unreviewably? There is no other area of decision making which has total immunity from Court intervention.

As a matter of fact, the Mafia's code of conduct contains a prohibition against any "appeal to the state's authorities for justice" (de Champlain 2004, 89–90).

When Abbott (2000, 303) reflected on the Chapter 11 provisions of NAFTA, he had reservations similar to those of Wilberforce concerning limited review in the Model Law: "The question under NAFTA is whether we have the proper institutions to serve the ECJ [European Court of Justice]-

type function. It is very questionable that we do. Are we comfortable with three private arbitrators ruling on critical questions of public health, even if their decisions only involve compensation, and not changes to legislation? I suspect not, because there are no adequate provisions for transparency, continuity or appellate review (except under New York Convention public policy exceptions)."

While Wilberforce doubted the wisdom of giving international commercial arbitrators "total immunity from Court intervention," Dezalay and Garth doubted that the requirements of domestic and international law were so different as to warrant the construction of an autonomous realm of private justice. Since the key players in all the arenas tend to be drawn from the same pool, various features of domestic laws frequently appear in international laws and international commercial arbitration systems. It is, after all, in the personal interest of every practitioner to try to increase the value of his or her own expertise and experience by persuading others of the universal importance and applicability of precisely such expertise and experience. Thus, in the "intense and wide-open competition for the business of business disputes":

> Competitors and participants promote their own definitions and the alliances they have formed, seeking to gain predominance for the approach that favors them and what they embody – retired judges, pure mediators, traditional arbitrators, litigators, business courts, legalized mediation. Some competitors are close to the domain of courts and formal law. They emphasize legal principles and what courts might do, thereby reinforcing the power and authority of the legal system. Others, without the capital of legal authority, for example the "pure mediators", are much closer to the market and the business domain ... The competition between the various players, in any event, builds the field and serves to give it credibility and legitimacy. The relative winners will succeed in making their approach seem the natural and normal one – the one embodied also in leading institutions. (Dezalay and Garth 1996, 173)

Although parties to the AIT did not have to worry about litigation in foreign courts, Doern and MacDonald (1999, 140–1) reported that all of the ministers agreed that any courts should be avoided. Apparently the ministers did not trust the courts any more than they trusted each other (149). When Swinton reflected on reasons for the AIT parties excluding courts, she focused on tradeoff issues:

It is easy to understand the reason governments want to keep this agreement out of the courts. First, judges are not well-suited to oversee the many obligations to meet and negotiate ... It would be a virtually impossible task for courts to oversee governmental negotiations, which require difficult tradeoffs between supposed economic gains from the removal of a barrier and competing policy considerations.

Second, even when provisions are stated in more direct terms, there can be a variety of interpretations involving complex public policy considerations, which governments are understandably reluctant to trust to the courts. Take, for example, the obligation in [AIT] Article 403 that "each Party shall ensure that any measure it adopts or maintains does not operate to create an obstacle to internal trade." In fact, an action that obstructs trade could be permitted by the agreement if the government were pursuing a "legitimate objective" and the measure was not "unduly" trade restrictive (Article 803). Deciding the appropriateness of a governmental action in these situations requires a difficult judgment about the burden that should be placed on trade when balancing it against other values, such as the optimal level of consumer protection. (Swinton 1995, 202–3)

While reading these passages, remember that with the AIT dispute settlement procedures, the only place one might want to see courts involved is when panels are involved. As explained in chapter 10, the AIT procedures were designed to bring parties together for an informal resolution of their disputes. Panels, or courts if they were permitted, would only be invoked as a last resort. Accordingly, it is a red herring to suggest that courts should be avoided because judges would make poor negotiators as they would not be able to properly interpret undefined concepts such as "unduly restrictive trade practices" or to weigh and balance competing values concerning such things as trade and consumer protection. When courts or panels would be called in, negotiations would have given way to adjudication, and the expertise of judges as well as all the other features of well-designed judicial systems would be the best protection of all interests of all affected parties. There is no good reason to suppose that relatively dependent, party-friendly panelists would make better adjudicators than relatively independent, objective judges. On the contrary, one would predict that the latter would be much more likely than the former to render judgments in the interest of the public good. "Judges traditionally serve even in private litigation as protectors of unrepresented public interests, whereas private arbitrators properly define their responsibilities exclusively in terms of the interests of the parties appearing before them" (McConnaughay 1999, 495–6). As well, even before adjudication is required some sort of parliamentary, or quasi-parliamentary, harmonizing procedure would likely do a better job than an ad hoc panel or tribune of interpreting undefined concepts, weighing and balancing diverse values, and delivering judgments broadly protecting the public good.

2 The second most frequently mentioned advantage of international commercial arbitration is its secrecy. Paterson and Thompson (1987, 1) wrote that "Arbitral proceedings are routinely surrounded by secrecy and confidentiality and the publication of international commercial arbitral awards is limited and irregular." According to the Law Reform Commission of British Columbia (1982, 3), a major "advantage of arbitration is that hearings can be held in private. This may be of importance to businessmen who do not wish to open the way in which they conduct business to the scrutiny of their competitors, or the general public." Of course, the Mafia also have an interest in not opening "the way in which they conduct business to ... the general public." "The rule of secrecy is a basic and essential requirement of all members of Cosa Nostra" (de Champlain 2004, 80).

Brower and Steven (2001, 197) claimed that the investor-state dispute resolution procedures in NAFTA were superior to state-to-state adjudication procedures because the latter tended to be "politically explosive" since "diplomatic protection has the distinct disadvantage of pitting two States against one another in an inherently confrontational setting where, once a case is commenced, government officials cannot be seen as acting indifferently to the interests of their nationals. International 'incidents,' and the longstanding resentment and ill will between nations they generate, simply are not as likely to occur when the private investor itself has the right and the responsibility to prosecute its own claim and hence only one government is actively involved in the litigation."

This is an odd piece of reasoning. Rather than risk governments acting too vigilantly against foreign investors by trying not to appear to be acting indifferently toward their nationals, Brower and Steven would have tribunals acting in relative secrecy in any way that seems appropriate to them. I would think that the threat of creating a possible "international incident" would be an added inducement for investors and states to be especially careful in their dealings with one another, which would do more to reduce the chances of such incidents than allowing individual investors to challenge states in relative privacy. Abouchar and King (1999, 212–3) concurred with this view, asserting that state-to-state dispute resolution was preferable precisely because states are "bound by diplomacy." They agreed with environmentalists who argue that "public policy considerations [involving environmental protection measures] ought to be considered (if at all) in a public forum before publicly accountable decision-makers."

For Jakubowski, the issue is a matter of principle. The Principle of Confidentiality is derived from the Principle of Autonomy:

> Arbitration is a matter between parties, a problem *inter partes*. The external world should not be involved in this matter.
>
> The subject of arbitration is a matter in which the parties are sovereign (parties' autonomy) and must not depend on third persons except arbitrators, experts, or witnesses whom they decide to involve. The external world is not entitled to interfere, because of the direct or indirect property (patrimonial) nature of the dispute.
>
> Let's remember that the potential claimant may decide whether he renounces legal prosecution of the claim or even renounces the claim itself. The law allows the parties to submit to arbitration. It's logical that the arbitration proceedings are a private matter of the parties and the exclusion of the public is not at all strange. Ad hoc arbitrations are held *in camera*. This principle, the principle of confidentiality, is adopted by many permanent arbitration institutions and associations. (Jakubowski 1982, 182)

Notice that the "principle of confidentiality" (or secrecy) considered in these passages is different from Jakubowski's "principle of confidence" mentioned earlier. The latter is a product of the character of arbitrators, while the former is a logical consequence of the presumed autonomous character of the arbitration process itself. I have already explained the inappropriateness of regarding the Principle of Autonomy as the foundation of arbitrations in which there are significant impacts or externality costs for people who are not parties to the arbitration. The fact that even gangsters would find it in their interests to "renounce legal prosecution" reminds us that particular parties' interest in secrecy concerning the resolution of their disputes is not sufficient to justify it as a routine matter of public policy. While it would be foolish to suppose that privacy is never appropriate, it seems to me even more foolish and even dangerous (from the point of view of protecting the public good) to assume it is appropriate (i.e., morally right and reasonable) to exclude everyone but the directly participating parties in every case of international commercial arbitration.

Building that assumption into the Model Law and its templates practically gave people whose primary interests were their own private profits a license to pursue those interests regardless of the impact on the public at large.

3 The third most frequently mentioned advantage of international commercial arbitration is the security of enforcement (Law Reform Commission of British Columbia 1982, 3, Paterson 1987, 114). For Chibueze (2001, 193), "By far the most important convention on international commercial arbitration is the Convention on the Recognition and Enforcement of Foreign Arbitral Awards ... The New York Convention put into place a treaty system, which now assures the recognition and enforcement of foreign arbitral awards within contracting states."

In his view, the Model Law provided even stronger enforcement protection (194).

Similarly, Wilberforce (1987, 10) wrote: "Apart from inter-European judgments, governed by the 1968 Convention, it can probably be said that arbitration awards are generally more easily enforced than Court judgments. The New York Convention gives a much more convenient and effective method of enforcing arbitration awards than anything you can find as regards Court judgments except, as I have said, the European judgments."

He congratulated the British Columbians for using the Model Law as a template for the enforcement provisions in their Act. Because of Article 7(2) of the New York Convention, when new agreements with even stronger provisions than the Convention are initiated, those agreements take precedence over the Convention (Sono 1987, 25).

An excellent review of judicial standards used in u.s. federal and state courts to determine whether or not commercial arbitration awards might be overruled ("vacated") may be found in Hayford (1996). Very briefly, he mentioned the four grounds listed in Section 10(a) of the u.s. Federal Arbitration Act:

> where an award was procured by corruption, fraud, or undue means ... there was evident partiality or corruption in the arbitrators, or either of them ... the arbitrators were guilty of misconduct ... [or] exceeded their powers, or so imperfectly executed them plus one or more "nonstatutory" grounds warranting vacatur of an otherwise valid commercial arbitration award. Primary among those nonstatutory grounds are a "manifest disregard" of the law by the arbitrator, a conflict between the award and a clear and well established "public policy," an award that is "arbitrary and capricious" or "completely irrational,"

and a failure of the award to "draw its essence" from the parties' contract ... vacatur under the "public policy" ground requires something more than a mere error or misunderstanding of the relevant law by the arbitrator. Under all of the articulations of this nonstatutory ground, the public policy at issue must be a clearly defined, dominant, and undisputed rule of law. (Hayford 1996, 738–9, 782)

Notwithstanding the usual requirements for application of the "public policy" grounds for vacatur, some judges have expressed concerns about the "inferior system of justice" provided by commercial arbitration processes (Hayford 1996, 807). It is indeed questionable whether superior systems of justice should be dragged in only to enforce decisions of commercial arbitration tribunals or panels when those decisions may have been poorly supported and ill-conceived, and have grave consequences for third parties who were denied representation in the arbitration proceedings. Park and Paulsson were right when they wrote that "The commercial community desires finality in private dispute resolution. But national judicial systems may wish to protect other values, such as the integrity of the adjudicatory process and respect for the rights of third parties ... the commercial community's need for finality in the resolution of private disputes inevitably competes with the desirability of uniform application of law ... Wisdom dictates that the State of arbitration exercise some control over the integrity of the proceedings and the interests of third parties" (Park and Paulsson 1983, 254, 284–5).

4 The flexibility of international commercial arbitration procedures compared to court litigation is almost always emphasized as an advantage, e.g., Dezalay and Garth 1996, 158; Law Commission of New Zealand 1991, 59; Chibueze 2001, 192. "Flexibility" is a euphemism for "user-friendly procedures" from the point of view of those engaged in commercial trade. Brower and Steven (2001, 197) claimed that the investor-state dispute resolution procedures in the NAFTA were superior to state-to-state adjudication procedures as the latter tended to produce arbitrary decisions because "the exigencies of time, money, political priorities, and the whims of individual bureaucrats may cause a government to downgrade, or even ignore, meritorious claims." As revealed in chapters 10–12, the flexibility of the investor-state rules of the NAFTA also opened the door for arbitrary decisions that probably would have received much more public scrutiny in a state-to-state forum. As well, as I illustrate in chapter 16, the AIT rules of procedure were in some ways too flexible to provide clear

guidance to all parties regarding exactly what was procedurally required and what was merely recommended. The panel was therefore left to pick and choose those provisions and interpretations that seemed most appropriate to them, which, as one might have expected, led to some controversial judgments.

5 International commercial arbitration is typically regarded as faster than litigation, e.g., Hoellering 1987, 20–1; Law Commission of New Zealand 1991, 59; Chibueze 2001, 192. As indicated earlier, speed is often mistaken for efficiency (Dezalay and Garth 1996, 141). Brower and Steven (2001, 197) claimed that the investor-state dispute resolution procedures in the NAFTA were superior to state-to-state adjudication procedures as the latter tended to produce inefficiencies because "governments are pressured to prosecute, or at least investigate, a great number of frivolous claims that would not otherwise be pressed if the responsibility and cost of prosecution remained with the individual investor." However, such costs could be passed on to individual investors just as, for example, the EPA demanded industrial research at the expense of industries directly involved with and standing to gain from the sale of certain products (see chapter 5). Furthermore, not only frivolous but preposterous claims challenging parliamentary privilege were introduced in the NAFTA MMT case (see chapter 11). On the other hand, the Ethyl Corporation was able to get its "day in court" under the investor-state provisions of NAFTA Chapter 11 after failing to get the U.S. government to proceed against the Canadian government under the state-to-state provisions of Chapter 20 (Clarkson 2002b, 380).

Granting that "a speedier hearing is ... theoretically possible," the Law Reform Commission of British Columbia (1982, 2–3) noted that the advantage was "not always realized." According to Dezalay and Garth (1996, 57), when there are strategic reasons and/or the likelihood of greater profits from delays, international commercial arbitration procedures may be easier to exploit than court procedures. From the point of view of the parties' lawyers, one aim is paramount, namely, "winning a good result" for their clients. Thus "To get that result, they are ready to exploit any procedural tactics and forums available to them. They are willing to create difficulties for their colleagues and the arbitral tribunal and even to damage the image of this justice – which had pretended to be rapid and less costly because informal" (57).

When their actions are challenged, the lawyers retreat to a species of the demonstrably unsound Loyal Agent's Argument (Michalos 1979). "The litigators respond matter-of-factly that it is only a matter of fulfilling their duty as lawyers and protecting, by all legal means at their disposal, their clients' interest" (Dezalay and Garth 1996, 57).

As argued earlier and later in this book, if the perceived appropriate recipient population for decision-makers engaged in international commercial arbitration is considerably smaller than the population adversely affected by resulting awards, there is good reason to doubt the appropriateness of that procedure as an instrument of public policy-making. A decision procedure that systematically neglects the interests of people affected by it cannot be regarded as reasonable, moral, or suitable for making public policy in purportedly democratic societies.

6 The superior technical expertise of arbitrators compared to ordinary judges is another frequently mentioned advantage of international commercial arbitration, e.g., Law Reform Commission of British Columbia 1982, 2; Law Commission of New Zealand 1991, 59; Jakubowski 1982, 181. According to Brower and Steven (2001, 200) "The arbitrators participating in [international commercial arbitration] are highly competent members of academia and the international bar, with experience and expertise in the relevant areas of law exceeding that of the vast majority of the domestic judiciary in each of the three NAFTA countries." While the AIT was crafted to manage domestic trade disputes, it was "based on the premise that the experts who know the subject matter intimately should try to resolve [issues] in the first place" (Miller 1995, 153). According to Howse (1995, 175), "A progressive feature of the Agreement on Internal Trade is that panels dealing with environmental disputes are required by Article 1510(2) to make use of environmental experts and that rosters of panelists must include such experts ... The use of ad hoc panels to decide disputes under the agreement also raises the concern of whether a sufficiently large roster of eligible persons can be found to handle the caseload. This is already becoming an issue in the FTA and the NAFTA Chapter Nineteen panels."

As it turned out, none of the panelists for the AIT case concerning MMT was expert in any relevant environmental sciences or automotive mechanics. In fact, at least one of the panelists explicitly acknowledged the relative absence of scientific expertise on the panel.

The Law Reform Commission of British Columbia (1982, 3) reminded us that if important issues of law rather than fact are involved in a case, the technical expertise of judges might well be superior to that of an arbitrator. Lord Wilberforce (1987, 13) also remarked that it is often difficult to decide "what is an error of law and what is an error of fact."

As assessed by Dezalay and Garth, businesses consider the most attractive and preferred technical expertise for international commercial arbitration is a sympathetic understanding of the interests of business. Since the interest of business and arbitrators is primarily profit, it is not difficult for each group to find suitable partners. According to Max Weber, the increasing importance of particularism in law, especially in commercial law ... comes from pressure exercised by merchants to have their legal affairs treated by specialized experts. Arbitration responds effectively to this need, since it permits merchants to choose arbitrators who are either directly or indirectly familiar with their business problems. The arbitrators may even be predisposed to listen sympathetically to business arguments of the major players in order to protect their careers as arbitrators" (Dezalay and Garth 1996, 117).

I did not see any evidence that members of the NAFTA tribune and the AIT panel listened "sympathetically to business arguments ... to protect their careers," but it does appear unwise, if not immoral, to craft a conflict resolution procedure to protect the public good such that the main users of the procedure may select judges generally sympathetic to their interests, whether or not those interests place the public good above all others. Who would suppose that the biased justice that might result from arbitrators who possess the preferred "technical expertise" would necessarily be advantageous for the public good?

7 Finally, international commercial arbitration is alleged to be less expensive than court litigation, e.g., Dezalay and Garth 1996, 156; Law Reform Commission of British Columbia 1982, 2; Law Commission of New Zealand 1991, 59. Although the two commissions mentioned the standard argument, they both acknowledged that arbitration can also be more expensive than litigation. Here again, flexibility may work for or against parties (Allison 1986). Wilberforce (1987, 10) remarked that while courts are relatively free, "one notices the difference when three arbitrators have to be paid." For Nemetz (1987, 4), "the question of costs is an open question. I have in mind the complaints of a number of corporations as to the mounting costs of arbitration. In a recent commercial case in British Columbia the matters arbitrated went on for almost a year ... It was suggested to me that the entire matter could have been resolved much faster and at a lesser cost in Court."

Reflecting on the philosophical and socio-economic roots and the most frequently alleged advantages of international commercial arbitration, one clearly sees that all of the procedures and supporting institutions were socially constructed by a wide variety of architects with an equally wide variety of personal, public, professional, and commercial interests. If the systems remain fragile, as I think Dezalay and Garth showed, it is partly the result of their disparate and controversial foundations. Although widely accepted by proponents of the most salient systems of international commercial arbitration, the Principle of Autonomy has some very problematic implications that cannot be ignored. Near the end of their excellent report, the authors of the Law Commission of New Zealand reminded us of the great unanswered question" "How is the balance between party autonomy and the general law to be struck? If choices are to be made in the drafting and later in the application and interpretation of the law, should the present emphasis on autonomy continue? That is a pervasive matter which arises throughout the Report" (70).

I suppose everyone will accept the proposition that the scope of application for private arbitration is fundamentally a policy choice that governments have to make (Paterson and Thompson 1987, 2). Not everyone will accept my version of moral consequentialism as the final standard against which the legitimacy of a system of international commercial arbitration based on the Principle of Autonomy should be tested. Given the complexities involved in applying it, reasonable people accepting the standard might disagree about any particular application, i.e., they might disagree about the alleged benefit-cost ratio contingently calculated for a question like "All things considered, is it (morally) right to use international commercial arbitration procedures to resolve disputes involving parties not represented in those procedures?" Nevertheless, these difficulties do not remove our burden of trying to answer the question.

In Graham's detailed analysis of the Model Law, he noted that a long list of considerations that judges might have regarded as relevant to their decisions concerning the enforcement of arbitration provisions was rendered inapplicable because of Article 8. According to that article, "(1) A court before which an action is brought in a matter which is the subject of an arbitration agreement shall, if a party so requests not later than when submitting his first statement on the substance of the dispute, refer the parties to arbitration unless it finds that the agreement is null and void, inoperative or incapable of being performed. (2) Where an action referred to in paragraph (1) of this article has been brought, arbitral proceedings may nevertheless be commenced or continued, and an award may be made, while the issue is pending before the court" (Graham 1987, 84–7).

According to Graham:

I think that the classes of non-arbitrable cases should be kept to a minimum and that the following principle should guide our Courts in considering this issue: arbitration should be allowed unless some clear
injustice would result. In other words we should foster a bias in favour
of arbitration rather than against it. Otherwise we will be failing to
recognize the special nature of these international commercial arrangements and failing to give effect to the clear signal sent by the British
Columbia legislator that this new law represents a radical break from
the past. No other interpretation, it is submitted, can be drawn from
the preamble to the statute which expressly recognizes that "British
Columbia has not previously enjoyed a hospitable legal environment
for international commercial arbitrations" ... This liberal approach to
international commercial arbitration in particular is the correct
approach. (Graham 1987, 91)

I wonder what could be more clearly an act of injustice than a procedure
that adversely affects your well-being but prevents you from even voicing
your opposition, let alone taking direct action to avoid the adverse affects.
Consistent with the Principle of Autonomy and the provisions of the Model
Law, in the NAFTA and AIT MMT cases, consumers whose diagnostic systems
controlling their motor vehicle emissions may have been adversely affected
– with possible adverse effects on their own health and that of others close
to them – were simply excluded from the dispute settlement proceedings.
Regardless of the actual harm suffered by those consumers and others, did
they not have a moral right to a voice in the proceedings? Insofar as the
likelihood of satisfying the moral consequentialist standard would have
been decreased in their absence and increased in their presence, it is difficult
to resist the conclusion that such people would have had a moral right to a
voice. While there is no more certainty concerning this conclusion than
there is in the widely held view that democracy is superior to all other
forms of government precisely because it gives everyone in the community
an equal voice, it seems to me that this widely held view is probably true.

In contrast to Jakubowski's notion that the legitimacy of a system of
international commercial arbitration is ultimately derived a priori from its
philosophical foundations, Dezalay and Garth claimed that the legitimacy
of international commercial arbitration is established a posteriori in competitive struggles among "moral entrepreneurs":

A central theme in sociolegal research is how the legitimacy of law is maintained so that it can provide a basis to govern matters that involve powerful economic and political entities ... The study of international commercial arbitration allows us to see how international private justice – lacking the legitimacy of the state court system – has become established and recognized almost universally as legitimate for business disputes. Competition among key actors and groups ... serves to construct legal legitimacy and at the same time promote law in the service of merchants. The competition, however, is not simply a matter of striving for business by offering better services. International commercial arbitration is a symbolic field, and therefore the competitive battles that take place within it are fought in symbolic terms among moral entrepreneurs. Battles fought in terms of legitimacy and credibility then serve a double role. They build careers and markets for those who are successful in this competition, and they build the legitimacy and credibility of international legal practices and international institutions. (Dezalay and Garth 1996, 33)

Thus, in this account, moral entrepreneurs provide the leadership in the social construction of the moral legitimacy of dispute resolution procedures that are commercially attractive enough to survive in a free market for such procedures. The moral legitimacy of the procedures has a foundation insofar as it flows partly from the status of the moral entrepreneurs selling the procedures. However, unlike the logical account described by Jakubowski, that foundation is not sufficient to legitimize the procedures. Commercial success provides the additional necessary condition which, in combination with the status of the supporting moral entrepreneurs, is sufficient to legitimize the procedures. While this "sociolegal" account does not exclude the logical account, it is empirically more accurate. Most importantly, the latter account introduces a nonmoral element into the concept of legitimacy being applied. One cannot help but wonder how the two elements are weighed in that concept. Would the status of the moral entrepreneurs still be necessary regardless of the size of the commercial success of the procedures? Would the Mafia's kangaroo courts require both elements? Reflecting on the question of why the parties were "willing to ignore NAFTA violations by one another that clearly would be proper matters for the Agreement's dispute resolution systems," Lopez (1997, 207) considered the growth in trade over the first few years of the agreement and wrote, "Apparently, a lot of isolated trade conflicts can be overlooked for average revenue increases of $40 billion annually."

Dezalay and Garth (1996, 204–5) described the delicate balance that must be maintained between the moral and nonmoral elements: "The autonomy necessary to legitimate a more expansive business justice requires a distance – or, more precisely, the public perception of distance – with respect to the vulgar logic of business and commerce. Here, as elsewhere in the legal field, the legitimacy of law and justice is poorly served by a too strict or too visible involvement with power and money ... But behind the façade of condemnation of the market we can find multiple ties between the universe of business and that of law."

Besides moral, legal and economic legitimacy, one may add an element of social legitimacy. Using an example particularly relevant to our story, Macdonald (2002, 82) explained the subtle pursuit of this sort of legitimacy by the oil and automotive industries:

the issue of climate change, once it is posed as a transportation and land-use issue, poses a threat to the basic economic interests of the oil and automotive industries. Cars manufactured today generate far less pollution per mile driven than ever before. The automobile industry has also come to pursue a policy interest of co-operation with governments in the regulation of both per-mile pollution and pollution generated during car production, the latter ... to be done on a voluntary basis. On the other hand, it has worked with the oil industry to engage in defensive lobbying on the issue of climate change. Effective policy measures to reduce fossil fuel emissions, such as the increased land-use density needed to make transit systems viable, would result in a reduction in the total number of miles driven each year and, therefore, cars and gasoline purchased. Neither of these sectors has proposed voluntary measures to achieve that objective.

The conclusion to be drawn is that business has primarily worked to achieve social legitimacy by making those behaviour changes that are already in accordance with its own value of increased efficiency. When the goal of legitimacy has clashed too strongly with the fundamental objective of the firm, profit maximization, legitimacy has had to take second place.

These findings have implications for both applied environmental policy-making and academic understanding of that process. In terms of theoretical understanding, they point to the need for a more sophisticated conceptualization of the interest of the actors ... Second, the connection between self-interest and contribution to the larger good must be carefully considered in each case. It seems reasonable to assume that policy actors seek both, but to determine how they balance the two goals when they are in contradiction we must examine specific cases, opening up the black box of the interest group, government department, or firm to determine how each establishes its policy objective.

In the MMT cases we will examine, the oil and automotive industries seem to have found themselves in a zero-sum game in which only one side could achieve its own "fundamental objective." Roughly speaking, the automotive industry had the federal government on its side, while the oil industry had the provinces and the terms and procedures of the NAFTA and AIT agreements on its side. When the broader interests of the public good were weighed in the balance against the narrower interest of minimally restricting trade, the latter carried more weight, first in the AIT case and then in the NAFTA case. Proponents of the agreements would say that insofar as the terms and procedures of the two agreements served to minimally restrict trade, everyone's economic interests were served. What's more, since those interests are positively correlated with many other interests, the NAFTA and AIT provisions are not only economically legitimate but also socially legitimate. Thus, examination of the MMT cases suggests a simple resolution of the balancing problem for the two industries as they pursued the goals of "self-interest and contribution to the larger good." If everyone wins when trade wins (Trebilcock 2001; Hart and Dymond 2002), then the dispute settlement procedures of the NAFTA and AIT effectively removed the need for anyone to consider balancing interests. Each side could put all its resources into the pursuit of its own interests and, with a nod to the ghost of Adam Smith's invisible hand, rest assured that whichever side won, the greater public good was served. Allison (1986, 393) provided a quotation from Justice Black in *Northern Pacific Railway Co. v. United States* (1958) that wonderfully illustrated this optimistic view: "The Sherman Act was designed to be a comprehensive charter of economic liberty aimed at preserving free and unfettered competition as the rule of trade. It rests on the premise that the unrestrained interaction of competitive forces will yield the best allocation of our economic resources, the lowest prices, the highest quality and the greatest material progress, while at the same time providing an environment conducive to the preservation of our democratic political and social institutions."

Unfortunately, we have seen (chapter 3) some pretty persuasive evidence that the visible hand of the NAFTA tends to undermine the work of Smith's invisible hand. In chapter 16, I try to show that the visible hand of the AIT may be equally destructive. For present purposes it is enough to remember that Macdonald's main point was that the social legitimacy of an action or policy might be established by showing that it achieved some sort of appropriate balance between "self-interest and contribution to the larger good." He did not specify exactly who would do the calculation, using what array of answers to some or all of the nineteen basic questions listed in chapter 2, but he gave us enough to distinguish his approach to constructing legitimacy from those of Jakubowski and Dezalay and Garth.

Swinton (1995) and Howse (1995) suggested that the AIT in general and the dispute resolution procedures in particular might be legitimated "in political practice." In the latter's view, "the higher the quality of dispute rulings and the more they are grounded in a coherent and consistent interpretation of the agreement, the more politically difficult it will be for governments to walk away from their commitment to free internal trade" (171). According to the former, "the agreement is likely to gain legitimacy over time, as some governments, at least, commit themselves to its obligations. That process is likely to be accelerated if the monitoring and dispute settlement processes are kept as open as possible, allowing public participation and oversight of compliance. Therefore, this is a document that will probably have significant effects on government action, whatever its technical legal status" (205).

In short, given enough time and perceived acceptable practice, the AIT and presumably the NAFTA dispute resolution procedures might achieve political legitimacy. Regarding the NAFTA, Clarkson (2002b`, 381–6) reached a very different conclusion. In his view, "several basic values held dear in the common law tradition are violated" by the investor-state provisions of Chapter 11.

Transparency is the first victim in this secret world of commercial arbitration ... *Arbitrariness* is another quality of this new corporatized justice ... *Neutrality* is another legal value that falls by the wayside ... *Judicial sovereignty* is still another victim of this extraordinary addition to the Canadian legal order ... NAFTA was unlikely to enjoy high legitimacy among the public so long as it empowered the continental market ... by reducing member states' capacities and by making it possible for capital to discipline governments that stood in its way.

Exclusion of citizens from a privatized continental justice system is a further de-legitimizing feature ... The restriction of standing to corporate and governmental players further skews the course of continental justice ... The democratic deficit accompanying NAFTA's legal deficit also involves the organized role of citizens ... Given that citizens and their

NGOs can neither launch a complaint nor be involved until the matter reaches the panel stage, the public is effectively shut out of the various dispute settlement processes of continental governance ... The whole principle of endowing foreign corporations with rights to sue national governments in an international commercial legal order is equivalent to gangrene. The problem can only be resolved by surgically removing the investor-state dispute process from Chapter 11.

Apparently, from Clarkson's point of view, the clash between our basic values and the provisions of Chapter 11 is so great that there cannot be any reconciliation.

Dispute Settlement in the NAFTA and AIT

This chapter provides a general overview of the most salient features of the dispute settlement provisions in the NAFTA and AIT, and of critical assessments of those features. Four chapters of the NAFTA have dispute settlement provisions. Generally speaking, Chapter 11 provisions apply to investment, Chapter 14 to financial services, Chapter 19 to anti-dumping and countervailing duty, and Chapter 20 to interpretations and applications of the NAFTA. Chapter 11 is divided into three sections. Section A describes the general scope of the chapter, including relatively standard international trade treaty rules for such things as national treatment, most-favored nation, minimum standards and, as we have already seen, performance requirements. Section B describes "a mechanism for the settlement of investment disputes ... among investors of the Parties in accordance with the principle of international reciprocity and due process before an impartial tribunal" (NAFTA 2002, Article 1115). Article 1118 instructs parties to "first attempt to settle a claim through consultation or negotiation" and, if that fails, to proceed to arbitration according to the regime explained in Articles 1119 to 1138. Article 1136.1 gives awards made by tribunals "no binding force except between the disputing parties and in respect of the particular case," while Article 1136.4 ensures that "Each Party shall provide for the enforcement of an award in its territory." Section C contains a list of basic definitions.

Article 1122.1 says that "Each Party consents to the submission of a claim to arbitration in accordance with the procedures set out in this Agreement" (NAFTA 2002). In Eklund's view:

This pre-commitment to arbitration by the Parties represents one of the most innovative aspects of NAFTA and illustrates a strong commitment

to the efficient resolution of investor-State disputes. By virtue of Article
1122, the consent and submission of a claim to arbitration under Chapter Eleven also satisfies the technical requirements of the Convention on the Settlement of Investment Disputes Between States and Nationals of Other States (ICSID Convention) [18 March 1965], the United Nations (New York) Convention on the Recognition and Enforcement of Foreign Arbitral Awards (New York Convention [10 June 1958]), and the Inter-American (Panama) Convention on International Commercial Arbitration (Inter-American Convention [30 January 1975]). Each of these Conventions represents an integral part of the dispute resolution mechanism under Section B, that being the enforcement of Chapter Eleven awards. (Eklund 1994, 136)

As one would expect, I believe that the notion of efficiency referred to by Eklund is too narrow to support any general argument for the efficiency of the investor-state arbitration mechanism in the robust sense of this term as required by my version of moral consequentialism. However, others apparently take the same narrow view of efficient action, which has led to a deep division of opinion regarding the legitimacy of the mechanism. Unfortunately, this particular problem applies equally to arbitration in the NAFTA and in the AIT.

According to Article 1120.1, "a disputing investor may submit the claim to arbitration under:

(a) the ICSID Convention, provided that both the disputing Party and the Party of the investor are parties to the convention;
(b) the Additional Facility Rules of ICSID, provided that either the disputing Party or the Party of the investor, but not both, is a party to the ICSID convention; or
(c) the UNCITRAL Arbitration Rules". (NAFTA 2002)

NAFTA Chapter 11 does not exclude judicial review, but it does not have its own provisions for appealing tribunal awards. The ICSID and UNCITRAL rules do have such provisions. Article 32.2 of the UNCITRAL Arbitration Rules makes Tribunal awards "final and binding on the parties," but Article 33 allows the parties to designate all applicable law (UNCITRAL 2002), including that of review. The NAFTA MMT case was arbitrated under the UNCITRAL Arbitration Rules, but was settled without a tribunal final decision or appeal. Had there been an appeal of a final decision, Canadian national law would have applied.

In Canada, Article 34 of the Federal Code provides for judicial review of international arbitration awards. A competent court may set aside an arbitral award if, *inter alia*, the party making the application furnishes proof that it was not given proper notice of the appointment of an arbitrator; the award deals with a dispute not contemplated by or falling within the terms of the submission to arbitration; or, the award is in conflict with the public policy of Canada. There are few reported cases which address the judicial review of arbitration awards under the Federal Code. However, case-law considering provincial legislation in Canada clearly reveals that Canadian courts will defer to the decision of the tribunal and will not interfere in international commercial arbitration awards in absence of sufficiently compelling circumstances ... The current law in British Columbia, and by analogy, other jurisdictions in Canada, bodes well for the autonomy of arbitral decisions made by Chapter Eleven Tribunals. (Eklund 1994, 154–5)

Eklund was relatively enthusiastic about the NAFTA dispute settlement "mechanism," and about the autonomy of arbitral tribunals. Here is a fair summary statement of her position, which is shared by several other writers:

Given the specialized nature of NAFTA investor-State disputes and the established expertise of arbitrators who adjudicate them, it is inconceivable that an investor would elect to litigate a Chapter Eleven dispute before a national court ... Concerning the review of an award, the impossibility of judicial review during or after proceedings makes arbitration under the ICSID Rules the most appealing of the Rules. Until such time as Canada and/or Mexico become signatories to the ICSID Convention, no Chapter Eleven investor-State disputes will be decided under the most efficient, and arguably the most cost-effective regime for the resolution of Chapter Eleven investor-State disputes – the ICSID Rules. (Eklund 1994, 157–8)

Because the NAFTA case was settled without a complete set of hearings and final award on the merits, most of the provisions from section B that might have played a crucial role had little impact. The limited role that they did play is discussed in chapters 11 and 12. At this point, my contextualizing aims can best be served by presenting an array of controversial issues that have been raised by many writers since the initial discussions of the NAFTA. Some of them reach all the way back to the initial discussions of the CUSTA.

An excellent report by Public Citizen and Friends of the Earth (Public Citizen 2001) reviewed a number of objections that have been raised against the NAFTA Chapter 11 (cf. Sornarajah 2003 and Clarkson 2003). Some of the issues raised may be illustrated by the MMT case.

1 The investor-to-state dispute resolution procedure allows investors to sue governments and, if successful, to win compensation from the taxpayers of a country without going through "the country's domestic court system and domestic laws" (Public Citizen 2001, i, iv). Although the Ethyl Corporation sued the Canadian government for U.S.$251 million, it was finally awarded only U.S.$13 million (C$19.3 million) (Soloway 1999, 55).

2 Investors can use the dispute resolution procedure to press cases already lost in domestic courts, thereby undermining state/provincial and municipal laws, e.g., to challenge "sovereign immunity" (Public Citizen 2001, ii, iv, vi, vii).

3 If Chapter 11 provisions are extended to the Free Trade Agreement of the Americas (FTAA), as currently proposed, the harms being done in the three NAFTA countries could be multiplied to thirty-one more countries (Public Citizen 2001, iii).

4 Because the Fast Track procedure was used in the United States, many members of Congress who supported the NAFTA were unaware of the provisions in Chapter 11 (Public Citizen 2001, iii).

5 Because cases adjudicated under Chapter 11 are "decided behind closed doors," it is difficult to get information on the proceedings and, therefore, difficult to know exactly what, if any, immediate or long-term damage was done (Public Citizen 2001, iii). This objection was addressed by the governments of Canada and the United States in an announcement released in both countries on 7 October 2003:

> Having reviewed the operation of arbitration proceedings conducted under Chapter Eleven of the North American Free Trade Agreement, Canada [and the United States] affirms that it will consent, and will request the consent of disputing investors and, as applicable, tribunals, that hearings in Chapter Eleven disputes to which it is a party be open to the public, except to ensure the protection of confidential information, including business confidential information. Canada [and the United States] recommends that tribunals determine the appropriate logistical arrangements for open hearings in consultation with disputing parties. These arrangements may include, for example, use of closed-circuit television systems, Internet webcasting, or other

forms of access. (http://www.dfait-maeci.gc.ca/NAFTA-alena/ open-hearing-en.asp)

Presumably, the excessive warranty claims that motor vehicle manufacturers shared with parties to the MMT cases for malfunctioning catalytic converters would have been regarded as "business confidential information" and, therefore, not subject to public disclosure. If so, the new dispensation would still allow businesses to have greater protection than consumers, which seems to me to at least require some reasonable effort at justification.

6 Because there is no requirement to give notice to anyone that a Chapter 11 case has been filed, many cases may have been filed and settled without public knowledge, regardless of what damage may have been done to some public interest (Public Citizen 2001, iii–iv). According to the International Institute for Sustainable Development and World Wildlife Fund report, "The consequence of secrecy at this stage is important: it provides foreign investors and their companies operating in the host state with privileged but private access to government decision-makers on actual or proposed measures. In effect, the virtually cost-free notice of intent to arbitrate is an exclusive opportunity to lobby, influence, maybe even to threaten, the government on any measure a foreign investor does not like, far from the prying eyes of the public" (IISD/WWF 2001, 42; VanDuzer 2002, 64, apparently agreed).

7 Foreign investors who are made to comply with certain domestic laws in the United States can use Chapter 11 provisions to claim compensation from the U.S. government on the grounds of "regulatory takings," although American citizens and companies cannot make such claims (Public Citizen 2001, iv–v, 5; cf. Kukucha 2003, 73). "In 1993, the U.S. Supreme Court ruled that 'our cases have long established that mere diminution in the value of property, however serious, is insufficient to demonstrate a taking'" (Public Citizen 2001, 4). As late as 31 July 2001, when the trade ministers from the three NAFTA countries (i.e., the Free Trade Commission) met, no change was made in the regulatory takings provisions of Chapter 11 (Public Citizen 2001, x).

William Greider called this particular feature "the most disturbing aspect of Chapter 11":

NAFTA's new investor protections actually mimic a radical revision of constitutional law that the American right has been aggressively pushing for years – redefining public regulation as a government "taking" of private property that requires compensation to the owners, just as when government takes private land for a highway or park it has to pay its fair value. Because any new regulation is bound to have some economic impact on private assets, this doctrine is a formula to shrink the reach of modern government and cripple the regulatory state – undermining long-established protections for social welfare and economic justice, environmental values and individual rights. Right-wing advocates frankly state that objective – restoring the primacy of property against society's broader claims ... "NAFTA checks the excesses of unilateral sovereignty," Washington lawyer Daniel Price told a scholarly forum in Cleveland. He ought to know, since he was the lead US negotiator on Chapter 11 a decade ago. As for anyone troubled by the intrusions on US sovereignty, he said, "My only advice is, get over it". Price, who heads international practice at Powell, Goldstein, Frazer & Murphy, a premier Washington firm, says that contrary to the widely held assumption that suits like Methanex's [see Sinclair 2007] represent an unintended consequence of NAFTA, the architects of NAFTA knew exactly what they were creating. "The parties did not stumble into this," he said. "This was a carefully crafted definition" ...

I asked Christopher Dugan, lead lawyer for Methanex, why the company did not pursue its complaint in US courts ... "We wanted an impartial tribunal," he said. "If you look at it, foreign investors do have a substantial reason to avoid the US judicial process. NAFTA does clearly create some rights for foreign investors that local citizens and companies don't have. But that's the whole purpose of it." (Greider 2002, 2–8)

Excellent reviews of the legal issues and history concerning "takings" legislation in international law generally and in the United States, Canada, and Mexico in particular may be found in Wagner (1999) and Cordes (1997). Contrary to Greider, Brower and Steven (2001, 200) wrote:

Canada effectively has agreed with those public interest groups that interpret investor claims under Article 1110 as a cynical and illegitimate attempt to bypass the domestic political process and undermine environmental and other public interest laws, regulations, and procedures.

Understandable as it may be, this concern is short-sighted and misplaced. What the NAFTA Parties set out to accomplish – the protection and promotion of investment through the uniform application of rules and guarantees in all three NAFTA countries – can best be sustained through the enforcement of Chapter 11 by independent and impartial international tribunals.

As we saw in chapter 9, Brower and Steven believed that hired arbitrators are better equipped than ordinary judges to adjudicate cases of international commercial arbitration.

Soloway (2003) claimed that since "there has been only one successful expropriation claim under Chapter 11," "there is no clearly established need for change" (6, 29). Besides, she reviewed several possible ways to try to improve the particular article creating the problem (Article 1110), but could not find an acceptable one. She rejected the "Domestic Law" approach because she thought it would undermine "the rationale for including the rules regarding expropriation in NAFTA" (25).

Examination of the summary of cases presented in Sinclair 2007 reveals that:

> There have been 46 claims, with a roughly equal number against each country (15 against Canada, 14 against the U.S. and 17 against Mexico) ... In the four decided cases against the U.S. to date, the investor's claims have been dismissed. By contrast, tribunals have awarded damages to the complaining investors in both decided claims against Canada. Canada also settled a third claim (the MMT case) "out of court" ... Tribunals have awarded damages to the complaining investors in two claims against Mexico, while five claims against Mexico have been dismissed ... A high number of claims (13 of 46) involve challenges to environmental protection measures ... Foreign investors are also aggressively challenging measures that governments maintained were not covered by NAFTA. For example, there are ongoing challenges related to water exports, log export controls, public postal services, Canada's agricultural supply management system, Canadian cultural policy, and other matters which were supposedly excluded from the NAFTA. (Sinclair 2007, 14)

Without a careful analysis of each claim, it is impossible to decide whether this is as good as Soloway thinks or as bad as critics think. But I doubt that one should judge a law primarily on the basis of the actual harms resulting from its use, rather than on the basis of the potential harms its use might allow. A law that would allow the cold-blooded murder of innocent people in a community of saints might satisfy Soloway's test regardless of its moral repugnance.

McGuire (2002) had a particularly insightful view of the issues. She felt that:

[Chapter 11 did not place governments under any] obligation to provide superior treatment to foreign investors on matters of expropriation. That is not what is meant by according treatment "under international law." There simply is no "international definition" of expropriation to be applied to foreign investors.

Nor, I would argue, should there ever be one definition. The definition of expropriation, and especially indirect expropriation, is but one aspect of the balance of property rights and obligations created in each state. That balance and, therefore, that definition will vary from state to state. If a domestic court – such as the US Supreme Court – cannot settle on one, definitive statement on the line between a taking and a regulation, why would one expect to find such a statement in international law? (McGuire 2002, 172)

8 The possibility of government compensation provides an incentive for investors to push the envelope in a variety of areas to see which laws and/or rulings may be overridden in NAFTA trials (Public Citizen 2001, viii). One of the most important areas in which the Ethyl Corporation tried to "push the envelope" in the NAFTA MMT case involved parliamentary privilege (see chapter 11 for details). If the challenge had been successful, the Government of Canada would have had to compensate Ethyl for any damage done to its reputation resulting from public debates in the House of Commons as well as for comments made by Members of Parliament outside the House in discussions with news media people about federal government policies.

9 Because the ICSID and UNCITRAL rules used by NAFTA tribunals were designed to "arbitrate private cases between contractual parties in narrow commercial disputes," they are poor procedures to use to adjudicate matters of general public interest and public policy (Public Citizen 2001, v, 3, 7; Soloway 2000, 109). Much more than the NAFTA/UNCITRAL rules, the AIT rules are clearly designed to accommodate broader discussions involving the general public interest. However, in spite of such provisions, the MMT panel working under the AIT rules tended to take a narrow commercial focus (see Chapter 16).

10 The "potential cost" to taxpayers resulting from NAFTA panel decisions could be disastrously large for governments (Public Citizen 2001, vi; Soloway 2000, 102). This is especially the case if, like the MMT tribunal, other tribunals are allowed to erroneously adjudicate "trade in goods"

cases by procedures designed for "investment" cases, contrary to explicit NAFTA rules (cf. IISD/WWF 2001, 16). Clarke and Barlow (1998, 37) crafted a version of a "potential cost" argument leading from the NAFTA MMT case to the now defunct Multilateral Agreement on Investment (MAI):

The MMT case is the first in the world where a national government has been forced by an international agreement [NAFTA] not only to reverse a law it had enacted but also to pay compensation to the transnational corporation that had challenged that law. Under the MAI, potentially every country in the world would be subject to this kind of challenge from every corporation in the world. And citizens would have to foot the bill. It doesn't take a great leap of imagination to foresee a day when corporations build into their business plans a strategy to seek compensation from the public for the cost of complying with health or environmental regulation.

Notwithstanding the neglect of the role of the AIT MMT case in the outcome of the NAFTA MMT case, the suggestion that the dispute settlement provisions of a trade agreement might function as a profit-making factor of production for private corporations is not at all far-fetched, as indicated in chapter 9.

11 Because NAFTA tribunals are liable to make arbitrary decisions, governments face considerable uncertainty about what actions are or are not legal under NAFTA (Public Citizen 2001, vi). The MMT cases adjudicated under both NAFTA and AIT rules illustrate problems of arbitrariness and uncertainty (see chapters 12 and 16).

12 The uncertainty that governments face is bound to make them reluctant to introduce legislation based on a precautionary principle that might be warranted to protect public health or the environment, i.e., uncertainty might have a "chilling effect" on some types of legislation (Public Citizen 2001, vii; IISD/WWF 2001, 1). According to Wagner (1999, 520–1):

To distinguish between legitimate environmental measures and disguised illegitimate measures, it is reasonable to require that the existence of the risk to the environment be scientifically supported. It is essential, however, that the need for scientific support not become a requirement that the government demonstrate that its measure is supported by "most," "best" or "most widely accepted" scientific evidence. Such a requirement is contrary to the precautionary principle and inconsistent with the nature of science. More importantly, it would

seriously interfere with the ability of governments to protect against
risks of environmental harm ... Pursuant to this principle, countries
have the right to regulate activities that may be harmful to the environment even if the scientific evidence concerning the connection between
the activity and the harm is inadequate or inconclusive – that is, even if
scientists do not agree or cannot explain exactly whether, how or to
what degree the harm is caused. This principle has been part of domestic and international law for several decades and has become a
"broadly accepted basis for international action."

Good analyses of issues related to the precautionary principle may be
found in Sands (1994) and VanderZwaag (1998, 1999). Audley (2002, 4)
asserted that "The U.S. government does not recognize the precautionary
principle in international law, but believes that the U.S. practice of taking
precaution when regulating is consistent with WTO trade:
Regarding the Government of Canada, Canadian Minister of Health,
Alan Rock, wrote:

19 Environment Canada and Health Canada follow a risk-based scientific decision making process to carry out their responsibilities under
CEPA [Canadian Environmental Protection Act] and other statutes. That
is, before risk management measures (e.g., a ban, control or pollution
prevention plan) are taken on a substance, a risk assessment is completed. Simply put, the process consists of two parts. First, the hazard
posed by the substance itself (e.g., determination of neurotoxicity or
carcinogenicity) and the extent of the exposure of Canadians or ecosys-
tems to the substance is determined. Then, this information is used to
assess the risk posed by the substance. If the risk is significant, risk
management measures are developed in consultation with interested
parties.
20 A risk assessment always involves a degree of uncertainty, the
extent of which depends on the quantity and quality of the data and
information available. The *Canadian Environmental Protection Act,*
1999, [preamble] requires that the Government of Canada, including
Environment Canada and Health Canada, "exercises its powers in a
manner that protects the environment and human health, (and) applies
the precautionary principle that, where there are threats of serious or
irreversible damage, lack of full scientific certainty shall not be used as
a reason for postponing cost-effective measures to prevent environmental degradation." This precautionary principle compliments [sic] the

risk management process; it is risk-based, not hazard-based. That is, knowing that a substance is poisonous, for example, is insufficient to justify regulatory action under the *Canadian Environmental Protection Act*, 1999. (Commissioner of the Environment and Sustainable Development 2001, 4)

Although the AIT rules explicitly allow for the application of a precautionary principle or a precautionary approach and although those provisions in the AIT were appealed to by the Government of Canada, the panel adjudicated the case paying no attention to them at all (see chapter 16). Abouchar and King (1999, 213) expressed the view that the precautionary principle articulated as Principle 15 of the Rio Declaration, 1992, fully supported the Canadian government's "banning the import of MMT." Given the relative importance and clarity of a precautionary principle or approach in the AIT compared to the NAFTA, the "chilling effect" danger connected to the latter must be even greater than that connected to the former.

Following Vogel (1995) to some extent and notwithstanding critics like Bernstein (2002) and others cited in chapter 4, Soloway (2003, 19) examined the new environmental acts enacted in Canada since the NAFTA came into force and concluded that "As the volume of new legislative instruments continues to expand, we can presume that the environmental regulatory framework continues to function in Canada (as it does in Mexico and the United States), despite the alleged 'chill' that Chapter 11 has caused."

On the contrary, Tollefson (2003, 49) thought it was "hazardous" to judge the adequacy of the framework without a careful examination of the "content" of the acts passed rather than the mere "volume." What is even more difficult, if anyone should undertake the latter investigation, some measure of the marginal increase or decrease in regulatory protection should be constructed.

In contrast to those troubled by a possible "regulatory chill," Schwanen (2002, 46) claimed that the provisions of Chapter 11 "resulted in what I would call 'deregulatory chill' – a phenomenon potentially inimical to economic efficiency and growth. This is because governments in some cases have found experimenting with deregulation and privatization more difficult politically since the NAFTA, since their ability to re-intervene in the future to correct any course of action once it is taken is severely questioned by some legal analysts. The debate of three years ago over expanding the role of private health clinics in Alberta is an example of this difficulty."

13 Because a NAFTA tribunal (S.D. Myers case, Sinclair 2007) has decided that a "market share was a legitimate investment," the principle has been

established that if an investor has ever been able to do something then the investor has a right to do it (Public Citizen 2001, viii).

14 Because a NAFTA tribunal has decided that the environmental protection obligation given in the preamble of NAFTA need not take precedence over other considerations (S.D. Myers case, Sinclair 2007), the obligation is relatively worthless (Public Citizen 2001, viii). The MMT case adjudicated by the NAFTA tribunal illustrates this problem (see chapters 11 and 12).

15 Corporations are using Chapter 11 provisions to try to "carve out more favorable market conditions or market share" (Public Citizen 2001, x).

16 "Chapter 11 can require governments to pay compensation to polluters to stop polluting, even if their activities have an adverse impact on public health and welfare." In effect, this turns "'the polluter pays' principle into a 'pay the polluter' principle" (IISD/WWF 2001, 1, 33; CCPA 2001, 4; Trebilcock 2002, 9).

According to Wagner (1999, 469), "Internalizing environmental costs – meaning shifting the cost of environmental harm from society at large to the person causing the harm – is a fundamental element of environmental protection. This principle, called the 'polluter pays principle,' was recognized internationally in the Rio Declaration on Environment and Development."

According to Runnalls (1994, 62), "Internalization of environmental costs is essential to achieve efficiency. Despite the substantial practical difficulties this entails, high priority should be attached to its implementation. As costs are progressively internalized the contribution of all economic activity, including trade, to the efficient utilization of resources is enhanced."

Macdonald (2002, 74) claimed that firms were always prepared to offer up "some behaviour change as a means of appeasing and forestalling those demanding a much greater degree of internalized cost." However, Cosbey (2004, 32) was certainly right when he wrote that "most people would agree that taxpayers should not be paying investors to alter behaviour that is contrary to the public interest." Clarkson (2002a, 349) claimed that in the MMT case, "Chapter 11's expropriation clause led to the polluter's being paid to keep on polluting." As already indicated, and explained in more detail below, because of the AIT panel's negative decision, the NAFTA tribunal did not have to address the "expropriation clause" (NAFTA Article 1110). However, if one were going to pick a particular clause leading to a "pay the polluter principle" in the MMT cases, it would be more accurate to select the AIT's "least trade restrictive" clause (AIT Article 404c). After all, giving panels the discretionary authority to strike down measures that they believe are "more trade restrictive than necessary" allows them to permit practically any level of pollution to continue in the interests of sustaining some preferred level of trade. Presumably, then, the costs of that pollution would be paid by someone other than the polluter.

17 Finally, as Abouchar and King (1999, 213) explained, an important issue concerning regulatory risk is involved:

> The ability of foreign corporations to simply launch dispute panels on their own initiative raises some unsettling questions about the extent to which foreign corporations are able to shift the burden of regulatory risk to the governments of the countries in which it plans to carry on business. There are compelling reasons for ensuring that such risk be borne by corporate actors – namely, providing an incentive to carry out comprehensive environmental due diligence before embarking on investments, and encouraging the use of regulatory risk insurance for environmentally sensitive operations (e.g., PCB import/export, purchase of toxic waste disposal sites, etc.). It its current form, Chapter 11 provides no incentives to do either.

Summarizing its own analyses of the shortcomings of Chapter 11, which are very similar to those of Public Citizen and Friends of the Earth, the International Institute for Sustainable Development and World Wildlife Fund report said:

> There is no apparent need for such shortcomings, and little apparent benefit to them. In short, the investor-state process as currently designed and implemented is shockingly unsuited to the task of balancing private rights against public goods in a legitimate and constructive manner.
>
> Valid arguments can be made for providing public access to dispute resolution processes to enforce international law. Indeed, in many other areas of international law, such access is available in different forms and expansions of this approach are actively encouraged by civil society organizations and academics. The real issue is to match an appropriate and genuinely accessible process to the nature and scope of the issues that may arise for adjudication. On this level, the investor-state process in Chapter 11 fails, unequivocally. (IISD/WWF 2001, 46)

Clarkson (2002a, 64–8) echoed several of the above criticisms, following these summary remarks:

Chapter 11 has established a new zone of privatized adjudication which has politicized issues that would previously have escaped most public notice. Not only has it added to the Canadian constitution a new corporate property right which treats firms unequally depending on their nationality. It has introduced an existing arbitration mechanism designed to handle international corporate disputes, turning it into a device to constrain government capacity.

Cases initiated against a municipal, provincial, or federal government under the investor-state provisions of Chapter 11 are not heard before a Canadian court using Canadian jurisprudence. These "investor-state" disputes go to arbitration before an international panel operating by rules established under the aegis of the World Bank or the United Nations for settling international disputes between transnational corporations. Since each of these forums operates according to the norms of international commercial law, Chapter 11 actually transfers adjudication of disputes over government policies from the realm of national law to international commercial law, with several serious implications. (Clarkson 2002, 64)

It is precisely the illegitimate transformation of issues of broad public interest into issues that allegedly involve only private commercial interests that has mobilized so many people against the Chapter 11 provisions. When people can see that their interests are being set aside, officially regarded as irrelevant and beyond judicial review, while those of private investors are carefully protected in fora with self-selected laws, adjudicated by self-selected panels, they are quite naturally outraged. As Clarkson wrote, Chapter 11 "created a sinister forum of judicial decision-making in secret ... [its] investor-state dispute mechanism is so egregiously offensive to Canada's constitutional norms that its supraconstitutional status could be targeted for defiance" (Clarkson 2002a, 410, 418).

The dispute settlement provisions of the AIT are a little more flexible than those of the NAFTA, although in many ways the former were modelled on the latter (Howse 1995, 170). The announced objective of the AIT is given in Article 100: "It is the objective of the Parties to reduce and eliminate, to the extent possible, barriers to the free movement of persons, goods, services and investments within Canada and to establish an open, efficient and stable domestic market" (AIT 2002).

The agreement is based on six general rules (Part III, Chapter 4) designed to "prevent governments from erecting new trade barriers and to reduce existing barriers." The rules involve:

- *non-discrimination*: Establishing equal treatment for all Canadian persons, goods, services and investments.
- *right of entry and exit*: Prohibiting measures that restrict the movement of persons, goods, services or investments across provincial or territorial boundaries.
- *no obstacles*: Ensuring provincial/territorial government policies and practices do not create obstacles to trade.
- *legitimate objectives*: Ensuring provincial/territorial non-trade objectives which may cause some deviation from the above guidelines have a minimal adverse impact on interprovincial trade.
- *reconciliation*: Providing the basis for eliminating trade barriers caused by differences in standards and regulations across Canada.
- *transparency*: Ensuring information is fully accessible to interested businesses, individuals and governments. (Internal Trade Secretariat 2002b, 1–2)

Article 300 provides a clear "Reaffirmation of Constitutional Powers and Responsibilities": "Nothing in this Agreement alters the legislative or other authority of Parliament or of the provincial legislatures or of the Government of Canada or of the provincial governments or the rights of any of them with respect to the exercise of their legislative or other authorities under the Constitution of Canada" (AIT 2002).

Lest there be any doubts about the scope of jurisdiction of dispute settlement panels, Article 1722 says that "For greater certainty, a Panel has no jurisdiction to rule on any constitutional issue" (AIT 2002).

The website of the Secretariat for the AIT lists forty-five disputes considered between 1995 and July 2007. Of these, fourteen were resolved by the disputants themselves, eight complaints were upheld by panels, three were denied, two were ruled not subject to the AIT, three were withdrawn, and fifteen were pending.

As early as the 1985 *Report of the Royal Commission on the Economic Union and Development Prospects for Canada* (Macdonald Commission) there were allegations of significant and unnecessary economic costs resulting from trade barriers among the provinces and territories. Some producers apparently found it easier to sell their products in another country than in another province, according to Doern and MacDonald (1999, 39, quoting from the Macdonald Commission Report). Unfortunately, reliable and valid evidence was in short supply and estimates of the actual size of the unnecessary losses varied widely from 1 per cent of GDP ($6.5 billion) to 0.05 per cent of GDP (Lee 2000, 2; Trebilcock and Behboodi 1995, 22;

Copeland 1998). In 1995 McCallum published a paper in the *American Economic Review* showing that "1988 interprovincial merchandise trade flows were more than twenty times more intense than were those between provinces and states," a finding that has stood several "tests of replication and still persists in Canada" (Helliwell 2002, 10, 18). Summarizing a considerable amount of research, Helliwell (2002, 30–2) came to conclusions that would have delighted Adam Smith:

> Within Canada, much attention has been paid to the existence and possible effects of barriers to interprovincial trade. Recently improved measures of intraprovincial trade distances have permitted more useful estimates of the relative size of interprovincial and international border effects, which had previously been found to be insignificant for all provinces (Helliwell 1996, 23–6). These new data show that, for the four largest provinces, there is no evidence that interprovincial trade is less dense than is intraprovincial trade, and for no province are the interprovincial border effects more than a fraction as large as are the international ones (Helliwell and Verdier 2001). Thus even the provincial differences of language, networks, and regulations have very little importance compared to those across national borders.
>
> What are the likely causes of the separation of national markets? ... Because studies have found that policy barriers are not an important cause of the remaining border effects among the industrial countries, the reasons must lie elsewhere ... Being further from home usually means being less well connected to local networks, less able to understand local norms, and less able to be sure how much to trust what people may say ... If networks and trust are important in facilitating trade, and if the strength of these networks diminishes with distance and as borders are crossed, then this would be sufficient to explain why both distance and national borders mark steep reductions in the intensity of trade linkages. This explanation is probably increasingly accepted.

Compare the preceding paragraph to the following comments that appeared a couple pages before the famous "invisible hand" passage from *The Wealth of Nations,* published over two hundred years earlier:

> every individual endeavours to employ his capital as near home as he can, and consequently as much as he can in the support of domestic industry; provided always that he can thereby obtain the ordinary, or not a great deal less than the ordinary profits of stock.

Thus, upon equal or nearly equal profits, every wholesale merchant naturally prefers the home trade to the foreign trade of consumption, and the foreign trade of consumption to the carrying trade. In the home trade his capital is never so long out of his sight as it frequently is in the foreign trade of consumption. He can know better the character and the situation of the persons whom he trusts, and if he should happen to be deceived, he knows better the laws of the country from which he must seek redress. (Smith 1776, from an excerpt in McCullough 1995, 10)

In the light of the research reviewed and the conclusions reached by Helliwell, one might well wonder with Lee (2000) about the point of reopening discussions over internal trade barriers. Celebrating the AIT's fifth anniversary, Schwanen (2000) thought the agreement deserved another "push." In Lee's view, which I suspect is still accurate today, "The main objective of current negotiations, like the original AIT, is to promote an agenda of privatization and deregulation that will handcuff governments in the future. A second objective is to facilitate Canada's international trade commitments – NAFTA, the WTO, and other bilateral agreements" (Lee 2000, 1).

Since Doern and MacDonald (1999) wrote a fine history of the negotiations leading to the AIT, and Trebilcock and Schwanen (1995) assembled an equally fine collection of analytic studies of most aspects of the agreement, I will only provide enough background material to supplement the detailed discussions of the MMT case. One of the remarkable twists of fate about this case is that it pitted the two biggest proponents of the AIT, the federal government ("the main demandeur" of the agreement according to Doern and MacDonald 1999, 159) and the government of Alberta, against each other. Of the three provincial NDP governments at the time of the negotiations over the agreement, the government of Saskatchewan was probably the most skeptical. Nevertheless, Saskatchewan joined Québec as an intervener in support of Alberta in the MMT case. As it turned out, the first casualty of the AIT's first formally settled dispute was a legislated Act of "the main demandeur" of the agreement.

Doern and MacDonald (1999, 35) speculated that with respect to areas such as the environment, the AIT might reduce the pursuit of relatively "narrow, provincially defined interests." In their view, the AIT offered "some hope in response to the recent trend towards political, geographical, and social decentralization." Monahan was equally enthusiastic and hopeful: "The agreement reflects a belief – however tentative – in the primacy of Canadian citizenship and identity over local attachments. Because the obligations set out in the agreement are reciprocal and are to be enforced through a process that is transparent and fair, it represents one of the few politically acceptable avenues by which Canadian attachments can be permitted to prevail over local or provincial ones. In a country as fractious as Canada, that is no small achievement" (Monahan 1995, 217).

On the contrary, "provincially defined interests," "local attachments," and the forces of "decentralization" were apparently paramount in the MMT case.

The AIT Chapters 5 through 15 contain provisions particularly relevant to the specific range of issues (e.g., procurement, investment, labour mobility) in each chapter related to resolving disputes. Usually these are in a section entitled "Consultations." Chapter 16 describes (a) the supervisory Committee on Internal Trade, whose members are "cabinet-level representatives of each of the Parties"; (b) the Working Group on Adjustment, which annually reviews the operation of the agreement and makes recommendations for alterations; and (c) the permanent Secretariat, which provides "administrative and operational support" for all aspects of the agreement, including the work of dispute settlement panels. Chapter 17 gives general procedures for government-to-government (Part A) and person-to-government (Part B) disputes, and Chapter 15 gives procedures for disputes concerning environmental issues. The MMT case was settled under the rules of Chapter 15 and its details are described here in chapters 13 to 16.

As Miller remarked, the AIT "reflects a strong antilitigation bias," with most chapters specifying "a dispute resolution process consisting of consultation, mediation, and conciliation to be followed in disputes concerning the specific sector discussed in that chapter" (Miller 1995, 152, 169). The language of the first two articles of Chapter 17 reveal the agreement's general approach.

Article 1700: Cooperation
1   The Parties undertake to resolve disputes in a conciliatory, cooperative and harmonious manner.
2   The Parties shall make every attempt through cooperation, consultations and other dispute avoidance and resolution processes available to them to arrive at a mutually satisfactory resolution of any matter that may affect the operation of this agreement.

Article 1701: Application
1   Subject to paragraph 6, this Chapter applies to the avoidance and resolution of disputes between Parties, or persons and Parties, regarding the interpretation and application of this Agreement.

2 Before a Party initiates dispute resolution proceedings under Part A of this Chapter [concerning disputes between governments], it shall select and proceed only under the one Chapter in Part IV of this Agreement [Chapters 5 through 15] that it considers to be most applicable to the matter. (AIT 2002)

From the perspective of the political philosophy behind Canadian federalism and the provisions of the *Constitution Act, 1867*, and the *Constitution Act, 1982*, Article 1700 would seem to be redundant. What else are member governments of a federation committed to if not to cooperation? Doern and MacDonald (1999, 26, 140) claimed that "there are probably well over forty policy areas in which the federal and provincial governments engage in some form of joint or coordinated policy process" and "within the federal government and within provincial governments, there are many line departments and central agencies also involved as disputes or issues or work programs wend their way through thirteen governments."

Swinton (1995, 197) noted that the whole AIT joined "hundreds of other intergovernmental agreements." For our purposes, Article 1701.2 is especially important, since it directs parties to "proceed only under the one Chapter ... that it considers to be most applicable." Accordingly, the provisions of the environmental Chapter 15 became authoritative for the MMT case.

Different people have assessed different features of the dispute settlement regime of the AIT in different ways. Although Miller (like Monahan 1995, 216) thought that it was advantageous to hold consultations between parties in private, summarizing the general rules of procedure for the operation of panels given in Article 1706, he expressed the view that "the parties have attempted to establish an independent, timely, transparent, and administratively fair panel process. Emphasis is placed on the openness of proceedings and documents are made available to the parties to encourage public confidence in the system and participation by interested parties, where that participation is appropriate" (Miller 1995, 159).

The relative "openness of proceedings" is specified by Article 1706.1(b), which says that "All proceedings before a panel shall be public and all documents filed with a panel shall be accessible to the disputing Parties or their agents, except as otherwise provided in the Rules" (AIT 2002).

Article 1706.1(d) specifies the most important exception, i.e., "Disputing Parties shall be afforded the opportunity to ensure the confidentiality of documents that are commercially sensitive or otherwise protected by law and to protect documents the disclosure of which could impair international relations or obligations" (AIT 2002).

Although 1706.1(d) provides a significant escape clause for the openness provided in 1706.1(b), most analysts commend the authors of the agreement for including the latter provision. For example, Howse (1995, 176) said that "Public proceedings should give rise to an expectation among affected citizens that the result of the process will be a reasoned and principled adjudication of the claims at issue, not some kind of diplomatic saw-off or compromise. In providing for public proceedings, the agreement embodies a significant improvement over the cloak-and-dagger tradition of executive federalism in Canada. The arguments governments make in the dispute settlement process will now be subject to democratic scrutiny."

Also, as Schwanen (1995, 14) remarked, panel proceedings with international agreements are typically not public. Presumably, my analysis of the AIT MMT case would count as part of Howse's "democratic scrutiny." Certainly my work on this book would have been much more difficult and less complete without 1706.1(b) and its implementation.

Regarding the timeliness or speed of dispute settlement with the AIT rules, in a very useful comparative study of the AIT, NAFTA, and WTO provisions, Clendenning and Clendenning (1999, 42, 45–6) concluded:

The AIT dispute settlement mechanism involves more steps and processes and is much more time consuming than the mechanisms under NAFTA and the WTO. The unique process involved in the AIT is the initial dispute avoidance and resolution process that must be undertaken in each chapter of the agreement before a dispute can be brought before the general dispute settlement mechanism. The AIT then proceeds to consultations between the parties prior to seeking assistance from the Committee on Internal Trade and requesting the establishment of a panel, which are similar to the steps undertaken in NAFTA. The WTO mechanism, however, proceeds directly from the consultations stage to the establishment of panels. Because of these additional steps and the longer time frame between steps under the AIT the time to bring a dispute to resolution through the entire process is much longer than under either NAFTA or the WTO ... The time frame for bringing disputes to a resolution under the AIT dispute settlement mechanism should be reduced by moving disputes more quickly to the panel stage, by reducing the time permitted between processes and by strengthening and accelerating the implementation of panel reports. The addition of appeal procedures to the process, although requiring time, could also add credibility and certainty to the final outcome and strengthen compliance with panel rulings.

Of course, if all other things are equal, the reduction of any costs for dispute resolution would be a good thing. I have already mentioned that some people confuse speed with efficiency, and this problem is more fully addressed in chapter 17 concerning the use of a model of commercial arbitration in both the AIT and NAFTA.

Articles 300, 1719 (Implementation of Panel Report) and 1720 (Non-Implementation – Publicity) pretty clearly indicate that decisions and recommendations of panels may have political and/or moral force, but they are not legally binding. According to James Ogilvy, Director, Internal Trade, Alberta Federal and Intergovernmental Affairs, "When a government has gone astray, when it has stepped outside the bounds of that agreement, there is at least a moral obligation to make the necessary changes" (SSCEENR 2/11, 1996, 27). Howse (1995, 170) remarked that, "there is no provision for binding enforcement through an award of damages, an injunction, or some equivalent order." Some regard this as a significant weakness. For example, de Mestral (1995, 96) wrote:

A major flaw with the agreement is that it is deemed to be a political text; as such, it is not anchored in any legal system, whether it be federal law, provincial law, international law, or Canadian constitutional law. This is more than just a lawyer's quibble since the dispute settlement system implies that there will be a process of application and interpretation of the text of the agreement *vis-à-vis* provincial and federal laws. This being the case, the dispute settlement panel will have no guidance whatsoever as to the nature of the law in which the text is grounded. This appears to be what private international law theorists term a *contrat sans loi*, which most regard as a theoretical and practical impossibility.

Making matters even worse, according to de Mestral, the non-legally binding agreement "contrives to apply the wrong sort of law":

The text is drafted in a style reminiscent of the Canada-US Free Trade Agreement, the North American Free Trade Agreement (NAFTA), or the GATT. The underlying assumption appears to be that the provinces are totally independent sovereign actors and that it is appropriate for them to make mutual concessions on interprovincial trade barriers comparable to concessions made by governments in the GATT or NAFTA. I find this truly extraordinary, and it is all the more extraordinary that the federal government should be aiding and abetting the process ... the text contains a number of clearly unconstitutional provisions. Much of it relates to provincial action in relation to interprovincial trade, yet interprovincial trade comes under federal, not provincial, jurisdiction. The dispute settlement provisions contain the absurdity of inviting a province that has suffered from an interprovincial trade barrier in another province to take retaliatory measures [Article 1710.3]. These measures, if they are aimed at interprovincial trade, would clearly be *ultra vires* the province that takes them. (de Mestral 1995, 97)

Since Article 1710.10 (a) says that "this Article does not allow a Party to take retaliatory action that is inconsistent with the Constitution of Canada," it is unclear what interprovincial trade-related action is envisioned in 1710.3. Howse (1995, 178–9) had some difficulty with this question too. To be more precise, the invitation to take retaliatory measures only applies to Part A (government-to-government proceedings), not to Part B. Miller (1995, 166) correctly observed that, unlike Part A: "Part B makes no provision for third-party participation at any stage of the proceedings, whether the third parties be governments or public interest groups ... where a panel report has not been complied with by a government and no mutually satisfactory solution of the dispute has been agreed on, there is obviously no retaliation. The private party must rely on the moral suasion of the panel report, which is made public, and the good faith of the noncomplying party."

De Mestral's overall assessment of the AIT was that "It contrives at one and the same time to involve no law, bad law, and the wrong kind of law" (de Mestral 1995, 95). Taking his charges at face value, one might conclude that the AIT is at best a redundant political agreement based on a perverse notion of the sovereign status of provinces and at worst an ungrounded legal agreement, with absurd provisions inviting provinces to transgress well-established constitutional law. Since all the internal textual evidence and practically all writers agree that the agreement has no legal force, I believe de Mestral's best alternative is closest to the truth. I suspect that the central defects of the agreement are a product of its proponents and authors pursuing commercial aims in the absence of any clear appreciation of the political, legal, and moral implications of what they were doing. That it was possible to treat the question of what to do about the use of MMT in unleaded gasoline as primarily a matter for commercial arbitration under the rules of the AIT rather than primarily a matter for federal legislation under the rules of Canadian constitutional and environmental law reveals the extent of the confusion in the assumptions, aims and methods of the agreement.

It would be unreasonable and unfair to expect anyone to accept the preceding sentence as true until I have thoroughly examined all the evidence relevant to this question. First, however, an elucidation of the background material necessary to that thorough examination is required.

II

Ethyl Corporation's Claims against the Government of Canada under the NAFTA

In this chapter and the next I review and evaluate the claims and counter-claims of the disputants in the NAFTA MMT case, and of the tribunal.

Ethyl Corporation filed its *Notice of Intent to Submit a Claim to Arbitration under Section B of Chapter 11 of NAFTA* on 10 September 1996, and its *Notice of Arbitration under the Arbitration Rules of UNCITRAL and NAFTA* on 14 April 1997.

In accordance with UNCITRAL Article 3, Ethyl Corporation demanded arbitration, named itself as claimant and the Government of Canada as respondent, described the nature of the claim, and asked for the arbitration to be held in New York City or Washington, D.C., for compensation of U.S. $250 million, and for a three-person arbitration tribunal with "Charles N. Brower, President of the American Society of International Law, as its party-appointed arbitrator." Describing "the nature of the claim," Ethyl maintained that the Government of Canada breached three obligations specified in Chapter 11, namely, Article 1102 on National Treatment, Article 1110 on Expropriation and Compensation, and Article 1106 on Performance Requirements (Appleton 1997a). The full text of the relevant sections of these articles is given in appendix 1. Below are some of the key issues and assertions from the *Notice of Arbitration*.

To meet the procedural requirements of NAFTA Articles 1118–1120, on 10 September 1996 Ethyl asked the Government of Canada for a meeting to try to negotiate a mutually acceptable resolution of their grievance. A meeting was held on 12 November 1996, which Ethyl claimed, but the Government of Canada denied, fulfilled its obligations for consultation or negotiation under Article 1118. Then, regarding Article 1102, Ethyl claimed:

Bill C-29 constitutes disguised discrimination, aimed at Ethyl Corporation, and its investment, Ethyl Canada. This measure constitutes a violation of the Government of Canada's national treatment obligation to NAFTA investors as set out in Article 1102 ... The intention to ban the importation and interprovincial trade in MMT is a completely arbitrary measure. On the introduction of Bill C-94, the Minister of the Environment, Sheila Copps M.P., acknowledged that Bill C-94 may not remove MMT from use in gasoline. MMT may still be made and used locally ... There would be no difference in nature and kind between MMT produced and used in a Canadian province and MMT imported for use in Canada. All that Bill C-94, and its successor C-29, prohibits is the sale of foreign-made MMT in Canada. This is a completely arbitrary measure aimed at harming Ethyl Corporation and favouring products manufactured in Canada. (Appleton 1997a, 9)

Regarding Article 1110, Ethyl wrote:

A fundamental obligation contained in the NAFTA Investment Chapter relates to expropriation ... The NAFTA does not define the term expropriation but it is clear that it is designed to protect against direct and indirect measures by extending its coverage to "measures tantamount to expropriation." In international law, expropriation refers to the act by which governmental authority is used to deny some benefit of property ... An expropriation therefore exists whenever there is a substantial and unreasonable interference with the enjoyment of a property right ... Article 1110 of the NAFTA does not prevent governmental regulatory actions. It requires governments to compensate investors for interference with their property rights as set out in the NAFTA ... In his letter of February 23, 1996 to the Minister of the Environment, Canada's Minister of International Trade [Eggleton 1996] pointed out that Canada's proposed legislation could constitute a measure tantamount to expropriation. Minister Eggleton's letter also indicates that the Government of Canada knew that its import prohibition (Bills C-94 and C-29) could be inconsistent with Canada's NAFTA obligations, including NAFTA's investment obligations. The Government of Canada's actions unreasonably interfere with the effective enjoyment of Ethyl Canada's property. This constitutes a measure tantamount to expropriation under the NAFTA. (Appleton 1997a, 10–12)

Regarding Article 1106, Ethyl claimed:

> The Government of Canada ... has not banned the use of MMT in
> unleaded gasoline explicitly or directly; rather, the Government of
> Canada seeks to prevent its importation and interprovincial trade. A
> domestic manufacturer, if there were any, could manufacture and dis-
> tribute MMT for use in unleaded gasoline entirely within a province and
> not violate Bill C-29 ... Bill C-29 violates Article 1106 (1) (b), which
> prohibits government measures that require investors to include in their
> products or services any amount of goods or services that originate
> within the Party ... If Ethyl Canada wanted to stay in the MMT supply
> business, it would have to purchase all of the MMT supply from Cana-
> dian producers in each province. This is a requirement to purchase
> domestic goods or services in contravention of Article 1106 (1) (c).
> (Appleton 1997a, 13)

After all of the above, Ethyl turned to what seems to me to be the most
extraordinary part of their complaint. They provided a list of specific
harms the two companies had suffered through the whole affair:

> From the winter of 1995 onwards, there have been a number of state-
> ments and actions made as part of the official duties of senior govern-
> ment officials. These statements have resulted in harm to Ethyl
> Corporation and Ethyl Canada. The Canadian actions include:
> • Public statements by the Deputy Prime Minister of Canada on
>   February 17, 1995.
> • The introduction of Bill C-94 into the House of Commons on May
>   19, 1995.
> • Statements by the Deputy Prime Minister to Parliament on May 19,
>   1995.
> • Public statements by the Deputy Prime Minister of Canada on May
>   19, 1995.
> • An article published in the Ottawa Citizen newspaper written by the
>   Hon. Sergio Marchi in September 1996.
> • Statements by the Parliamentary Secretary to the Minister of the
>   Environment, in Parliament on October 10, 1996.
> • The introduction of Bill C-29 by the House of Commons on an accel-
>   erated basis on April 22, 1996.
> • The passage of Bill C-29 by the House of Commons on December 2,
>   1996.

- The introduction of Bill C-29 in the Canadian Senate.
- The passage of 2nd reading of Bill C-29 in the Canadian Senate on Dec. 16, 1996.
- Final passage of Bill C-29 in the Canadian Senate on April 9, 1997.

... Taken in their entirety, the actions of the Government of Canada indicate a systematic practice by the Canadian government to discriminate against American MMT manufacturers and to advantage domestic producers ... The definition of the term "investment" in Article 1139 establishes that government measures that harm an investor's intangible property can constitute a measure tantamount to expropriation. The term "measure" as defined by Article 201 includes 'any law, regulation, procedure, requirement or practice." (Appleton 1997a, 16–17)

What is extraordinary about the list of harms is its inclusion of routine activities of elected members of parliament. The mere introduction and debate about proposed legislation in properly constituted legislative bodies (the Canadian House of Commons and the Senate) are challenged as harms demanding material compensation. It is difficult to imagine a more egregious attack on democracy and democratic process. Presumably the authors of the attack were either unfamiliar with or unimpressed by the idea of parliamentary privilege. In *Erskine May's Parliamentary Practice*, it is defined as:

the sum of the peculiar rights enjoyed by each House collectively ... and by Members of each House individually, without which they could not discharge their functions, and which exceed those possessed by other bodies or individuals ... [The right of free speech] includes the power to initiate, and consider in such order as it pleases, matters of legislation or discussion, as well as the privilege of freedom of debate proper ... [Every Member may state] whatever he [or she] thinks fit in debate, however offensive it may be to the feelings, or injurious to the character, of individuals; and he [or she] is protected by his [or her] privilege from any action or libel, as well as from any question or molestation. (Infonet@parl.gc.ca, 1 January 2002)

As indicated in chapter 10 regarding the eighth problem with NAFTA Chapter 11 according to Public Citizen (2001), the provisions of the chapter practically encourage investors to see what they can get away with. On this issue, IISD/WWF (2001, 19) wrote: "While it is certainly true that Chapter 11 does not exclude a foreign investor from the obligation to follow applicable laws in the host state, it is also true that Chapter 11 has provided these investors with special rights to challenge those very laws, or any proposed laws that might affect their interests. There are no counterbalancing rights of governments or obligations on foreign investors that limit the scope or exercise of the rights ... The granting of rights without commensurate responsibilities is inherently dangerous. This is no less the case when those rights come from international law."

I do not know what provisions one could include in the NAFTA to prevent investors from attacking a doctrine as important to democracy as parliamentary privilege. It would be a mockery of the doctrine to use a provision against frivolous complaints to challenge morally outrageous complaints. The alleged losses suffered by Ethyl were listed as follows.

1 Lost sales and profits since the date of introduction of Bill C-94;
2 Loss of value of its investment in Ethyl Canada;
3 Loss of value in its intellectual property;
4 Loss of value of goodwill in Ethyl Corporation;
5 Loss of world-wide sales due to other countries relying on those measures taken by the Government of Canada which are inconsistent with its NAFTA obligations;
6 The cost of reducing operations in Canada;
7 Fees and expenses incurred to defend itself against allegations made by Canada;
8 Fees and expenses of various professional services incurred to defeat Bills C-94 and C-29; and
9 Tax consequences of the award to maintain the integrity of the award. (Appleton 1997a, 18)

Following the *Notice of Arbitration*, on 2 September 1997 a tribunal was formed according to the provisions of NAFTA Chapter 11 and UNCITRAL. A month later (2 October 1997) Ethyl filed its *Statement of Claim*. According to UNCITRAL Article 18, the latter should include the same information as the former plus more detailed information about the facts supporting the claim and the key points at issue. Among other things, the compensation demand was increased by $1 million, and it was noted that "There is one basic point at issue: Has the Government of Canada taken measures inconsistent with its obligations under Section A of Chapter 11 of the NAFTA?" (Appleton 1997b, 13). Ethyl also included the full text of Bill C-29, the *Manganese-based Fuel Additives Act* (MMT Act).

While the list of specific harms given in the *Notice of Arbitration* is not repeated in the *Statement of Claim*, paragraphs 25 and 26 of the latter document assert that:

> 25 The reckless behaviour of the Government of Canada has adversely affected the company's goodwill both inside and outside Canada. The public statements of public officials in their official capacity constitute evidence of governmental practices. These government measures resulted in harm to Ethyl's property, including its goodwill regarding use of MMT.
>
> 26 The damage to the commercial reputations of Ethyl and Ethyl Canada by the defamatory statements of Canadian officials constitute expropriation as defined in the NAFTA of the goodwill of Ethyl Canada. These government measures have detrimentally affected the ability of the investor to sell its products in other jurisdictions. (Appleton 1997b, 7–8)

The most notable omission in the *Statement of Claim* is any reference to the alleged damage that MMT might do to catalytic converters or on-board diagnostic equipment. The very first paragraph of the *Notice of Arbitration* ends as follows: "Various groups have alleged that MMT harms the diagnostic systems on automobiles or that MMT is a risk to human health. Health Canada has concluded that MMT does not pose a threat to human health and no independent studies have concluded that MMT harms automobile diagnostic systems" (Appleton 1997a, 4).

I do not know whether Ethyl backed away from the equipment issue because it was regarded as unnecessary or because it was indefensible, or both. Chapters 12 and 15 demonstrate that the equipment issue was of immense importance to the federal government's cases for both the NAFTA and the AIT.

The remaining major additions in the *Statement of Claim* provide evidence supporting the claim "that MMT does not present a risk to human health or the environment." In particular, reference is made to three authoritative reports, Health and Welfare Canada (1978), The Royal Society of Canada's Commission on Lead in the Environment (Commission 1986), and Wood and Egyed (1994). The following quotation from the *Statement of Claim* is cited there from page v of *Lead in Gasoline: Alternatives to Lead in Gasoline* (February 1986), which has the same ISBN as Hotz (1986). But the quotation does not appear on page v of Hotz (1986) or in the Commission's final report (1986), and I have not been able to locate a copy of the February 1986 report. Hotz (1986, 11) does include a suggestion from A. Barbeau that is somewhat similar to the material in the quotation.

> Manganese is one of the more abundant elements in the earth's crust [more precisely, the twelfth most abundant element and fifth most abundant metal], and its high concentrations in soils, water and air reflect this fact. National Health and Welfare Canada has predicted that *the average additional individual intake of manganese resulting from the use of mmt in gasoline is likely to be no greater than 0.3 micrograms per day (mg/day). This compares with an average individual uptake from food, water and respiration of about 100–140 mg/day. By comparison with these large amounts already handled by the body, the extra loading on the public at large from* MMT *is and will remain very small.* (Quoted from Appleton 1997b, 5, emphasis in original)

Hotz's (1986, 2) conclusion about MMT was that "the general public has a wide margin of health safety with respect to the worst case use of MMT in gasoline."

The commission's explicit recommendation was clearly favourable to MMT: "We recommend that MMT ... and MTBE [methyl tertiary butyl ether] ... be regarded as environmentally acceptable substitutes for TEL (tetraethyl lead) as octane improvers in gasoline. The same applies to methanol and ethanol used as additives or blending components" (Commission on Lead in the Environment 1986, xxi; see also remarks by Alain Perez, President of the CPPI, in SSCEENR 2/4, 1997a, 17).

Much more is said about ethanol in chapters 14 and 15. Methanol, an alcohol fuel most often produced from natural gas, is a basic component of MTBE. The latter product is central to another nasty NAFTA Chapter 11 case involving the Canadian-based Methanex Corporation and the United States of America. On 9 August 2005 a NAFTA tribunal dismissed the investors' claims (Sinclair 2007, 5). Excellent reviews and documents relevant to the case can be found at the website of the International Institute for Sustainable Development. In Mann's (2002) view, MTBE is "a sunset product" that may not merit further support by Methanex. Several environmental and legal issues related to MTBE are reviewed in Walker (2002), including its probable links to cancer in humans.

Health and Welfare Canada sponsored two literature reviews before the Wood and Eyged (1994) review, namely, Meek and Bogoroch (1978) and an update by the Midwest Research Institute (1987). For our purposes, the most important conclusion of the latter review was that "The experimental animal data on [manganese exposure from] MMT exposure are not very useful for determining the risk of long-term human exposure to low levels of MMT. Lifetime or carcinogenicity studies have not been done by inhalation or any other route. The very high doses used and the unusual exposure routes other than inhalation, dermal, or ingestion make extrapolations to human exposure difficult. Clearly, however, ambient manganese exposure from unburned MMT in the atmosphere … should not be a problem" (Midwest Research Institute 1987, 75).

The Wood and Eyged health-risk assessment of MMT impressed me as very thorough and persuasive, and also relatively favourable to MMT. Here is a brief summary of their findings:

The major health concern arises, not with MMT itself … but with the airborne manganese oxides produced upon combustion of the additive. Manganese, although considered an essential element in small amounts, is neurotoxic at higher doses, particularly when inhaled, since self-limiting homeostatic mechanisms are most effective for manganese derived from gastrointestinal uptake … From a multi-media exposure perspective, inhalation represents less than 2% of total daily uptake of manganese for all age groups and all percentiles of the population, as well as occupational groups such as taxi drivers and service garage mechanics. The remainder is derived primarily from natural levels of manganese in dietary sources. For individuals exposed to very high levels of manganese in an occupational setting (e.g., battery plant workers), air represents more than 90% of total manganese exposure.

Thus, all analyses indicate that the combustion products of MMT in gasoline do not represent an added health risk to the Canadian population. (Wood and Eyged 1994, 66–9)

In contrast to these assessments, Elizabeth May, Executive Director of the Sierra Club of Canada, testifying before the Senate Committee, was very critical of Health Canada and the Wood and Eyged report, and strongly endorsed the MMT Act and the need for a precautionary approach. The following passages provide a good sample of the views she brought to the committee:

The Health Canada study is flawed. It is out of step with much of the work being done internationally. This is actually a core part of the problem with the Canadian regulatory response to MMT. Health

Canada allowed the use of MMT initially knowing that they had big data gaps. They have never addressed those gaps ...

Senator Buchanan: ... Why is this bill a trade bill and not under the environment act?

Ms May: I think that is because Health Canada has done a terrible job on this file ... I think CEPA would have been a better route, but the bill is before you, having passed through the House of Commons ...

Senator Buchanan: ... would you agree there should be an environmental assessment before this bill passes?

Ms May: No, and I will tell you why. A poison is being added to our gasoline. A poison is reaching children every day. The legislative process of this country grinds slowly. I want to see MMT out of gasoline as quickly as possible ... Both Environment and Health agree it is a hazard to the environment ...

We know [manganese] is a neurotoxin. We know that it has serious effects when it is used on lab animals. We know that it has effects occupationally. We know that the studies looking at chronic low level exposure give us cause for worry. Do we turn a blind eye to those studies and say, "Since we are not sure, it is probably all right," or do we say, "All the evidence points to a significant neurotoxic effect, so we ought to be careful about exposing the entire human population – and particularly vulnerable groups like pregnant women, young children, the elderly, asthmatics and people with respiratory illnesses – to this particular substance, especially when alternatives are available?" ...

The definition of "toxic" under CEPA is that it constitutes or may constitute a danger to human life or health. Given the medical studies and the opinion of experts around the world, I think MMT fits that definition. (SSCEENR 2/5, 1997d, 57–60)

CEPA and the problems in applying it to MMT are discussed further in this chapter and in chapter 14. The U.S. National Physicians for Social Responsibility (1996) issued a scathing resolution on MMT. Among other things, the group said that:

Whereas: Manganese is recognized as a nervous system toxin at high levels of exposure, is also a pulmonary toxin, and may also be a reproductive and developmental toxin; and

Whereas: No available health data indicate that the widespread use of MMT as proposed is safe; and

Whereas: The widespread commercialization of MMT, without clear evidence of its safety, would represent a population-wide toxicologic experiment, performed without the informed consent of those who would be exposed, in violation of accepted norms of medical ethics; and ...

[the EPA found] that available data preclude adequate assessment of MMT's risks;

Be it therefore resolved: The Physicians for Social Responsibility deplores the use of MMT in the U.S. gasoline supply without clear evidence of safety, and urges the U.S. Congress and applicable state agencies to ban the addition of MMT into gasoline until its safety is clearly documented;

urges all refiners and sellers of gasoline to refrain from adding MMT to their products until its safety is clearly documented; ...

urges all refiners and sellers of gasoline to label their product, at the point of retail sale, with regard to MMT content, so consumers will know whether they are purchasing gasoline with MMT added; ...

urges further research into the health effects of manganese exposure, emphasizing the effects on vulnerable populations, with financial support from Ethyl Corporation but carried out completely independently of that corporation.

If all or most of the opinions of experts were consistent about the issues before us, there would have been no controversy over MMT. Part of the disagreement between the assessment of May and Wood and Egyed, for example, was that the former focused on studies of the direct effects of manganese on the health of animals and people while the latter focused on the residual and marginal effects of the combustion of a manganese-based additive in gasoline. There was no apparent disagreement about the toxic effects of manganese or about the need for more research and monitoring of various kinds, especially involving vulnerable populations of workers, young people, pregnant women, the very old, and so on. Health Canada officials certainly did not regard the Wood and Egyed study as a licence to forget about MMT. In a response to a petition sent (3 July 2001) to the Commissioner of the Environment and Sustainable Development, under Section 22 of the *Auditor General Act*, Alan Rock, Minister of Health, wrote (on 23 July 2001):

22 It is important to correct the statement in the petition that "Health Canada continues to support the use of MMT in Canadian gasoline."

Health Canada's analysis of the scientific information on the health effects of MMT are [sic] contained in its risk assessment (available at www.hc-sc.gc.ca/air) in which it was concluded that "airborne manganese resulting from the combustion of MMT in gasoline-powered vehicles is not entering the Canadian environment in quantities or under conditions that may constitute a health risk."

23 Health Canada conducted the 1994 (and previous) risk assessments of MMT to respond to Part 5, paragraphs 68(b) and 68(c) of the then CEPA (1988) to assess whether or not a substance is "CEPA toxic" in the Canadian environment.

24 Based on the 1994 risk assessment, which reviewed the pertinent scientific literature on the direct health effects of manganese and MMT, Health Canada has no objection to the use of MMT in gasoline ...

32 Health Canada will continue its study of the scientific literature regarding manganese and MMT in the context of CEPA and will take, in conjunction with Environment Canada and stakeholders, any action indicated by the scientific evidence. (Commissioner of the Environment and Sustainable Development 2001, 5–6)

A more guarded statement would be difficult to construct. Responding to the same petition, David Anderson, Minister of the Environment, said, "In announcing that Canada would lift its restrictions on the interprovincial trade and import of the gasoline additive MMT in 1998, the federal Ministers of the Environment and Industry underlined the government's continued commitment to protect the health and environment of Canadians. The federal government will assess the results of future tests on the effects of MMT or any other fuel additive on automobile tailpipe emissions. If subsequent federal action is warranted, it will be taken under CEPA" (Commissioner of the Environment and Sustainable Development 2003, 2).

Every official whose opinion was recorded in all of the literature I reviewed fully supported the *MMT Act*, essentially on the basis of a precautionary approach similar to that articulated by May. The bottom line for all health-related proponents of the *Act*, as well as the federal government (see chapters 12 and 15), was quite simply that it is better to be safe than sorry. The main area of disagreement was about how much more manganese actually reached people in a potentially damaging way as a result of MMT being burned with gasoline. Exact measurement of MMT's contribution is difficult because, among other things, it is "impossible to distinguish between directly emitted Mn from automobiles, Mn enriched road dust and the naturally occurring Mn in crustal material" (Zayed 2001). In a study designed precisely to help sort out the relative contributions of manganese from various sources, Bhuie and Roy (2001, 1300) wrote: "In conclusion, this extensive study did not show any statistically significant relationship between Mn levels in soil and distances from the highway at any of the sites despite the heavy traffic volumes and, thus, increased MMT usage at the urban sites. This could be due to the natural abundance of Mn in nature causing compounding of the variation among the sites, indicating that the contribution of Mn from MMT is very low and does not significantly increase soil background levels in the Canadian terrestrial environment. The authors are studying the impacts of Mn leaching into the deeper layers of soil and toxicity levels in plants, and the findings will be reported later."

May brought the committee's attention to a good review article published three years after the Wood and Egyed review, i.e., Frumkin and Solomon (1997). The former review was much longer, more detailed, and had one hundred references, while the latter had seventy-seven, including seven dated after 1994 and excluding Wood and Egyed.

Frumkin and Solomon (1997, 107) strongly urged caution: "Common sense and prudence ... dictate that MMT not be used until further data are available and its safety is confirmed." In response to Ethyl's claim that "'MMT is the most tested fuel additive in history' and that evaluations by Health Canada and the U.S. EPA had shown MMT not to pose a health risk," Frumkin and Solomon wrote, "In fact, no systematic epidemiological studies have been conducted on the effects of MMT use. While it is possible that MMT use would not pose a population hazard, absolutely no empirical evidence supports this claim" (112).

The truth of the first quoted sentence depends heavily on one's interpretation of a "systematic epidemiological study." In principle I have no objection to a fairly robust definition of the phrase, although probably plenty of worthwhile epidemiological studies are not strictly robust. Different kinds of studies make different kinds of contributions to what becomes generally accepted as well-warranted information or knowledge, and the history of science is a history of controversies over the preferred methods for studying diverse phenomena (Durbin 1980). Nevertheless, if one thinks of a "systematic epidemiological study" as one in which the impact of manganese particles from combusted MMT on some sort of human health outcomes for a general population, measured objectively (e.g., examining brain, liver, lung tissue) or subjectively (e.g., examining people's self-reported health status), are assessed under rigorously controlled circumstances, then Frumkin and Solomon are right. So far as I have been able to determine, nothing of the sort has even been described yet. Even the EPA's detailed proposal in Oge (1999) is short of that mark. A review of the most relevant and thorough studies from Wood and Egyed (1994) and Frumkin and Solomon (1997) reveals that while they all dealt with exposure to manganese in one form or another, either there was careful measurement of the level of exposure from burning MMT but no measurement of health outcomes, or there was careful measurement of health outcomes but no measurement of the level of exposure from burning MMT. This applies to studies discussed in both reviews (e.g., Iregren 1990; Loranger and Zayed 1994, 1995; Mergler et al. 1994; Roels et al. 1987, 1992; Siegl and Bergert 1982; Wennberg et al. 1991) and to studies only discussed in the later review (e.g., Hua and Huang 1991; Iregren 1994; Lucchini et al. 1995; Sierra et al. 1995; Sjogren 1996; Zayed et al. 1994). It even applies to studies described in a more recent review (Zayed 2001), in which the author lists several studies published since the 1997 review and several crucial pieces of information that have to be assembled before a thorough evidence-based risk assessment can be completed.

The truth of Frumkin and Solomon's second sentence is more difficult to assess because it involves at least two claims: (1) It is possible that the use of MMT does not "pose a population hazard," i.e., that the use of MMT is safe for the general population; (2) There is "absolutely no empirical evidence" supporting the claim that MMT is safe for the general population. Because it is granted in the first claim that MMT may be safe, one should not assume that Frumkin and Solomon would use the second claim in a fallacious argument appealing to ignorance (Michalos 1970a). That is, they are not arguing that the absence of evidence showing that MMT is safe should be regarded as the presence of evidence showing that MMT is not safe. Rather, they are arguing that the presence of evidence showing that manganese can be harmful to one's health is sufficient to take a precautionary approach to the use of MMT because when it is burned with gasoline it releases manganese particles that may find their way into human beings and, over time, cause serious health problems. This was the fundamental argument for the MMT Act, which was essentially an act of precaution.

The problem is that even people granting the reasonableness of precaution might disagree on exactly what particular precautionary measures ought to be employed. Chapter 16 outlines a wide variety of measures that were considered and, for one reason or another, discarded by key players in the dispute. Before we reach a conclusion about the fundamental argument, every measure will be explored. Here I only want to mention an objection that opponents of the MMT Act would raise against the claim that there is "absolutely no empirical evidence" supporting the claim that MMT may be safe, i.e., that acceptance of this claim depends on one's willingness to totally discount the empirical evidence showing the *relatively low increment* of manganese exposure to people resulting from the combustion of MMT in gasoline. In spite of all the uncertainties regarding the most reasonable RfC, the most likely rates of exposure, inhalation, absorption and so on for anyone, Wood and Egyed (1994, 48) reported that the PM_{10} ambient manganese data for 1992 for one area of the cities of Hamilton and Sault Ste Marie, Ontario, had an annual daily mean of 0.100 μm Mn/m³ (i.e., 0.100 micrograms of manganese per cubic metre) and 0.158 μm Mn/m³, respectively. Assuming the average daily level of ambient manganese in Canadian and American cities mentioned earlier of 0.03 to 0.04 μm Mn/m³, any problems faced by average citizens would be multiplied by at least 3.33 and 5.27 for citizens in those high level areas of Hamilton and Sault Ste Marie, respectively. Assuming that the annual average daily level of exposure is closer to the 9.2 ng/m³ (i.e., 9.2 nanograms per cubic metre; one nanogram equals 10^{-9} or one thousand millionth of a gram) estimate of the RTI (1998) report described in chapter 15, the residents of those high level areas are (or would be if the 1992 figures applied later) even worse off, relatively speaking. Thus, opponents of the *MMT Act* could argue that because levels of manganese exposure (lasting perhaps a lifetime for some residents) are relatively very high in parts of Hamilton and Sault Ste Marie compared to any levels of manganese exposure resulting from burning MMT in gasoline, and because, so far as we know, these residents do not suffer more ill effects of exposure than residents of any other areas, it is reasonable to entertain the hypothesis that the levels of exposure to manganese from burning MMT may really be not only relatively harmless, but just plain harmless.

Frumkin and Solomon addressed this objection: "even if the average American would absorb relatively little additional manganese following the introduction of MMT, there is potential for toxicity for large numbers of people. Without rigorous evidence demonstrating safety, the increased exposure to manganese posed by MMT cannot be assumed to be safe" (112).

They were especially concerned about the people who were vulnerable because of their work, age, pregnancy, liver problems, and so on. For such people, the small additional exposure might be enough to "push them over the edge." While that is true, this consideration would not normally be given much weight in other circumstances. We know, for example, that for some people exposure to just a bit more alcohol, sugar, or television might be very dangerous to their health compared to that of most other people, but this is not generally regarded as good grounds for banning alcohol, sugar, or television; even a staunch defender of the precautionary principle would be reluctant to use it to justify such bans. Thus it would not be reasonable to totally discount the evidence showing the relatively low increment of manganese exposure resulting from the combustion of MMT in gasoline. Nor would it be, nor was it, reasonable for the federal government to press its case for the *MMT Act* so aggressively and to completely ignore the potential dangers from manganese exposure in Hamilton and Sault Ste Marie. What is worse, one of the saddest admissions written by any official about such exposures came out of a response by Alan Rock to the petition cited earlier: "Although Health Canada concluded in the 1994 document that air manganese levels in most urban centres did not represent a threat to the health of Canadians, it was stated that levels in cities with manganese-emitting industries can be above the reference concentration. Hence, Health Canada has developed a protocol for a study of personal exposure to manganese and other metals in a city with industrial emissions, *and is seeking funding for such a study*" (Commissioner of the Environment and Sustainable Development 2001, 4; emphasis added).

Against the background of all the resources that have been found to create and sustain trade deals that seem to protect investors' profits over everything else, it is very distressing to hear that residents in the cities with manganese-emitting industries will have their health properly protected only if the Minister of Health is lucky enough to find funding for the needed research.

12

Government of Canada's Response to Ethyl's Claims under the NAFTA and the Tribunal's *Award on Jurisdiction*

The Government of Canada filed its *Statement of Defence in the Matter of an Arbitration under Chapter 11 of the North American Free Trade Agreement Between Ethyl Corporation (Claimant/Investor) v. Government of Canada (Respondent/ Party)* on 27 November 1997 (Hughes, Evernden, and Tyhurst 1997). Strictly speaking, the *Defence* replied to both the *Notice of Arbitration* and the *Statement of Claim*. Briefly, Canada's position was that the NAFTA tribunal was "without jurisdiction to entertain Ethyl's claim," the *MMT Act* was "legitimate regulation," no national treatment obligation had been breached, no performance requirement was imposed, no investment was expropriated, no measure was taken that was "tantamount to expropriation," and, therefore, Ethyl was not entitled to compensation (Hughes, Evernden, and Tyhurst 1997, 1–2). Apparently, the Government of Canada was not prepared to give an inch.

Its *Defence* began by explaining that before proposed legislation becomes effective law (capable of producing legal effects) in Canada it must be passed by the House of Commons and the Senate, and receive Royal Assent. Besides being debated on the floors of the House and Senate, proposals are routinely examined and revised in parliamentary committees, as Bill C-29 was in the House of Commons Standing Committee on Environment and Sustainable Development and the Senate Standing Committee on Energy, Environment and Natural Resources. Sometimes, as in the case of Bill C-29, the law comes into force some weeks after receiving Royal Assent. As we have seen already, Ethyl Corporation was one of the participants in the Senate Hearings and was free to lobby for its position not only throughout the legislative process which formally began in June 1995 with the introduction of Bill C-94, but also in the several years before that when

MMT was being used and evaluated by various bodies in various fora in Canada and the United States.

Following this explanation, the *Defence* asserted that Ethyl's complaints against the Government of Canada changed from its *Notice of Intent* and *Notice of Arbitration* to its *Statement of Claim*. In the first two documents it was charged that the Government of Canada breached its NAFTA obligations with ministerial "statements" about MMT and a proposed law banning its use. In the *Statement of Claim* it was charged that the government breached its NAFTA obligations by passing Bill C-29. Besides asserting that the basis of complaint had changed over time, the *Defence* claimed that Ethyl's letters granting consent to arbitration and waiving its right to adjudication in some other forum, dated 8 July 1997, were in fact delivered on 2 October 1997. Armed with these apparent anomalies, the Government of Canada proceeded to defend itself on the grounds of procedural irregularities.

In particular, the government argued that Chapter 11 required (a) a measure by a party that breached a NAFTA obligation *and* "incurred loss or damage by reason of, or arising out of, that breach" (Article 1116); (b) a six-month waiting period from the time of "the events giving rise to a claim" to the submission of a claim to arbitration (*Notice of Arbitration*) (Article 1120); (c) a ninety-day waiting period from the date of submission of its *Notice of Intent* to its *Notice of Arbitration* (Article 1119); and (d) consent and waiver letters delivered when the *Notice of Arbitration* is delivered (Articles 1121 and 1137). Because these requirements were not met, "the claim set out in the Statement of Claim is null and void and this Tribunal is utterly without jurisdiction to entertain it" (Hughes, Evernden, and Tyhurst 1997, 6–9).

Conditions (c) and (d) were straightforward. Since the *Notice of Intent* was dated 10 September 1996 and the *Notice of Arbitration* was filed 14 April 1997, condition (c) was clearly satisfied. It has already been explained that Ethyl failed to satisfy condition (d). Conditions (a) and (b) were more complicated. Neither was satisfied if "the events giving rise to a claim" are those mentioned in the *Statement of Claim*, because the *Notice of Arbitration* was dated 14 April 1997 and Bill C-29 came into force several weeks later on 24 June 1997. If, on the other hand, the offending "events" are those mentioned in the *Notice of Intent* and the *Notice of Arbitration* then, the government asserted, conditions (a) and (b) were still not satisfied because "statements" are not "measures" as defined by NAFTA. It was not denied that as early as 12 October 1994 Minister Copps told a Canadian press reporter that if the oil industry did not voluntarily remove MMT before August 1995, she would introduce legislation requiring its removal. Nor was it denied that there were also "statements" from February and May 1995 quoted above from the *Notice of Arbitration*. Nevertheless, if "statements" were not "measures" then conditions (a) and (b) could not be satisfied.

Assuming that the offending "events" were those specified in the *Statement of Claim*, i.e., the passing (read "coming into force") of Bill C-29, it was asserted that "Ethyl's submission to arbitration is void in that the legislation complained of in the Statement of Claim had not been enacted or come into force at the time the claim was submitted. There was therefore no measure nor was there any measure relating to an investment or an investor in effect upon which Ethyl could found an alleged breach of any obligation under Chapter 11 (Hughes, Evernden, and Tyhurst 1997, 10).

If the offending event was the coming into force of the MMT Act on 24 June 1997, then at the time of the "submission to arbitration" (either by the *Notice of Intent* on 10 September 1996 or the *Notice of Arbitration* on 14 April 1997) the event did not exist and therefore it could not have had any effects at all. A nice point, if the offending event was the one mentioned in the antecedent of the conditional proposition. Unfortunately, the tribunal did not share the government's view of the offending event.

Assuming that the offending "events" were "statements" as specified in the *Notice of Intent* and *Notice of Arbitration*, the government relied on its understanding of Article 201 to defend its claim that "statements" were not "measures". Article 201 says that a "measure includes any law, regulation, procedure, requirement or practice." It is difficult to interpret most remarks made by members of parliament inside or outside the House or Senate about the alleged environmental and health effects of MMT as "measures" as defined in this Article. In any case, if the offending "events" were "statements," the government backed up its claim that "statements" were not "measures" with what strikes me as an even stronger argument, which was also endorsed by a brief from the Government of Mexico. In this supporting argument, the Government of Canada claimed that insofar as any "measure" was involved, "it relates to trade in goods within the meaning of Chapter 3 of the NAFTA," and Article 1112 (1) says that "In the event of any inconsistency between this Chapter and another Chapter, the other Chapter shall prevail to the extent of the inconsistency" (Hughes, Evernden, and Tyhurst 1997, 11).

The Government of Mexico offered its view of the issues in accordance with Article 1128, which allows any of the three contracting parties to "make submissions to a Tribunal on a question of interpretation of this Agreement." The key points made are remarkably consistent with those of the Government of Canada, and lead to the same conclusion, namely, that "the Tribunal is utterly without jurisdiction to entertain" the *Statement of Claim*. Thus:

> On the facts, this case involves a measure relating to trade in goods. The enforcement of rights that may accrue under Chapter Three accrue not to the Claimant but to the United States. If the United States is of the view that Canada has imposed a measure which constitutes an import barrier under Article 309 ... it is entitled to commence dispute settlement proceedings under Chapter Twenty. As in other potential international trade cases, the present Claimant is fully entitled to petition the United States authorities to commence such proceedings. However, it is not open to the Claimant to use the investor-State mechanism to launch what is in reality a challenge against a trade measure in the guise of an investment dispute.
>
> ... The opening language of Article 1101 (1) (a) states that the chapter "applies to measures adopted or maintained by a Party relating to ... [investors or investments]". Thus, to properly be the subject of an investor-State arbitration, *the measure at issue must have been in effect at the time that the arbitral process was initiated*. Given the express contemplation of proposed measures in other parts of the NAFTA, this language cannot be interpreted to reach proposed measures. In Mexico's submission, therefore, the use of the verbs "adopt" and "maintain" means that the measure complained of must already be in existence at the time that the proceeding is initiated, i.e., at the time the notice of claim is filed pursuant to Article 1119. This is particularly so in the case of Chapter Eleven, since a measure that has not yet produced legal effects cannot cause damages for which compensation or restitution may be due.
>
> ... Mexico is also of the view that arbitral tribunals established under Chapter Eleven must adhere to the requirements of Section B ... With respect to this particular case, this means that the *appropriate waivers must have been filed at the proper time*, and that the *claimant not be permitted to change its claim from a non-arbitrable "non-measure" to an arbitrable measure during the process*. The language of Articles 1119 and 1120 is clear. The Agreement has to have been allegedly breached at the time that the Notice of Intent is filed and six months must have elapsed "since the events giving rise to a claim." (quotation taken from Böckstiegel, Brower, and Lalonde 1998, 23–4; emphasis added)

In the view of the International Institute for Sustainable Development and the World Wildlife Fund (IISD/WWF 2001, 24), practically anything, "statements" included, might be a "measure" according to Article 201. "In essence," the report said, "any new governmental act, at any level of government, that impacts on an investor may fall within what is covered." If so, the vagueness of the concept would function as a dangerous incentive for investors to try to resist government regulatory efforts.

Following its discussion of procedural irregularities, the Government of Canada proceeded to review its problems with MMT. It claimed that "The public health and environmental impacts of long-term, lower dose exposure to airborne respirable manganese and unburned MMT are unknown." On 28 July 1997 Canada's Motor Vehicle Safety Regulations were amended to:

> harmonize the national standards for HC, CO and NO$_x$ with those in the United States and require that light duty vehicles and trucks be equipped with OBD systems to monitor engine and emission control equipment ... Faced with tightening auto emissions standards, Canadian vehicle manufacturers and others pressed the Government of Canada to eliminate MMT from unleaded gasoline ... The vehicle industry and petroleum refiners were unable to agree on acceptable measures for addressing the problems associated with the use of MMT in gasoline. The Government of Canada encouraged these parties to resolve the issue among them, participating in numerous meetings with them at senior levels. The parties met and made various proposals in early 1995 but were unable to resolve their differences.

> The vehicle industry presented evidence that MMT: plugged catalytic converters, reduced catalyst life, increased the emission of CO and HC and increased warranty costs; increased spark plug misfire and reduced spark plug life; and caused the malfunctioning of both oxygen sensors and of state-of-the-art OBD systems scheduled for introduction into new vehicles in 1996. [To review the House Committee presentation and discussion, see HSCESD10/24, 1995b.]

> ... Balanced against these considerations, Parliament had to consider factors including the claims made by Ethyl that MMT was environmentally beneficial, and the potential costs to refiners of increasing octane levels in unleaded fuels without using MMT.

> Parliament weighed the foregoing considerations together with Canada's NAFTA obligations. It concluded that the public interest necessitated regulating the use of manganese-based fuel additives in unleaded

gasoline and the method chosen was to regulate the importation for commercial purposes, and interprovincial trade in, those additives ...

Given the evident indirect potential effects, as opposed to direct toxic effects, of manganese-based fuel additives on the environment, the *Canadian Environmental Protection Act* was not an appropriate mechanism for addressing the regulation of MMT and other manganese-based fuel additives ...

In any case, Canada says that the Act was intended to be, and is, an effective way of removing MMT from all gasoline produced in Canada. (Hughes, Evernden, and Tyhurst 1997, 13–31)

Besides all of the above, the government specifically brought up the commitments made in the preamble to the NAFTA and the relationship of those commitments to the NAFTA's objectives. It was noted that:

The preamble to the NAFTA states that the Parties resolved to carry out stated objectives "in a manner consistent with environmental protection and conservation" and to "strengthen the development and enforcement of environmental laws and regulations" ...

The negotiation of the NAFTA included unprecedented consideration of environmental protection. The agreement contains numerous provisions which recognize and preserve the ability of the parties to protect the environment and health of their citizens. Such provisions were negotiated in the light of the objectives and commitments expressed in the general statements cited above. (Hughes, Evernden, and Tyhurst 1997, 26)

Among the "numerous provisions," Article 1114 is probably the most explicit:

1 Nothing in this Chapter shall be construed to prevent a Party from adopting, maintaining or enforcing any measure otherwise consistent with this Chapter that it considers appropriate to ensure that investment activity in its territory is undertaken in a manner sensitive to environmental concerns.

2 The Parties recognize that it is inappropriate to encourage investment by relaxing domestic health, safety or environmental measures. Accordingly, a Party should not waive or otherwise derogate from, or offer to waive or otherwise derogate from, such measures as an encouragement for the establishment, acquisition, expansion or retention in its territory of an investment of an investor. (NAFTA 2002)

Finally, the government insisted that the MMT *Act* did not breach any national treatment obligations because it treated everyone trading in MMT the same; that it did not impose any performance requirements because it did not specify any given level of domestic content of anything; that it did not do anything "tantamount to expropriation" because the regulations did not take anything away from anyone; and that, therefore, "the Claimant suffered no compensable loss or damage as a consequence of ministerial support for, or the passage and enforcement of, the Act" (Hughes, Evernden, and Tyhurst 1997, 28–34).

The tribunal issued its *Award on Jurisdiction* on 24 June 1998. The first six sections of the *Award* identified the parties to the dispute i.e., the claimant and respondent, (section 1), summarized the dispute (2) and the relief sought (3), and reviewed the chronology of relevant events, arbitral proceedings, and major legal arguments of the parties and Mexico regarding the jurisdiction of the tribunal, along the lines of the discussion above. It was also noted that by a letter of 14 July 1997 the Government of Canada appointed the Honourable Marc Lalonde (P.C., O.C., Q.C., former federal Minister of Health) as arbitrator, and by agreement in letters the claimant and respondent confirmed the appointment of Professor Karl-Heinz Böckstiegel (Professor of Transnational Law, University of Cologne) as presiding arbitrator or chair of the tribunal on 2 September 1997. Dezalay and Garth (1996, 140) described Böckstiegel as "one of the best known and most active arbitrators in the ICC [International Chamber of Commerce] world."

The tribunal's arguments, official conclusions, and final award were given in the remaining sections 7 and 8. First came a list of the relevant sections of the applicable laws or rules the tribunal was "required to apply in interpreting and applying NAFTA." In particular, Article 1131 (1) required that "A Tribunal established under this Section shall decide the issues in dispute in accordance with this Agreement and applicable rules of international law." The latter included the UNCITRAL Arbitration Rules reviewed above, and the Vienna Convention on the Law of Treaties that entered into force on 27 January 1980 and is accepted by the three parties to the NAFTA. The most important sections of that Convention were Article 31:

1 A treaty shall be interpreted in good faith in accordance with the ordinary meaning to be given to the terms of the treaty in their context and in the light of its object and purpose.
2 The context for the purpose of the interpretation of a treaty shall comprise, in addition to the text, including its preamble and annexes: [any additional agreements or instruments accepted by the parties] ...

3 There shall be taken into account, together with the context:
(a) Any subsequent agreement between the parties regarding the interpretation of the treaty or the application of its provisions;
(b) Any subsequent practice in the application of the treaty which establishes the agreement of the parties regarding its interpretation;
(c) Any relevant rules of international law applicable in the relations between the parties.
4 A special meaning shall be given to a term if it is established that the parties so intended.

and Article 32:

Recourse may be had to supplementary means of interpretation, including the preparatory work of the treaty and the circumstances of its conclusion, in order to confirm the meaning resulting from the application of article 31, or to determine the meaning when the interpretation according to article 31,
(a) Leaves the meaning ambiguous or obscure; or
(b) Leads to a result which is manifestly absurd or unreasonable.
(Böckstiegel, Brower, and Lalonde 1998, 26–7)

Second, it was insisted that, according to Article 31(1) of the Vienna Convention, the tribunal had to examine the issues of the case in the light of the "object and purpose" of the NAFTA Article 102 (Böckstiegel, Brower, and Lalonde 1998, 29). That article says:

1 The objectives of this Agreement, as elaborated more specifically through its principles and rules, including national treatment, most-favored-nation treatment and transparency, are to:
a) eliminate barriers to trade in, and facilitate the cross-border movement of, goods and services between the territories of the Parties;
b) promote conditions of fair competition in the free trade area;
c) increase substantially investment opportunities in the territories of the Parties;
d) provide adequate and effective protection and enforcement of intellectual property rights in each Party's territory;
e) create effective procedures for the implementation and application of this Agreement, for its joint administration and for the resolution of disputes; and

f) establish a framework for further trilateral, regional and multilateral cooperation to expand and enhance the benefits of this Agreement.

2 The Parties shall interpret and apply the provisions of this Agreement in the light of its objectives set out in paragraph 1 and in accordance with applicable rules of international law. (NAFTA 2002)

Unfortunately, once the tribunal introduced NAFTA Article 102 as a reasonable implication of Article 31(1) of the Vienna Convention, Article 31(2) was completely neglected. Most importantly, the tribunal neglected to give any weight to the "context" of the treaty which, as indicated above, includes the treaty's "preamble and annexes." No attention was paid to the Government of Canada's claim (quoted above) that the "object and purpose" of the treaty were negotiated given the assumption (i.e., in the "context") that the three parties were committed to preserving their ability "to protect the environment and health of their citizens." Since Article 31(3)(b) directs tribunals to take into account "any subsequent practice in the application of the treaty which establishes the agreement of the parties regarding its interpretation," the failure of this particular tribunal to give any weight to the "context" of the treaty set a very dangerous precedent. It is not an exaggeration to say, as suggested in chapter 10 in criticism 14 of Public Citizen (2001), that the commitments to environmental and health protection made in the preamble and Article 1114 were rendered practically worthless. Even if future tribunals are not absolutely bound by decisions made by this one, Weiler (2000, 188) was no doubt correct when he wrote that "awards made in the early claims submitted to arbitration promise to establish a pattern for how the NAFTA's investor-state provisions will work in practice" (cf. IISD/WWF 2001, 41–2).

Given the mixed bag of scientific evidence for and against the harmful effects of MMT, one can appreciate why reasonable people might disagree about whether the additive should have been eliminated from unleaded gasoline. So it is both sad and ironic that a dangerous precedent was set about the relative status of the "contextual" versus "object and purpose" provisions of the NAFTA. A poor interpretation of the NAFTA text led to a poor precedent for future disputes and to a poor safety assessment of the product at the centre of the dispute.

The report of the International Institute for Sustainable Development and World Wildlife Fund commented on two other NAFTA cases in which tribunals failed to take proper account of the context of the agreement. In the Metalclad case the tribunal ignored "the counterbalances included in the preamble of NAFTA relating to environmental protection and sustainable development as equal goals" and created "a high risk of an imbalanced interpretation of Chapter 11s obligations." "The Tribunal went so far as to argue that it was the objective of Chapter 11 to *ensure the successful implementation* of investment initiatives, although this objective is never stated in NAFTA itself" (IISD/WWF 2001, 17–18; see also Public Citizen 2001, 14).

In the S.D. Myers decision, the NGO's report said that even though the tribunal "noted the environmental objectives expressed in the preamble," it:

> went on to incorporate actual trade rules from other parts of NAFTA directly into the interpretation of Chapter 11. It also went on to use NAFTA's trade objectives to help interpret two international environmental agreements relating to the transboundary movement of hazardous waste that were negotiated in a completely unrelated context, leaving them subject to a distorted interpretation.

> These cases show how broad objectives related to trade liberalization can impact on the interpretation of investment rules (and even on international environmental agreements). When the objectives are not balanced, or are invoked in an unbalanced manner, the effect is unbalanced interpretations. This highlights the need to have specific objectives for an investment agreement or an investment chapter in a larger agreement. It also highlights the need to ensure that such objectives are clearly and expressly balanced. (IISD/WWF 2001, 18–19)

The problem of inappropriately drawing on trade rules to interpret investment rules was subsequently addressed by the North American Free Trade Commission in its *Notes of Interpretation* issued 31 July 2001. However, since no rule book exists to instruct tribunals in the art and science of weighing objectives and considerations to ensure a "balanced" assessment, how will "unbalanced" assessments be identified and prevented? What is worse, in the light of research on perceived fairness (Michalos 1990), assuming that trade lawyers are relatively more sensitive to trade than to environmental issues, it is likely that trade lawyers will tend to perceive decisions favouring trade over the environment as "fair." Granting that environmental lawyers would be biased in the opposite direction, it would be reasonable and fair to try to ensure that tribunals are staffed with an eye to balancing their interests and expertise. However, while such staffing might be a reasonable necessary condition of fair adjudication, it would not be sufficient. A second necessary condition would be the addition of an objective about the protection of health and the environment to Article 101.1. Clearly, Article 101.1 in its current form privileges trade over health and the environment, among other things.

Third, the tribunal said that it was necessary to distinguish "jurisdictional provisions," which were "limits set to the authority of this Tribunal to act at all on the merits of the dispute," from "procedural rules," violations of which by a claimant might delay proceedings or even lead to dismissal of a claim. The Government of Canada believed its objections concerned the former, and Ethyl believed those objections concerned the latter. Since UNCITRAL rules stipulate that "the sole basis of jurisdiction under NAFTA Chapter 11 ... is the consent of the Parties," the question of the exact nature of the government's objections rested on the question of whether or not both parties granted consent. Then, since Ethyl's initiation of the proceedings clearly indicated its consent, the question was really only about the Canadian government's consent. The tribunal decided that because the allegations made by Ethyl against the Government of Canada were made by "an investor of a Party" within three years of the time when it discovered a "loss or damage," the "Claimant's Statement of Claim satisfies *prima facie* the requirements of Article 1116 to establish the jurisdiction of this Tribunal" (Böckstiegel, Brower, and Lalonde 1998, 31). That is, because the claim was apparently of the sort that the Government of Canada a priori supposed should be adjudicated by the NAFTA's dispute settlement procedures, it could be assumed that the government implicitly granted consent.

The tribunal's decision regarding this consent issue strikes me as very peculiar, although Sornarajah (2003, 13) suggested that it would not be extraordinary. It seems to be based on the principle that two parties never have to explicitly grant consent: as long as one party makes a prima facie legitimate claim, it may be assumed that the other party gave a priori consent simply because it signed the treaty. But this is inconsistent with Article 1122 (2) (a), which requires "written consent of the parties." Also puzzling is that the Government of Canada had to provide written consent to establish a tribunal to hear the case for jurisdiction, but it apparently did not have to provide written consent for the tribunal to decide that the government had granted jurisdiction to the tribunal a priori by merely signing the treaty. If the tribunal's interpretation of Article 1122 (2) (a) is appropriate, then the article ought to be changed or deleted rather than allow action that is literally inconsistent with it be treated as if it were not inconsistent.

Fourth, regarding the claim of the Government of Canada, which was supported by the Government of Mexico, that the *MMT Act* was about "trade in goods" and that, therefore, in accordance with Article 1112 (1), any dispute involving such trade had to proceed under the rules of Chapters 3 and 20, the tribunal decided that:

> The argument made is that issues of trade in goods under Chapter 3 give rise to government-to-government dispute settlement procedures under Section B of Chapter 20, and, it is contended, thereby necessarily exclude the possibility of investor-State arbitration under Chapter 11. Canada cites no authority, and does not elaborate any argument, however, as to why the two necessarily are incompatible ... As Ethyl has pointed out, Canada indicated at the Hearing on jurisdiction that this was not "an issue that was absolutely critical to be disposed of at [that] hearing". In the circumstances, further treatment of this issue, if any, must abide another day. The Tribunal cannot presently exclude Ethyl's claim on this basis. (Böckstiegel, Brower, and Lalonde 1998, 32–3)

On this issue, it seems to me that the tribunal was spectacularly short-sighted. It did not see that every case of "trade in goods" involves investment although every case of investment does not involve "trade in goods." Thus, following this tribunal's precedent, whenever a case involving "trade in goods" arises, another Tribunal can treat it as a case involving investment, effectively undermining not only Article 1112 (1) but also Chapters 3 and 20. If "trade in goods" involved precisely the same range of issues as investment, then there would be no need or justification for separate Chapters and provisions in the NAFTA regarding them. But the authors of the NAFTA clearly believed such Chapters and provisions, including the dispute settlement procedures, were needed. Therefore, "trade in goods" and investment do not involve the same range of issues. Thus, unless tribunals are determined to undermine Article 1112 (1) and Chapters 3 and 20, they must grant that when a claim involves "trade in goods" then government-to-government arbitration is appropriate and investor-state arbitration is inappropriate. The two arbitration procedures are necessarily incompatible because and exactly insofar as application of Chapter 11 procedures in cases involving "trade in goods" can only be made at the expense of making Article 1112 (1) and Chapters 3 and 20 relatively worthless. The tribunal's failure to see these devastating implications of their position on this issue is surprising, as is the Government of Canada's willingness to allow that the issue was not "absolutely critical." One can appreciate the tribunal's reluctance to examine issues that were not regarded as "critical" to the respondent (Weiler 2000, 201), but this does not excuse their inability to see the wholly unacceptable and undesirable consequences of their position.

Weiler (2000, 197) quoted from another tribunal's award (*Pope & Talbot*, Sinclair 2007) that clearly recognized "the fact that a measure may primarily be concerned with trade in goods does not necessarily mean that it does not also relate to investments or investors." Unfortunately, that tribunal also failed to explore the logical implications of that fact as explained above, as did VanDuzer (2002, 59–61). The relatively large number of adjudications under Chapters 3 and 20 compared to the few under Chapter 11 indicate that the majority of disputants share my view of the proper use of the alternative procedures. Although VanDuzer did not see the particular difficulty with these decisions, he was troubled by "the fact that the three most important decisions under Chapter 11 so far, *Metalclad*, *S.D. Myers*, and *Pope & Talbot* [Sinclair 2007], all contained interpretive errors" (VanDuzer 2002, 97).

Fifth, regarding the government's claim that "statements" are not "measures," the tribunal was sympathetic. However, granting that "statements" are not "measures" and, therefore, by implication, the government's arguments against the alleged breaches cited in the *Notice of Intent* and the *Notice of Arbitration* were sound, the tribunal concluded that "Ethyl 'jumped the gun'" filing its *Statement of Claim* but that the "jump" was relatively unimportant to its decision regarding jurisdiction. In its own words, "In any event, the MMT Act is, as of 24 June 1997, a reality, and therefore the Tribunal is now presented with a claim based on a 'measure' which has been 'adopted or maintained' within the meaning of Article 1101" (Böckstiegel, Brower, and Lalonde 1998, 36). Nevertheless, the tribunal suspected that the challenge to its jurisdiction might not have arisen at all if Ethyl had not "jumped the gun," and that was important: "Had Ethyl first awaited Royal Assent to Bill C-29, and then bided its time another six months, the Tribunal would not have been required to deal with this issue. The Tribunal deems it appropriate to decide, therefore, that Claimant shall bear the costs of the proceedings on jurisdiction insofar as these issues are involved" (Böckstiegel, Brower, and Lalonde 1998, 41).

We have no way of knowing exactly how much "these issues" cost Ethyl. In any case, while the tribunal was flexible (practically cavalier) regarding its requirements for Ethyl to follow "procedural rules," it apparently wanted to send a message that somebody should pay a price for that flexibility and, in this case, the somebody was the claimant. A similar conclusion was reached regarding the government's charge that written consent and waivers were not delivered as required by Article 1121 (Böckstiegel,

Brower, and Lalonde 1998, 44–5). In a footnote, Weiler (2000, 194) remarked that a later tribunal (in *Pope and Talbot and the Government of Canada*, 24 February 2000) had "stated that the waiver and consent requirements are duplicative of common arbitral practice: that the submission of a claim to arbitration constitutes both consent to the arbitration and the 'constructive waiver' of all claims in domestic courts." If that is the case, the tribunal's apparent pique in the MMT case is difficult to understand. The tribunal for the case of *Waste Management (Acaverde) v. Mexico*, 2 June 2000) was more sympathetic to Mexico's stricter interpretation of the "procedural rules" (IISD/WWF 2001, 82–3).

Raising what was perhaps the most disingenuous question in the whole *Award on Jurisdiction*, the tribunal wrote: "There is no doubt that Chapter 11 embodies certain requirements that an arbitrating investor must meet before a Tribunal can proceed to consider its claim. The question rather is whether the NAFTA Parties intended that any of these conditions must be fulfilled prior to or simultaneously with delivery of a Notice of Arbitration in order for a Tribunal's jurisdiction to attach" (Böckstiegel, Brower, and Lalonde 1998, 38).

Furthermore, it was asserted that if the NAFTA parties wanted to rule out a simultaneous interpretation of Articles 1119 and 1120, "they explicitly could have required passage of six months 'since the adoption or maintenance of a measure giving rise to a claim'" (Böckstiegel, Brower, and Lalonde 1998, 41).

The tribunal's question is disingenuous because the assumption that the temporal requirements specified in Articles 1119 and 1120 might be met simultaneously is vacuous, and contrary to the spirit and letter of Article 1118. The latter says that "The disputing parties should first attempt to settle a claim through consultation or negotiation." The assumption that the conditions specified in Articles 1119 and 1120 might be met simultaneously is vacuous because if a *Notice of Intent* is filed 90 days before the *Statement of Claim* as per Article 1119 (and 90 more days from the offending events as per Article 1120), it would mean that the claimant had decided to go to arbitration while good faith negotiations, which might lead to no *Statement of Claim* being filed, were supposed to be going on. Thus the assumption that the temporal conditions of the two articles might be satisfied simultaneously implies that the claimant intends to go to arbitration and to possibly not go to arbitration. So one cannot seriously entertain the tribunal's question about a simultaneous interpretation of the temporal requirements of Articles 1119 and 1120 unless one assumes that the authors of the treaty intended to allow Notices of Intention to be vacuous, which would make the assumption of good faith negotiations absurd. I find the attribution of such intentions to the authors of the treaty highly implausible.

In his testimony before the Senate Standing Committee Hicks implied that there was no intention to file a *Statement of Claim* when Ethyl filed its *Notice of Intent*. The latter was merely a device for informing the Canadian Government of its "fact situation." Why it was necessary to use the legal machinery of the NAFTA to provide this information in the form of a false declaration of an intention is unclear. He said: "The reason we filed the notice of intent when we did was simply to be above board. We were not aware of this provision in NAFTA [i.e., the provisions of Chapter 11 that might allow compensation for damages to a company's reputation as a result of a Minister's negative comments about its products] until late spring last year. We looked into it and decided it was legitimate and that our fact situation fit. Therefore, we thought the proper thing to do was to file the notice of claim [sic] as soon as possible so that people who were considering this bill would know that that is another factor out there. We contend that our damages would be in the order of U.S. $200 million" (SSCEENR 2/5, 1997d, 18).

Sixth, regarding the government's charge that Ethyl changed its complaint from the *Notice of Intent* and *Notice of Arbitration* to the *Statement of Claim*, the tribunal decided that the changes made were merely "amendments" and that such amendments were acceptable under Article 20 of the UNCITRAL Arbitration Rules. Considering the tribunal's treatment of the Government of Canada's charge regarding the procedural rules involved in this sixth point, Weiler (2000, 200–1) wrote:

What is perhaps most interesting about the tribunal's approach to Canada's "new claim" argument, however, is that the tribunal did not concern itself with the requirements of NAFTA Article 1119 regarding the contents of Ethyl's Notice of Intent ... In light of this tribunal's findings, it would appear that should a future investor's Notice of Arbitration contain an element different from that found in the Notice of Intent (such as a higher claim amount or an additional ground of liability) NAFTA parties would be well advised not to waste time in a fruitless challenge based upon the alleged inconsistency. So long as the Notice of Intent enables the investor and the NAFTA party to engage in meaningful discussions, any differences found between it and the Notice of Arbitration should be of little significance to a tribunal ... This is because it is the Notice of Arbitration that initiates the arbitration. The Notice of

Intent only serves as a basis for the consultations or negotiations envisioned under NAFTA Article 1118, which is most likely why the tribunal did not even mention the differences between the Statement of Claim and the Notice of Intent.

As indicated above, the tribunal did not even mind the differences between the *Statement of Claim* and the *Notice of Arbitration*, since such things seem to be permitted by the UNCITRAL rules. If that is the preferred interpretation of Article 1119, then it ought to be re-written to make that clear, rather than allow future litigants to try to second-guess tribunals' interpretations.

Following the *Award on Jurisdiction* on 24 June 1998, on 20 July 1998 Industry Minister John Manley and Environment Minister Christine Stewart lifted restrictions on inter-provincial trade and import of MMT, and agreed to pay Ethyl U.S.$13 million to cover the costs of the NAFTA litigation and lost revenue. Since this came a month after the tribunal's award, it is understandable that most people assume that the tribunal's decision was the cause of the Government's capitulation. Granting that the tribunal's decision was an important consideration, I believe that the decision made twelve days earlier by the panel established under the AIT was much more important, although it is usually neglected entirely when the MMT story is told. Having lost the domestic struggle with the provinces, MMT might be produced (i.e., not merely blended) in any province and distributed across the whole country. So, a NAFTA victory over Ethyl Corporation that prevented the importation of MMT could not have kept the product out of Canada or solved any of the environmental, health, or consumer problems that the *MMT Act* was supposed to solve. Since that must have been perfectly clear to those who invented the strategy of eliminating the product by banning it from all border-crossing, one cannot possibly agree with Hufbauer et al. (2000, 12) that the aim of the *MMT Act* was to discriminate between domestic and foreign producers. That seems as implausible as the WTO tribunal's decision that "U.S. laws governing emission controls on gases emitted by oil refineries constituted a non-tariff barrier that discriminated against foreign oil refiners" (Goldring 1998, 8).

In Stephen Clarkson's general assessment of the AIT and its dispute settlement mechanism in particular, he claimed that:

Borrowed from NAFTA, this mechanism was born weak, because it did not allow claimants to pursue awards for damages, injunctions, sanctions, or even retaliation. Nor would panel determinations formally bind the disputing parties, whose compliance with rulings was to be voluntary. Thus the AIT's neoconservatizing impact on the federation may turn out to be more apparent than real ... It remains virtually invisible to the public because of the general silence about it in political discourse. Most members of the business community barely understand it. Those who are aware of its existence find it too complicated and functionally inaccessible. It enjoys very little credibility even among policymakers, who remain equivocal about its provisions and uncommitted to its application. The Agreement on Internal Trade is admittedly only in its infancy. New rounds of negotiation may enhance its privileging of commercial, government-restraining values over environmental or social, government-enhancing functions. (Clarkson 2002a, 87–9)

Although Clarkson was fully aware that the AIT panel decision preceded the NAFTA tribunal decision, he still wrote that: "The [NAFTA] MMT case revealed how Canadian environmental policy, once thought to be the purview of the sovereign legislature, has been taken hostage by continental governance. Under the supraconstitutional aegis of Chapter 11, the issue is no longer the classic Canadian question of *which* level of government – federal or provincial – can initiate an environmental regulation. The issue now became *whether any* level of government could initiate such legislation if it jeopardizes the interests of a foreign company" (Clarkson 2002a, 349).

I believe that my analysis of the events and issues leading to the NAFTA and AIT cases over MMT reveals that the AIT provided precisely the sort of leverage needed to allow the Ethyl Corporation to triumph over the Canadian government in the parallel NAFTA case. We will never know what might have happened in the latter case in the absence of the former, but in the light of what is disclosed here about the impact of the AIT case on the NAFTA case, nobody should ever underestimate the importance or the danger of the AIT.

Interesting as the first NAFTA case was, its impact was limited because it never got past the *Award on Jurisdiction* to the *Award on Merits*. The claimant's and respondent's controversial claims about the violation of Article 1102 on National Treatment, 1110 on Expropriation, and 1106 on Performance Requirements were simply not addressed by the tribunal. The claim in Public Citizen (2001, 5) that the tribunal expressed the view that 1110 may have been violated seems to have been based on the tribunal's willingness to consider the claimant's claims "in the context of the merits" (Böckstiegel, Brower, and Lalonde 1998, 37), which never occurred. When

Ivan Feltham, Q.C., Consultant in International Trade Law and Competition Law, testified before the Senate Standing Committee on the NAFTA Chapter 11 and Article 1110 in particular, he said:

> Throughout the history of our country and more particularly in recent years … every new regulation imposes costs on industry … It is inconceivable to me, honourable senators, that the negotiators for the Government of Canada and the other two countries could have come to the conclusion that every regulation which imposes costs on industry should give that industry a right to compensation for whatever additional costs or losses it might suffer. That just has not been the case in the world to date. Whatever the notion of creeping expropriation is, which is how it is described in some of the literature, it has not gone so far as to justify that. (SSCEENR 2/19, 1997g, 22; see also Hufbauer et al. 2000, 14–15 for a similar view)

When Minister Marchi testified before the Senate Standing Committee, he reminded its members that: "Within the investment chapter, articles 1106.6 and 1114 refer specifically to the ability of states to enact measures for the protection of the environment" (SSCEENR 2/20, 1997h, 11).

These important provisions were also not addressed by the North American Free Trade Commission's *Notes of Interpretation of Certain Chapter 11 Provisions* released on 31 July 2001 (www.dfait-maeci.gc.ca/tna-nac/NAFTA Interpre-e.asp). According to the brief report of the International Institute for Sustainable Development on the *Notes*, the latter clarifies the interpretation of Article 1105 by indicating:

> that the obligation for a "minimum standard of treatment" is no more onerous than that granted under customary international law. It further says that a breach of some other NAFTA provision, or of the provisions of some other international agreement, do not necessarily constitute a breach of Article 1105 … In several Chapter 11 cases the argument has been made that because a government breached rules in other parts of NAFTA, or even in non-NAFTA law such as the WTO's Technical Barriers to Trade Agreement, it has automatically breached its obligations on minimum standards of treatment. This broad interpretation of minimum standards of treatment – essentially giving firms the right to litigate any international law obligation – has not been seen outside of the NAFTA context. The statement puts an end to this. (http://www.iisd.org/pdf/2001/trade_NAFTA_ aug2001.pdf)

13

Alberta's Claims against the Government of Canada under the AIT

In this and the two following two chapters I review and evaluate the claims and counter-claims of the disputants in the AIT MMT case.

On 28 April 1997 the Government of Alberta (complainant) requested consultations with the Government of Canada (respondent) in accordance with the AIT Annex 1510.1. This action was undertaken in response to a request from the oil refiners of Alberta, acting through the CPPI. Neither Ethyl Canada nor Ethyl Corporation are members of the CPPI (PD9/22, 1995c, 4), although CPPI members are certainly Ethyl's biggest customers and all three share many common interests. The federal government's strategy was to eliminate MMT from the Canadian market by prohibiting it from crossing provincial as well as national borders, but if the AIT could be used to prevent the prohibition of interprovincial sales, that would effectively destroy this strategy. In the absence of such a prohibition, Ethyl might have followed the well-established tradition of setting up a branch plant in any province and servicing the whole country from that site.

Consultations were initiated on 12 May 1997 and ended on 11 June 1997. The next day, the complainant informed the respondent that the consultations had not been successful within the mandated forty-day period since the initial request. The two parties then agreed to invoke the procedures of Chapter 17 as soon as the mandated additional fifty-day waiting period expired. Thus, on 5 August 1997, in accordance with Article 1702, Alberta requested a second round of consultations which proved to be as unproductive as the first. (The AIT has since been amended to allow a complaining party to skip the second set of consultations if consultations took place under the applicable Chapter provisions. Ref. 1702.1 (c).) Accordingly, on 8 September 1997 the two parties agreed that further consultations would be useless and that a panel should be requested from the

Committee on Internal Trade according to Article 1704. On 16 October 1997 the Government of Alberta officially requested a panel, which turned out to consist of Clay Gilson (former Vice President Academic of the University of Manitoba) as chair, Claude Castonguay (Fellow of the Royal Society of Canada and Vice-Chairman of the Board, Laurentian Bank), Kathleen Kelly (Arbitration Lawyer), Arthur Mauro (Former Chairman and CEO of the Investors Group), and Bob Rae (former Premier of Ontario). According to a report from the National Round Table on the Environment and the Economy, Clifford Lincoln (MP from Lachine-Lac-Saint-Louis) thought "the federal government was given only a single vote on the panel, in his opinion biasing the proceedings against the federal position" (NRTEE 2001, 65).

Most readers will recognize the names of some panel members, all of whom have had distinguished careers in public service and/or private industry. Because Mauro served as "the neutral chair of the main negotiating table" during the negotiations that created the AIT, he deserves a bit more attention. According to Doern and MacDonald (1999, 78–9):

> The role of Arthur Mauro ... was ... crucial to the 1993–4 negotiating process. Mauro is a respected and experienced lawyer-businessman from Winnipeg who had been chief executive officer of a regional airline company, chair of a royal commission on transportation, chancellor of the University of Manitoba, and a legal practitioner whose work frequently involved arbitrating disputes. Politically he was a nationally well-connected Progressive Conservative but was not seen as a partisan party man ... his name had received unanimous support from all ministers and governments involved ... [he] is credited ... with being especially important in three respects. First, he was among the main movers to insist fairly early on that the negotiations needed a text to work from ... He also saw the dispute-resolution provisions as being crucial to the integrity of the agreement ... [and third] In the end-game and in the final phase in June 1994, the meetings themselves became very trying and combative, with tempers on edge ... if an additional final trust factor was needed to get through this final stage, Mauro helped supply some of it.

Doern and MacDonald also refer to Mauro as "a partial surrogate business voice" (63).

Hearings before the panel were held six months later in Ottawa, on 15 and 16 April 1998. Appendix 4 contains a full list of participants. At the outset, the chair informed everyone that this was "the first formal panel under the Agreement on Internal Trade" and "the first experience that I have had with a panel of this type and importance. It is certainly the first dispute, as I understand it, that has come forward under Chapter 17 of the AIT Dispute Resolution Procedures. In other words, the panel starts with few established precedents, if you like, in this particular area" (AIT Hearings 1998a, 1).

Later on, James Ogilvy, Internal Trade Representative for Alberta, remarked that "We, like the panel, as you commented earlier, are very much aware of being part of and actually making history today and tomorrow or in this whole proceedings" (AIT Hearings 1998, 48).

Later still, he said, "Alberta regards the dispute resolution process as efficacious ... The fact that we are here as part of the first ever dispute to go before a Panel is remarkable because there are 35 disputes that have been officially recorded; 31 of them have been resolved at an earlier stage, consultation or some other stage, and there are only four at the moment pending" (AIT Hearings 1998a, 57).

In accordance with Annex 1706.1, the complainant had to:

(a) specify the actual or proposed measure complained of;
(b) list the relevant provisions of the Agreement;
(c) provide a brief summary of the complaint;
(d) explain how the measure has impaired or would impair internal trade; and
(e) identify the actual or potential injury or denial of benefit caused by the actual or proposed measure. (AIT Annex 1706.1.25)

The Government of Alberta claimed that the MMT Act failed to comply with the Government of Canada's obligations under the AIT, that the Act was inconsistent with the general and specific provisions of the agreement, that it impaired internal trade and injured Alberta refiners, and that it could not be justified or excused under the special AIT provisions regarding measures associated with legitimate objectives. In particular, Alberta sought a determination from the panel that:

- the Act is inconsistent with Articles 401, 402 and 403;
- the Act's prohibition of interprovincial trade in or importation for a commercial purpose of MMT does not serve a legitimate objective under the AIT within the meaning of Article 404(a);
- the prohibition impairs unduly the access to MMT (Article 404(b));

- the measure is more trade restrictive than necessary to achieve the stated objective (Article 404(c));
- the measure is a disguised restriction on trade (Article 404(d)); and
- the Act fails to fulfill the requirements of Articles 405 and 1508 (which are not subject to the legitimate objectives test).

In a letter to Minister Copps dated 18 April 1995, Ty Lund, Alberta Minister Responsible for Forests, Parks and Wildlife, said: "Alberta is concerned that the actions of the federal government to affect the interprovincial trade of MMT appear to contradict the provision found in the Energy Chapter of the draft Agreement on Internal Trade. Article 1209, Section 1 of the draft agreement currently states, 'No party shall restrict, prohibit or hinder access to its petroleum markets or its petroleum products markets'. It is our understanding that the intent of the federal/provincial agreement was to remove inter-provincial barriers to trade in petroleum products" (Lund 1995, 1).

Presumably that claim was dropped because the AIT energy chapter was not adopted. It still has not been adopted, as of 28 August 2007.

Following all that, Alberta asked the panel to recommend that:

- the Parliament of Canada repeal the Act;
- the federal, provincial and territorial governments work through CCME and any other appropriate bodies, together with industry stakeholders, employing disinterested science, to investigate MMT as a gasoline additive; and
- in the interim the federal government delist MMT from the Schedule of Controlled Substances under the Act. (Government of Alberta 1997, 1–2)

Unlike in the NAFTA MMT case, Alberta made it clear from the beginning that the offending measure was the MMT *Act* itself. Undoubtedly the MMT *Act* was a measure for purposes of the agreement. Article 200 of the AIT asserts that "**measure** includes any legislation, regulation, directive, requirement, guideline, program, policy, administrative practice or other procedure" and even that "**environmental measure** means a measure the primary purpose of which is to protect the environment or to prevent danger to human, animal or plant life or health"(AIT 2002).

It was strategically important for the Government of Alberta to establish that the MMT *Act* was an environmental measure as defined above because procedural requirements for such measures specified in Article 1508 were allegedly violated by the Government of Canada. In support of its claim Alberta asserted that (1) both Bill C-29 and C-94 were proposed by succeeding Ministers of the Environment (first Copps and then Marchi); (2) inside and outside parliament, the ministers usually said that the MMT *Act* was supposed to protect the environment and the health and safety of Canadians; (3) the Government of Canada never challenged Alberta's characterization of the *Act* as an environmental measure during any of the consultations; (4) in those consultations "the only line department specialists in attendance were officials from Environment Canada"; (5) in the *Statement of Claim* in its constitutional challenge to the MMT *Act*, dated 23 June 1997, Ethyl Canada said that the Government of Canada had mentioned "protection of the natural environment" as one of its purposes, and the government granted that point in its *Statement of Defence* of 23 July 1997. In Ethyl Canada's *Statement of Claim* filed in the Ontario Court (General Division), it was asserted that the MMT *Act* was *"ultra vires* the Parliament of Canada insofar as it is inconsistent with the provisions of the *Constitution Act, 1867"* and "an interlocutory and permanent injunction" was demanded "enjoining [the Defendants, the Attorney-General of Canada and the Minister of the Environment] from enforcing the provisions of the *Act"* (Ethyl Canada 1997, 2–3).

The specific procedural requirements that were supposed to have been violated are given in AIT Article 1508.1: "The Parties shall endeavour to harmonize environmental measures that may directly affect interprovincial mobility and trade, following principles such as those set out in the *Statement of Interjurisdictional Cooperation on Environmental Matters* (Winnipeg: CCME, 1991[sic]) and *Rationalizing the Management Regime for the Environment: Purpose, Objectives and Principles* (Winnipeg: CCME, 1994) any other applicable principles established by the Council, and this Agreement" (AIT 2002).

The CCME formed a Cleaner Vehicles and Fuels Task Force to investigate such things as benzene, sulphur, aromatics and, notably, MMT. Unfortunately, according to the Alberta complaint, the assessment of MMT "was dropped as a result of the federal government's unilateral decision to legislate against it" (Government of Alberta 1997, 17). That was confirmed in the testimony given to the Senate Standing Committee by Nicole Pageot, Director General, Road Safety and Motor Vehicle Regulation, Transport Canada:

With respect to gasoline the CCME task force was aware of the concern over the compatibility of 1998 model year vehicles with fuels containing MMT. However, since the Manganese-Based Fuel Additives Act, now Bill C-29, had already been tabled in the House of Commons, the task force did not address the issue of this additive's continued use in Canadian gasoline ... Following extensive consultation with stakeholders, the government determined that Bill C-29 was necessary to protect the health of Canadians from the potential adverse impact of the fuel additive MMT on vehicle emission-control systems and, ultimately, on vehicle emissions. It is on that basis that Transport Canada supports Bill C-29. (SSCEENR 2/6, 1997e, 17)

The Government of Alberta claimed that the MMT *Act* was also inconsistent with AIT Article 405.1, which says: "In order to provide for the free movement of persons, goods, services and investments within Canada, the Parties shall, in accordance with Annex 405.1, reconcile their standards and standards-related measures by harmonization, mutual recognition or other means" (AIT 2002).

In Alberta's view, the *MMT Act* declared "that the only acceptable level of MMT in gasoline is zero, expressed in either absolute or relative quantities. Thus the *Act* is a 'standards-related measure,' in the language of the Agreement" (Government of Alberta 1997, 18).

According to Article 200, "**standard** means a specification, approved by a Party or by a recognized body, including those accredited as members of Canada's National Standards System, that sets out the rules, guidelines or characteristics for goods or related processes and production methods, or for services, service providers or their related operating methods; [and] **standards-related measure** means a measure that incorporates a standard and may also set out the requirements and procedures to ensure conformity or compliance" (AIT 2002).

During the AIT Hearings (1998, 73–5), Lorne Ternes, Counsel for Alberta, asserted that "Alberta suggests that ... Canada, through its measure – through its embargo measure – has instituted a new standard. Why do I say that? I say that because prior to this legislation being enforced Alberta, together with a good number of other Canadian jurisdictions, subscribed to the Canadian General Standards Board standard that there would be no more than 18 milligrams of manganese per litre in unleaded fuel which uses MMT as an octane enhancer. That was the standard ... There is a standard. And if there is a standard, 405.1 obligates the parties to harmonize. There is a process ... [which] was not used."

Provinces are not required to adopt standards set by the Canadian General Standards Board but they often do (AIT Hearings 1998a, 77).

Alberta further claimed that because the MMT Act treated the fuel additive MMT less favourably than it treated the fuel additives MTBE, Ethyl Tertiary Butyl Ether (ETBE), and ethanol, the Act was inconsistent with Article 401.3(a), which says "With respect to the Federal Government ... it shall accord to the goods of a Province treatment no less favourable than the best treatment it accords to like, directly competitive or substitutable goods of any other Province or non-Party" (AIT 2002).

So far as the Government of Alberta was concerned, any "octane enhancer" was a "like, directly competitive or substitutable good" insofar as they "served the same need" or had "common end-uses." WTO Appellate Body reports were cited that agreed with this view (Government of Alberta 1997, 14).

Because Article 402 said that "no Party shall adopt or maintain any measure that restricts or prevents the movement of persons, goods, services or investments across provincial boundaries"(AIT 2002) and the MMT Act "prohibits interprovincial trade in MMT as well as the importation of that good," Alberta claimed that the Act was clearly inconsistent with the AIT article. By prohibiting interprovincial trade, the Act was also said to be inconsistent with Article 403, which requires each party to "ensure that any measure it adopts or maintains does not operate to create an obstacle to internal trade" (AIT 2002).

Recognizing that some legitimate national, provincial, and territorial objectives might be inconsistent with the objective articulated in Article 100, Articles 401, 402, and 403 are explicitly made subject to the "legitimate objectives" provisions of Article 404. Rugman, Kirton, and Soloway (1997, 136) claimed that the provisions of this article were largely adapted from NAFTA Chapter 9. AIT Article 404 says:

Where it is established that a measure is inconsistent with Article 401, 402 or 403, that measure is still permissible under this Agreement where it can be demonstrated that:
(a) the purpose of the measure is to achieve a legitimate objective;
(b) the measure does not operate to impair unduly the access of persons, goods, services or investments of a Party that meet that legitimate objective;
(c) the measure is not more trade restrictive than necessary to achieve that legitimate objective; and
(d) the measure does not create a disguised restriction on trade.
(AIT 2002)

According to Article 200:

legitimate objective means any of the following objectives pursued
within the territory of a Party:
(a) public security and safety;
(b) public order;
(c) protection of human, animal or plant life or health;
(d) protection of the environment;
(e) consumer protection;
(f) protection of the health, safety and well-being of workers; or
(g) affirmative action programs for disadvantaged groups. (AIT 2002)

Thus, Alberta's case against the MMT *Act* would not be complete unless it
was shown that the *Act* did not satisfy each of the four necessary conditions for a legitimate objective as specified in these two Articles. Accordingly, the complainant argued, first, that Article 404(a) was not satisfied
because "if the purpose of the measure is purportedly to protect human
health, to protect the environment or to protect consumers, the Act is not
structured to achieve any of these objectives. As recognized by federal officials, the legislation does not prohibit the domestic use of MMT" (Government of Alberta 1997, 30).

Whatever harms MMT caused would not be prevented by the MMT *Act* as
long as the product was sold and used in the province or territory where it
was produced. So, it was claimed, the *Act* did not meet its alleged objectives.

Second, the complainant argued that the *Act* did not satisfy Article
404(b) because:

The Act uses severe criminal sanctions to enforce prohibition of the importation of the good or of the interprovincial trade of the good. Certainly the
measure severely impairs the movement of and the ability to obtain MMT
lawfully which, prior to the enactment of the Act, was imported, processed and marketed freely ... The Act severely impairs access to, and interprovincial movement of, a legal good by imposing a trade measure ... The
measure has caused refiners great expense, has unduly impaired access of
MMT and yet has not met the stated objectives. Alberta submits that ... the
measure even on the basis of this failure alone would not be permissible
under the AIT. (Government of Alberta 1997, 30–1)

Since the good was legal to produce and sell, the main net effect of the
Act was to "unduly impair access" to it, contrary to Article 404(b).

Third, the complainant argued that the *Act* did not satisfy Article 404(c) because:

If the measure is not excessive, the federal government must demonstrate that it took into account the need to minimize negative trade effects when choosing among equally effective and reasonably available means of achieving that objective ... [In fact, there is] evidence pointing to the federal government's avoidance of less trade-restrictive actions proposed by CPPI, not once but on several occasions. CPPI went further, providing written undertakings to phase out MMT voluntarily if the science supported the need. This offer is summarized most recently in the letter of July 7, 1997 from Alain Perez to the presidents of the CVMA and the Association of International Automobile Manufacturers of Canada and copied to the federal government:
   "Our members will voluntarily phase out MMT if an independent study, either a government sponsored study or a study carried out jointly by the automobile and petroleum industries, supports your allegations on the effect of MMT on the performance of current, or future, automobile equipment." (Government of Alberta 1997, 31–2)

That is, since the MMT producers' withdrawal of the product from the market if independent tests showed it harmed automobile equipment was supposed to have been less trade-restrictive than an *Act* restricting trade in the product, the federal government's measure was "not more trade restrictive than necessary." So, Article 404(c) was not satisfied.

Fourth, Alberta argued that the *Act* did not satisfy Article 404(d) because "the tight focus on MMT can be seen as a disguised restriction: while the legislation purports to deal with a full range of manganese-based substances, its progressive internal narrowings show that it targets a single substance, a single industry, and in fact a single supplier" (Government of Alberta 1997, 34).

Thus, since satisfaction of each of the four conditions is necessary in order to pass the legitimate objectives tests of Article 404 and, according to the complainant, the *Act* fails to pass every one of them, the measure in question is inconsistent with the AIT provisions.

Besides all of the alleged inconsistencies with the AIT provisions, the Government of Alberta (1997, 28) argued that, contrary to the federal government's claims about harmonizing policies with the United States, the *Act* would create disharmony. Perhaps the most important document in support of the Complainant's position was a letter from the International Trade Minister Eggleton to Minister Marchi, dated 23 February 1996:

I understand that you are considering the re-introduction of Bill C-94 in the upcoming session. My department continues to have certain reservations concerning this measure, which I wish to draw to your attention.

One of the original arguments favouring the ban on MMT was that the United States already prohibited its use as a petroleum additive. Recently, the U.S. Court of Appeal overturned the U.S. ban. This has effectively removed harmonization arguments in support of Bill C-94. Indeed, since adding MMT to petroleum products is now permissible in the U.S., harmonization would now be promoted by introducing no new Canadian regulations.

An import prohibition on MMT would be inconsistent with Canada's obligations under the WTO and the NAFTA: (1) it would constitute an impermissible prohibition on imports, particularly if domestic production, sale or use is not similarly prohibited; and (2) it would not be justified on health or environmental grounds, given current scientific evidence ...

There has been heated debate surrounding the exact effects of banning MMT. The claims of the automotive and petroleum industries conflict markedly, with little common ground between them. Testing is only now starting in the United States, with unambiguous results some years away.

In view of the Presidential and Congressional elections this year, American politicians are particularly sensitive to any foreign initiative which might injure their domestic industries.

In conclusion, let me stress my department's belief that Bill C-94 should not be re-introduced as it could have many adverse implications for Canadian trade, without compensating environmental benefits. (Eggleton 1996, 1–2)

In Ternes words, "The very thing that supposedly as a legitimate objective was driving Canada, the federal government, to deal with MMT, has flipped around. Now the proposed act is creating disharmony with the U.S. situation" (AIT Hearings 1998a, 93).

14

Claims of the Governments of Québec and Saskatchewan against the Government of Canada under the AIT

In accordance with Article 1704.9, the Governments of Québec and Saskatchewan entered into the dispute. That article says that "Any Party that has a substantial interest in the matter in dispute, within the meaning of paragraph 10, is entitled to join the panel proceedings on delivery of written notice to the other Parties and the Secretariat within 15 days after the date of delivery of the request for establishment of a panel" (AIT 2002).

Article 1704.10 says that "A Party shall be deemed to have a substantial interest in the matter in dispute where: ... (b) in the case of a Party that is a Province, it has a significant number of persons carrying on business in the Province who are or will be affected by the measure at issue" (AIT 2002).

I will consider the specific claims of Québec first and then those of Saskatchewan. Strictly speaking, Alberta is the sole complainant, and Québec and Saskatchewan are intervenors, but I will refer to all three as complainants. In both cases the complainants tried to avoid repetition and to emphasize their most important points, and I will follow that approach.

Québec claimed that "the approach used during the process that led to the enactment of the Act" was inconsistent with Article 405 on Reconciliation, Annex 405.1.13 and 405.1.14 on Standards and Standards-Related Measures, Annex 405.2.9 on Regulatory Measures and Regulatory Regimes and Article 1508.1 on Harmonization (see appendix 3 for details).

"The federal government did not give the Parties, including Québec, any real opportunity to jointly review these new measures which create barriers to internal trade. Nor did it undertake with them any serious and constructive consultations and discussions to find better solutions" (Government of Québec 1997, 4).

As a matter of fact, since 1971, Québec had had its own *Petroleum Products Trade Act*, which includes measures for octane ratings and lead content.

Most importantly, "under Article 17 and Schedule 1 of the Petroleum Products Regulations, the quality standards for gasoline provide for a maximum manganese content of 18 mg/litre ... Further, over the years Québec has shown a definite interest in the standards applied outside its boundaries and has not hesitated to act collaboratively with others and to harmonize its standards so as not to unduly hinder the petroleum products trade" (Government of Québec 1997, 6).

The *Brief from Québec* listed notable examples such as the complainant's collaboration with the Canadian General Standards Board, the CCME, Environment Canada, governments of other provinces, and the CPPI. If such collaboration could produce agreements on the maximum sulfur content in fuels, lead tetraethyl in gasoline, and the underground storage of petroleum products, it probably could have produced agreement on MMT. After all, the Québec standard of 18 mg/litre for manganese in gasoline was precisely the same as that set by the Canadian General Standards Board (AIT Hearings 1998a, 73; AIT Hearings 1998b, 211). "Although these discussions were sometimes spread out over fairly long periods of time," it was insisted, "perseverance and joint effort were the guarantors of the successes achieved" (Government of Québec 1997, 7–8).

To document the federal government's intransigence, the complainant listed the clear signals that were sent and allegedly ignored. The Québec National Assembly unanimously passed a motion in May 1996 asking the federal government to "suspend passage" of the MMT Act. The provinces of Alberta, Prince Edward Island, Manitoba, New Brunswick, Nova Scotia, Saskatchewan, the Northwest Territories and the Yukon "made similar requests." Dissenting members of the Senate Standing Committee "drew attention to the automotive industry's offer to complete existing studies so as to resolve the uncertainties and inaccuracies present." And yet, "These examples of the good will and openness of the Parties and of third parties, such as the CPPI, to avoid a deadlock and find avenues for solution in relation to this file, did not meet with any support from the federal government. The latter elected to pursue a unilateral and precipitous [sic] approach in contempt of its commitments to its partners in the Agreement" (Government of Québec 1997, 8).

The complainant reminded the panel that Article 1509.1 (a) instructs the CCME to "facilitate a process for the harmonization of environmental measures in accordance with Article 1508" (AIT 2002). So, the federal government should have appealed to the CCME. Also, because the respondent did not give the provinces "notice of the measures it intended to implement," there was a violation of Articles 406.2 and 1506. The former says, "A Party proposing to adopt or modify a measure that may materially affect the operation of this Agreement shall, to the extent practicable, notify the other Party with an interest in the matter of its intention to do so and provide a copy of the proposed measure to that Party on request." The latter says, "A Party required to notify any other Party of a proposed environmental measure under Article 406.2 (Transparency) shall instead notify the Council [of Ministers of the Environment] and the Council shall notify the other Parties" (AIT 2002).

The complainant granted that parties could have obtained copies of the proposed new *Act*, but expressed some distress because the AIT was "intended to improve on the old system" of information-sharing and the federal government clung to that old system rather than initiating the new one. As a result, "The inadequacies of the process also have implications for the validity of the measures legislated by this Act. Given the provisions provided for in the Agreement, the failure of the federal government to adopt an approach which would have optimized the accuracy of the information and knowledge at its disposal and which would have made it possible to identify a broader range of solutions, actually undermines the possibility of justifying the merit of this Act" (Government of Québec 1997, 9).

So, a poor process produced a poor product, and petroleum companies in Québec would be saddled with additional costs of doing business in the neighborhood of $15 million annually. "This is far from negligible. In fact," the complainant said, "it is a recurring expense, a permanent increase in production costs" (Government of Québec 1997, 10).

After noting inconsistencies between the MMT *Act* and Articles 401, 402, and 403, the *Brief from Québec* zeroed in on the federal government's failure to satisfy the legitimate objectives tests, especially Article 404 (c). The complainant was sure that the federal government had not vigorously searched for a measure that would "minimize negative trade effects." As far as anyone knew, besides the MMT *Act*, the two-pump solution was the only alternative entertained, and the reason for the poverty of ideas was the federal government's alleged "unilateral and precipitous [sic] approach." While "major oil companies were, to a certain degree, given the opportunity of presenting their views through CPPI", many others were left out. Those left out were said to be independent petroleum product retailers, owners of filling stations, consumer associations, the Canadian Automobile Association, automobile manufacturers and provincial governments (Government of Québec 1997, 11–13).

The complainant then listed some apparent alternatives to the MMT *Act* and the two-pump solution that might have passed the test of Article

404 (c). These included fiscal incentives, different filling stations with different kinds of gasoline, much reduced levels of manganese, tradable permits, and direct regulation.

> In short, the unwarranted sense of urgency and the inadequacies of the federal government's consultation process greatly limited the number of options that should have been examined before going ahead with the measures. More verifications, consultations and analysis should have been done before adopting such drastic and trade restrictive legislative measures ... As they now stand, the provisions of the Act do not even allow the federal government to achieve its stated objectives. They permit the continued use of MMT. The alleged pollution problems are therefore likely to persist, since the provinces have not decided to prohibit the use and sale locally of fuel containing MMT and since each of them has the right, according to Articles 300 and 1505.2 of the Agreement, "*to establish its own environmental priorities and levels of environmental protection in its territory in accordance with this Agreement and to adopt or modify its environmental measures accordingly.*" (Government of Québec 1997, 15, emphasis in the original)

Finally, the Government of Québec asked the panel to find that the *MMT Act* should be repealed or that MMT should be removed from its schedule. If the federal government was still keen to investigate the environmental and health impacts of MMT, it should "reopen the file" in accordance with the AIT and "allow all Parties to participate in real discussions on the various issues at stake, possible solutions and deadlines for their implementation, this being done in respect of the legislative authority of each of the governments and in compliance with the provisions of the Agreement" (Government of Québec 1997, 17).

Under AIT Article 1704.10 (b), the *Submission on Behalf of the Government of Saskatchewan* was filed by Robert Perrin and Linda Zarzeczny on 15 January 1998 (Perrin and Zarzeczny 1998). Since MMT was not produced in Saskatchewan, the *MMT Act* made it unavailable in that province. That had a very adverse effect because the Consumers' Cooperative Refinery Limited (CCRL), a wholly owned subsidiary of Federated Co-operatives Limited (FCL), used MMT in "virtually all" the gasoline it produced, more in the summer than in the winter. Collectively, those co-operatives were owned by 900,000 individual members and CCRL produced about "1.3 billion litres of gasoline," 70 per cent of which was used in Saskatchewan.

The MMT trade ban required CCRL to segregate gasolines between in-province (which gas could, and did, contain MMT) and out-of-province (which gas, in accordance with the Act, did not contain MMT). This segregation occurred until supplies of MMT were exhausted. Currently, the octane loss due to the MMT trade ban is being replaced by other methods and components. The least costly method is to operate the CCRL gasoline reformer (which takes low octane gas and converts it to higher octane gas) at a greater severity. Essentially, this requires increasing the operating temperatures of the reforming unit, which results in a higher octane level in the gas produced. However, this also results in a reduced yield – the greater the octane improvement, the greater the yield loss. This means more fuel and crude oil consumption, a higher benzene level in the gasoline and less gasoline ultimately produced ... In some circumstances, it is necessary to purchase more costly high octane blending components such as (MTBE) ... The MMT ban increases the cost of producing gasoline. Like other refiners, CCRL will have to absorb this, resulting in lower patronage dividends to the 900,000 members mentioned above. Alternatively, it is reasonable to assume that the effects of the Act may ultimately be passed on to consumers in the form of increased gas prices. (Perrin and Zarzeczny 1998, 3–4)

After this brief but informative lesson in ecological economics, the complainant summarized the abortive attempts made to get the federal government to change its course since early in 1995. "Ministers and officials of several departments, including Environment, Energy and Intergovernmental and Aboriginal Affairs" had asked for more "reliable information." Letters were sent to the Minister of the Environment by FCL on 9 March 1995 (with copies to over a dozen other officials) and by the Saskatchewan Minister of Environment and Resource Management (30 May 1995); to the Deputy Minister of the Environment (5 May 1995) by the Saskatchewan Deputy Minister of Environment and Resource Management); to the Chair of the House of Commons Standing Committee on Environment and Sustainable Development (20 October 1995) and the Chair of the Senate Standing Committee on Energy, the Environment and Natural Resources (16 November 1995) by the Saskatchewan Minister of Environment and Resource Management; to the new Minister of the Environment (5 June 1996) by the new Saskatchewan Minister of Environment and Resource Management; to the Prime Minister (16 September 1996) by the Premier of

Saskatchewan; to the Minister of the Environment (5 March 1997) by the Saskatchewan Minister of Environment and Resource Management, to the Saskatchewan Minister of Environment and Resource Management (27 April 1995) by the Deputy Minister of the Environment; and to the Premier of Saskatchewan (16 October 1996) by the Prime Minister. Copies of all these letters are part of the public record in AIT 1998b.

Besides all of this activity, "The province also participated in the consultation meetings on May 23, June 5 and September 8 of 1997, pursuant to the consultation provisions in Chapters 15 and 17 of the AIT. This process did not resolve the matter for Saskatchewan or any of the other provinces or stakeholders opposed to the federal MMT legislation. Consequently, Alberta requested the establishment of these Panel proceedings, which Saskatchewan joins" (Perrin and Zarzeczny 1998, 5).

While Québec complained about the absence of and the need for "real discussions" (see also AIT Hearings 1998b, 219–36.) and Nova Scotia complained that the CCME was never properly engaged (SSCEENR 2/11, 1996, 2), Saskatchewan seemed to have had at least enough exchanges to conclude that they were not going to produce the desired result.

Following the complainant's brief history of the events leading to the call for a panel, it was asserted that "Saskatchewan agrees with, and adopts, all arguments made by Alberta" in its *Submission.* Accordingly, the only task to be performed was to "highlight ... compelling reasons for this Panel to award the relief requested by Alberta" (Perrin and Zarzeczny 1998, 5).

First, there were doubts that the legitimate objectives tests were passed, and these doubts were reinforced by recalling Article 1505.7, which says: "Further to Article 404(c) (Legitimate Objectives) and Annexes 405.1(5) and 405.2(5), an environmental measure shall not be considered to be more trade restrictive than necessary to achieve a legitimate objective if the Party adopting or maintaining the measure takes into account the need to minimize negative trade effects when choosing among equally effective and reasonably available means of achieving that legitimate objective" (AIT 2002).

The complainant did not believe that the federal government took account of "the need to minimize negative trade effects." From the Government of Saskatchewan's point of view, "A Party claiming a legitimate objective is required to show that it has gone through a fair and rigorous process ... Saskatchewan is not aware of any evidence that would suggest that the federal government took into account the need to minimize negative trade effects or the requirement to ensure proportionality, as required by these provisions. On the contrary, suggestions for how to do so, such as obtaining independent testing, and working with industry and the provinces to resolve the MMT issue, were rejected by the federal government" (Perrin and Zarzeczny 1998, 7).

The *Submission* asserted that the following less trade restrictive measures were recommended to but not adopted by the federal government: "multi-stakeholder technical testing of MMT"; getting "input from the CCME task force on cleaner vehicles and fuels"; examining MMT "within the whole spectrum of fuel formulations to clearly evaluate the costs and benefits"; and using the provisions of the Canadian Environmental Protection Act (CEPA) for dealing with toxic substances (especially section 11, subsections 12.1 and 12.3, and section 15). In the complainant's view, the assessment process described in section 15 "is tailor-made for the MMT issue. The CEPA contemplates exactly the type of reasoned investigation, science, and consultation that has been suggested by the provinces, and refused by the federal government, throughout the curious history of this case" (Perrin and Zarzeczny 1998, 7–10).

Section 11 was not mentioned again by the complainant, Canada, or the panel, but in the AIT Hearings (1998c, 270) Tom Wallace, Internal Trade Representative for the Government of Canada, said, "With respect to the specific point regarding CEPA and the use of Section 11 of CEPA, the reason CEPA was not used was because of a determination by Health Canada that MMT was not toxic in the concentrations emitted. Eighty per cent of it stays in automobiles." Later on John Tyhurst, Counsel for the Government of Canada, said, "It is because we are dealing with indirect effects that the toxic section of the CEPA could not be relied on" (AIT Hearings 1998c, 366).

The complainant then took issue with the federal government's characterization of the situation as some sort of an "emergency." A letter from the Deputy Minister of Environment Canada dated 27 April 1995 to the Saskatchewan Minister of Environment and Resource Management, stated that the introduction of the *MMT Act* was "the only effective solution to the problem *on a priority basis*." Again a letter from the Prime Minister to the Premier of Saskatchewan dated 16 October 1996 asserted that "Federal intervention was identified as the only effective solution to the MMT issue *on a priority basis*" (Perrin and Zarzeczny 1998, 10–11; emphasis in original). As far as the Government of Saskatchewan was concerned, no "emergency" existed.

As the documents filed by Alberta and Saskatchewan indicate, the MMT issue dates back to 1992. There was, we submit, nothing that occurred since then to cause any government to reasonably believe that immediate action was critical for health, environment or consumer protection reasons. On the contrary, despite that passage of time, the federal government was unable to marshal any evidence that would provide it with a non-trade hook for MMT legislation. It did not avail itself of the *priority* procedures in the CEPA for allegedly toxic substances. One is necessarily left to conclude that the decision to pass the Act, some five years after the identification of the alleged issue and in the absence of reliable evidence of harm to the environment or to the health of Canadians, stemmed from the effective efforts by the auto manufacturers, not the mutable justifications offered over that time by the federal government.

Saskatchewan submits that on any reasonable standard of proof, the federal government will be unable to satisfy the onus upon it to show a legitimate objective for this measure.

In addition to the arguments above, Saskatchewan asks that this Panel bear in mind what Saskatchewan believes is a critical and telling fact in this dispute. The federal government has alternatively characterized this measure as one for environmental, health and consumer protection purposes, with the first being the primary justification ... If any of these purposes were the real reason behind the federal government's action, why does it remain legal to produce and use MMT in Canada? ... Saskatchewan asks the Panel to note that using trade legislation to fill a gap in the federal government's legislative constitutional authority is not a legitimate objective recognized by the AIT. (Perrin and Zarzeczny 1998, 11–12)

Saskatchewan was pulling no punches. In these passages the federal government was effectively described as at least a lackey for the auto manufacturers and at most an ineffective empire-builder. I do not know what sort of impact such ad hominem imputations of nefarious motives should be expected to have on arbitrators, but they did tend to change the flavour of the *Submission*.

Perrin raised another ad hominem argument, this time accusing the federal government of making biased assessments of MMT because of the government's announced policies supporting ethanol:

this particular government always had the intention to ban MMT, regardless of the science or lack thereof. We refer the panel to the background attached to the federal government's press release at tab 81 of Canada's documents. And I quote from that: [Perrin's quotation is not quite accurate. So the correct version from the *Backgrounder* to the

Minister of the Environment's *News Release* dated 18 April 1996 has been substituted.] "Such a policy would be consistent with the Red Book commitment in the Liberal Party of Canada Agricultural Policy Paper to eliminate MMT from gasoline, and with a U.S. federal policy which is intended to create additional demand for renewable fuels, like ethanol."

This commitment was also referred to by Senator Whelan, on page 24 of a document which is 48 pages of tab 82 in Canada's document. And I quote: "In the Red Book, from September 24, 1993, it was clearly indicated that the Liberals were committed to banning the use of MMT in Canadian automotive fuels."

Panel, we have a copy of that agricultural policy paper and ask you to note that as early as May 1993, the Liberal party, now the federal government stated: "Liberals are committed to banning the use of MMT in Canadian automotive fuels."

How, in the light of this, can it be said that this federal government was interested in finding out the real story about MMT, or that it could be objective when it came to the conflicting evidence in the four years that followed this statement? It was simply following its agenda: Ban MMT and promote ethanol ... One cannot help but be a bit cynical about the weighing and balancing of evidence process described in the federal submission ... it is abundantly clear that the government's mind was made up long before any of this evidence even existed. (AIT Hearings, 1998a, 153–5)

Although an investigation of the *Red Book* commitment to ethanol requires a deviation from our main story, it is both relevant and interesting in itself. A careful reading of the Liberal *Red Book* of 1993 reveals no reference to MMT or ethanol. In that particular remark made in the meeting of the Standing Senate Committee on Energy, the Environment and Natural Resources on Wednesday, 5 February 1997, Senator Whelan's memory failed him (SSCEENR 2/5, 1997d, 31). It failed him earlier too (SSCEENR, 2/4, 1997a, 46). The error was also made by Minister Marchi, according to Monique Guay (MP, Laurentides), who reproduced it (PD9/25, 1996a, 10), and by Jerry Pickard (MP, Essex-Kent, PD10/28, 1996f, 2).

However, Perrin correctly quoted from the second page of the Liberal policy paper called *Food Security for Canadians and A Fair Return for Canadian Farmers*, which was released 10 May 1993. The same sentence about banning the use of MMT is repeated on page two of the *Backgrounder* that accompanied the main paper.

Hill and Leiss (2001, 83) quote a letter from Jean Chrétien, then Leader of the Opposition, to the Honourable Don Mazankowski, dated 17 April 1991, which clearly states support for banning MMT and replacing it with ethanol:

> Given the fact that Canadian crude oil reserves are being rapidly depleted and the government had promised on two occasions ... to bring in Environmentally Friendly ethanol blended fuels since 1984, will you take the necessary action to require that all automotive gasoline based fuels contain 3.2% oxygen content. Such a move would create a market for between 5,000,000 to 8,000,000 bushels of grain, and the by-products can be utilized either as an animal feed or human food that is particularly suited for persons needing a diet of low calories, high fibre and protein ... I respectfully request that you take immediate action on this issue to provide a new market for Canadian Grain Growers, to cut the level of hydro-carbon emissions, and to ban the use of MMT in Canada that will eliminate the use of a substance that threatens the health of millions of Canadians, particularly our children."

In the parliamentary debate over Bill C-94 (19 September 1995, 3–6; hereafter PD9/19, 1995a, 3–6), Julian Reed also recorded support for the ethanol agenda and the *MMT Act*. After informing the House that Henry Ford's Model T ran on pure ethanol, Reed said:

> a Canadian ethanol industry has potential to be one of the great things for Canadian agriculture.
>
> Since the government did its little arrangement about a year ago, about $300 million has been committed in Ontario alone for ethanol development. If ethanol were to replace MMT at the rate of 10 per cent in Canada, it would take approximately 10 investments of the size that are taking place in Ontario right now in order to fill that need. One can see that there is great potential ... About two years ago there were 50 outlets selling gasoline containing an ethanol additive. Right now there are 500 and the prognosis is that there will be 5,000 within the next two years ... some refineries have already made the switch to ethanol ... Mohawk adopted this some time ago and promoted it in Ontario ... in the United States 39 cities mandate the use of gasolines containing ethanol for environmental reasons ... In 1995, 45 new ethanol plants are being built in the United States.

I suppose the "little arrangement" referred to was the national bio-ethanol program. Andy Scott, Liberal MP for Fredericton-York-Sunbury, described it as a program to

> support the development of ethanol production through a refundable line of credit to qualified candidates who want to establish bio-ethanol fuel production plants in Canada. Managed by the Farm Credit Corporation, the program will guarantee up to $70 million in loans between 1999 and 2005 ... There will be no subsidies, no megaprojects ... This is a fiscally responsible way to help turn wood chips, straw, grain and other biomass derived waste into energy which can be used to fuel our vehicles.
>
> Properly blended ethanol gasoline can reduce carbon monoxide emissions which degrade urban air quality. It can reduce carbon dioxide emissions which are a primary source of greenhouse gases. It can reduce benzene emissions, a substance declared toxic under CEPA, into the atmosphere.
>
> The program is targeted to encourage ethanol production in every region of the country. This is a sound example of the concept of sustainable development. We can deal with an environmental problem and create jobs at the same time. (PD9/26, 1995d, 6; see also Soloway 1999, 70 for more on the virtues of ethanol)

But even if as early as April 1991 Chrétien and presumably the Liberal Party favoured a policy of banning the use of MMT and boosting the ethanol industry, and by the time Bill C-94 was introduced the Liberal Party strongly supported such a policy, it still does not follow that the Leader or the Party made a biased assessment of any or all of the evidence about the problems MMT was supposed to create for OBD systems. It is not only logically possible but also a necessary condition of accepting parliamentary debates and hearings as reasonable means for resolving disagreements that people with strong beliefs may still make unbiased assessments on the basis of good evidence and sound arguments. Of course, this does not prove that anyone ever has or that Liberals did so in the current case. Hill and Leiss (2001) were apparently convinced that what they referred to as "the ethanol caper" (98) was the original rationale for the Liberals' attack on MMT. In addition to the policy and program items already mentioned, they were suspicious about the connection between the private member's bill (C-333) proposed by Liberal MP Ralph Ferguson in October 1990 mandating "a minimum level of oxygen content in gasoline, thereby encouraging the use of ethanol as an octane enhancer" and, three years later, "an announcement of a proposed new $170 million corn-to-ethanol plant to be built in Chatham, Ontario (Ferguson's home area) by Commercial Fuels of Brampton" (Hill and Leiss 2001, 83).

It would not be fair to the ethanol critics to allow Chrétien's reference to the "environmentally friendly ethanol" or, for that matter, to the whole idea of a potentially booming ethanol industry to go unchallenged. The following sample will illustrate the critics' case. First, Keith Martin, Reform MP from Esquimalt-Juan de Fuca, claimed that ethanol "requires a government subsidy in the order of eight cents per litre in order to get to market" (PD9/19,1995a, 2). A month later, Perez raised it to twenty cents per litre (HSCESD10/19, 1995a, 13).

Soloway (1999, 71) claimed that ethanol has been "heavily subsidized and protected" in the United States "not for its dubious environmental benefits, but because it increases farm income and reduces U.S. dependence on imported oil". She quoted a study from the National Academy of Sciences claiming that "while [ethanol blends] would reduce carbon monoxide emissions by 25 percent, hydrocarbons would increase by as much as 50 percent and nitrogen oxide by 15 percent ... ethanol may also contribute to ozone pollution (smog) because it evaporates relatively quickly ... using ethanol as a blending agent in gasoline ... would not achieve significant air-quality benefits and, in fact, would likely to be [sic] detrimental" (Soloway 1999, 72).

David Chatters, Reform MP from Athabasca, said that "We hear time and time again that [ethanol] is a product which is available to replace MMT and that it will produce cleaner air. Again it is hogwash. People from the refineries tell me that ethanol is not a substitute for MMT. It will not replace MMT when MMT is banned. Gasolines will simply be further refined to reach the octane rating that can now be obtained with MMT. Further refining will cause higher pollution and higher costs both for the consumer and for the refining industry" (PD9/26,1995d, 8).

This is a slightly different spin; i.e., the federal government's ethanol agenda is a non-starter because the refiners simply will not co-operate. If, as indicated above, Mohawk can make money using ethanol and thirty-nine American states mandate its use, this spin may represent more bluster than fact. Nevertheless, testifying before the House Standing Committee on Environment and Sustainable Development regarding Bill C-94, Perez said:

We believe the bill is counter-productive because, first, from an environmental standpoint, the removal of MMT will force refiners to operate refineries differently and use more energy, and this will result in higher emissions for greenhouse gases ... vehicle emissions will also increase, particularly in nitrous oxide ... the removal of MMT will add about $90 million of cost to our refining operations. Any alternatives that we have to produce octane, such as ethanol or MTBE, are more expensive. In the case of ethanol, even though it's subsidized, it's as expensive, and if subsidies stop, it will be even more expensive.

More importantly, MMT is an additive and you add very small amounts. Ethanol and MTBE are replacements for gasolines, and you would add up to 10% or 15%, or more, of the volume. Therefore you would lose 10% to 15% of your refinery output and raise the cost of your refinery considerably. (HSCESD10/19, 1995a, 1– 2)

The trouble with the problem explained above is that it may not apply to any refineries in Canada. A few minutes after he made those comments, Perez said:

if MMT became a banned substance after the adoption of Bill C-94, the industry would not replace MMT with ethanol or MTBE. Given the technology at our disposal, it would be cheaper for us to simply change our refining methods.

If we can't use MMT to increase the octane level in gas, we will simply increase the amount of energy and the temperature in our units to extract those molecules from crude oil ... Ethanol and MTBE are solutions for refineries – and as far as I know, it's not the case in Canada amongst members of the CPPI – who would not have the ability to do that. Those companies [i.e., that are not members of the CPPI and may not exist at all in Canada] would have to substitute 10 or 15% of their production with ethanol or MTBE. (HSCESD10/19, 1995a, 6)

The real problems would arise not because ethanol would be used, resulting in lost output, but because it would not be used. Ferland elaborated on Perez's earlier remarks:

As Mr. Perez explained, if MMT were banned, refineries would have to increase the intensity of their refining operations. This means they would have to buy more crude oil to produce the same amount of fuel as before.

Since refining operations would be more intense, Canada would become even more dependent on outside oil, particularly eastern Canada.

If we bought more crude oil, our refining operations would increase, and we would have to produce and burn more fuel to sustain the increase in refining operations. This would result in more gas being released into the atmosphere.

These issues have to be seen in their overall context. On one hand, people are trying to ban MMT, but that would lead to increased car pollution because they would burn fuel without MMT. As well, pollution would increase because refinery operations would intensify and more oil would be burned to feed them. You have to look at the big picture before making that kind of decision. (HSCESD10/19, 1995a, 6)

Reed was baffled. He asked "How is it that MMT has been out of use in the United States for eighteen years? How is it that it was considered advisable, beneficial and desirable to use a product like ethanol, which you consider undesirable and unacceptable, and now in the United States the volume of sales of gasoline using ethanol blends has risen to 8% and is growing by leaps and bounds? It has taken off. This year in the United States 45 new ethanol production plants are in construction" (HSCESD10/19, 1995a, 10).

Paul Steckle, Liberal MP from Huron-Bruce, asked "Why has the petrol industry in the United States of America chosen to go the ethanol route? Were they not challenged, as you, I have to think, are somewhat challenged by the fact that there's a margin of volume that you're going to lose by going to ethanol? Is that a concern? Why is it not a concern to the Americans? Why have American gasoline prices been marginally or in some cases substantially lower than Canadian prices given the fact that they're using a more costly product, using your own analogies here on this?" (HSCESD10/19, 1995a, 11–12).

Brian Fischer, Senior Vice-President, Products and Chemicals, Imperial Oil Ltd. answered both Reed and Steckle: "If you study the full cost of producing ethanol versus conventional gasoline with today's technology, it is twice as costly as conventional fuels ... Our studies of ethanol through its full life cycle would say it has no environmental benefits over conventional gasoline when you consider production through to end use, and I believe there are many in the U.S. who would also support that view" (HSCESD10/19, 1995a, 10–12).

When I tracked down some studies of the "full cost of producing ethanol versus conventional gasoline," I found considerable controversy. The province of Manitoba established the Manitoba Ethanol Advisory Panel on 2 July 2002 to examine the "social, environmental, financial and economic development considerations associated with introducing a mandate for ethanol-blended fuels consumed in Manitoba."The final panel's report included a section reporting results of reviewing "full cost" studies, with the following conclusion: "A number of studies have been conducted in the U.S. and Canada that have examined the energy balance associated with ethanol production. Only one researcher has shown a significant negative energy balance. The majority of current information indicates a positive energy balance and a trend to improving energy balances. In fact, the most recent study released in 2002 found that corn-based ethanol production results in 34 per-cent more energy produced than is consumed inclusive of all energy used – from seed in the ground to ethanol in the vehicle tank" (Ethanol Advisory Panel 2002, 11).

A chart in the Advisory Panel's report summarizing the results of ten studies (12) lists four studies as finding a negative energy balance (Ho 1989; Keeney and DeLuca 1992; Pimentel 1991; and Pimentel 2001). A fact-sheet produced by the U.S. Department of Energy asserts that "Ethanol is a renewable resource that yields a positive energy balance. Whether it is produced from corn or other biomass feedstocks, the ethanol fuel cycle generates more energy than it consumes" (U.S. Department of Energy 1999, 4).

A U.S. Department of Agriculture study by Shapouri, Duffield, and Wang (2002) supports the use of ethanol and claims it would have a positive energy balance. On the contrary, Pimentel (2001, 163–4) wrote, "Numerous studies have concluded that ethanol production does not enhance energy security, is not a renewable energy source, is not an economical fuel, and does not insure clean air. Further its production uses land suitable for crop production and causes environmental degradation ... about 70% more energy is required to produce 1,000 liters of ethanol [from corn fermentation] than the energy that actually is in the ethanol."

In a more recent study Pimentel (2003, 127) wrote:

In the U.S. ethanol system ... about 29% more energy is used to produce a gallon of ethanol than the energy in a gallon of ethanol. Fossil energy powers corn production and the fermentation/distillation processes. Increasing subsidized ethanol production will take more feed from livestock production, and is estimated to currently cost consumers an additional $1 billion per year. Ethanol production increases environmental degradation. Corn production causes more total soil erosion than any other crop. Also, corn production uses more insecticides, herbicides, and nitrogen fertilizers than any other crop. All these factors degrade the agricultural and natural environment and contribute to water pollution and air pollution. Increasing the cost of food and diverting human food resources to the costly inefficient production of ethanol fuel raise major ethical questions. These occur at a time when more than half of the world's population is malnourished. The ethical priority for corn and other food crops should be for food and feed. Subsidized ethanol produced from u.s. corn is not a renewable energy source.

When I asked Pimentel about the discrepancy between his findings and those of the USDA, he wrote me a short note (1 April 2003) saying:

> The reason that the USDA achieves a positive energy return on ethanol is because of the following manipulations:
> 1) They do not include any energy for the production and maintenance of the farm machinery – a large input.
> 2) They do not include any energy for the production of the hybrid corn.
> 3) They do not include any energy for irrigation.
> 4) They use only one-half of the energy for the production of the nitrogen fertilizer.
> 5) They use old, out-of-date data (1991) and only for a select 9 states, not 50 states.

Because Pimentel's analyses are based on corn as the feedstock, and may not apply equally to other kinds of feedstock, e.g., woody and herbaceous cellulosic plants (Wang, Saricks, and Santini 1999), I wrote him (16 September 2003) asking "Can a similar case be made regarding biomass as from, say, forest industry leftovers of which this province has plenty?" He replied the very next day saying: "Unfortunately, converting wood into ethanol is worse than using corn or wheat. However, wood can be converted into methanol and the energetics appear positive. The prime problem is that enormous plants are needed for economies of scale. In addition, I do not know of a single methanol plant in the world [producing methanol from wood]. Thus, the potential only looks good on paper."

In the presence of such complications and disagreements among experts, it is difficult to know what to think. I have not examined the literature thoroughly enough to make a well-informed judgment one way or the other, but I am inclined to accept Pimentel's assessment because of the broad array of factors that he takes into account.

Later on in the AIT Hearings, Perrin raised another objection to the Canadian government's case against MMT that was not repeated in the written *Submission*. His remarks were based on issues 7 to 10 regarding question 1 of *The Minority Opinion* of 4 March 1997 (see chapter 8). Confident of the strength of his argument, Perrin followed it with the remark, "You may be wondering why, if the evidence is so inconclusive, the auto manufacturers pushed so hard for this MMT law" (AIT Hearings 1998a, 170). He thought that at least part of the answer to this question could be found in testimony given by Hicks to the Senate Standing Committee on 5 February 1997 (I quote from the Senate record rather than from the AIT Hearings transcript because the latter is badly scrambled):

The auto industry does not like to be told what to do, and it does not like variables. I described the waiver process for getting a fuel additive approved in the United States, and I have a chart which I would like to hand out showing all the fuel additives that have been approved under this waiver proceeding in the United States under this section of the Clean Air Act. It includes MMT, ethanol, MTBE and methanol. It is helpful to see how big our fleets were compared to some of the other fleets. I specifically wish to draw your attention to the fact that the auto industry opposed everyone one of them by written comments in front of the EPA. It opposed MMT, ethanol and MTBE.

In a hearing before the House of Commons standing committee a year ago October, one of the auto representatives held up a clear pitcher of water and said, "This is what we would like all gasoline to look like." They want no additives. They want one fuel so they can build one car which can run anywhere. (SSCEENR 2/5, 1997c, 11)

Hicks's memory of what was said in the House Standing Committee was not quite accurate. The main exchange was between Chatters and Rick Colcomb, Director of Engineering and Future Product Planning for GM Canada. Here are the essentials:

Mr. Chatters: I just wanted to ask one question ... Has not the failure of the OBD-II technology in the United States been unacceptably high, requiring considerable warranty expense where MMT fuel does not exist? Was there not in fact a need to reduce standards to allow licensing of these systems in the U.S.? ...

Mr. Colcomb: Let me try to answer. Yes, there are always problems with new technology, and the guys with greyer hair than me sitting back there are guys trying to do on-board diagnostics. It's the toughest challenge we've ever had ... It requires us ... to monitor every single system in the vehicle. It requires mathematical modelling and understanding of how catalysts are supposed to convert, comparing oxygen storage, and ... pieces of hardware that are deteriorating, that are plugging or wearing or getting old and tired and not working any more. Yes, there are issues; there are always issues with new technology, MMT only compounds those issues.

We don't know how to do some things with fuel that's as pure as this water. Anything in the fuel hurts us. Sulphur hurts us, manganese hurts us. We're not asking for completely clean fuel. We'll have issues and we'll learn, and it's extremely tough ... It's a very difficult issue. We'll continue to learn. That's part of the problem – you just can't do an independent study on something that's being invented as we speak. (HSCESD 10/24, 1995b, 21–2)

Contrary to Hicks's recollection, Colcomb's central points were not that motor vehicle manufacturers do not like to be told what to do or that they want fuel without any additives, though nobody likes to be told what to do and manufacturers might indeed like to have fuel without additives. The central points were that, first, even if fuel as pure as water were available, it would not solve all their problems; second, that the development of new technology is fraught with failures; third, that developers learn on the job; and fourth, that because technology development is open-ended and incremental, it is a mistake to imagine that there could be a single independent study that would function like the classical, textbook crucial experiment challenged by Duhem.

Hicks's characterization of motor vehicle manufacturers' objections to MMT reminded me of Ralph Nader's complaints in his 1965 classic *Unsafe at Any Speed: The Designed-in Dangers of the American Automobile*. In that book, Nader claimed that the manufacturers resisted the introduction of such safety equipment as stop lights, directional signals, windshield wipers, safety glass, seat belts, and pollution control devices (Michalos 1981a, 176). In the presence of that history (not to mention the infamous Pinto case (Gioia 1992)), Hicks's proposed sweeping explanation does not appear totally incredible, but it does not do justice to what Colcomb actually said. Lest anyone fail to notice it, Perrin added the following explicitly economic argument. "The automobile industry believes that the ban on the importation and interprovincial sale of MMT in Canada serves its economic interest by eliminating a variable that would otherwise have to be considered when designing and certifying vehicles to meet current and future emission standards" (AIT Hearings 1998a, 172–3). Jack Donald, President and CEO of Parkland [refining] Industries offered the same argument (SSCEENR 2/19, 1997g, 45).

Given Perrin's historical and economic arguments in the preceding paragraph, one might forget that the question at issue is whether the Canadian government had sufficient environmental and health reasons to bring in the MMT Act. Insofar as the last two arguments show, at best, that motor vehicle manufacturers historically, and perhaps in the current case of resisting MMT, have tried to serve their own interests, they contribute little more than ad hominem attacks. Even if auto manufacturers' actions are typically motivated by narrow self-interest rather than the public interest, truth, or doing the morally right thing, it does not follow that the Canadian government did not have sufficient environmental and health reasons to pursue its policy regarding Bill C-29.

In the end, the complainant asked the panel to recommend removing MMT from the MMT Act's schedule, repealing the Act, seeking "independent third party information" about MMT's alleged harms, and insisting that the federal government collaborate with all "interested Parties and persons" to find a "reasonable resolution" of the outstanding issues (Perrin and Zarzeczny 1998, 13–14).

15

Government of Canada's Response to Provincial Claims under the AIT

The Government of Canada filed its written *Submission of the Responding Party* on 26 January 1998. Following a brief introduction, the *Submission* begins with an explanation of the respondent's view of the onus of proof, the standard of review, and the manner of weighing evidence that the panel ought to apply. In the third section the facts of the case are described as the respondent saw them. Next comes a section containing a point-by-point response to each of the Government of Alberta's claims, followed by a section challenging certain additional alleged factual claims. A short conclusion includes Canada's "request to the Panel." I will summarize the essential points of each section in turn, integrating relevant additional material from the AIT Hearings.

Against the background of the federal government's insistence on proper process in the NAFTA case, it is striking that in the AIT Hearings its representative, Wallace, asserted very early on that "In our view the role of the panel is really not to reach a view on whether the process followed by the federal government in managing this difficult file conformed to what certain parties' views might be on what constituted appropriate federal-provincial relations. The issue, really, is whether the measure is inconsistent with the agreement, in light of the specific language of the agreement's provisions ... In short, this dispute is, or should be in our view, about substance, not process" (AIT Hearings 1998c, 254–5).

Given the NAFTA background and the fact that the AIT includes procedural rules, which complainants charged the federal government violated, this disclaimer of their significance is difficult to take seriously. It is noticeably absent from the written *Submission*.

Regarding the onus of proof, Canada agreed with Alberta that the latter had the burden of demonstrating that the *MMT Act* is inconsistent with the

AIT. Both parties agreed that Canada had the burden of demonstrating that any measures inconsistent with the AIT satisfied the requirements of the legitimate objectives tests of Article 404.

Regarding the standard of review, the respondent gave four reasons for believing that the AIT did not require panels to make "a full-blown re-examination of all the facts reviewed before the *Act* came into force." First, Article 1505.8 emphasized that "scientific certainty is not required to justify a measure." Second, Article 404(a) "requires only that the 'purpose' (as opposed to the effect) of a measure be a 'legitimate objective'." Third, "The Panel process was intended to be expeditious and dealt with through the filing of briefs and the submission of oral argument. The Panel is expert in matters of trade and commerce, but not in the science of auto emissions control and monitoring systems. The Panel simply cannot be expected to engage in delicate balancing of conflicting facts or engage in the weighing of conflicting scientific evidence" (Canada 1998, 3).

Fourth, "The assessment of whether a measure furthered the legitimate objective was a policy and legislative decision. Under our constitutional regime, the legislative process involves debate and analysis of information in a political forum, and the exercise of judgment. It is neither feasible nor appropriate for the Panel to weigh the decision taken by Parliament for correctness on the basis of the scientific evidence. This would involve reproducing the proceedings before Parliament, supplementing them with additional information and debating the sufficiency of the evidence yet again" (Canada 1998, 3).

Although Canada did not go as far as it did in its NAFTA defence to challenge the jurisdictional authority of the AIT panel, it came close insofar as it challenged the panel's scientific expertise and its political legitimacy. The fundamental question Canada thought the panel should answer was simply: "Was there a reasonable basis for the legislative action taken?" If the panel had accepted the respondent's view, it would have granted not only that a "full-blown" review was redundant but also that the panel was incapable of carrying out such a review and that if it persisted, the standard it would apply ("correctness on the basis of scientific evidence") would be inappropriate anyhow. As it turned out, the panel agreed that a "full-blown" review was not necessary, but disagreed that it was therefore committed to a standard of "correctness" rather than "reasonableness." After all, the applicable standard and the robustness of the review had no logically necessary connection. Nevertheless, as will be seen below, the panel apparently proceeded to apply a standard of "correctness."

Regarding the manner of weighing evidence, the respondent claimed that the panel should be guided by Article 1706.3, which says "All procedures before a panel shall be dealt with as informally and expeditiously as the circumstances and considerations of fairness permit" (AIT 2002). In the hearings (1998a, 14), Brian Evernden, Counsel for Canada, said "I suppose on one level what that means is that you can allow pretty well anything you want to come before you, providing you consider it credible and trustworthy." The *Submission's* language was more circumspect. It regarded this article as reflecting "general principles of administrative and arbitral law," as might be found in Macaulay and Sprague (1996). In the *Submission's* exact words, "This provision recognizes that the dispute resolution provisions of the *Agreement* were intended to permit expeditious proceedings not burdened by legal challenges over the technical rules of evidence. A panel is clearly the master of its own proceedings and may accept evidence in any form suited to the proceeding before it. The panel process was not intended to be a trial" (Canada 1998, 4).

To anyone not trained in law who reads the AIT and documents supporting the claims of complainants and respondents in any dispute, the previous quotation is incredible. Although there is plenty of room for disagreement over the interpretation of specific aspects of the agreement, every step in the process appears to be prescribed and/or justified by some provision in the AIT. Still, Canada only insisted on three "minimum principles": first, that "there must be some evidence, and not mere assertion or argument"; second, that "evidence received should be assigned weight depending on whether it is credible or trustworthy"; and third, that disputes must be resolved on the basis of evidence that the panel "considers most credible and trustworthy" (Canada 1998, 5). Regarding the concept of "weight of evidence" in international commercial arbitration, Brower (1994, 47–53) claimed that:

> International law has no hard and fast rules governing the character or weight of evidence in international arbitrations. Further, proceedings before arbitral tribunals are subject to no "international rules of evidence" that in any manner resemble the technical rules often followed in proceedings before domestic courts ... As a general proposition, therefore, "rules" of evidence followed by arbitral tribunals tend to be more liberal than those followed by domestic courts. The traditional practice of international tribunals is thus to admit virtually any evidence, subject to evaluation of its relevance, credibility, and weight ... While parties may present whatever evidence they deem appropriate to

prove their claims, the arbitrators determine the sufficiency of the evidence proffered and have the discretion to evaluate it however they wish ... The value of the available evidence is only as good as the arbitrator, based on his or her own value system, determines it to be.

So far as I have been able to discern, Brower's remarks apply with full force to the "rules" and weight of evidence in AIT arbitration proceedings.

Among the facts of the case, as they appeared to the respondent, that have not been mentioned already, great emphasis was put on the role of the MMT Act in the federal government's overall strategy and commitments to the "conservation of clean air." The strategy and commitments are outlined here. Nearly half of the fifty-five-page *Submission* is devoted to the impacts of MMT use on air pollution. Clean air is described as "an exhaustible natural resource" and the transportation sector is described as "the single leading source of air pollution in Canada." This sector contributes:

more than 60% of the nitrogen oxides (NO_x), whose direct effects include lung irritation and immune system suppression, and more than 30% of the human-produced volatile organic compounds (VOCs), which include compounds, such as benzene, which are known to be toxic or carcinogens. Vehicles produce approximately one-half of benzene emissions ... Automobiles and trucks also are responsible for approximately 60% of the carbon monoxide (CO), which reduces the ability of blood to carry oxygen, particularly in smokers and persons with heart disease or anaemia ... NO_x and VOCs (which include hydrocarbons (HC)) also produce indirect effects on health and the environment because they interact with sunlight to produce ground-level ozone. Ground-level ozone has been shown to contribute to decreases in lung function, increase in respiratory symptoms, such as cough and pain in deep breathing, chronic lung disease and death. It has also been shown to damage forests and other vegetation and reduce crop yields by up to 20%. NO_x is also a contributor to acid rain. (Canada 1998, 7–8)

Because of these dangerous pollutants from the transportation sector, Canada and many other nations have entered into international agreements to reduce motor vehicle emissions. Among other things, the respondent mentioned the United Nations Economic Commission for Europe *Convention on Long-range Transboundary Air Pollution*, ratified by Canada in 1981, and the U.S.-Canada *Agreement on Air Quality*, which was concluded in March 1991. The "key component" of these agreements was "the requirement for stringent national emissions control standards for automobiles based upon the best available vehicle technology or specified emissions control levels" (Canada 1998, 10). Domestically, the respondent noted that "Initiatives taken by the CCME have included developing 1990 and 1997 Smog Management Plans, which recommend tighter federal standards for NO_x and VOC emissions from motor vehicles, and preparing a long-term strategy for reducing acid rain by controlling and reducing sulphur dioxide (SO_2) and NO_x emissions ... [In sum] Various federal/provincial and provincial initiatives also control fuels and emissions. The control of vehicle emissions by the Government of Canada is thus part of a broader strategy to control air pollution and protect the health of Canadians and the environment" (Canada 1998, 11).

Besides these initiatives, the federal government has been cooperating with the United States government in harmonizing their vehicle emissions control programs. The American requirements have tended to be more stringent. In Canada, as reviewed in chapter 6, "the standards were set initially by informal Memoranda of Understanding with the vehicle industry and, more recently, by regulation." Among the pollution control devices introduced since the 1970s by the motor vehicle industry, the respondent mentioned catalytic converters, oxygen sensors for the converters, and on-board diagnostic equipment, which resulted in the reduction of tailpipe emissions "by 90 to 95 percent or more since the 1970s" (Canada 1998, 12).

In spite of the technological advances leading to lower emissions per vehicle, the continued increase in the total numbers of vehicles and kilometres driven means that, "more stringent emissions standards are required as the ground gained through technological improvements is lost" (Canada 1998, 12). What is worse, the situation described in Canada and the United States is also true of all the countries in the Organization for Economic Cooperation and Development (OECD 1994; Michalos 1997a).

Because well-functioning emissions control equipment promises to replace much more labour-intensive, expensive inspection and maintenance routines, anything that puts such equipment in jeopardy would have to be taken seriously. Unfortunately, as early as 1978 the U.S. EPA had found reasons for believing that MMT was precisely such a harmful agent (see chapter 5). The most recent release available from the EPA on this topic was posted on the web on 2 March 2007. Here are its most relevant passages:

In its decision on the use of MMT in the U.S., the Agency determined that MMT at 1/32 gpg Mn [1/32 grams manganese per gallon of gasoline] will not cause or contribute to regulated emissions failures of vehicles. Some have expressed concerns that the use of MMT may harm on-board diagnostic equipment (OBD) which monitors the performance of emissions control devices in the vehicle. As of this time, the Agency believes the data collected is [sic] inconclusive with regard to OBD ... modeling indicates that, as a result of MMT use in unleaded gasoline, certain portions of the population may be exposed to levels in the same range as the Reference Concentration (RfC or safe level for a lifetime exposure with an order of magnitude uncertainty). Because the expected exposure is not much higher or much lower than the RfC, a definitive conclusion about risk is impossible to reach. Long-term animal testing and exposure research are needed to more accurately define the risk.

Under the Clean Air Act authority to require testing of motor fuels and additives, EPA has required the Afton Corporation to perform testing to help fill in data gaps and potentially provide information that would result in a more definitive risk evaluation ... In addition to the already completed tests, the manufacturer is now in the process of developing physiologically based pharmokinetic (PBPK) models for manganese that are being derived from data generated from the complete testings. Afton anticipates that the PBPK models will be completed in 2008.

After submission of this additional information, the Agency will study the results. The Agency may then be able to refine its risk evaluation or may ask for further testing ... With funding from Afton, Research Triangle Institute (RTI) has also completed a study of manganese exposures in Toronto, Canada where MMT is used. The Agency is also evaluating this study to determine what impact it might have on any evaluation of risk associated with use of the additive. (EPA 2007)

At this point (August 2007), the RTI (1998) study does not appear to have had an "impact ... on any evaluation of risk" by the EPA. The following quotations and comments from the report provide a fair summary of what RTI did and found.

The EPA requested that additional information be obtained to improve the risk assessment for MMT use in unleaded gasoline in the U.S., including a more robust exposure analysis ... A primary objective of the [RTI] study was to estimate the distribution of manganese exposures over a 12-month period in a population for which such exposures included effects of the gasoline additive MMT ...

Toronto, Ontario, was chosen as the study site because MMT has been used as a gasoline additive in Canada for about 20 years; the metropolitan Toronto area has a large, diverse population; and it includes diverse traffic densities. These factors taken together provided a sufficiently wide range of variability. Additionally, Toronto exhibited no known active major industrial point sources of Mn emissions. A wealth of historic Mn data available for ambient air and some historic personal exposure data were available.

The inferential or target population was defined in terms of the household population at least 16 years of age resident in the Toronto study site from June 1995 through August 1996 ... The spatial dimension of the study site ... encompassed approximately 600 square kilometers (230 square miles) and a household population of approximately two million people. (RTI 1998, ch. 2, 1)

The researchers were primarily interested in examining the relative amount of manganese particles with aerodynamic diameters of less than 2.5 micrometres in size ($PM_{2.5}$) per cubic metre that entered the air as a result of the combustion of gasoline containing MMT. Earlier research had revealed that at least 85 per cent of the particles resulting from such combustion were of that size. Air samples were drawn from monitoring devices worn on 1,143 residents, as well as from fixed sites inside people's residences, in yards or areas immediately outside their residences, and from "three long-term, outdoor fixed-site monitoring stations." Because study participants' tolerance for wearing monitoring devices was limited, samples were taken from diverse sets of individuals covering 3-day periods. Data from the four different sampling procedures then had to be used in different statistical models, with different assumptions, to estimate average annual exposure levels for average citizens. According to the report, "average citizens" were a subset of the total sample of respondents who did not have extraordinary occupational exposures, e.g., were not metal workers or welders. For such average citizens, the estimated mean annual daily exposure was 9.2 ng/m^3, rising to 14.1, 16.3, and 21.5, respectively, for those in the 90th, 95th and 99th, percentiles (RTI 1998, ch. 1, 9; ch. 2, 22).

Testifying to the Senate Standing Committee, Lynam said that Health Canada's "safe exposure level for manganese" was 110 nanograms per cubic metre and that "the current WHO guideline" was 1,000 nanograms per cubic metre (SSCEENR 2/5, 1997d, 9). Based on those figures, RTI's estimated mean annual exposure rate was about twelve times lower than Health Canada's "safe" level and about 109 times lower than WHO's "safe" level. On the other hand, the RTI study also found that manganese "levels were 428 ng/m^3 in the subway and 9.7 ng/m^3 outdoors (a ratio of about 44)"(RTI 1998, 2–38). So Toronto subway users were (and probably still are) routinely exposed to airborne manganese particles at nearly four times Health Canada's estimated "safe" level, as a result of "the grinding of the steel rails and brakes," not of MMT. One would think that, at a minimum, such figures would demand careful investigation.

The Government of Canada went on to produce letters from the Manufacturers of Emissions Controls Association dated 19 July 1990, 7 September 1990, and 3 October 1991 indicating that the use of MMT would "adversely affect motor vehicle emissions control performance" (AIT 1998b). Similar submissions and evidence from owner's manuals were provided by GM, Chrysler, Ford, Porsche, and Honda over the next few years (Canada 1998, 20–4). On the other side, the complainant produced a briefing note about the 1994 Toyota study (see chapter 8, argument 25).

In June 1993 the Joint Government-Industry Committee on Transportation Fuels and Vehicle Emissions Control Technology was formed with a mandate to examine the evidence concerning the impact of MMT on emissions control equipment more carefully (see chapter 6). Besides crafting the "consensus statement" on harmonization, it concluded that available evidence about MMT was "inconclusive" and that more research should be undertaken.

That was not good enough for the motor vehicle manufacturers. On 14 October 1994, the MVMA sent a letter to the CPPI telling them that if MMT was not eliminated from gasoline, then warranties on emission control devices would be altered (see chapter 8). In response to that letter, the CPPI wrote to Minister Copps on 11 November 1994, congratulating her "on the success of the recent CCME meeting held in Bathurst, New Brunswick," explaining that they were "encouraged by the initiatives to be undertaken in connection with federal-provincial program harmonization, emissions and fuel quality standards, and the emphasis on voluntary actions to address climate change," and recommending more research (CPPI 1994b). The Minister replied with a letter dated 18 November 1994 asking the two industries to resolve their problems with MMT by the end of the year (Copps 1994).On 19 December 1994 the MVMA and the AIAMC "made a presentation and provided data to the petroleum industry regarding the adverse effects of MMT on emissions control and monitoring hardware" (Canada 1998, 18).

After asking Copps for a deadline extension on 31 December 1994, on 6 January 1995 the "CPPI and 11 of its members agreed to: form a technical task force; review the available data; issue a report by February 28, 1995;

and respond appropriately to its findings." The Technical Task Force was composed of one CPPI staff member, five representatives from CPPI member companies, a representative of Irving Oil, and three consultants. So formally, at least, it was not a group of disinterested, unbiased observers. It met in Toronto, 17–19 January 1995, and heard presentations from the MVMA and AIAMC. As one might have expected, "The information received from Ethyl and the OEMs [original equipment manufacturers = auto manufacturers in the present case] is best described as diametrically opposed. The two sides did not agree on anything of substance except that manganese oxide accumulates in the engine and exhaust system" (CPPI Technical Task Force 1995, 1–2, 13).

Over objections from the vehicle manufacturers, Copps extended the deadline by a month. On 6 January 1995 the MVMA wrote to Copps complaining that "Although we will continue to provide information to CPPI as well as to individual companies, now and in the future, we cannot accept further delays. MMT-free gasoline is already being purchased by our manufacturing facilities on a daily basis, in large volumes. We cannot understand why it is not being made available to the general public for purchase nor are we convinced that MMT-free gasoline will be made available" (Canada 1998, 19).

On 26 January 1995 Chrysler Canada "shared highly sensitive warranty data with CPPI regarding the adverse effects of MMT on vehicle equipment," and five days later the MVMA sent a letter to Copps rejecting the CPPI's offer "to reduce maximum allowable levels of MMT to 9mg/l (9 milligrams per litre) from [what was] the current 18 mg/l of gasoline." Since 9 mg/l was roughly the average level of use of MMT in gasoline in Canada, the offer was little more than an offer to do nothing. In case that was not clear, the day after the MVMA sent its letter to Copps, the CPPI sent her a letter (1 February 1995) saying that the elimination of MMT from gasoline "would only take place if required by legislation."

Seven days later, the MVMA and AIAMC proposed a "two pump solution" to the CPPI, which was rejected two days later, along with yet another proposal for further research, which the MVMA and AIAMC rejected on 17 February 1995. On 28 February 1995, the CPPI Technical Task Force presented its *Report*. It could not "reconcile the differences between the data presented by the vehicle industry and by Ethyl," and it proposed more research (Canada 1998, 19–21).

The very next month, the Government of Canada received reports from two independent analysts, the Carter Report of 2 March 1995 and the Walsh Report of 16 March 1995.

Both experts stated that while the data provided by both the vehicle industry and Ethyl Corporation were inconclusive, MMT tended to degrade emissions systems performance. They further stated that MMT could increase consumer costs … The Walsh Report questioned Ethyl's testing methodology and concluded that real world data indicate that the use of MMT in gasoline is causing an increase in hydrocarbon emissions from vehicles in Canada and that the laboratory studies carried out by Ethyl tended to reinforce this conclusion … The second technical opinion, provided by Stephen A. Carter of ORTECH Corporation (the "Carter Report"), concluded that, while the data are incomplete and contradictory, the equipment manufacturers' original data was [sic] more relevant and credible. Mr. Carter was the independent expert also engaged by CPPI to gauge the aforementioned data as part of its Task Force which found that the data was [sic] inconclusive. (Canada 1998, 26)

During the AIT Hearings (1998c, 349–50), Tyhurst reminded everyone that, notwithstanding the neutral conclusions reached by the task force, "Two independent analyses, admittedly commissioned by the federal government but of recognized experts, one of whom [Carter] was a member of the CPPI task force, come to the conclusion that the [federal] government is making the right decision to remove MMT from gasoline. I have not seen a shred of evidence — perhaps my friends will take me up on this – attacking those studies, but I am certainly not aware of any evidence attacking the Walsh or the Carter analysis. And the Walsh analysis, as I pointed out, does contain risk assessment."

In the afternoon of the same day, Ternes took up Tyhurst's challenge and offered the group a reason to place less weight on those "independent analyses" than Tyhurst would have preferred. Since the dates of the Task Force, Carter, and Walsh reports were, respectively, 28 February 1995, 2 March 1995 and 16 March 1995, it was obvious that neither Carter nor Walsh had enough time to do any significant independent research for their own reports. This does not prove that their conclusions were incorrect, but it does suggest that they might have limited value. Regarding Carter's report, Ternes said, "He prepared this report very quickly … he spent two days preparing this report … this isn't independent research; what this is is a commentary or analysis of the CPPI Technical Task Force. It's not new, independent research."

About Walsh's report, he said it took only until "March 16, two weeks after, to do this independent study. Again, it's not really a scientific study;

it's not independent science. It's a comment on the CPPI Technical Task Force ... His disclaimer says this: 'This memo reflects my best judgement of the issues based on a short but intense review of the available information'." (AIT Hearings 1998c, 405–6)

There is no indication of how impressed the Panel was by Ternes's reply to Tyhurst's challenge. However, even though independently collecting and analysing one's own data (depending on the researchers' particular expertise, among other things) may offer some advantages over simply analysing someone else's data, I would not make much out of Ternes's remarks. Again, depending on researchers' particular skills, a secondary or later analysis of data might be much more revealing than the first. The history of science is full of examples of people examining data collected by others from different perspectives and reaching not only different but also more appropriate conclusions (Durbin 1980).

Besides commissioning the reports by Carter and Walsh, the respondent hired Abraham and Lawless to examine the evidence for Ethyl's claim that MMT reduces NO_x emissions (see chapter 8, argument 6). Apparently leaving no stone unturned, the respondent addressed the Wood and Egyed (1994) report reviewed above in chapter 8, which found no direct threat to human health from MMT. "The Health Canada report addressed neither the indirect health or environmental effects resulting from deposits of manganese oxides on sparkplugs, catalytic converters and OBD systems through increased air pollutants (i.e., VOC's, NO_x, resulting ground level ozone and particulates); nor did it consider their effects on Canada's ability to reduce air pollution through the use of new technology or stronger emissions standards. Health Canada supports a ban on MMT given these indirect effects" (Canada 1998, 28).

The *Submission* also indicated that while the industrialists were searching for solutions, in November 1994 the CCME formed a Task Force on Cleaner Vehicles and Fuels "to develop options and recommendations for a national approach to new vehicle emissions, fuel efficiency standards and fuel reformulations for Canada." That Task Force *Report* was released in early October and endorsed by the CCME on 23 October 1995. Among other things, the task force emphasized:

(a) the need for harmonization of Canadian and U.S. emissions standards;
(b) the need for compatibility between the fuels used by motor vehicles and the increasingly complex and sophisticated pollution control and monitoring technologies being introduced to meet the stringent emissions standards required under the U.S. Clean Air Act; and,

(c) the importance of on-going inspection and maintenance programs to ensure emissions control systems remain in good working order. (Canada 1998, 13–16)

In the AIT Hearings (1998c, 296), Bob Rae expressed the view that "The agreement seems to imply a degree of consultation [through the CCME, in accordance with Article 1509] which, certainly from what I have heard, didn't take place in precisely the way that it was anticipated by the agreement. Am I wrong? I don't know.

Mr. Wallace [replied]: I guess [Article] 1509 talks about obligations of the council, rather than the obligations of the party. And, indeed, the council has done what is in 1509.

I guess with respect to this dispute, the obligations of the parties, then, I guess come back to 1508. I guess in my remarks I said that 1508.1 is important, but so is 1508.2 and the definition of harmonization."

As we will see below and in chapter 16, the federal government's argument regarding "1508.2 and the definition of harmonization" seems to be very strong, although the panel completely ignored it. Regarding Rae's point about the absence of an appropriate "degree of consultation," refer back to testimony given to the Senate Standing Committee by Nicole Pageot:

The Motor Vehicle Safety Act is defined as an act to regulate the manufacture and importation of motor vehicles and motor vehicle equipment to reduce the risk of health, injury and damage to property and the environment. It is this act that provides federal legislative authority for setting standards to limit emissions from vehicles ... Since 1971, Transport Canada's Road Safety and Motor Vehicle Regulation Directorate has promulgated progressively more stringent national emission standards for on-road motor vehicles under the authority of the Motor Vehicle Safety Act to address the environmental issues associated with vehicle emissions ...

Vehicle manufacturers and importers are required to comply with Transport Canada's emission standards as a condition of the importation or the interprovincial shipment of new motor vehicles in Canada ... While it is Transport Canada that holds the legislative authority to promulgate motor vehicle emission standards, several federal government departments play an important role in and contribute to the process of establishing the most appropriate standards for Canada ...

Transport Canada promulgates the standard for new motor vehicles under the Motor Vehicle Safety Act.

Environment Canada provides environmental policy input and environmental impact assessment to support motor vehicle emission regulations. Environment Canada also regulates national fuel quality under the authority of the Canadian Environmental Protection Act, in part to ensure compatibility of fuels and vehicles.

Health Canada provides input on the effects of various emission constituents and the reaction of products on human health.

Natural Resources Canada provides input on the effects of new standards on fuel supply, demand quality, and the fuels producing industry.

Industry Canada provides input on the effects of new standards on Canadian industry, employment and trade agreements.

Aside from the federal government, a broad cross-section of Canadian society has definite views on environmental issues, including motor vehicle emissions. These include provincial governments, particularly through the auspices of the Canadian Council of Ministers of the Environment, ... as well as industries, environmental groups, public health groups, consumer groups and labour unions. Through a process of interdepartmental and public consultation, new emissions standards promulgated by Transport Canada represent a fair and balanced consensus of all involved federal departments and include consideration of input from the provinces, interested private sector groups, organizations and the public. (SSCEENR 2/6, 1997e, 14–15; emphasis added; cf. testimony of P.J. Monahan below)

Over a four-day period (18, 19, 24, 26 October 1995), the House Standing Committee on Environment and Sustainable Development heard evidence from Environment Canada, the Canadian Automobile Association, the CPPI, Consumers' Co-operative Refiners Limited, Ethyl Canada Inc., General Motors, the MVMA, Toyota, Honda, and the AIAMC about Bill C-94 and MMT. Contrary to the Québec *Brief*, Richard Godding, Vice-President, Canadian Automobile Association, said the CAA supported Bill C-94 and thought that "The petroleum manufacturers ... have certainly been consulted more than enough – as we understand it – and CAA respectfully suggests that their concerns over process should not be a reason to hold up a worthwhile piece of legislation. CAA has been able to secure enough technical information on this subject from Environment Canada and industry sources to proclaim its support for the merits of eliminating MMT" (HSCESD10/19, 1995a, 26).

From 11 February 1996 to 4 March 1997 the Senate Standing Committee on Energy, the Environment and Natural Resources heard evidence from all those who appeared before the House Committee plus:

> the Minister of the Environment, Imperial Oil, Petro-Canada, Shell, Husky, Ultramar, Parkland Industries, Ford, Chrysler, Nissan, Mercedes-Benz, the Canadian Auto Dealers Association, the Sierra Club, Health Canada, Transport Canada, Pollution Probe, the Learning Disability Association of Canada, the Allergy/Asthmatic Association, the Government of Alberta, the Government of Nova Scotia, and others. The Senate issued a majority report on March 4, 1997, which concluded: "Based on the preponderance of evidence, the government was justified in invoking the precautionary principle and introducing Bill C-29 as a prudent, responsible course of action' ... Overall, the legislation [Bill C-94 and Bill C-29] was before Parliament from May 1995 to April 1997. (Canada 1998, 31–2)

As indicated above, the Government of Canada then followed up on this work by amending the *Motor Vehicle Safety Regulations* on 28 July 1997, so that, beginning with the 1998 model year, all new motor vehicles sold in Canada would meet the u.s. emissions standards for HC, CO, and NO$_x$, and "would be equipped with an OBD system to monitor emissions control equipment for proper functioning" (Canada 1998, 16). The respondent could hardly have backed away from the *MMT Act*, given these amendments, the intransigence of the industrialists, the reports of independent analysts, the work of the CCME and its task force, the hearings in committees of the House and Senate, the debates on the floor of parliament, and the still inconclusive but worrying evidence about the harmful effects of MMT on catalytic converters and on-board diagnostic systems. Indeed, the respondent went so far as to assert that "the legislation in question effectively harmonizes Canadian unleaded gasoline with that of the u.s.," even though the u.s. Court of Appeals ordered the EPA to grant a waiver for the use of MMT as a fuel additive as early as November 1995 (Canada 1998, 31).

After this relatively long review of the environmental case for eliminating MMT from unleaded gasoline, the *Submission* briefly noted that, contrary to the complainant's charges, "The offences and penalties found in the *Act* are comparable with those of other federal environmental legislation" (Canada 1998, 33). It then proceeded to a point-by-point rebuttal of Alberta's allegations regarding inconsistencies between the *MMT Act* and the AIT. I will now review each point in turn.

First, it was asserted that the *MMT Act* did not violate Article 401 because "it treats all gasoline containing MMT equally, wherever it is produced" (Canada 1998, 34, 37). In response to the complainant's charge that MMT, MTBE, ETBE, and ethanol were "like, directly competitive, or substitutable goods" in the language of Article 401.1 (b), the respondent raised at least twelve objections:

[1] Some 80% of the manganese contained in MMT remains in the engine-emissions control and monitoring system after combustion, while other gasoline additives, such as oxygenates, are completely consumed in the combustion process. [2] Evidence presented by the vehicle industry demonstrates that these different by-products from combustion result in different effects on emissions control systems and engine performance and, therefore, [3] result in different impacts on the environment and human health. [4] Oxygenates on the other hand can be used as blend stocks or impart other properties to fuels. The only gasoline additives which are potentially "like, directly competitive or substitutable" with MMT are other manganese-based additives, and these are all treated in the same manner by the Act.

[5] Refiners would not object to the elimination of MMT if it were a seamless substitute for other gasoline additives. [6] Refiners, therefore, apparently do not consider other octane enhancers to be directly substitutable for MMT, which has [7] different costs, [8] differing octane enhancing properties and [9] requires a different capital cost structure to produce.

[10] The evidence presented by the vehicle industry of the effect of MMT enhanced gasoline on vehicle emissions systems and on-board diagnostics equipment also distinguishes such gasoline from MMT-free gasoline.

[11] Alberta's argument, taken to the extreme, implies that actions to ban lead as a gasoline additive would violate Article 401, despite its generally accepted deleterious effects on the environment and human health, simply because it did not treat lead in the same manner as other octane enhancers. [12] Canada submits that Article 401 was not intended to prevent regulatory distinctions from being made between products which have different effects on the environment and human health … [Thus,] the available evidence demonstrates distinctions which show that MMT and MMT-enhanced gasoline are not "like, directly com-

petitive or substitutable" with other additives and MMT-free gasoline, respectively, on the plain meaning of those words. (Canada 1998, 38–9)

The "different costs" referred to above include the estimated relative costs in 1985 Canadian dollars of "raising the rating of one barrel of fuel by one octane number" using various enhancers. Using tetraethyl lead at 0.29 g/l the cost would have been 6 cents; using MMT at 0.016 g/l the cost would have been 15 cents; for reformulation, 30 cents; for aromatics (benzene, toluene, xylene), 42–92 cents; for MTBE, 40–90 cents (Commission on Lead in the Environment 1986, 106). The idea that, say, MTBE could be regarded as "like, directly competitive or substitutable" with MMT given the very different costs of using them for the same "end use" seems farfetched. Nevertheless, this did not prevent Ogilvy from claiming that:

It is interesting too that both of these products, the gasoline containing MMT and the gasoline not containing MMT, are substitutable for each other and definitely competitive. They [1] sell to the customer for roughly the same price, depending on location more than on refinery; they [2] can be used in any automobile and [3] are directly competitive; [4] they are certainly substitutable for each other. They are also [5] subject to identical legislation; it is the one Act. It is equally legal – identical legislation, but ... although it is applied identically to the products or to manufacturers, it has discriminatory impact ... Alberta consumes only 42 per cent of its production; so it depends very heavily on exports across the country ... Ontario, on the other hand, consumes over 95 per cent of its production, and the out-of-province transfers are the flip side of that ... in order to serve their markets, Alberta refiners would have to continue the present practice ... of split-run distribution, while Ontario refiners could happily satisfy their full market with MMT-enhanced gasoline ... The indirect impact of the legislation clearly discriminates between manufacturers in different markets. Thus Article 403 cannot be dismissed as having only marginal application to the matter before the panel. (AIT Hearings 1998, 65–8)

According to Clarkson (2002a, 70), the Appellate Body of the WTO once "memorably compared the concept of 'likeness' to 'an accordion, which may be stretched wide or squeezed tight as the case requires'." Because "similarity" or "likeness" is, from a logical point of view, a three-place predicate (*A* is similar or like *B* by virtue of having or lacking properties

P_I-P_n.), the difficulties in using Alberta's "end-use" criterion as a sole discriminating property were predictable. In fact, any attempt to completely characterize any product in terms of any single property would be problematic because there is no generally agreed upon perspective from which every product must be viewed (cf. the discussion of "in like circumstances" in NAFTA, IISD/WWF 2001, 26–7).

Second, it was granted that the *Act* did violate Articles 402 (right of entry and exit) and 403 (no obstacles to trade).

Third, it was claimed that because the *Act* was not a "standard-related measure" as defined in Article 200, Annex Article 405.1 was not applicable. In the respondent's view, "A standard consists of, for example, detailed rules for composition or quality that may be adjusted or modified to suit regulatory purposes ... There is no procedure for adjusting the quantity of MMT used in gasoline, even if Canada wished to do so. Therefore, the premise of Article 405.1, that adjustment and reconciliation of standards can occur, is not present in the *Act*" (Canada 1998, 42).

Notwithstanding this argument, the Government of Canada went on to argue that if the panel insisted on treating the MMT *Act* as a "standard-related measure" then all that was required was that the procedures indicated in Article 405.1 for reviewing and reconciling standards should be met. Furthermore, since those procedures were met, the respondent claimed, there was no violation of the Article. The most interesting part of the respondent's line of argumentation is the following:

With respect to the question of proportionality, the obligation under Annex 405.1.5 is to ensure that the trade restrictiveness of the standard is no greater than necessary to deal with the risk. Canada's objective could have been achieved in three ways: voluntary elimination by the refining industry; regulation by the provinces; or, regulation by the federal government. Canada was unable to achieve the objective through voluntary action or action by the provinces, and, therefore, put its own legislation in place. Canada anticipates that the effect of the legislation will be to eliminate MMT from all domestically consumed gasoline. Canada notes that each of the three alternatives discussed above is equally trade restrictive. Canada has satisfied the proportionality condition. (Canada 1998, 44)

Fourth, because in the federal government's view the MMT *Act* was a "regulatory measure" according to the definition given in Article 407, i.e., "a measure that does not contain a standard and that pertains to commercial activity" (AIT 2002), Annex Article 405.2 was applicable. Most importantly, then, if that were the case, then the panel would have to obey Annex Article 405.2.10, which says that "Chapter Seventeen (Dispute Resolution Procedures) does not apply to this Annex" (AIT 2002).

Taking the respondent's third and fourth points together its argument was: (1) The measure in question was "standard-related" or not. (2) If it was "standard-related" then AIT obligations were not breached because the procedures of Article 405.1 were met and the panel had no jurisdiction to hear the case. (3) If it was not "standard-related" then according to Article 405.2, the panel had no jurisdiction to hear the case. So, on either alternative, the panel had no jurisdiction to hear the case.

Since the Canadian General Standards Board had a standard for the allowable amount of manganese per litre of gasoline, it is perhaps understandable that someone might regard a prohibition against cross-border trade in a product containing manganese as setting a new standard. However, no new standard for the allowable amount of manganese per litre of gasoline was set. Nothing in the *MMT Act* says anything about how much manganese can be used in gasoline and, therefore, no new standard of usage of MMT in gasoline is set by the *Act*. This is a fairly subtle argument based on a subtle distinction, but it appears to me to be sound. It is true that the *Act* has the effect of eliminating MMT from gasoline, but the effect is not achieved by setting a new standard of usage. What is new is the regulation against cross-border trade in MMT, which would effectively eliminate it from gasoline, given the economic impracticalities of producing and selling it in every province.

Fifth, the respondent claimed that "the essence of this dispute is whether the legislation meets the conditions described in paragraphs (a) to (d) of Article 404 [the 'legitimate objectives' tests], as qualified by the interpretive provisions in Chapter 15" (Canada 1998, 34). The most important qualification was articulated in Article 1505.8, i.e., "For greater certainty, an environmental measure shall not be considered to be inconsistent with this Agreement by reason solely of the lack of full scientific certainty regarding the need for the measure" (AIT 2002). This was supposed to be the federal government's ace in the hole, and the reason that half the *Submission* was occupied with a review of all the apparently relevant considerations that had to be taken into account to determine what federal public policy and what implementation instrument should be adopted. Accordingly, the respondent recited the provisions of Article 1505.1–8, reviewed the considerations outlined above, and concluded that "Against this background and in view of the context set out in Section III [i.e., the considerations],

Canada submits that it has met all of the conditions enumerated in 404 (a) through (d), as interpreted in conjunction with Article 1505" (Canada 1998, 45–7).

The respondent then proceeded to consider each of the four tests of Article 404 in turn.

In the light of the extended review of the environmental issues considered above, it was relatively easy to show that the test in Article 404 (a) was passed because "The protection of the environment, the protection of human health and consumer protection are legitimate objectives as defined in Article 200" (Canada 1998, 47).

Regarding Article 404 (b), the respondent claimed that because the MMT Act only applied to manganese-based fuel additives, it was not "broader than necessary" (Canada 1998, 49).

Regarding Article 404 (c), it was claimed that the measure was "not more trade restrictive than necessary" given the five available options:

- First, the "two pump solution" proposed by the MVMA, which was rejected by the CPPI.
- Second, the CPPI's offer to reduce MMT levels to 9 mg/l – a non-solution insofar as that was already the average level of MMT in gasoline in Canada – which was rejected by the MVMA. One might argue (as Hill did in correspondence) that if the allowable level of MMT had been reduced to 9mg/l, there would have been a reduction in the average level actually used and that level might have been acceptable to both sides. However, inspection of the wording of the CPPI's offer in Brouillard's letter to Copps (1 February 1995, quoted above) reveals that the offer was far from clear, and there is no evidence that the MVMA was prepared to accept any reduced level of MMT usage.
- Third, the CPPI's repeated suggestion to have more research, which was rejected because the respondent thought the available research evidence was adequate and "the timing of more stringent emissions regulations" was too short to wait for more studies. Besides, it was believed that "The results of further study would also in all likelihood have been disputed by at least some of the major parties involved in this matter" (Canada 1998, 50). Addressing the same issue in the AIT Hearings (1998c, 270–2), Wallace said:

further scientific study would be unlikely to resolve the controversies that had existed with respect to the use of this product for over 20 years, really, when the automobile manufacturers and Ethyl have been at loggerheads over this.

... We doubted very much whether it would be possible to arrive at a conclusive scientific study in the short term. We are also very conscious of the expense of these studies. They are not cheap, by any stretch of the imagination. Right now I believe the u.s. program is a $10 million study. As you may have seen, Ethyl is also financing very expensive studies ... but there continues to be considerable scientific debate between Ethyl's new studies ... and the auto industry ... [In any case,] With respect to Article 404 (c), the point I would like to make is further scientific study would not have removed MMT from gasoline. Therefore, it cannot be considered as a less trade restrictive option which would have met Canada's objective.

• Fourth:

The only other available option was to ban the use of MMT outright, which would have required the concurrence of all the provinces. While there was initial support for the legislation from some provinces [Newfoundland, Ontario, and British Columbia], Canada was unable to secure assurances from all the provinces that they would enact complementary legislation to reinforce the federal measure. As such, this option was not reasonably available to Canada and, in any event, would have been equally trade restrictive.

Alberta, itself, has not proposed any options for addressing this issue with the exception of further discussion and a complete ban on MMT. The former would not have addressed the matter and the latter would have been equally trade restrictive.

... In summary, Canada submits that it has met the requirement under both Article 404 (c) and Article 1505.7 ... there were no less trade restrictive options reasonably available to it *which would also have allowed the achievement of its legitimate objective.* (Canada 1998, 50–1; emphasis added)

Unfortunately, the trade option Canada finally selected to achieve its purpose proved to be no more acceptable than the other four. The defect in the fourth option should be stressed, because some members of parliament were and perhaps still are unaware of it. For example, James Moore of the former Canadian Alliance Party (now Conservative Party) mistakenly claimed in the House of Commons on 1 May 2001 that "If the federal government had outright banned the use of MMT in Canada, regardless of where it was made, Ethyl would not have been able to prove the discrimination that was central to winning its case" (Moore 2001, 4). Peter Underwood, Deputy Minister, Department of the Environment, Government of Nova Scotia, made the same mistake (SSCEENR 2/11, 1996, 2, 4), as did Réal Ménard (MP, Hochelaga-Maisonneuve, PD9/27, 1996b, 11).In the presence of Article 1505.2, without the consent of all provinces, such a ban would have been impossible (see chapter 14).

Regarding Article 404 (d), it was asserted that "the measure is completely open and transparent and is, therefore, not a disguised measure" (Canada 1998, 51). In the AIT Hearings, Wallace denied the complainant's claim that if trade legislation was used "to accomplish an environmental objective" then it was a "disguised barrier." On the contrary, he said, "A disguised barrier to trade occurs often when you use a non-trade measure ostensibly for the purpose of achieving a legitimate objective, but when your real motivation, your real rationale, is to promote or protect a local interest ... There is nothing in the agreement that suggests that trade legislation is in any way less preferable to other legislation as [a] means of addressing environmental concerns. The issue is not the form of the legislation. The issue is whether the tests are met. If the tests are met, it doesn't matter whether it is trade legislation or non-trade legislation that meets it" (AIT Hearings 1998c, 275–6).

Regarding the issue of using trade legislation to address environmental concerns, during the Hearings on Bill C-29 before the Senate Standing Committee, Ogilvy challenged the bill on the grounds that "It is a widely held and widely respected convention that legislation be applied directly to the problems that exist, if problems are discovered, not indirectly as with this bill. In this case, there has not been the opportunity to apply health legislation or environmental legislation because the evidence simply does not exist that that type of legislation is appropriate or necessary. Instead, the bill is a trade bill. It seeks to achieve indirectly what cannot be justified and accomplished directly. On the face of it, I suggest that indirect legislation can be seen as a symptom of a poorly conceived objective and becomes the product of a poorly executed process" (SSCEENR 2/11, 1996, 7).

However, in his *Brief* to that committee, Monahan (1997, 2, 7) claimed that:

The Parliament of Canada has exclusive legislative authority to regulate interprovincial and international trade, pursuant to its authority under section 91(2) of the *Constitution Act, 1867*. The corollary to the proposition is that the provincial legislatures have no power to regulate such trade. Provincial legislative power to regulate trade matters applies only to transactions, activities or persons located "in the province", which has been interpreted as not including the power to regulate the importation of goods into the provinces ... Parliament has exercised its plenary authority to regulate importation and interprovincial trade in a wide variety of contexts for many different social, economic, health and other policy objectives. There have never been any doubts raised about the constitutional validity of these enactments.

As reported in chapter 3, section 91(2) of the Constitution Act, 1867 says, "it is hereby declared that (notwithstanding anything in this Act) the exclusive Legislative Authority of the Parliament of Canada extends to all Matters coming within the Classes of Subjects next hereinafter enumerated; that is to say ... 2. the Regulation of Trade and Commerce."

In support of his claim that many precedents exist for the Federal Government's strategy, Monahan listed sixteen Acts (Monahan 1997, 2–4, 7). In fact, the *Motor Vehicle Safety Act* functions exactly as the MMT *Act* would have functioned. Monahan's account of the former is clearly applicable to the latter:

> It is settled law that Parliament may validly affect local trade, as long as its regulation applies only to interprovincial or international trade ... Consider, for example, the *Motor Vehicle Safety Act* which establishes standards that are mandatory for vehicles that cross provincial borders. Because 95 per cent of all motor vehicles produced in Canada cross a provincial border, the standards are in practical terms effective to control the production of all vehicles, whatever their intended market. However, these "effects" on local production of vehicles cannot be the basis of a constitutional challenge, since the federal legislation only applies on a mandatory basis to interprovincial or international movement of vehicles. (Monahan 1997, 8)

Quite apart from any problems that Ethyl might have had with Monahan's interpretation of the law, it made Senator Gérald Beaudoin "extremely nervous": "If I take Patrick Monahan's argument that Parliament can do whatever it wants with interprovincial trade, then it can become the Trojan Horse of Canadian federalism. What will be left to the provinces? It will always be possible, for whatever reason, to use trade

powers and to control the way things are done within the provinces"
(SSCEENR 2/19, 1997g, 11).

The following exchange then took place:

Mr Monahan: With all due respect, senator, it is not a Trojan Horse. It
is not a case of being able to say, "Now we can prevent the selling of
apples that local growers are growing in British Columbia." That is not
the case because MMT is not produced here.

Senator Beaudoin: I have no quarrel with that. When we are dealing
with the importation of manganese, of course it is federal. However,
once the manganese is in Canada and it is dealt with interprovincially,
then it is federal. When it is not interprovincial trade, what happens?
Does it become federal by the ancillary power?

Mr Monahan: No. You have admitted, senator, my exact point. Of
course, they can control the importation of a good. All I am saying is
that we will control the importation into a province either from the
United States or from another province, and there is nothing which prevents you from doing anything you want with it in that province ... All
they are doing is preventing you from bringing it in, which is exactly
my point ...

If you have this product in a province, you can do anything you want
with it. This bill does not tell you that you cannot do something in a
province. There is not a word in the bill about that. That is exactly my
point, senator. (SSCEENR 2/19, 1997g, 11)

A few minutes later, Jacques Frémont, Faculty of Law at the University of
Montreal, offered the following general reflections on the afternoon's discussion:

I am glad to hear your comments. I will share with you the secret which
I share with my first-year students. Normally, by the end of the year,
they have had a demonstration of it. If you still think that constitutional law is something other than politics, then you are wrong ...
Judges, like politicians, are questioning or debating morality and fairness ... Constitutional law is simply politics disguised, and it is a second
guess given to judges, important people in our society, to try to ensure
that things do work properly according to the basic social contract and,
in this case, to the federal contract we have in this country. It might
very well pass the test. I suggest it might raise some serious problems.
We will see. (SSCEENR 2/19, 1997g, 19)

Monahan probably would have been sympathetic to Frémont's point. Over a decade earlier, he wrote:

within the sphere of Canadian federalism, it is impossible to draw any meaningful distinction between doctrinal and political discourse. The choices confronting the constitutional adjudicator are ultimately indistinguishable from those of the political actor ... It might be thought that the continuity between legal and political reasoning means that the received legal understandings of Canadian federalism are unpatterned or incoherent. But this would be to mistake the nature and potential of the argument that law is politics ... [The point is] that federalism disputes are at bottom disagreements over the terms of our collective life. (Monahan 1984, 48–9)

After making its case concerning the four tests of Article 404 (a)–(d), the federal government challenged Alberta's charges that "Canada 'abandoned' science ... knowingly neglected to employ impartial scientific enquiry ... [and] refused to sponsor impartial scientific study" by listing again some of the evidence reviewed in chapters 7 and 8. For good measure, the respondent added the following moral and political point: "The CPPI's view is understandably different from that of the federal government. It did not have to take into account risks which reached beyond its industry interest group in its assessment of the evidence. The task of weighing the evidence in light of all the impacts on the public interest of all Canadians fell to the federal government" (Canada 1998, 52).

Unfortunately, again, the results of that task were then submitted to the AIT panel to weigh in a different balance, with the possibility of reaching different results.

The government also challenged the charge that its "rationale for the legislation shifted over time" from aiming to eliminate MMT from the market to protecting the environment and human health. From the beginning, it was claimed, all the efforts made to work with the CCME and the industries involved in the dispute demonstrated its fundamental concern with the environment and human health. Besides, "The CPPI, in its correspondence suggesting options for resolving the issue relied upon by Alberta, did not question the environmental rationale for the legislation – it merely questioned the scientific conclusions and suggested further study" (Canada 1998, 52–3).

The Government of Alberta's position would have been incoherent if it had been calling for "further" (additional) scientific studies and believed there had been no scientific studies already.

The respondent did not think that the u.s. Court of Appeals's decision to allow the sale of gasoline with MMT "removed the harmonization of gasoline standards with the United States as a rationale for the legislation" because (a) the EPA standards for assessing the failure of emissions control devices was too "tolerant"; (b) neither the court's nor the EPA's decisions considered the effects of MMT on OBD systems; (c) the federal government believed, correctly as it turned out, that MMT was not going to be adopted widely in the United States anyhow; and (d) "the EPA decision may be reversed if new evidence of health or other effects is brought forward" (Canada 1998, 53).

Regarding (c), according to Clarke (1997, 29) "Amoco, B.P., Chevron, Exxon, Mobil Penzoil, Shell, Sun and Texaco, representing approximately 85% of the u.s. gasoline market share by volume ... indicated that they do not intend to use MMT." When Marchi moved to have Bill C-29 read the third time in the House of Commons, he mentioned those nine companies as well as Anchor, ARCO, Conoco, Hess, Marathon, and Philips (PD9/25, 1996a, 4; see also AIT Hearings 1998c, 313–14). In fact, "the semiannual fuel surveys conducted by the American Automobile Manufacturers Association (AAMA) and later by the Alliance of Automobile Manufacturers have not detected manganese in any of the us gasoline sampled, except for one fuel in January 2002" (Benson and Dana 2002, 2). Besides Canada, the only countries using MMT in unleaded gasoline that were mentioned in the literature were Ukraine and Bulgaria (SSCEENR 2/11, 1996, 16).

One might also have added (e) to the respondent's rationale:

While the ruling will allow the introduction of MMT in unleaded u.s. fuels, much lower concentrations than in Canada will be permitted and none in areas where air quality is a problem. Furthermore, MMT is still specifically banned, such as in the State of California ... In Canada, the Canadian General Standards Board limits the manganese content in unleaded automotive gasoline to a maximum of 18 mg manganese per litre of gasoline. By contrast, even after Ethyl Corporation's success in the American waiver process, less than half the concentration of MMT is permitted in the u.s., that is, only 8.26 mg per litre of gasoline. (Clarke 1997, 28)

Note that part of the dispute between the complainant and respondent arose because they assessed "harmonization" with the United States on the basis of different criteria, and the AIT offers no guidance about which is preferable or consistent with the agreement. The Government of Alberta, like

Eggleton (and Keith Martin, PD2/25, 1996a, 15), applied a legalistic criterion according to which Canadian and American regulations had to be harmonized. The Government of Canada, and Whelan (MP, Essex-Windsor)
PD2/25, 1996a, 22) applied a more inclusive criterion that was sensitive not
only to codified regulations but also to actual market conditions (referred to
as "de facto" harmonization by Tyhurst in the AIT Hearings 1998c, 358).
According to the latter, the practices of the Canadian and American petroleum and refining industries had to be harmonized. Historically, environmentally relevant practices sometimes create a demand for new legislation
and new legislation sometimes creates a demand for changes in environmental practices (Vogel 1995). The author of at least one memorandum to the
Minister of the Environment thought that the decision of the U.S. Court of
Appeals on 20 October 1995 might allow the Ethyl Corporation to expand
its sales of MMT into 70 per cent of the U.S. gasoline market (McCloskey
1995, 1). That would certainly be a prize worth fighting for and would
explain Ethyl's persistence in seeking EPA waivers over many years. However,
the *Affidavit of Alain Perez* (1997, 6–7) suggests a good reason for doubting
that such expansion would ever occur. In Perez's view:

When facing the decision as to how to compensate for the loss of
octane occasioned by the elimination of MMT in unleaded gasoline,
petroleum refiners will be required to optimize both their investment
and operating costs. This will result in several refineries making capital
expenditures. For those several petroleum refiners who choose the capital investment route to replace the octane lost from MMT, there would
be substantial economical disincentive to revert back to the use of MMT
as a means for enhancing octane in the event that the ban on the use of
MMT in Canada were ultimately lifted.

If Perez was right, then some of those companies mentioned in chapter 4
that suspended use of MMT in 2004 may never use it again.

Given the importance of harmonization to all the players in our story
and to its role in the AIT, it is remarkable that the panel simply disposed of
the issue with two sentences: "The Respondent made reference to the need
for harmonization with the regulatory environment in the United States. It
is open to the Respondent and other Parties to the *Agreement* to consider
establishing standards in Canada at levels not to exceed those permitted in
the United States" (Gilson, Castonguay, Kelly, Mauro, and Rae 1998, 12).

As if the perfunctory treatment of the harmonization issues just reviewed
were not enough, the panel totally ignored the Government of Canada's

most ingenious argument concerning harmonization (see chapter 16.). I will present the argument using as much of the language of the hearings as possible, although it seems a bit garbled, and then try to sharpen it. After calling the panel's attention to Article 1508.1 again, Wallace invited them to consider 1508.2, which says, "In harmonizing environmental measures, the Parties shall maintain and endeavour to strengthen existing levels of environmental protection. The Parties shall not, through such harmonization, lower the levels of environmental protection" (AIT 2002): and 1511: "In this Chapter: harmonization means to adjust environmental measures to minimize unnecessary differences between the Parties without compromising the achievement of the legitimate objectives of each party" (AIT 2002).

He continued:

The concept, therefore, is one of essentially prohibiting harmonization down. The chapter only allows for harmonization up.

If we are talking about [the fact that] the federal government should have harmonized its legislation with the legislation of the provinces, within the meaning of the Agreement on Internal Trade, the type of harmonization envisaged is one of bringing up the provinces to the same standards of the federal government, as opposed to, through that process, forcing the federal government to compromise the achievement of its legitimate objectives to coincide with the level of environmental protection that may be thought appropriate by some of the provinces.

The point is that to the extent that we talk about Article 405 (1) and harmonization, to the extent we talk about Article 1508, we have to bear in mind 1508 (2), and that the concept of harmonization within the environmental chapter is a concept of harmonization, as long as no party is required to lower their standards of protection that they deem most appropriate as a result of that harmonization. (AIT Hearings 1998c, 276–8)

Thus, the argument seems to be that, granting the need for harmonization as specified in Article 1508.1, if "The Parties shall not, through such harmonization, lower the levels of environmental protection" (1508.2), then any harmonization that occurs must favour the party with the highest environmental standard, which in the present case is the federal government. If this is a legitimate way to interpret these articles, then the AIT is a much more progressive document than it appears to be, to me at least. It is a pity that neither the panel nor anyone else seems to have paid any attention to this argument.

The force of Article 1511, as it relates to the federal government's argument in the previous paragraph, is unclear. The essence of Article 1511 seems to be that "the achievement of the legitimate objectives of each Party" must not be compromised in the interests of harmonization. If so, the complainant in the current case might argue that its interest in continued trade is as legitimate as the federal government's interest in the protection of health and the environment and that, therefore, the first premise of the federal government's argument involves a misleading oversimplification. In effect, the complainant's objection would be that because 1511 takes precedence over 1508.2, the federal government's argument is unsound. This interpretation would make the AIT less progressive than the interpretation suggested in the previous paragraph, but that would not, of course, make it an incorrect interpretation. Unfortunately, we have no way of determining which interpretation is correct and no way of guaranteeing that the correct interpretation would make the AIT logically coherent.

Regarding the complainant's charges that "a number of internal federal government memoranda ... question the reliability of OBD systems and the *bona fides* of the vehicle industry," the respondent claimed that those memoranda "cannot be taken as setting out the government position," that suspicions about vehicle industry motives were merely the result of accusations of the Ethyl Corporation, and that the memoranda failed to mention the Report of the California Air Resources Board (CARB) of 25 October 1996 indicating that the OBD systems "have proven very effective in detecting emissions-related problems in-use" (Canada 1998, 13, 53).

One of the apparently most damaging of "government memoranda" was a Briefing Note from a Transport Canada official dated 1 March 1995 (AIT Hearings 1998a, 85–6):

The President and General Manager of General Motors of Canada (GM), V. Maureen Kempston Darkes, has written to the Minister to advise him of GM's plans to disable emission control systems on 1996 GM vehicles in Canada because they feel their vehicles are not compatible with MMT ... Transport Canada is not aware of the full implication on vehicle emissions of disconnecting the OBD-II system warning light, so is therefore not able to determine whether or not the vehicles will comply with the 1988 standard. TC and GM officials are in contact on this matter.

If GM believes that MMT will cause failures in spark plugs, oxygen sensors and catalytic converters, it is not clear how disabling the light which signals a failure in these parts will protect consumers from the adverse effects of MMT. The GM strategy seems designed to protect GM from warranty claims whether attributable to MMT or not.

Further work on resolving the MMT issue, as suggested by GM, should be channeled through Environment Canada who is responsible for fuel quality. (Desjardins, 1995, 1–3)

Colcomb told the House Standing Committee that it was "the spark plug warranty experience – up to 50 times higher in Canada than in the northern United States" that led to the investigation of the problem with MMT (HSCESD10/24, 1995b, 4). The respondent did not address the question of "how disabling the light which signals a failure in these parts will protect consumers" (raised again by Perrin in AIT Hearings 1998a, 186), but one need not look far for an answer. As indicated earlier, the OBD system monitors "virtually all the power train and system components and all of the inputs and outputs of [the GM] entire emission system in the order of 100 different variables" (HSCESD10/24, 1995b, 4). The OBD warning light is supposed to flash to inform the vehicle driver that the catalytic converter is not operating properly. However, insofar as MMT makes the OBD system unreliable, the warning light signals are unreliable. With the warning light disabled, consumers would have to resort to routine manual inspections of the converter to determine its condition. The unpleasantness and expense of such inspections was revealed through the Air Care Program in the lower mainland of British Columbia (AIT Hearings 1998c, 321–2). When such inspections revealed failures in converter functions, consumers would be informed that their fuel emissions were making unacceptable contributions to the production of dangerous smog and would be able to take remedial action. That action would lead to fixing or replacing the converters, some of which might still be under warranty. Consumers fortunate enough to discover a problem within the warranty period would be able to claim the full value of the warranty, which is how disabling the warning light protects them, i.e., by ensuring periodic inspections. Whether the systems were covered by warranties or not, the routine manual inspections would help protect all of us from increases in smog that are preventable with current technology. In the AIT Hearings (1998c, 302), reference is made to "a speech by the Minister [of the Environment] of Ontario in which it was mentioned that smog contributes to 1,800 premature deaths in Ontario alone annually."

During the hearings, another objection was raised on behalf of the Government of Alberta regarding the federal government's concerns about warranties. Since it was not raised in the Government of Alberta's *Submission* or in the panel's *Report,* its importance and impact are unclear. However, it is worth reviewing briefly in case MMT or some other additive becomes an issue in the future. According to Ternes (AIT Hearings 1998, 95–114):

Cars are certified to operate on fuels. The Minister for the Environment, when he reintroduced the bill ... said, "We're worried about Canadian warranty claims because of MMT". I am confused, too. Vehicles that are certified with a fuel for MMT that does not cause or contribute to component failure, why should there be additional warranty claims? ... If warranties are such a concern, I want you to look at the language. Here is Ford 1997 Crown Victoria ... it starts off with: "Your vehicle was not designed to use fuel [with] ... manganese-based additives such as MMT ... Repair of damage caused by using a fuel that your vehicle was not designed for may not be covered by your warranty." There's their warning ... That's as strong as they get.

Well, in point of fact, vehicles are designed for that; otherwise, they wouldn't be certified, they wouldn't get past the EPA ...

"Chrysler recommends using gasolines without MMT."

"Because it is not indicated on the pump, you should really ask your retailer whether or not it has MMT." That's basically it. That's what Chrysler says ...

Honda [says] "In Canada, some gasolines contain an octane-enhancing additive called MMT. If you use such gasolines, your emission control system performance may deteriorate and the [MIL] ... may turn on. If this happens, contact ... for service."

Porsche [says] "If repairs are required due to the use of fuels containing MMT, Porsche reserves the right to deny coverage of those repairs under warranty."

For such strong concerns that were registered by the automotive industry, the warranties are not that threatening ...

I would love to be the lawyer representing the owner of the automobile if warranty was denied because of MMT, a legal substance that an automobile was designed to pass or to be certified for. I would love to be in that room ... These cars are certified to run on this fuel. How are they going to refuse warranties?

The next day in the hearings, Tyhurst took issue with Ternes: "the way that the vehicles are certified, the regulatory process is not as Alberta described it ... the fuel that they actually use to certify the vehicles is an MMT-free fuel. The cars actually don't have to be designed to function with MMT to meet the certification standard which permits you to get the car on the road, so that we are not creating an inconsistency by having the presence of some MMT in the United States. That's not creating a regulatory inconsistency, as I think was suggested by Alberta" (AIT Hearings 1998c, 307–8).

Tyhurst makes two points. First, contrary to Ternes assertion, vehicles are certified to run on MMT-free fuel, not on fuel containing MMT. If that is the case, then Ternes's claim that EPA certification requires manufacturers to honour warranties allegedly harmed by MMT is false. Second, if the certification standard merely involves MMT-free fuel, then any similar standard set in Canada would not create "a regulatory inconsistency," again contrary to Alberta's submission. Also, because gas stations almost never indicate the presence or absence of MMT in their products, how could consumers know what gasoline to buy to protect their warranties and, therefore, how might any court assign responsibility for OBD malfunctioning (AIT Hearings 1998c, p.346–7)?

Testifying before the Senate Standing Committee, Huw Williams, Director of Public Relations for the Canadian Automobile Dealers Association, said:

the dealers in British Columbia are subject to the highest environmental standards across Canada. They have taken the lead and followed the California emissions standards ...

We received a legal opinion from a local law firm, which we have since run past a number of other lawyers, that makes it clear that the liability for the warranty in the province of British Columbia rests with the seller of the vehicle or the retailer.

Yesterday senators asked the presidents of the big three: Will you honour that warranty in the 1998 model year? I am here to tell you that, if they do not honour that warranty, the liability for that comes on to the dealer. Dealers in the province of British Columbia will be faced with one of two things. They can either sell vehicles with disconnected OBD-II systems, which do not meet the warranty standards and they will therefore be subject to fines, or they will not be able to sell cars at all because they do not want to be subject to fines. Something has to budge, either the provincial legislation or the federal legislation. (SSCEENR 2/5, 1997c, 3–4)

When the chair of the committee challenged the legal opinion, Ted Knight, Chairman of the Canadian Automobile Dealers Association, replied "That is the opinion we were given ... I can assure you that the Canadian consumer is paying more for maintenance on their vehicles than consumers in the United States" (SSCEENR 2/5, 1997c, 5). An interesting exchange followed between Knight and some senators about a fundamental issue in business ethics, namely, simple honesty between sellers and buyers:

> Senator [Colin] Kenny: You have told us this tongue in cheek, but you really mean it. You are making a hell of a lot more money in your service end than your counterparts in areas that do not have MMT in the gasoline. Do your customers understand that? When they come in with a problem, do you communicate to them or does anyone communicate to them that they are paying more dough than comparable users elsewhere?
>
> Mr. Knight: No, sir, I am a businessman. Chrysler and GM will pay the warranty, and the customer will pay the tune-up. If your car in Canada requires more work than the American's car, that is the cost of doing business and the cost of maintenance. If I said to every customer, "Do you know that your counterpart in the United States probably does not have to do this work because of this problem," I think there would be a lot of reaction out there. However, the consumer does not know.
>
> Senator Kenny: ... If your customers do not understand why they are paying the dough, how would you advise us to communicate the problem to them?
>
> Mr. Knight: ... Selling is such an interesting profession. If everyone sat down and talked to the consumer about MMT, you would find over a period of time that people would say, "What is this all about?" People do not know. Very honestly, as a car dealer, until the issue arose, I did not know because I have other things to worry about.
>
> Senator Kenny: You are also telling us that it is not in your interests to tell people about it.
>
> Mr. Knight: I am not sure if that would be a fair comment on my part ...
>
> Senator [John] Buchanan: ... I know a lot of dealers. They are like politicians; they have to satisfy their customers to get them coming back.
>
> Mr. Knight: That is right ...
>
> Senator [Eugene] Whelan: ... Why do you say MMT should be banned?
>
> Mr. Knight: It is not good for a number of reasons. It is not good for the environment. It is not good for automobiles. It is not good for

consumers. If we went on a campaign and told every consumer in this country that this stuff will cost them $100 per new car per year for the next 10 years, there would be an uprising. We are already viewed as being right below lawyers and politicians on the credibility scale. (SSCEENR 2/5, 1997c, 7–13)

In an effort to confirm or disconfirm Ternes's claims about the significance of EPA certification of additives for vehicle warranties, on 2 December 2002 I wrote to Elizabeth Craig, Deputy Assistant Administrator, EPA Office of Air and Radiation. Among other things, I said:

If EPA certifies a car for use with a certain kind of gasoline (in this case, with or without MMT), does that imply that if a vehicle component is harmed by that kind of gasoline that the manufacturer must honour its warranty for that component? Car manufacturers were putting warnings in their owner's manuals saying things like "the on-board diagnostic system in this car may be damaged by gasoline containing MMT. So owners should avoid using such gasoline because that might void their warranty on those systems". Lawyers for Ethyl claimed that if EPA certified a gasoline additive then such warnings would not have any legal force if owners insisted on making the manufacturers honour their warranties. I couldn't find any evidence that certification carried that implication.

Craig sent my note to Don Zinger, in the U.S. Office of Transportation and Air Quality, and he replied on 10 December 2002 as follows:

To answer his [Michalos's] question ... if a motorist uses a fuel that is registered by EPA, even if the auto company recommends against its use, the emissions warranty should not be voided. But, this whole area of fuel and fuel additives and their potential effect on warranties, is a major "gray area" in the law. Some auto companies go further in their owners manuals in recommending or not recommending certain fuels than we think is appropriate, but we have never had the occasion to force the issue through some kind of legal action. In the case of MMT, the auto companies have been negative on its use from the very beginning. EPA also fought to keep it out of U.S. gasoline but we lost a court case 5 years ago so we were forced to register it for legal use. The fact of the matter is that almost no MMT has ever been used in the U.S., so we do not have to deal with it from a warranty context. Canada is a different matter, since a lot of MMT is used there. To answer his final question, EPA has not and does not plan to do any MMT studies or testing. The manufacturer of MMT, Ethyl Corp., is doing some extensive health effects testing on MMT, as required by EPA regs. Finally, the auto companies recently released a large report on the effects of MMT on the emission control systems of vehicles.

Zinger's remarks indicate some uncertainty about the status of the warranties, though he thinks they would have to be honoured given registered fuels or additives. We will have to leave the matter in that relatively uncertain state.

Finally, the federal government asserted that the estimated costs of failing to introduce its measure would be much greater than the estimated costs of introducing it. "The periodic costs of replacing MMT-fouled sparkplugs alone in the 14 million or so vehicles across the nation could easily balance, or far outweigh, [the] alleged costs [to the petroleum industry]. When one adds in the costs of hospitalization, loss of employment and other environmental and health costs of increased pollution, the case for action against MMT becomes overwhelming" (Canada 1998, 54–5).

In case anyone was not persuaded by this argument, Wallace reminded the panel that so far as the complainants' side was concerned:

the estimated costs have jumped around quite a bit over time. The initial estimates of the estimated capital costs to refiners in the Kellogg study of a couple years ago were $115 million in capital costs and $50 million in ongoing operating costs. The most recent evidence submitted by Alberta on February 13 [1998] has the capital costs at $32 million. We have had almost a $100 million swing in the capital cost estimates of the cost in the past couple years. The operating costs have come down from about $50 million to $32 million.

The only point we want to make is that there is a lot of uncertainty about this. (AIT Hearings 1998c, 281–2)

If Wallace had looked at the Senate Standing Committee hearings, he might have found Jim Pantelidis claiming that "estimates developed by the U.S. EPA suggest that the removal of MMT would result in an overall 8 per cent increase of nitrogen oxide emissions from vehicles. This would result in a significant downturn in the Canadian air quality, especially for large urban areas. For refiners to offset this NO_x increase through fuel formulation, we would have to severely limit the sulphur content in gasoline, at a cost of roughly $2 billion" (SSCEENR 2/4, 1997a, 19).

Robert Routs, President of Shell Canada, also endorsed the $2 billion figure (SSCEENR 2/4, 1997a, 24). Later on in that hearing he addressed the cost issue from another point of view: "With regard to economics," he said, "I do not know if most people around this table are aware that this industry makes large volumes of fuel. Any issue can be made ridiculous in terms of cents per litre and cost. The minister [Copps] has said 'this issue will cost the industry .2 cents per litre, so what are they worrying about?' Our profits are less than 1 cent per litre. Some members of the industry make more, some make less. If you put it in that context, you can see that .2 cents on 1 cent is quite a bit" (SSCEENR 2/4, 1997a, 27).

16

AIT *Report of the Article 1704 Panel*

On 12 June 1998 the AIT panel filed its *Report of the Article 1704 Panel Concerning a Dispute between Alberta and Canada regarding the Manganese-Based Fuel Additives Act.* The *Report* summarized its authority, the complaint process followed, relevant provisions of the AIT, operating principles, background of the complaint, its views on the complainant's and respondent's specific issues, its final determinations, and a dissenting opinion. Its appendices listed all participants and official documents, and summarized written submissions.

When the panel met with advocates for both sides on Wednesday, 15 April 1998, one of the first issues the chair introduced involved the disposition of a report that was received after the official deadline for submissions (AIT Hearings 1998a, 18–43). For our purposes, the most interesting thing about the discussion concerning the report was that everyone around the table seemed happy to dispose of its scientific aspects. A sample of remarks will illustrate my point.

Speaking on behalf of the federal government, Evernden said: "one of the foundation arguments that we make [is] that there is no scientific certainty here and that we will never develop a consensus on that."

On behalf of Alberta, Ternes said, "the affidavit information is not a question of establishing full scientific certainty, scientific certainty, reasonable scientific certainty or any of those levels of certainty. There are facts in there that will help you to understand where we are really at."

Evernden then floated the idea that "If my friends really take the position that the science is irrelevant, at least the science as it is described in the Roos affidavit is irrelevant, then presumably that could be either redacted or removed from the affidavit and we could address only those parts of the affidavit which they believe are still of some utility to you ... That is, what we are trying to help you do here is get rid of this extra paper burden, if we can do it."

The other side was pleased to unload the "burden." Zarzecny said, "We meant what we said: We are not filing the Roos affidavit for the science; we are filing it to answer some other matters that were raised by the federal material."

Granted that the "extra paper burden" was not onerous simply because it involved scientific analysis, the latter seemed to contribute to people's uneasiness about it and willingness to do without it. The next day, Bob Rae said, not entirely facetiously, that "I agree with the fact that none of us on this panel, with maybe one or two exceptions, could tell a catalytic converter from a gas cap. So we are really not equipped to deal with that issue" (AIT Hearings 1998c, 298).

Later on the same day, Tyhurst said, "I would like to turn, then, to a subject we all would like to avoid here, and that is the question of conflicting science" (AIT Hearings 1998c, 332).

Then he proceeded to call everyone's attention to the very detailed but conflicting reports prepared by the MVMA and the AIAMC (MVMA/AIAMC 1995) evaluated in chapter 7 and the CPPI Technical Task Force (1995) report. As reported in chapter 15, the latter prefaced its apparently reasonable review of the "Key Unanswered Questions" and "Proposed Testing Program" with the following summary comments: "It is clear that the OEMs and Ethyl have approached their analyses of the potential impacts of MMT in different ways, using different scientific techniques and achieving very different results. Neither data set is judged to be inherently incorrect, they are just different. The Task Force finds that it cannot reconcile these differences and thus cannot make sound recommendations on the future use of MMT in Canadian gasolines" (CPPI Technical Task Force Report 1995, 22).

Since the Task Force was sponsored by the CPPI, one might have expected a more enthusiastic endorsement of the use of MMT. To its credit, the Task Force dealt even-handedly with the material placed before it and reached a fairly neutral position calling for still more, fairly specific, research. So far as I know, nobody has undertaken the research program precisely as recommended. However, that is not the main point I want to make. What I have tried to illustrate is that because of the advocates' and panelists' particular expertise and because of the complicated conflicts in the scientific analyses offered by the disputants, the a priori chances of scientific research playing a decisive role in the panel's final decisions were slight.

Following the compromise solution regarding the material that arrived after the deadline, the panel disposed of the respondent's claim that "the issue in dispute is one of substance, and beyond specific provisions of the Agreement" by remarking that "Articles 1705 and 1707 state that the mandate of a Panel is to determine if the measure under review is consistent with the *Agreement*. Therefore, the question is not whether the *Act* is consistent with a specific chapter, or even with Parts III (General Rules) and IV (Specific Rules), but whether the *Act* conforms to the Agreement, including the principles and process contained therein" (Gilson, Castonguay, Kelly, Mauro, and Rae, 1998, 5).

Article 1707.2(b) says that "The [panel] report shall contain ... a determination, with reasons, as to whether the measure in question is or would be inconsistent with this Agreement" (AIT 2002). Since the Agreement is nothing more than a collection of particular provisions, I do not see how consistency with the Agreement could mean anything but consistency with each and every one of those provisions.

Following the issue regarding the disposition of the late report, the panel's second main issue concerned the complainant's charge that the MMT *Act* was inconsistent with Article 401. The Panel declared that:

The *Act* treats MMT less favourably than other octane enhancers, and MMT-enhanced gasoline less favourably than MMT-free gasoline. The intent of Article 401.3 is to prevent the Respondent from favouring goods from one province over the goods of another province. The Panel finds that there is no geographical discrimination in the *Act*. MMT-enhanced gasoline was produced in all provinces with refineries when the *Act* came into force, and all refineries in Canada could produce MMT-free gasoline with the proper equipment and process adjustments. Accordingly, market discrimination is more appropriately addressed under Article 403. The *Act* is consistent with Article 401. (Gilson, Castonguay, Kelly, Mauro, and Rae, 1998, 6)

Soloway (1999, 81–2) thought the panel might have found "geographical discrimination" in that the *Act* "favored Canada's primary auto-producing region (Ontario) over its primary oil-producing region (Alberta)," but I think the fourth sentence in the quotation immediately above would be true if "regions" were substituted for "provinces," which would make her suggestion untenable.

Third, it was asserted that "The Panel agrees with the Respondent and finds that the *Act* is inconsistent with Articles 402 and 403" (Gilson,

Castonguay, Kelly, Mauro, and Rae 1998, 7). Thus, everyone, both disputants and the panel, agreed that the MMT Act was inconsistent with those
two articles and that, therefore, at some point the battle would have to be
fought over the four "legitimate objectives" provisions of Article 404.
Before that, the panel addressed the charges regarding Articles 405 and
1508.

We have already seen that Article 1508.1 instructs parties to harmonize
environmental measures following principles and procedures constructed
and agreed upon by the CCME and/or its task forces and committees. Article
1508.3 says that "In the event of an inconsistency between Article 405
(Reconciliation) and this Article, this Article prevails to the extent of the
inconsistency" (AIT 2002). After the panel drew our attention to this provision, and emphasized that "The evidence before the Panel established that
the Respondent did not follow the process provisions of the Agreement,
and this disregard for process resulted in this dispute," it went on to say
that "a breach of the Chapter 15 process does not of itself lead to a fatal
inconsistency with the Agreement." More importantly, the panel saw no
need to consider the question of whether or not the Act was, as alleged by
Alberta, a "standards-related measure" as specified by Article 405, because
if it failed to pass the "legitimate objectives" tests of Article 404, it was
clearly dead in the water anyhow (Gilson, Castonguay, Kelly, Mauro, and
Rae 1998, 7–8). Accordingly, our fourth point about the *Report* is that no
determination was made about the *Act's* status with respect to Article 405,
and the panel proceeded immediately to the issues concerning Article 404.

Consider the panel's reason for believing that "the Respondent did not
follow the process provisions of the Agreement" regarding Article 1508.1.
What the panel said was, "In the present case the Respondent failed to
exhaust the established process for consultation, reconciliation and harmonization" (Gilson, Castonguay, Kelly, Mauro, and Rae 1998, 8). Remember, the Government of Alberta claimed that the CCME's Cleaner Vehicles
and Fuels Task Force dropped its assessment of MMT, the Government of
Québec claimed that the federal government should have appealed to the
CCME, and the Government of Saskatchewan claimed that the federal government should have had input from the Task Force. As explained in chapter 15, the CCME Task Force began its work in November 1994 and
presented its *Report* to the CCME in October 1995. The CCME endorsed the
Report on 23 October 1995 and agreed to implement its recommendations.
The CCME recommendations and the federal government's follow-up of its
consultations with the CCME are also explained above. In the presence of
these facts, the whole burden of the panel's belief in the respondent's failure

seems to rest on the idea that the latter did not "exhaust the established process." One must ask: Exactly what would it take to "exhaust" the process? Québec's *Brief* indicated that the processes sometimes required considerable "perseverance," and the definition of "consensus" in the CCME By-law No. 1991, 1.01(d) calls for "narrowing an issue until there is no dissent" (see chapter 6). If the latter is read strictly, one might suppose that the consultation process is only exhausted when "there is no dissent." But "dissent" about what? About issues in the original dispute or about a crafted resolution or set of recommendations? One would think that, if not earlier, at least when the CCME announced its recommendations, a consensus had been reached, since the CCME includes all fourteen environmental ministers. Hence, I think the panel's judgment that the prescribed process had not been exhausted was unwarranted, and even unreasonable, insofar as the AIT has no criteria for "exhaustion" of a process.

Recall Wallace's claim that, contrary to the assumption in the preceding paragraph, Article 1508 does not prescribe or require that new measures must proceed through the CCME: "there is nothing in this [1505 or 1508], in a process sense, that says you cannot introduce a standard or a measure for environmental protection that is not in harmony with the measures of the other parties without going through a CCME process. It doesn't say that. What it says in 1508 is that there is an obligation on the parties, and it is really a collective obligation, to endeavour to try to harmonize their standards, but in a way which increases the level of environmental protection, not reducing it" (AIT Hearings 1998c, 375).

To me, a careful reading of Article 1508 supports Wallace's claim. Article 1508.1 talks about trying to harmonize environmental measures "following principles *such as those* set out ... [and] *any other applicable principles* established by the Council, and this agreement" (emphasis added). Clearly, if the drafters of the AIT meant to insist upon a single path for the introduction of new measures or standards, they could, should, and probably would have written "following only the principles set out." So I do not believe the assumed prescribed process is a correct interpretation of the AIT. If I am wrong and it is correct, then the language of Article 1508.1 should be changed accordingly.

Fifth, regarding the first "legitimate objectives" test, the panel found that "While the evidence on the effects of MMT is not conclusive, there was sufficient evidence to determine that the Respondent had a reasonable basis for believing that the *Act* would achieve a legitimate objective, and therefore meets the requirements of Article 404(a)" (Gilson, Castonguay, Kelly, Mauro, and Rae, 1998, 7–8).

This is a remarkably sympathetic view of the federal government's position, and flatly opposed to Alberta's complaint as explained above. MMT is only manufactured in the United States and blended in Canada, and few people believed it would be economically feasible to establish manufacturing plants in any province to service only that province. (On one occasion Perez claimed MMT might be manufactured and sold within "two or three provinces (SSCEENR 2/4, 1997a, 43)). If the product could not be shipped across provincial or national borders, then once existing stockpiles were exhausted, it was most likely not going to be blended, sold, or used at all (AIT Hearings 1998a, 121–2; 1998c, 261–2, 308–11). At that point, no refiners in any province would have an advantage over any other with regard to exporting their product, effectively removing complaints raised in the hearings (AIT Hearings 1998c, 260–2). Therefore, any harmful effects MMT might have and, what is at least as important, any worries anyone might have about such possible effects appearing some time in the future would be eliminated, which was precisely the "legitimate objective" sought by the Canadian Government through the *MMT Act*. From this perspective, the *Act*'s supporters appear to have been politically astute as well as economically sensible. In response to the question: If the aim was simply to remove the additive from gasoline, why not just ban it outright as a reasonable precaution in the presence of considerable uncertainty but potentially significant harms to future generations?, the respondent replied: "Alberta also argues that banning MMT would have been a... less access-impairing measure ... Canada submits that this is demonstrably not the case. Banning the use of MMT outright would have equally impaired access to MMT" (Canada 1998, 49; see also AIT Hearings 1998c, 269–70).

In any case, we know that the respondent did not have the authority to ban the product.

Sixth, regarding Article 404(b), the panel briefly compared the history of leaded gasoline with that of MMT and found the federal government's actions precipitate and excessive. Noting again that the problems around MMT centre on its effects on "the latest generation of emissions control devices," and its long-term environmental and health effects, the panel wrote:

> In the recent past, a similar situation existed in the case of leaded gasoline. At that time, automobile manufacturers designed vehicles to operate on unleaded gasoline, while older vehicles could still use leaded gasoline. Even though it was established that lead was directly toxic,

the phased elimination of this substance from gasoline took place over a number of years.

The Respondent has not demonstrated that there existed a matter of such urgency or a risk so widespread as to warrant such comprehensive restrictions as the *Act* provides on internal trade. If the legitimate objective of the *Act* is as stated, to prevent MMT from being used in newer model vehicles in major urban areas, then total elimination of MMT was unduly restrictive.

In light of these factors, the Panel has determined that the Act is inconsistent with Article 404(b). (Gilson, Castonguay, Kelly, Mauro, and Rae 1998, 9)

Two points should be noticed about these last quoted passages. First, the panel's description of the federal government's alleged "legitimate objective" is a gross oversimplification and distortion of the respondent's position. The respondent never said that its "legitimate objective" was "to prevent MMT from being used in newer model vehicles in major urban areas." What was said is this:

The protection of the environment, the protection of human health and consumer protection are legitimate objectives as defined in Article 200.

The risks and potential impacts on the public interest associated with the continued use of MMT, which the federal government had to weigh included:

(a) the adverse effects of MMT on catalytic converters, and the impact this would have on increased HC and CO emissions;

(b) the adverse effects of MMT on OBD systems and oxygen sensors and the impact this would have on the use and operation of the catalytic converter (and the resulting effects on the production of CO, NO_x and HC), as well as the general operation of the vehicle such as the correction for misfires (which reduce fuel efficiency and thus increase the production of greenhouse gases);

(c) the adverse effects of MMT on sparkplug performance and durability and the resulting effect on fuel efficiency and greenhouse gas production;

(d) the cost, to manufacturers and consumers, of repair or replacement of parts associated with the adverse effects of MMT, the effect on warranty coverage and the impact this would have on the program to move to more strict emission control requirements;

(e) the effect of malfunctioning OBD systems on: consumer acceptance and use of this important new technology (e.g., potential discon-
nection by the consumer of malfunctioning equipment); manufacturers'
reputations; and continuous (as opposed to sporadic) monitoring of
vehicle emissions;

(f) the concerns expressed by non-governmental organizations,
including the Learning Disability Association of Canada and environmental groups, about the potentially toxic effects of airborne manganese from vehicle exhaust, and about the lack of data on its direct
health impacts;

(g) the unfairness and impracticality of insisting on auto industry
compliance with new harmonized emission control standards requiring
new technology where such technology is not capable of operating
properly with unleaded gasoline containing MMT; and,

(h) Canada's inability to satisfy domestic and international targets
and obligations for the reduction of HC, CO, NO_x and greenhouse gases
if OBD and pollution control systems did not work.

Balanced against these considerations, the federal government had to
consider factors including the claims made by Ethyl that MMT was environmentally beneficial, and the potential costs to refiners of increasing
octane levels in unleaded fuels without using MMT.

Parliament, and government departments, weighed the evidence of
the numerous interests on both sides of the debate surrounding the
adoption of the *Act*. Through the committee process, Parliament
received testimony and reports, and questioned witnesses. Parliament
concluded that the risks associated with the continued use of MMT in
gasoline outweighed the costs or benefits attributed to its use. *Canada
submits that the foregoing considerations amply demonstrate that the
primary purpose of the measure was the protection of the environment,
human health and the consumer.* (Canada 1998, 47–9; emphasis
added)

The second point to be made about the quoted passages is that, like
many critics of MMT, the panel compared the MMT case to the lead case but
then drew a conclusion exactly the opposite from that of the critics. Critics
generally say that the lesson to be learned from the leaded gasoline case is
that it is better to be safe than sorry. So we should eliminate MMT now lest
we discover later that low-level exposure is seriously damaging in the long
run. The panel's view was that the lesson to be learned is that a relatively
slow, phased in elimination of MMT beginning perhaps with special pumps

and reformulated gas for newer model vehicles in major urban areas would be preferable to the blanket prohibition of the *Act*. Compared to the relatively slower, limited model of action, the blanket prohibition model appeared to the panel "to impair unduly" access to the product MMT. The relatively slower process would also have cost less in the short-run and allowed time for independent scientific review to possibly render a conclusive judgment about MMT's alleged effects. Hill and Leiss (2001, 97) supported such an approach.

The trouble with this reasonable-sounding but essentially two pump model is, as we saw above (8 and 10 February 1995), that the CPPI rejected it and if the CPPI rejected it, Alberta also would have rejected it. What is worse, it completely neglects the proportionality considerations required by Annex 405.1.5. The federal government's position was that when it weighed the evidence for and against eliminating MMT from gasoline, it appeared to be wiser and safer, all things considered, to insist on total elimination. That is to say, the decision to be made was not merely one of finding an effective way to prevent the possible harms that might be done by MMT but of finding the most cost-effective way. In the government's view, the *MMT Act* was the most cost-effective strategy because it held out the promise of the smallest cost to everyone affected. In terms invented in Michalos (1978), I would say that the federal government undertook a broad-based cost-benefit analysis using a recipient population including everyone affected by the government's action with a variety of different kinds of costs and benefits, while the panel's cost-benefit analysis used a much narrower recipient population involving those likely to suffer lost trade, or at least, some loss in the terms of trade, with costs and benefits measured primarily, if not exclusively, in dollars. Obviously, such different decision procedures would be unlikely to reach the same conclusion, but the question is: Which decision procedure was most appropriate for the AIT? I think the federal government's procedure was more appropriate, from a moral point of view, but I have been unable to find textual support in the AIT. Most importantly and more precisely, I have been unable to find textual support in the AIT for the crucial passages in the federal government's account of the standard of review according to Article 1706.3.

Given the apparent importance that the respondent assigned to its view of the appropriate standard of review, one would have expected the panel to give it considerable attention. On the contrary, it was indirectly blown away with the following comments focused on the issue of deference: "On the matter of process, reference was made to the inherent authority of Parliament and the deference due the Parliamentary process. In our view there is no issue relative to Parliamentary authority or Panel deference. The Parliament of Canada and the legislatures of the provinces and territories are not subservient to each other or to the Panel in the exercise of their Constitutional powers. However, they are Parties to this *Agreement*, and it is the *Agreement* which must prevail" (Gilson, Castonguay, Kelly, Mauro, and Rae 1998, 5).

Nothing was ever said explicitly about the issue of applying a standard of "reasonableness" versus one of "correctness," but the implication of the last sentence in the quoted paragraph seems to be that a standard of "correctness" in the sense of "consistency with the *Agreement*" should be applied. That is to say, granting that the application of the two standards might on some or even most occasions lead to the same conclusion, insofar as a conflict between them might arise, the panel's view was that the "correctness" standard should and, I believe did, prevail.

Speaking on behalf of the Government of Saskatchewan, Zarzecny took the position that the federal government's view was totally without foundation. She said:

> The arguments of Canada in that section [on standard of review] all have a common thesis. Less is required of the federal government in this case than the provinces. Canada argues that less stringent rules should be applied to them, that their burden of proof should be lower, that you should treat them with deference, and that the question for you is whether the MMT legislation is not whether or not it is inconsistent with the AIT, but only whether it is reasonable.
>
> It is Saskatchewan's submission that there is simply no basis in law or in the Agreement on Internal Trade for that kind of characterization ... Panel, to accept this argument of deference, you would have to accept that the federal government is somehow in these proceedings akin to an administrative tribunal. There is simply nothing to support that characterization. It is much more accurate, if any comparison is to be made here today, to say that you, the panel, are the administrative tribunal and the federal government, like the provinces, is just one party before you ...
>
> The question posed is: "Was there a reasonable basis for the legislative action taken?"
>
> We submit that this is not the question to be asked or answered. The panel not only has the right, but the obligation, to make the determination exactly as they are set out in Chapter 17 of the AIT. That chapter directs the panel to make a finding whether or not the measure in

question is inconsistent with the AIT. There is nothing in the agreement that requires the panel to tie its hands and look only at the reasonableness of the measure but, rather, is the measure inconsistent and then has it impaired internal trade.

Whether the measure was reasonable or practical or wise or anything of that nature is simply not an issue before the panel today. (AIT Hearings 1998a, 130–3)

As suggested above, I think Zarzecny is right about the absence of support in the AIT for a standard of review based on "reasonableness," which from a moral point of view seems to me to be a serious defect. On the other hand, I think it is a mistake to characterize such a standard as "less stringent" because, as I have explained in several places, it is extraordinarily difficult to do a thorough cost-benefit analysis for any real-life problem. I doubt that the federal government's suggestion about its deserving some deference is equivalent to or implies treating it as an "administrative tribunal" in the case instead of as a party to the dispute, but it does suggest giving it some sort of edge. Insofar as the parliamentary procedures used to assess the MMT *Act* were much more thorough and inclusive than that or probably any other panel could be, I think they do entitle the respondent's position to some sort of deference. This may be just another version of the fundamental problem that I have with the use of administrative tribunals or panels to make public policy (cf. IISD/WWF 2001, 39; Public Citizen 2001, 17).

The federal government said that part of the point of having the dispute settlement procedures established in the AIT was to allow for "expeditious proceedings" rather than "trials," but I suspect that the fundamental flaw in the procedures stems from the fact that "expeditious proceedings" are practically (not conceptually) antithetical to democratic proceedings. It seems to me that maximally inclusive, democratic decision-making with "reasonableness" as the standard of review is morally and politically appropriate for making public policy, and that because ad hoc panels cannot match that sort of process, they ought to show some deference to decisions made in accordance with that process. Clarke captured the essence of the democratic process when he said, "If I can speak to process for a moment, any policy, regulatory initiative or piece of legislation goes through a rather excruciating process in government before we get it onto the Order Paper. Everyone in this town has a kick at this cat. Every conceivable aspect of the policy is looked at, whether it is economics, trade, jobs, unity or the environment. To get anything on to the Order Paper requires superhuman effort. This bill [*MMT Act*] required a superhuman effort, as other bills do. It is a government bill, not an Environment Canada bill" (SSCEENR 2/4, 1997a, 6).

The obvious question "How much deference is appropriate?" has no nice answer at this point, and it is troublesome to allow that different people may reasonably settle on different degrees of deference. My basic position is that matters of broad public policy should be settled using parliamentary procedures rather than arbitration panels or tribunals. If some additional decision procedure is required to adjudicate a dispute, a domestic court or perhaps an international court would be preferable. I believe, though I could not prove it on the basis of the narrow range of issues examined in this book, that if the AIT and NAFTA (and WTO) dispute settlement procedures were abandoned in favour of public trials in domestic or international courts, the general public's interests or public good would be better protected. Arthur Mauro agreed with the respondent's view that "the courts show deference to the initial findings of policy makers or expert tribunals and apply a standard of reasonableness, not correctness. But the onus is on Canada to indicate that there was a reasonable basis for the policy decision that led to the legislation, to the creation of the barrier, because, alternatively, it would require Alberta to prove that the decision was frivolous, vexatious, without any real basis. And I don't think that the act contemplates that" (AIT Hearings 1998c, 288–9).

The Government of Canada, represented by Tyhurst at this point, agreed that the onus was on Canada but insisted "that the onus requires a reasonable basis, not that we have proved beyond reasonable doubt." This was accepted by Mauro.

Tyhurst then proceeded to explain two points about:

sources of law which suggest that deference should be accorded ... The first point related to the approach that is taken by courts in judicial review cases. As was mentioned, in questions of technical findings of fact, courts normally give deference to the technical finder of fact, for the reasons that I have already indicated.

That is particularly true, though, in the case of legislative decisions, because they are even more difficult in terms of balancing conflicting views. The courts tend to put legislative decisions even higher than the administrative decisions of a scientific nature. So the most deference is accorded to legislative decisions.

... The other point we make is the approach taken by international tribunals. There is a tendency for international tribunals to give deference to decisions of sovereign states. (AIT Hearings 1998c, 290–1)

Howlett concurred with Tyhurst: "the courts have consistently deferred to legislators in policy matters, including matters related to the environment. Not surprisingly, this deference has resulted in a rather patchy, ad hoc approach to administrative law on the part of the Canadian courts, but one still based on judicial self-restraint and unwillingness to become too closely involved in administrative decision-making" (Howlett 2002, 34; Coe 2002, 197, apparently agreed).

Hogg (1997, ch. 5, 28–28.1) offered a very clear justification for judicial restraint:

There can be no doubt that judicial review permits, indeed requires, non-elected judges to make decisions of great political significance. Yet Canada's adoption of the Charter of Rights in 1982 was a conscious decision to increase the scope of judicial review. It is hard to say whether public acceptance of judicial review flows from a belief in the myth of "a strict and complete legalism", or whether people really are content that some political choices be made by judges. Its seems to me, however, that the judges' lack of democratic accountability, coupled with the limitations inherent in the adversarial judicial process, dictates that the appropriate posture for the courts in distribution of powers (or federalism) cases is one of restraint: the legislative decision should be overridden only where invalidity is clear. There should be, in other words, a presumption of constitutionality.

In a fine article reviewing issues around the judiciary's presumption of constitutionality for legislative acts enacted by parliament, Magnet (1980, 104) emphasized the superior fact-finding capacity of legislatures compared to courts.

Where factual preconditions to the constitutionally valid exercise of legislative power exist, it would be unthinkable that the legislature would refrain from investigating the sufficiency of the necessary facts. The legislature has a formidable array of fact-finding machinery available for the purpose. It can summon experts before committees, procure special in-depth reports, or appoint royal commissions or other tribunals having wide investigatory powers under the Inquiries Acts. Judicial fact-finding tools pale beside the impressive resources of the legislature. (Hogg (1997, 5–27) expresses a very similar view)

These remarks have even more force if one compares the capacity of legislatures to that of tribunals and panels. Whether or not the Government of Canada or Zarzecny was right about the appropriateness of the panel displaying some level of deference to that government's point of view regarding the need for the MMT Act, the panel chose not to enter into an argument about it. So far as I could tell, the panel also chose not to display any sort of deference.

Following her critique of the federal government's position regarding the standard of review and deference, Zarzecny challenged its position regarding the "weighing of evidence." The panel was completely silent on this point, but Zarzecny said:

Canada suggests that the panel should accept the principle that there must be, and again I quote: "Some evidence and not mere assertion or argument to accept any contested fact as having been proven."

Saskatchewan submits that this is not the rule to be applied, particularly to what we believe are the two critical questions in the case before you today. The first question is: Is the MMT legislation inconsistent with any of the provisions of the Agreement on Internal Trade? ... [Canada] admitted that it is inconsistent with Articles 402 and 403 of the AIT.

Once that first question is answered, we get to the second question ... Has Canada established a legitimate objective for the legislation within the meaning of Article 404 of the AIT?

Panel, for both these questions, the party with the onus of proof must do more than offer some evidence. It must prove its case to you on a balance of probabilities. (AIT Hearings, 1998a, 133–4)

She went on to explain that "the balance of probabilities" means roughly that one position is shown to have "more evidence or evidence of greater cogency" (AIT Hearings 1998a, 134–6). Needless to say, "probabilities" and "evidence of greater cogency" were not defined, which is understandable, but lamentable. I suspect that carefully crafted definitions of these notions would probably take us very close to a standard of "reasonableness," which has also not been defined here (cf. "consensual rationality" in Michalos 1973, 1978).

To return to our examination of the panel's judgment concerning the issues in dispute, the seventh main point was that Article 404(c) is qualified by or must be interpreted according to Article 1505.7, and that the Government of Canada failed to meet the specified test:

Article 404(c) and Article 1505.7 have three requirements: "take into account the need to minimize negative trade effects", "equally effective" means, and "reasonably available" means. The onus is on the Respondent to demonstrate, on balance of probabilities, that it has met these requirements, and to demonstrate that no other available option would have met the legitimate objective.

Several options were identified as equally effective and reasonably available. From the evidence and the submissions of the Complainants, three of those options, namely, tradable permits, taxation, and direct regulation under section 46 of CEPA, did not require further study on the effects of MMT ... Therefore the Panel determines that the Respondent has not discharged the requirements of 404(c), as modified by 1505.7. (Gilson, Castonguay, Kelly, Mauro, and Rae, 1998, 10)

Monahan's (1997, 9) reading of the requirements of Article 404(c) and 1505.7 was more flexible than that of the panel: "the implication of Article 1505.7 is that even if such a less restrictive alternative were available, a government is merely obliged to take into account the need to minimize negative trade effects ... In other words, the government is not obliged to adopt a less restrictive alternative, even one that is an equally effective means of achieving its objective, as long as it has considered the need to minimize negative trade effects."

Although it is true that there is no provision in the AIT that explicitly says trade legislation is less preferable than other legislation for addressing environmental issues, the "least trade restrictive" requirement of Article 404 (c) practically guarantees that trade legislation will in fact be less preferable. Trade legislation especially, but any legislation that happens to conflict with Article 404 (c), is operating with a handicap, insofar as meeting that requirement may be regarded as a necessary condition of its acceptance. In other words, this particular test makes the minimization of trade reduction the paramount concern or value, and consequently makes trade legislation "less preferable" if not entirely useless for achieving environmental or any other non-trade goals. What is worse, even non-trade legislation might be undermined by Article 404 (c) if it inadvertently reduces trade. As early as

November 1994, Sinclair (1994, 7–8) noted that Article 403 provided "a basis to challenge non-trade policy measures" and Article 404 (c) "invited trade dispute settlement panels to substitute their judgment for that of policy-makers in determining whether a specific measure is 'necessary' to achieve a legitimate objective." The MMT panel accepted that invitation and decided that the policy-makers were wrong, but allowing the minimization of trade reduction to be a supreme value is morally indefensible.

Addressing this particular implication of the AIT, Cohen (1995, 270) wrote:

> The requirement that provinces must demonstrate that measures inconsistent with the agreement but which attempt to meet legitimate objectives are not more trade restrictive than is necessary will lead governments to adopt the least intrusive and perhaps relatively less effective measures. To use consumer protection legislation as an example, less intrusive regulatory measures – such as requirements for performance rather than design standards, insurance requirements and warnings or disclosure requirements rather than licensing or certification measures – may have significant adverse distributive consequences to particular groups of consumers and certainly present a risk of less effective regulatory impact than do the more intrusive regulatory instruments available to governments.

The *MMT Act* involved both environmental and consumer protection, and the options suggested by the panel were precisely of the sort predicted by Cohen. Explanations of the three options cited above (tradable permits, taxation, and direct regulation) are not given in the main document (Government of Alberta 1997). However, the first two are briefly discussed in the *Brief from Québec* (Government of Québec 1997) and the third is easy to construct. The taxation option is straightforward. The use of MMT-free gasoline might be increased and that of MMT-enhanced gasoline decreased by taxing the latter sufficiently higher than the former. Since this option would violate Article 401.1 (b) and 404 (d) as much as the *MMT Act* itself, it would not have been acceptable to the complainant. Regarding tradable permits, the *Brief* said:

> Why did the federal government not examine the advisability of establishing emission quotas or allowing tradable permits which, in other areas, have proven adequate means of controlling the release of harmful substances into the environment? In such instances, harmful sub-

stances have been controlled by regulating the total amount released into the environment. The allowable amount of pollutant can be specified in a set standard or it can decrease over time.

Assuming such a system were applied to MMT, refineries for whom reducing this additive would be a relatively costly endeavour, could purchase permits to use MMT from refineries where this additive can be removed at a lesser cost during the production process. In the United States, this system proved successful during the '80s as a means of reducing the cost of eliminating lead from gas.

A tradable permit system not only ensures that an environmental objective is achieved, but does so at a lesser cost and in a way certainly less detrimental to interprovincial trade. At the outset, the federal government, in consultation with the provinces, should have analysed the advantages of such a system with respect to internal trade, as well as its technical and economic feasibility. (Government of Québec 1997, 14)

Chapter 6 reviewed some of the critical literature regarding liberal environmentalism and market-friendly environmental policies. Schemes of tradable permits or emissions trading have been given considerable attention by the National Round Table on the Environment and the Economy (http://www.nrtee-trnee.ca/emissionstrading/en/overview_ABC) and the Tradeable Permits Working Group (http://www.nccp.ca/NCCP/national_process/issues/tradable_e.htn). Whatever one can say in their favour, no generally acceptable scheme is available today. In the National Round Table document just cited, a possible start-up date for some scheme concerning carbon trading in general is put at 2008. I am not aware of any discussions focused specifically on manganese emissions. Regarding the more general issue, the National Round Table overview said, "Governments would need to determine overall emissions limits, the allocation of permits, the eligibility of offsets, and time frames and penalties for non-compliance ... Emissions trading also requires brokers, analysts and certifiers of claimed emissions reductions ... development of a permit/credit registrar; the establishment of a market oversight body; ... determination of when such a system should be announced and begin operating; and agreement on how emissions reduction actions undertaken prior to the operation of the system should be recognized within the system."

As if these were not barriers enough, given the complainant's view of the alleged evidence for the adverse effects of MMT, this option would not have been any more acceptable than the *MMT Act*. Besides, since the adverse effects of MMT on emissions control and OBD systems result from the roughly 80 per cent residue remaining in the system rather than from the 20 per cent escaping in some form, it is unclear how a tradable permit system would work. Insofar as MMT poses a problem, it is not in refineries but in motor vehicles. Supposing that over time tradable permits might be adjusted to substantially reduce or even eliminate the use of MMT, this option seems to violate Articles 401.1 (b) and 404 (d) as much as the *Act* itself. As well, the likely dollar cost (probably more to the public purse than to industry) of putting such a system in place to support a product with a questionable future would be prohibitive.

In the AIT Hearings (1998C, 272–4) Wallace admitted that "tradeable emission permits ... [were] not looked at at the time ... [nor] proposed by any party to Canada's knowledge at that time in the debate surrounding the issue." However, as just explained, because a substantial part of the problem was not one of unacceptable emissions, it was unclear how they might be useful. Perhaps more importantly, Wallace was concerned that a permit system would have the refiners in lower mainland British Columbia getting MMT, and about any harmful effects it might have on air pollution and automobile emission systems. From the point of view of the federal government, and any unbiased observer for that matter, moving problems from one or more parts of the country to other parts was not an acceptable method of solving them.

Several clauses of Section 46 of CEPA could be directly applicable, and none would have the direct effect of removing MMT from the market. Here are the most relevant parts:

46. (1) The Minister may, for the purpose of conducting research, creating an inventory of data, formulating objectives and codes of practice, issuing guidelines or assessing or reporting on the state of the environment, publish in the *Canada Gazette* and in any other manner that the Minister considers appropriate a notice requiring any person described in the notice to provide the Minister with any information that may be in the possession of that person or to which the person may reasonably be expected to have access, including information regarding the following: ...

(b) substances that have not been determined to be toxic under Part 5 ... but whose presence in the environment must be monitored if the Minister considers that to be appropriate; ...

(f) substances that may cause or contribute to international or interprovincial pollution of fresh water, salt water or the atmosphere;

(g) substances or fuels that may contribute significantly to air pollution; ...

(2) The Minister may ... require that a person to whom a notice is directed submit the information to the Minister. (CEPA 1999)

These clauses clearly indicate that Section 46 is intended to allow a Minister of the Environment to collect more information about any substance that may be considered dangerous to the environment. So the suggestion that these provisions might have been used instead of the MMT *Act* is no more than a suggestion that the federal government might have insisted on having more research undertaken and more data collected. For the question at issue, namely, whether the time had come to remove MMT from gasoline or to continue investigating the consequences of not removing it, the suggested application of Section 46 as a viable alternative to the MMT *Act* is question-begging. It is nothing more than a recommendation to accept the position of the complainant rather than the respondent.

In sum, since two of the three proposed alternatives to the MMT *Act* would not have been acceptable to the complainant, even though the latter suggested them, the panel's willingness to regard them as viable options was unrealistic. Insofar as the third proposed alternative is simply another version of the complainant's call for more research, it is question-begging and therefore also not a viable option. Thus, the panel's argument regarding Article 404 (c) cannot be regarded as sound.

Eighth, regarding Article 404(d), the panel found that "the *Act* is transparent, and does not create a disguised restriction on trade" (Gilson, Castonguay, Kelly, Mauro, and Rae 1998, 10). Since no reason is given as to why the panel's view should be more acceptable than the complainant's view of the *Act's* transparency, it is difficult to see how the requirement of Article 1707.2(b) to "give a determination, with reasons" was satisfied. Presumably, the panel would insist (as above) that Articles 1705 and 1707 apply to the whole *Agreement*, rather than to specific articles. However, if that is true, why did the panel usually provide reasons for its other determinations regarding specific articles?

The panel's ninth major determination concerned the possibility that, while the MMT *Act* was introduced apparently as a measure to control international trade, its real intent was to control internal trade. Had that been the case, the *Act* would have been "a disguised restriction on trade" and would have failed to pass the test of Article 404(d). The panel did not believe that the Canadian Government was playing that game, but it did believe that the issues of international versus internal trade were separable and that the panel's "authority to make recommendations is limited to matters affecting interprovincial trade." Granting this limitation, the panel had to deal with the following interesting charge: "The Respondent contends that the Panel's jurisdiction is limited to a review of the interprovincial trade aspects of a measure, and cannot make a recommendation respecting international trade. Therefore, the Panel cannot recommend that the *Act* be repealed, nor can it recommend that MMT be removed from the Schedule to the *Act*, because either of those recommendations would impact on the international trade component of the Act" (Gilson, Castonguay, Kelly, Mauro, and Rae, 1998, 10–11).

In short, insofar as the panel's determinations would have a significant impact on international trade, such determinations would be beyond the panel's jurisdiction and therefore "null and void," to use the Government's earlier phrase. This was a serious challenge not only to this particular panel but to every Panel dealing with issues involving international as well as internal trade. In the panel's view:

If international trade agreements provide an absolute defence to disputes under the *Agreement* there would be no need for Canada to meet any of the Article 404 tests. A simple declaration that Canada has restricted international trade in a particular product would be sufficient justification to restrict internal trade.

Alternatively, in any dispute, the Panel having determined that the measure constrains international trade, could only conclude that the new barrier on internal trade was in fact "justified".

The provisions relative to requiring consideration of alternatives and the requirement that the legislation be no more trade restrictive than necessary must be made effective.

Subsequent events may establish that permitting interprovincial trade in MMT while prohibiting the importation does breach an international agreement but this will be determined in a different forum. Our task is limited to determining whether the *Act* in question is inconsistent with the *Agreement* and recommending appropriate steps to remove the barrier to internal trade. (Gilson, Castonguay, Kelly, Mauro, and Rae 1998, 11)

In other words, if the provisions of Article 404 are to have any point at all, disputants cannot be allowed to offer international trade restrictions as a justification for internal trade restrictions. Or more clearly, perhaps, the fact that the federal government protects a home industry by means of an international trade agreement cannot be used as a justification for the federal, provincial, or territorial governments protecting that industry by means of an internal trade agreement; e.g., the fact that a Québec dairy farmer might be protected against Vermont dairy farmers cannot be used as a justification for protecting Québec dairy farmers from Ontario dairy farmers. While it is apparently acceptable for disputants and panelists to cite rulings from arbitration panels for international agreements, as we have seen, such citations cannot be binding on AIT panels. Although I believe the panel's argument is sound, it is also an invitation to uncertainty at best and incoherence among internal and international agreements at worst. (On the need for coherence among international agreements, see Marceau 1999).

Immediately following these judgments regarding Article 404, the panel rendered its tenth and final, overall, determination:

> The Panel finds that the *Act* is inconsistent with the Articles 402 and 403 of the *Agreement*, and the inconsistency is not justified by the legitimate objectives test contained in Article 404 ... the Panel does not recommend repeal of the *Act* ... The Panel recommends that the Respondent remove the inconsistency of the *Act* with the *Agreement*. Pending such action, the Panel recommends that the Respondent suspend the operation of the *Act* with respect to interprovincial trade ... The Panel also recommends that the Respondent and the Complainants seek resolution of the outstanding harmonization and regulatory standards issues in conformance with the provisions of the *Agreement*, in particular by using CCME as a forum for discussion and resolution of the MMT issue. (Gilson, Castonguay, Kelly, Mauro, and Rae, 1998, 11–12)

Rules 51 to 54 of Annex 1706.1 deal with the allocation of costs. The allocation may or may not reflect the panel's views about the disputants' shares of responsibility for the dispute. The federal government was assigned 60 per cent of the panel's operational costs, Alberta was assigned 30 per cent, and Saskatchewan and Québec, 5 per cent each. Following the MMT case, the AIT was amended such that no disputant can be assigned more than 50 per cent of costs.

I suppose the panel's recommendation "that the Respondent remove the inconsistency of the *Act* with the *Agreement*" through the use of the "CCME as a forum for discussion and resolution" meant that some sort of liberal environmentalist resolution of the problem should be found. Such a resolution would have been consistent with the AIT and with the general trends toward harmonization of environmental policies agreed upon by a process of collaborative or cooperative negotiations. Whether this was reasonable and acceptable from a broad-based moral consequentialist point of view, or merely the best one could do assuming the necessity of minimally restricting trade, is an open question. As most readers would expect by now, in my view the panel's recommendation was at best only consistent with the latter alternative.

The panel did not address the Government of Québec's charge that many groups, including the Canadian Automobile Association and automobile manufacturers were not consulted. However, we have already seen that the MVMA was a major player throughout the NAFTA and AIT cases, and the Canadian Automobile Association made presentations to both the House and Senate Committees. And no committee could possibly contact every person that might be able to give testimony. So, one cannot give much credence to this sort of a challenge. The panel also did not address the charge that the measure permitted "the continued use of MMT." However, as explained earlier, because it was economically very difficult, if not impossible, to produce the product for a single province, given the MMT Act, it would have been practically impossible to continue to make the product available in Canada.

The panel did not address the Government of Saskatchewan's charge that the federal government rejected the suggestion about "obtaining independent testing," but we saw that reports were commissioned from the independent researchers Carter, Walsh, and Abraham and Lawless. Regarding the charge that no new "emergency" existed, as indicated in chapter 3, "Parliament can enact legislation to pre-empt or avoid an emergency" (Monahan 2002, 261). However, we did see some evidence of an emergency in the letters from the MVMA and the AIAMC in the latter half of 1994. An editorial in The Edmonton Journal, 15 January 1995 (A3), said "With the Big Three members of the Motor Vehicle Manufacturers' Association threatening to close plants, increase the price of 1996 model-year cars by up to $3,000 or rip out sophisticated anti-pollution equipment from cars sold in Canada, Copps asked the parties [MVMA and CPPI] last fall to resolve the issue. The Canadian Petroleum Products Institute and its 11 members have promised to study the issue and report back by the end of February. But automakers say that's too late for them to meet their 1996 production-line deadlines."

Notwithstanding this evidence, as late as February 1997, the president of Ethyl Canada told the Standing Senate Committee that the threat to "disconnect equipment ... is not new. It has been made since 1994, the first year that OBD systems were required under u.s. law. Four model years later, warranties remain intact and only GM has disabled the dashboard light and only on its 1996 models. There has been no market disruption, and that rationale, [for Bill C-29] like so many others, does not hold water" (SSCEENR 2/5, 1997d, 2–3).

The very next day, responding to a senator's question about the possibility of modifying the current OBD systems to accommodate MMT, the committee was told by D. Hrobelsky, Chief, Energy and Emissions Engineering, Transport Canada:

The difficulty we are facing is that it probably cannot be done in time. Our new, tighter standards are proposed for the 1998 model year. As some of the auto industry witnesses indicated, for them that starts as early as next week with the introduction of some early 1998 models. Given the short lead time for industries to comply with new requirements, the redesign of systems with regard to fuel effects is not a feasible option at this time ... We could tolerate MMT, or MMT effects, 10 years ago. Today, the standards are much more stringent and we require compliance to them for twice the mileage and time on "real world" fuels and under "real world" conditions, as opposed to in the laboratory under controlled conditions. (SSCEENR 2/6, 1997e, 22–3)

A few minutes later, when Pageot was asked what Transport Canada would do if Bill C-29 was not passed, she said, "We have a tight time frame. We will have to decide on our course of action. We may possibly postpone the promulgation of our standards. We believe that the fuel issue must be resolved before we can finalize our emission standards" (SSCEENR 2/6, 1997e, 24).

Hrobelsky added:

The department proposed tighter standards in June of 1996. Those have not gone to final regulation because the position of the department has been that the issue of MMT must be resolved before those standards can pass.

The legal situation we are in if this bill does not pass and we cannot go to new standards is that Canada reverts to emissions standards established in 1988. We can potentially fall 10 years back in emission control. What that would mean in practice is difficult to say. It will depend a lot on what vehicle manufacturers choose to do. They have told you that they are concerned enough with the effects of fuels on their vehicles that they are considering – and some are doing so now – disabling emission controls for Canada. The fact is that legally they will be able to do that as long as they do not exceed our 1988 standards, which is not a great challenge for them now ... There is a strong risk that vehicles will be modified back to 1988 standards, if manufacturers feel that is necessary. (SSCEENR 2/6, 1997e, 24)

As it turned out, Hrobelsky's worst fears were not realized. Though Bill C-29 did not succeed, the EPA "Tier 1 standards ... were fully introduced in the U.S. as of the 1996 model year and with only few exceptions, the same vehicles were sold in Canada" (Gourley 2002).

The panel did not address the question of why it remained "legal to produce and use MMT in Canada" if indeed there was some danger to health, the environment, or consumers, but we know that the MMT Act would have made it practically impossible to produce and use MMT even though it remained legal to do so.

Finally, the most remarkable aspect of the panel's determinations is that the federal government's ace in the hole Article 1505.8 was never mentioned at all. Like NAFTA tribunals (VanDuzer 2002, 93), AIT panels are under no obligation to address every argument raised by disputants, even if that means that the strongest arguments might be entirely neglected and justice denied, e.g., see Mexico's objections to the Metalclad award (Thomas 2002, 103). Recall that the AIT Article says that "an environmental measure shall not be considered to be inconsistent with this Agreement by reason solely of the lack of full scientific certainty regarding the need for the measure." The panel's decisions about the respondent's failure to satisfy the tests of Article 404 (b) and (c) presupposed that in the absence of "full scientific certainty regarding the need for the measure," the appropriate course of action was to do as little as possible to interrupt trade. The main effect of two pumps, tradable permits, taxation, and additional data collection would be to allow as much trade in MMT as possible until, presumably, there is "full scientific certainty" regarding the product's harmfulness. At that point, even the CPPI would come on side and voluntarily stop using MMT. If I am right about this presupposition of the panel's decisions, then those decisions were incorrect insofar as they assume the antithesis of Article 1505.8; and Ogilvy was wrong when he said, "I don't think any of the provinces have suggested that we would expect full scientific certainty. That was never sought by any of the provinces" (AIT Hearings 1998c, 392).

After all, the provinces and the panel were calling for precisely the same tests to be met, with precisely the same presupposition. My guess is that Wilson had the same presupposition when he told the Senate Standing Committee that "We believe there should be a firm science-based foundation for any action" (SSCEENR 2/5, 1997d, 2).

According to Monahan (1997, 10–12), "This proviso [Article 1505.8] recognizes that it is common for there to be disputes about the scientific validity of the evidence that is relied on by governments when they act to protect the environment. The purpose of the proviso would appear to be to prevent complaints being brought on the basis of such scientific disputes, assuming that the government in question is proceeding in good faith and on the basis of credible scientific evidence ... Article 1505.8 ... states that environmental measures are not subject to challenge on the basis of lack of full scientific certainty respecting the need for the measure."

It is a pity that the panel did not share his or my view of this Article.

In the Senate Hearings on Bill C-29, Nova Scotia's Deputy Minister for the Environment accepted "that there are times when action is necessary even though there is not full scientific certainty," but did not believe there was "a reasonable expectation of risk to public health or the environment" in the case of MMT. He went further in asserting that "It is incumbent upon Environment Canada to create a process which ensures increased certainty for triggering the use of the precautionary principle" (SSCEENR 2/11, 1996, 4). It is unclear to me what procedure and criteria one would use to establish the certainty of the sufficiency of scientific uncertainty to invoke a precautionary principle, but the demand for such certainty seems to be the beginning of an infinite regress, if one really accepts the legitimacy of such principles. Granting that it is sometimes wise to act in the presence of uncertainty, one ought to grant that it might be wise to act as if one's scientific uncertainty were sufficient to act even though one might not be certain that it was sufficient. Then our friend from Nova Scotia would demand a new process, leading to the same result, with no clear end in sight. Clearly, our friend is inviting us down the garden path to an infinite regress.

Some Members of the House were more direct in their demands. For example, Benoît Sauvageau (MP, Terrebonne) said, "Like all the members of this House, the members of the Bloc Quebecois are very concerned with the well-being of Quebecers and Canadians alike. That is why we have asked that the government give us *clear and irrefutable proof that* MMT *is harmful*" (PD10/28, 1996f, 7, emphasis added).

Francine Lalonde (MP, Mercier) said, "if the government truly wished to protect the environment, it would have seen to it that these conclusions [about the harmful effects of MMT] were accurate beyond all possible doubt, or at least beyond all reasonable doubt" (PD11/29, 1996g, 7).

Jay Hill (MP, Prince George-Peace River) used indirect language, but its implication was practically the same as that of Sauvageau and Lalonde: "If we in this place are going to ban products in Canada, which is what is going to be accomplished with this ban on the transportation of MMT, every time we think there is a potential for harm, how many lawsuits will the Government of Canada have to face? Ultimately how many millions of dollars will the taxpayers of Canada have to pay just because we feel there is some potential for a problem down the road?" (PD10/28, 1996f, 9).

One panel member disagreed with its judgments, and his or her views were summarized following the panel's overall determinations. That panel member would have "dismissed the application" on the grounds that all four tests of Article 404 were satisfied. All panel members agreed that Article 404(a) and 404(d) tests were passed, but only the dissenting member believed that Article 404(b) and 404(c) tests were passed. The following quotation reveals the source of the disagreement:

> There is no doubt that the legislation is by itself an impairment of internal trade. However, it is equally clear to me that the legislation satisfies the test set out in article 404. The purpose and effect of the legislation will be to get rid of MMT as a substance in gasoline. No other substances are so named or restricted, and therefore I would find that there has been "no undue impairment of access of goods", and I would also find that the measure is "not more trade restrictive than necessary to achieve the legitimate objective".
>
> I would also disagree with my colleagues that insofar as the process followed has been less than perfect, the entire blame for this should be placed at the door of the Respondent. This legislation was before the Parliament of Canada for over a year, and there was ample opportunity for other governments to put forward alternative measures. I note that the so-called "two pump solution" was rejected by the petroleum industry itself. We have no basis upon which to find that the differences between the parties would have been resolved if this issue had been discussed further. (Gilson, Castonguay, Kelly, Mauro, and Rae 1998, 13)

Clearly, the panel and the dissenting member applied different standards to determine whether or not there was "undue impairment" and the *Act* was "more trade restrictive than necessary." For the dissenting member, if only one of many octane-enhancing substances was banned from all interprovincial trade, then the tests of Article 404(b) and 404(c) were passed. For the panel, if any one of the alternatives of "tradable permits, taxation and direct regulation under section 46 of CEPA" was adopted, then those tests would have been passed. So, the dissenting member's standard focused on minimizing impairment to trade by minimizing the numbers of substances banned, while the panel's standard focused on minimizing impairment to trade by other means. Since, as I have tried to show above, the three other means were not viable options, I agree with the dissenting member regarding passage of the test in Article 404 (c). I also agree with the dissenting member in not holding only the respondent responsible for the failure of the CCME dispute resolution procedures to produce results.

Reports by Cosbey (2004), Mann and Porter (2003), and UNDP (2003) reveal that "necessity tests" continue to be a significant irritant for critics of trade treaties. However, Sinclair (1994, 10) offered a very interesting and relevant quotation from Professor David Wirth's testimony before the U.S. House of Representatives Committee on Science, Space and Technology in September 1992, regarding the use of the word "necessary" in provisions like Article 404 (c):

This "necessity" requirement is a difficult defence before trade dispute panels. For example, in congressional hearings on NAFTA one expert testified that "... I am unaware of a single GATT panel report that turns on the interpretation of this word [i.e., "necessary"] where the measure in question was held to be consistent with the GATT. The panel reports articulate, variously, a "least GATT-inconsistent" or a "least trade restrictive" test. Quite obviously, the word "necessary" has been interpreted to give dispute settlement panels a roving commission to second-guess domestic measures and to substitute their own judgment as to the desirability of a particular regulatory measure, an analytical approach that in practice virtually assures that a measure whose consistency with the agreement in question turns on this test will not pass muster.

In the presence of such testimony, it is difficult to believe that those who crafted such provisions did not realize that they were moulding the building blocks of kangaroo courts. As if it were not enough to make the minimization of trade reduction one's supreme value, under the guise of creating rules for an even playing field, they created rules for a biased playing field. (For a counter-opinion concerning the "least-trade restrictive requirement" in NAFTA, see Rugman, Kirton, and Soloway 1997, 138.)

17

Conclusion

I began with the question: In the NAFTA dispute settlement involving MMT, were the broader community interests of most people in Canada served better or worse than the relatively narrower commercial trade interests of investors? My attempt to answer that question was complicated by the initiation of the AIT dispute settlement. However, the answer to the basic question is that broader community interests, as assessed and defended by the Government of Canada, were crushed in favour of the narrower trade interests of the Ethyl Corporation and the petroleum industry, defended in one arena by the Ethyl Corporation and in the other by the Government of Alberta with the support of Saskatchewan and Québec. Since the NAFTA case never got past the Award on Jurisdiction to the determination of the Award on Merits, it is possible that the outcome might have been different. However, given the information we have about the deliberations and determinations of the NAFTA tribunal in the MMT case, it is highly unlikely that the federal government would have fared any better had the case been allowed to continue. That suggests that the answer above probably would have been reached anyhow.

I believe that the material considered here reveals that the NAFTA and AIT dispute settlement processes and substantive provisions are seriously flawed and that the adjudicators' decisions regarding the cases against the MMT Act were also flawed. The processes, provisions, decision-makers, and elements of the cases involving MMT, especially the confused and complicated science surrounding the product, were individually necessary and collectively sufficient to produce bad public policy.

The NAFTA and AIT and their dispute settlement procedures were very much the products of the *zeitgeist* of the last quarter of the twentieth century, which I think of as the Age of Avarice – a time in which someone could say that greed is good and few would dissent, at least few with a public profile. I do not believe we have left that age behind us. The existence of these trade treaties, others like them, and others proposed that are cut from the same cloth shows that that *zeitgeist* is still with us, still demanding vigilance lest further foundations of civil society are consumed by its insatiable appetite.

Reflecting on the great number and variety of issues considered in the preceding chapters, one must finally ask: What, if anything, should be done with the NAFTA and AIT dispute settlement procedures? What recommendations should be made? I think it has been shown here that the procedures are seriously flawed and based on equally flawed moral principles and economic science. The flaws are so deep that they are beyond reconstruction. At least I cannot imagine any reconstruction that would be acceptable to those who currently think they provide a road map for future developments and those who share my views of their flaws. I will indicate specific changes that should be made if most of the basic provisions are going to be maintained, but my first recommendation is for wholesale abandonment.

The AIT should be abandoned altogether, not just the dispute settlement provisions. We have seen how those provisions range from being totally useless to very dangerous. We have seen how they shift the focus of attention away from fundamental questions about the well-being of people affected by certain policies to questions about "undue" or "unnecessary" restrictions on trade. And we have seen how decisions made in settings disturbingly similar to kangaroo courts can have very real, costly, and destructive consequences. To what purpose, and for whose benefit? In an established federal state, with well-functioning legislative and judicial systems at all levels, councils of ministers for diverse sectors, hundreds of working committees, and accepted venues for formal and informal discussions, consultations, and negotiations, the AIT was not and is not necessary. If it were merely a useless layer of red tape, wrapped around the labyrinth of offices, procedures, and venues characterizing governmental decision-making in Canada, it might be tolerable. But it is more than that. It is the all-Canadian child of the Age of Avarice, non-legal, non-binding, and, most Canadian of all, non-threatening. But it is nonetheless dangerous. It helps make other deals and their provisions more acceptable, and facilitates the dismantling of democracy.

Because NAFTA's Chapter 11 has received and continues to receive so much attention from opponents and proponents alike, and the NAFTA MMT case was settled without the major claims and counter claims being addressed in an Award on Merits, relatively few recommendations can be made based only on the latter case. I will list those below. Taking into consideration all the material reviewed here regarding the provisions of Chapter 11 and the applications of those provisions in the MMT case and others, I am inclined to recommend total abandonment of NAFTA Chapter 11. If proponents of the Chapter would be willing to delete its most cherished provisions around such things as performance requirements, minimum trade restrictions, and secrecy, something in it might be salvageable, but almost certainly not enough to make the remnant acceptable to them. Besides, I think the Chapter rests on the morally unacceptable foundation of the Principle of Autonomy, whose unacceptability becomes particularly evident in cases involving environmental degradation, human health, and consumer protection. As indicated earlier, if the NAFTA MMT case had been played out to the end, its results would likely have been similar to those of the AIT case. Then I could have used those results to illustrate the points illustrated with the AIT case, and reached the same recommendation concerning Chapter 11.

Considering the above negative recommendations, readers will want to know what dispute resolution procedures I would recommend. Briefly, regarding domestic disputes, we have all the judicial remedies required to obtain justice for governments at all levels, for individuals, and for corporations. Insofar as justice is the paramount concern, rather than the creation of jobs and wealth for investors, arbitrators, and all of the components of the supporting infrastructure related to internal trade, the Canadian justice system was and is sufficient to the tasks. The AIT procedures did not fill any gaps, although they created undesirable opportunities for mischief at the expense of Canadian taxpayers. Regarding international disputes concerning the three NAFTA countries, the situation is more complicated, but the traditional procedures used prior to the 1958 *New York Convention* involving the "local remedies rule," domestic courts of host nations in which alleged transgressions occur and courts with international jurisdiction or a capacity to adjudicate disputes involving international law (e.g., the Commercial Court of London or the International Court of Justice) would be preferable to Chapter 11. Presumably an acceptable international court system could be constructed for the three countries, with full transparency, unbiased rules, a relatively permanent appellant body, and so on. That might not serve the interests of investors as well as Chapter 11, but if it served the broader public interests well, that would be its justification.

Regarding specific provisions, I think that the biggest flaws in both agreements, so far as they were revealed in our two cases, are at least the imprecision or obscurity of certain articles, and at most their logical incoherence or their bias in favour of commercial trade over the prevention of environmental degradation and the protection of human health and consumers. In particular, I believe examination of the two MMT cases shows that the following articles are flawed as described and need revision or outright deletion from the agreements.

NAFTA Articles

101.1   Objectives should include protecting health and the environment.

201   The term "measure" should be more precisely defined.

1112 (1)   Article should indicate that all trade in goods involves some investment.

1114   Some reference to this article should be included in the objectives.

1119   Simultaneous satisfaction of temporal conditions should be explicitly excluded.

1120   Simultaneous satisfaction of temporal conditions should be explicitly excluded.

1121   Temporal requirements for delivering consent and waiver letters should be made explicit.

1122(2)(a) If written consent is not required then the article should say so.

AIT Articles

401.1   Criteria for "like, directly competitive and substitutable" should be clarified.

404 (b)   Criteria for "impair unduly" and the status of this article versus Article 1505.8 should be clarified.

404 (c)   Criteria for "not more trade restrictive than necessary" and the status of this article versus Article 1505.8 should be clarified.

405   Differences between "standards-related measures" and "regulatory measures" should be clarified.

1505.2   This article should be made logically coherent or deleted.

1505.8   The status of this article with respect to Article 404 (b) and (c) should be specified.

1508   The article should specify that a particular process is not required.

1508.1   "Established process" and the meaning of "dissent" in By-law 1991, 1.01 (d) should be clarified.

1508.1 & 2 These articles should specify that the two provisions together are intended to prevent downward harmonization.

1511   The article should specify what kind of harmonization is required, as a matter of fact or law, and that 1508.1 & 2 take precedence over 1511.

Regarding my critique of the NAFTA tribunal's decisions, I argued that the tribunal failed:

1 To given any weight to the "context" of the agreement, as required by the Vienna Convention Article 31 (2);
2 To get "written consent of the parties" granting jurisdiction to the Tribunal, as required by NAFTA Article 1122 (2)(a);
3 To appreciate that the tribunal's interpretation of Articles 1112 (1) and Chapters 3 and 20 significantly undermines those provisions;
4 To appreciate that the tribunal's assumption that the temporal requirements of Articles 1119 and 1120 might be met simultaneously renders those provisions vacuous.

Regarding my critique of the AIT panel's decisions, I argued that the panel failed to notice that its:

1 Decisions regarding Articles 404 (b) and (c) presupposed the antithesis of the precautionary Article 1505.8;
2 Assumption about a phased elimination of MMT was another version of the rejected two-pump solution and not a viable option for purposes of Article 404 (b);
3 Assumptions about tradable permits, taxation, and direct regulation under Section 46 of CEPA were not viable options for purposes of Article 404 (c);
4 Judgment that the federal government did not apply the process specified in Article 1508.1 was mistaken.

Taking all these flaws together, it is impossible to believe that any broad community purposes were served by such dispute settlement procedures applied as they were (IISD/WWF 2001, 41). Clearly, investors' interests were served very well by the NAFTA procedures. After all, in that case taxes paid to the federal government were passed on to Ethyl in the final settlement. No wonder, then, as Sinclair (2001, 1) says, that:

> The U.S. corporate community has ... rallied behind the most extreme interpretations of the investment chapter. In an extraordinary letter released April 19 in Quebec [See full text in appendix 5], top U.S. cor-

porations strongly endorsed NAFTA's investor-state dispute provisions, including highly controversial protection against so-called "regulatory takings", or, as the letter puts it, "protection of assets from direct or indirect expropriation, to include protection from regulations that diminish the value of investor's assets"...

But to fully remove the threat to the governments' right to regulate and legislate in the public interest, the NAFTA investment chapter must be fundamentally changed. Now that its extreme policy consequences are clear, investor-state should be excised from NAFTA and other investment treaties. On sensitive matters such as expropriation, foreign investors should not have rights beyond those available to everyone else under domestic law, which already provides for prompt and effective compensation in cases of genuine expropriation ...

Therefore, corporate support for investor-state and the extreme interpretations of NAFTA's investment chapter must be publicly criticized and weakened. For example, the major auto companies were among the signatories to the April 19 letter. Are the major auto companies asserting that regulation to combat global warming or to reduce auto emissions are equivalent to expropriation if they reduce the value of the companies' assets? Is this the auto manufacturers' view of good corporate citizenship and sustainable development?

On the basis of the evidence presented above in the NAFTA case, Ethyl Corporation and the CPPI were clearly guilty of asserting precisely what Sinclair suggested the auto manufacturers were asserting. They did regard the federal government's "regulation to combat global warming ... equivalent to expropriation," and they proved that their bite was as good as their bark by challenging the government through Chapter 11.

An interesting exchange took place between Karen Kraft Sloan, Liberal MP for York-Simcoe and Hicks on the question of corporate social responsibility in 1995:

Mrs. Kraft Sloan: Mr. Hicks, you've been talking about Bill C-94 as some tip of the iceberg or whatever, implying that some other agenda is going on here, that the automotive industry wants to have control over the petroleum products industry around emissions. In the back of your mind, who is responsible for reducing emissions?
Mr. Hicks: I understand very well where I think I would be coming from if I were the automobile companies, because traditionally –
Mrs. Kraft Sloan: No. I'd like to know who is responsible for reducing emissions.

Mr. Hicks: I'm trying to answer your question, because traditionally in the United States the burden has fallen solely on the automobile companies. I understand their plight. They've been told by the United States government over the years to build cleaner cars, to build safer cars, to ratchet down the level of emissions that are allowed.

Other than the phase-out of leaded gasoline back in the 1970s, it was not until the 1990 Clean Air Act amendments, when reformulated fuels, oxygenated fuels, and those types of things came in as a mandate in the United States, that the burden shifted at all to the petroleum sector to help clean up the emissions that come out of cars.

Mrs. Kraft Sloan: You're suggesting the burden has shifted all to the petroleum industry?

Mr. Hicks: No, I'm saying that was the first time it shifted away from the auto manufacturers at all. I can understand where the auto manufacturers are coming from ... If I were them, I would try to do the same thing, too, and shift the burden as far to the petroleum industry as I could.

Mrs. Kraft Sloan: But my question is who has the responsibility for reducing emissions? I'm not asking what you feel the automotive industry is trying to do or not trying to do. I'm asking who you think has the responsibility for reducing emissions.

Mr. Hicks: From a legal standpoint?

Mrs. Kraft Sloan: No, I'm asking you in terms of that social responsibility.

Mr. Hicks: Well, it depends on which emissions. In automobiles, the automobile manufacturers have responsibility. In refineries or other stationary sources, the refiners have responsibility. So it depends on what kinds of emissions you're talking about, where they're coming from and what the law says. If we're talking about regulated automobile emissions, the auto manufacturers have to comply with the Clean Air Act standards.

Mrs. Kraft Sloan: I'm not talking about legal responsibility. I'm talking about any kind of social or environmental responsibility. I guess this is where the problem falls. The automotive industry is talking about a whole system approach, and if we are really trying to think environmentally – if we are really trying to address the kinds of problems we have in regard to environment and our human health – we have to understand who the players are.

I would suggest that people who have responsibility for reducing emissions are not just the automotive industry, but also the petroleum industry, the government and the consumer who uses those, as well. Forgive me if I'm wrong on that.

Mr. Hicks: I agree with you. (HSCESD10/24, 1995b, 46–7)

One should not make too much out of one exchange between an MP and a vice-president of Ethyl Canada, but the very idea of social responsibility seemed to be quite distant and foreign to Mr Hicks. Such unfamiliarity probably contributed to Ethyl Canada's corporate social performance regarding its endangered product MMT. However, a more general point can be made about corporate social responsibility as seen through the framework of NAFTA's Chapter 11.

Under Chapter 11, investors have only their self-interest to consider. To some extent, this may have political dimensions, for example, concerning their relationships with officials in the host state. Many companies, however, are quite comfortable operating in a context of legal "battle" with governments in the pursuit of their corporate interest. Indeed, trade law experts and negotiators have expressed the view that private participants in the trade law system are not constrained by anything other than their self-interest, which strongly differentiates them from governments that have to balance many public policy objectives in making any decision. (IISD/WWF 2001, 20)

In other words, Chapter 11 is crafted to allow investors to pursue their self-interests against the broader public interests that should be pursued by governments. Why is it reasonable or morally right that there should be a level playing field, let alone a biased playing field, between the interests of a private investor and the broader public interests? Why should a private investor's interests not be subject to the same laws as those of anyone else, and protected by democratic processes and public policy-making in which all interests have to be equally protected? From a broad-based consequentialist moral point of view, there is no good reason to support a dispute settlement system that privileges the protection of private wealth over the protection of our public environment or democratic public policy-making. From that point of view, the latter should be privileged.

The AIT case is more complicated than the NAFTA case, and it is not entirely clear whose interests are supposed to be served by its procedures. In the AIT case, the federal government's environmental strategy was undermined by that of provincial governments. The trouble is that Article 1505.2 explicitly allows each party (i.e., the federal government as well as the governments of each province and territory) to "establish [its] own environmental priorities and levels of environmental protection." This article is similar to that of Article 3 in the North American Agreement on Environmental Cooperation, where it makes some sense (Wagner 1999, 477). However, applied to Canada by itself, the article is incoherent. Since the territory of the federal government includes all the other territories, 1505.2 implies that the federal government's regulations should take precedence over those of a province or territory and that the latter should take precedence over those of the former, which is logically absurd.

An old and fairly deep problem with democracy and with any reasonable consequentialism is lurking here. From a moral and democratic point of view, we ought to pursue the greatest good for the greatest number, although the greatest number may not know what is the greatest good for themselves or anyone else. We certainly want to respect minority rights but, as John Stuart Mill (1859) explained, all rights must finally satisfy a general consequentialist principle. In chapter 2, I explained many of the very difficult problems with such principles, though I still believe they provide the basis for moral theories that are at least as good as any others. Soloway (1999, 91–4) touches on some of the same problems in measuring "domestic" versus "global welfare." In the fourteenth century the philosopher Marsilio of Padua made the democratic case about as well as anyone:

> As Aristotle said: "That is presumably right [i.e., in the laws] which is for the common benefit of the state and the citizens." But that this is best achieved only by the whole body of the citizens or by the weightier part thereof, which is assumed to be the same thing, I show as follows: that at which the entire body of the citizens aims intellectually and emotionally is more certainly judged as to its truth and more diligently considered as to its common utility. For a defect in some proposed law can be better noted by the greater number than by any part thereof, since every whole, or at least every corporeal whole, is greater in mass and in virtue than any part of it taken separately. Moreover, the common utility of a law is better considered by the entire multitude, because no one knowingly harms himself. (Marsilio of Padua 1324)

More recently, Schubert (1960, 204–5) wrote, "Decisions that are the product of a process of full consideration are most likely to be decisions in the public interest ... people accept democratic decision making processes because these provide the maximum opportunity for diverse interests to seek to influence governmental decisions at all levels."

The trouble is that Canada and other places where people believe in democratic rule by majorities are made up of diverse communities of diverse sizes and compositions, which occasionally produce more or less different visions of a good life and different laws to sustain it. So, for example, our city councils make collective decisions on behalf of their constituents, as do our provincial legislatures, federal parliaments, political parties, trade unions, and even NAFTA tribunals and AIT panels. Assuming, contrary to fact occasionally, that each collective decision is right for the group on whose behalf it is made, such decisions may not be right for other constituencies. In the AIT case, Ogilvy informed the panel that "for the citizens of Alberta, the Alberta government is best placed to determine the public interest in that territory ... This is not simply an interest group, this is the government that comes to you with a request to consider our submission" (AIT Hearings 1998a, 61).

Since Alberta does not issue passports and Canada does, those representing the Canadian government were at least as well positioned to argue that they were "best placed to determine the public interest in that territory," which happened to include Alberta.

I think the NAFTA tribunal and the AIT panel in the MMT cases made bad decisions for their constituents because I am assuming their constituents were not just the Ethyl Corporation and the Government of Canada in the former case and federal and provincial governments in the latter case. From a moral point of view, their constituents were everyone affected by their decisions, impartially considered. From that point of view, the Government of Canada's approach to weighing all the evidence was more appropriate.

Unfortunately, one must remember that the Government of Canada, along with the American and Mexican governments, agreed to NAFTA, just as the federal, provincial, and territorial governments agreed to the AIT. Those democratically elected governments, in imperfect democracies to be sure, invented and approved of those treaties, whose very existence created the necessary conditions for the poor decisions that were and will be made. Imperfect people crafted imperfect institutions in which other imperfect people operated to produce imperfect decisions and public policy. I believe that simply characterizes the human condition as it is and probably always will be, but I also believe we have a moral obligation to try to do better. Fortunately, we have the power to do better. Unlike the decisions of tribunals and panels in the NAFTA and AIT, respectively, the decisions of the Parliament of Canada are subject to public discussion and democratic control. This treatise is a modest contribution to that fundamental democratic process.

Relevant Parts of NAFTA

Article 1 102: National Treatment
1. Each Party shall accord to investors of another Party treatment no less favorable than that it accords, in like circumstances, to its own investors with respect to the establishment, acquisition, expansion, management, conduct, operation, and sale or other disposition of investments.
2. Each Party shall accord to investments of investors of another Party treatment no less favorable than that it accords, in like circumstances, to investments of its own investors with respect to the establishment, acquisition, expansion, management, conduct, operation, and sale or other disposition of investments.

Article 1106: Performance Requirements
1. No Party may impose or enforce any of the following requirements, or enforce any commitment or undertaking, in connection with the establishment, acquisition, expansion, management, conduct or operation of an investment of an investor of a Party or of a non-Party in its territory:
(a) to export a given level or percentage of goods or services;
(b) to achieve a given level or percentage of domestic content ...
6. Provided that such measures are not applied in an arbitrary or unjustifiable manner, or do not constitute a disguised restriction on international trade or investment, nothing in paragraph 1(b) or (c) or 3(a) or (b) shall be construed to prevent any Party from adopting or maintaining measures, including environmental measures:
(a) necessary to secure compliance with laws and regulations that are not inconsistent with the provisions of this agreement.
(b) necessary to protect human, animal or plant life or health; or
(c) necessary for the conservation of living or non-living exhaustible natural resources ...

Article 1110: Expropriation and Compensation

1. No Party may directly or indirectly nationalize or expropriate an investment of an investor of another Party in its territory or take a measure tantamount to nationalization or expropriation of such an investment ("expropriation"), except:

(a) for a public purpose;

(b) on a non-discriminatory basis;

(c) in accordance with due process of law and Article 1105(1); and

(d) on payment of compensation in accordance with paragraphs 2 through 6.

2. Compensation shall be equivalent to the fair market value of the expropriated investment immediately before the expropriation took place ("date of expropriation"), and shall not reflect any change in value occurring because the intended expropriation had become known earlier. Valuation criteria shall include going concern value, asset value including declared tax value of tangible property, and other criteria, as appropriate, to determine fair market value.

3. Compensation shall be paid without delay and be fully realizable ...

Article 1114: Environmental Measures

1. Nothing in this Chapter shall be construed to prevent a Party from adopting, maintaining or enforcing any measure otherwise consistent with this Chapter that it considers appropriate to ensure that investment activity in its territory is undertaken in a manner sensitive to environmental concerns.

2. The Parties recognize that it is inappropriate to encourage investment by relaxing domestic health, safety or environmental measures. Accordingly, a Party should not waive or otherwise derogate from, or offer to waive or otherwise derogate from, such measures as an encouragement for the establishment, acquisition, expansion or retention in its territory of an investment of an investor. If a Party considers that another Party has offered such an encouragement, it may request consultations with the other Party and the two Parties shall consult with a view to avoiding any such encouragement ...

Source: NAFTA 2002

Chronology of the MMT Case

Date	Actor	Event
1976	Canada	MMT begins replacing lead as octane enhancer in Canada
31 March 1977	EPA	U.S. Clean Air Act bans use of fuel or fuel additive in light-duty motor vehicles that is not "substantially similar" to those used in certifying 1975 models, unless an EPA waiver is obtained by showing the product "will not cause or contribute to a failure of any emission control device or system over the useful life of any vehicle.".
1978	Health Canada	Study concludes that there is no evidence at the time indicating expected ambient manganese concentrations would be a hazard to human health, making MMT an acceptable gasoline additive to replace lead.
17 March 1978	Ethyl/EPA	Ethyl Corporation makes first unsuccessful application to EPA for a waiver for MMT.
27 Jan. 1980	USA, Can., Mexico	Vienna Convention on the Law of Treaties comes into force and is accepted by Canada, USA and Mexico.
26 May 1981	Ethyl/EPA	Ethyl Corporation makes second unsuccessful application to EPA for a waiver, due to concerns about MMT increasing hydrocarbon emissions.
1970–90	Canada	Canada phases out lead in gasoline.
September 1985	Commiss. on Lead	Interim report of Royal Society of Canada Commission finds MMT an acceptable source of octane.

April 1986	CGSB	Canadian General Standards Board decides that MMT is not harmful to catalytic converters, other vehicle equipment, or urban air quality.
September 1986	Commiss. on Lead	Final report of the commission concludes that MMT is not likely to pose a threat to the environment or human health.
9 May 1990	Ethyl/EPA	Ethyl submits third waiver application but withdraws it on 1 Nov. 1990.
19 July 1990	MECA	Manufacturers of Emissions Controls Association (MECA) sends letter to Canadian Government indicating adverse affects of MMT on emissions control equipment performance.
July 1990	Environment Canada	Letter from John Buccini (EC) to EPA indicating that there is no evidence from car manufacturers or elsewhere that MMT causes significant problems for emission control systems.
7 Sept. 1990	MECA	MECA sends second letter to Canadian Government indicating adverse affects of MMT on emissions control equipment performance.
Oct. 1990	Ferguson	The Hon. Ralph Ferguson proposes a Private Member's Bill (C-333) in the House of Commons that would have banned MMT if it had passed.
5 Feb. 1991	NAFTA	Negotiations leading to NAFTA officially begin.
12–15 March 1991	NIEHS/EPA	National Institute of Environmental Health Sciences and EPA jointly hold international conference to determine research requirements to "improve its manganese health risk assessment."
12 July 1991	Ethyl/EPA	Ethyl Corporation submits fourth waiver application.
July 1991	Ethyl/EPA	EPA admits its tests were flawed, so Ethyl resubmits waiver application.
3 Oct. 1991	MECA	MECA sends third letter to Canadian Government indicating adverse affects of MMT on emissions control equipment performance.
8 January 1992	EPA/Ethyl	EPA rejects Ethyl's fourth waiver application in light of 1991 Ford Escort tests showing problems with hydrocarbon emissions.
13 Feb. 1992	Ethyl	Ethyl Corporation files petition for review in the U.S. Court of Appeals of the EPA decision of January 8.

20 Feb. 1992	Trans.Can/ MVMA/AIAMC	Transport Canada, Motor Vehicle Manufacturers Association (MVMA), and Association of International Automobile Manufacturers of Canada (AIAMC) sign Memorandum of Understanding denying warranty claims caused by "unique Canadian fuel composition."
5 June 1992	Ferguson	Ralph Ferguson, MP for Lambton-Middlesex, introduces private member's Bill C-226, Automotive Pollution Reduction Act
28 Oct. 1992	EPA	EPA holds public workshop to "assist the Agency in its attempt to formulate ... an emission testing program" likely to be applicable to future standards.
17 Dec. 1992	NAFTA	NAFTA is signed in Ottawa.
25 Feb. 1993	Parliament	Bill C-115, NAFTA legislation is first tabled in House of Commons.
6 April 1993	U.S. Court / EPA	U.S. Court of Appeals remands EPA's 8 January 1992 decision back to EPA for reconsideration.
June 1993	Ad-Hoc Committee	Ad-Hoc Joint Government-Industry Committee on Transportation Fuels and Vehicle Emissions Control Technology is formed to examine impact of MMT on emissions control equipment.
15 July 1993	Ethyl Corp.	Ethyl Corporation makes fourth request to EPA for waiver to sell MMT.
6 Aug. 1993	Ford	Ford Motor Company recommends that EPA deny the fourth application (15 July 1993) from Ethyl Corporation for a waiver for MMT.
17 Aug. 1993	Joint Gov. Industry Committee	Joint Government-Industry Committee on Transportation Fuels and Motor Vehicle Control Technologies asks government officials to draft a "consensus statement" on harmonization between Canada and USA.
30 Nov. 1993	EPA	EPA decides that MMT does not contribute to the failure of emission control systems, and allows Ethyl to resubmit its application on that date while EPA continues to investigate health risks.
1 Dec. 1993	EPA	Most recent RfC for inhaled manganese (i.e., $0.05\mu g\ Mn/m^{3)}$ comes into effect.

June 1993– Sept. 1994	Stakeholders	Five unsuccessful meetings are held between government and industry representatives to reach agreement on MMT issues, after which the issues returned to the responsible ministers.
1 Jan. 1994	NAFTA	NAFTA enters into force.
27 May 1994	EPA	Clean Air Act Amendments come into effect establishing "new health effects testing requirements."
13 July 1994	EPA	EPA denies Ethyl's waiver application of 30 November 1993, based on unresolved health issues related to manganese emissions.
18 July 1994	First Ministers	Agreement on Internal Trade (AIT) is signed by first ministers of the Government of Canada, 10 provinces, and two territories.
September 1994	MVMA	Vehicle manufacturers warn Environment Minister Sheila Copps of possible $3,000 cost per vehicle for damaged onboard diagnostic equipment if MMT is not removed from gasoline.
12 Oct. 1994	MVMA/CPPI	The MVMA and Canadian Petroleum Products Institute (CPPI) agree to harmonize their efforts to improve air quality following "consensus statement" of the Government-Industry Committee (17 Aug. 1993), and inform Transport Canada and Environment Canada.
12 Oct. 1994	Env. Canada	Copps tells Canadian press reporter that if oil industry does not voluntarily remove MMT before August 1995, she will introduce legislation requiring its removal.
14 Oct. 1994	MVMA	Informs CPPI that if MMT is not eliminated from gasoline then warranties on emission control devices will be altered.
27 Oct. 1994	CPPI	CPPI issues news release saying it will remove MMT from gasoline if an independent scientific panel determines that it harms air quality.
11 Nov. 1994	CPPI	CPPI congratulates Copps on a successful Canadian Council of Ministers of the Environment (CCME) meeting, rejects MVMA's request to eliminate MMT, and calls for further research.
18 Nov. 1994	Env. Canada Min. Copps	Copps asks vehicle and refining industries to resolve MMT issue by end of year.

24 Nov. 1994	EPA	Ethyl Corp. is informed that special Tier 2 testing will be required.
30 Nov. 1994	EPA	EPA says that "use of HiTEC 3000 [MMT] at the specified concentration will not cause or contribute to a failure of any emission control device or system.
November 1994	CCME	CCME Task Force on Cleaner Vehicles and Fuels begins to examine MMT but stops when Bill C-94 is introduced.
19 Dec. 1994	MVMA & AIAMC	MVMA & AIAMC present their case and data to CPPI showing adverse effects of MMT on emissions control and monitoring equipment.
December 1994	Health Canada	Wood and Egyed risk assessment report on MMT is released finding no significant threat to health posed by manganese in the environment resulting from using MMT in gasoline.
6 Jan. 1995	MVMA & CPPI	MVMA informs Minister Copps that MMT-free gasoline is being sold to manufacturing firms but not to the general public; CPPI agrees to form Technical Task Force.
17–19 Jan. 1995	CPPI	First meeting of CPPI Technical Task Force.
18 Jan. 1995	MVMA & AIAMC	MVMA & AIAMC present their case and data to CPPI showing adverse effects of MMT on emissions control and monitoring equipment.
28 Jan. 1995	Chrysler Canada	Chrysler Canada shows warranty data to CPPI indicating adverse effects of MMT on vehicle equipment.
1 Feb. 1995	CPPI	CPPI sends letter to Copps saying MMT would be removed from gasoline only if required by legislation.
8 Feb. 1995	MVMA & AIAMC	MVMA & AIAMC propose a two-pump solution to CPPI.
10 Feb. 1995	CPPI	CPPI rejects the two-pump solution and proposes further research.
17 Feb. 1995	MVMA & AIAMC	Letters are sent to Copps rejecting the CPPI proposal for further research.
17 Feb. 1995	Env. Canada	Press release from Copps saying Canadian Government will take action on MMT.
24 Feb. 1995	Industry Canada	Industry Canada advises Environment Canada that Ethyl Canada would lose millions of dollars and half its total sales revenue if it loses MMT business.

28 Feb. 1995	CPPI	CPPI Technical Task Force Report says it cannot reconcile differences between the vehicle industry and Ethyl, and recommends more research.
2 March 1995	Carter	Carter Report says "data are incomplete and contradictory," but equipment manufacturers' data are "more relevant and credible."
16 March 1995	Walsh	Walsh Report says lab and real world data indicate use of MMT in gasoline increases HC emissions.
5 April 1995	Env. Canada	Press release saying government plans to draft legislation to prohibit the importation of and interprovincial trade in MMT.
14 April 1995	U.S. Court	U.S. Court of Appeals rules that EPA had no right to reject Ethyl's waiver application based on health issues (see July 1994).
19 May 1995	Env. Canada	Bill C-94 (later C-29), the Manganese-based Fuel Additives Act that bans importation and interprovincial trade of MMT, is introduced (First Reading) by Copps in the House of Commons.
19 May 1995	Env. Canada	Copps holds press conference detailing government policy of banning inter-provincial trade and importation of MMT; Env. Canada issues press release to same effect.
1 July 1995	Canadian Governments	AIT comes into effect for federal, provincial, and territorial governments.
19 Sept. 1995	House of Commons	The House gives second reading to Bill C-94 and sends it to House of Commons Committee.
October 1995	CCME	CCME receives report from Task Force on Cleaner Vehicles and Fuels.
18 Oct. 1995	Abraham & Lawless	Independent review of Ethyl's data on MMT's reduction of NO_x emissions found to be not statistically significant.
18,19,24,26 October 1995	House of Commons	House Standing Committee on Environment and Sustainable Development holds hearings on Bill C-94.
26 Oct. 1995	House Committee	House Standing Committee on Environment and Sustainable Development concludes hearings on C-94, agrees to report to the House acceptance without any changes.

23 Oct. 1995	CCME	CCME endorses Task Force report and agrees to work on implementing the report's recommendations.
November 1995	U.S. Court/EPA	EPA is ordered by U.S. Court of Appeals to register MMT as fuel additive.
2 Feb. 1996	Parliament	Parliament prorogued; Bill C-94 dies on the order paper after debates over 8-day period.
23 Feb. 1996	Trade Ministry	Trade Minister Art Eggleton warns Environment Minister Sergio Marchi that Bill C-94 would be inconsistent with NAFTA and WTO obligations.
March 1996	Env. Canada	Marchi reintroduces Bill C-94 as Bill C-29.
18 April 1996	Env. Canada	Press release saying government will re-introduce Bill C-94 at Third Reading state; Marchi states his concerns about negative health and environmental effects of MMT.
22 April 1996	Env. Canada	Bill C-94 is re-introduced at Third Reading as Bill C-29
May 1996	Québec Nat. Assembly	The Assembly unanimously passes a resolution asking federal government to suspend passage of the MMT Act.
31 July 1996	Prime Minister	Prime Minister Jean Chrétien asks ministers of environment, trade, industry, and natural resources to review Bill C-29 and report in the fall.
10 Sept. 1996	Ethyl Corp.	Ethyl files Notice of Intent to submit a claim to arbitration under Section B of Chapter 11 of NAFTA, and asks Canadian government to negotiate a resolution of their grievance.
16 Sept. 1996	*Ottawa Citizen*	The paper publishes letter from Environment Minister saying MMT endangers "our children's health" and "the air we breathe and the water we drink."
25 Sept. 1996	House of Commons	The house begins debate on Bill C-29 covering a 10-day period.
10 Oct. 1996	Parliamentary Secretary	Parliamentary Secretary to Minister of the Environment says banning and replacing MMT will benefit Canadians, as opposed to "giving all of the money to an American firm."
25 Oct. 1996	CARB	California Air Resources Board (CARB) releases report saying OBD systems are "very effective in detecting emissions-related problems in-use."

12 Nov. 1996	Ethyl & Canada	Meeting is held between representatives of Ethyl and Canada, which Ethyl claims and Canada denies satisfied a NAFTA consultation requirement.
20 Nov. 1996	CPPI	Representing the Alberta refining industry, the CPPI asks the Government of Alberta to initiate a formal complaint under the AIT against Bill C-29.
2 Dec. 1996	House of Commons	Bill C-29 is passed by House of Commons (Third Reading).
3 Dec. 1996	Can. Senate	Bill C-29 is introduced to Senate for First Reading.
17 Dec. 1996	Can. Senate	Bill C-29 is given Second Reading and sent to Senate Standing Committee on Energy, the Environment and Natural Resources.
4 March 1997	Can. Senate	Senate Standing Committee issues Interim Report saying Bill C-29 was justified on precautionary principles, Minority Opinion is filed.
9 April 1997	Can. Senate	Bill C-29 is passed by Senate (Third Reading).
14 April 1997	Ethyl	Ethyl files Notice of Arbitration under NAFTA, appoints Charles N. Brower as its arbitrator.
25 April 1997	Env. Canada	Bill C-29 is given Royal Assent.
28 April 1997	Alberta	On behalf of Alberta refiners, Government of Alberta requests consultations with Government of Canada under AIT Annex 1510.1.
12 May 1997	Alberta	Forty-day consultation period begins under AIT Chapter 15.
11 June 1997	Alberta	Consultations under AIT Chapter 15 end.
12 June 1997	Alberta	Alberta informs Canada that consultations were unsuccessful.
23 June 1997	Ethyl Canada	Ethyl files a Statement of Claim in the Ontario Court (General Division) against the Attorney General of Canada and the Minister of the Environment asserting that the MMT Act is ultra vires the Parliament of Canada and enjoining the defendants from enforcing the Act.
24 June 1997	Canadian Government	Bill C-29 comes into force sixty days after Royal Assent.
7 July 1997	CPPI	CPPI sends letter to CVMA and AIAMC agreeing to voluntarily phase out MMT if science supported the need.

8 July 1997	Ethyl	Ethyl prepares letters giving consent to arbitration and waiving its right to proceed under alternative rules, but does not give these letters to the Government of Canada until October 2.
14 July 1997	Canadian Government	The government confirms appointment of Marc Lalonde as its arbitrator.
23 July 1997	Canadian Government	The government grants Ethyl's point from the constitutional challenge of 23 June 1997.
28 July 1997	Canadian Government	Amendments to the Motor Vehicle Safety Regulations come into force harmonizing U.S. and Canadian emissions standards for HC, CO and No$_x$, and requiring OBD systems on 1998 and future models.
5 August 1997	Alberta	Following 90-day Chapter 15 time limit, Alberta requests second round of consultations under AIT Chapter 17.
2 Sept. 1997	UNCITRAL /NAFTA	Tribunal is established under UNCITRAL/NAFTA, with Professor Karl-Heinz Böckstiegel appointed as presiding arbitrator.
8 Sept. 1997	Alberta & Canada	Complainants and respondent agree that further consultations would be useless.
15 Sept. 1997	Canadian Government	The government gives consent to Government of Alberta to request appointment of a Dispute Resolution Panel under AIT Article 1704.
2 Oct. 1997	Ethyl	Ethyl files Statement of Claim under UNCITRAL/NAFTA, and delivers letters dated 8 July 1997.
16 Oct. 1997	Alberta	Alberta files request to form a Dispute Resolution Panel under AIT Article 1704.
27 Nov. 1997	DFAIT	Canadian Department of Foreign Affairs and International Trade files its Statement of Defence against Ethyl Corporation in NAFTA case.
28 Nov. 1997	NAFTA Tribunal	Decision regarding the place of arbitration is made for Toronto.
1 Dec. 1977	Alberta	Alberta files written submission in support of complaint under AIT.
19 Dec. 1997	Québec	Québec files Brief from Québec, Interested Party under AIT.
15 Jan. 1998	Saskatchewan	Saskatchewan files Submission on Behalf of the Government of Saskatchewan under AIT.

26 Jan. 1998	Canada	Canada files written Submission of the Responding Party under AIT.
29 Jan. 1998	Canada	CCME's Canada-Wide Accord on Environmental Harmonization comes into force.
15–16 April 1998	AIT Panel/ Disputants	Hearings are held in Ottawa before AIT Panel.
12 June 1998	AIT Panel	Panel decides Bill C-29 is inconsistent with AIT Articles 402 and 403.
24 June 1998	NAFTA Tribunal	Tribunal issues its Award on Jurisdiction in Bill C-29 challenge, allowing case to go forward.
20 July 1998	Canadian Government	In response to AIT Panel decision, Industry Minister John Manley and Environment Minister Christine Stewart lift restrictions on inter-provincial trade and import of MMT, and agree to pay Ethyl $13 million to cover costs of NAFTA litigation and lost revenue.
25 Jan. 1999	EPA	EPA proposes specific Tier 2 "test program" for Ethyl to carry out regarding health effects of MMT.

SOURCES: This table was constructed using information from: Government of Alberta 1997; Hughes, Evernden, and Tyhurst 1997; Canada 1998; Clarke 1997; Böckstiegel, Brower, and Lalonde 1998; Gilson, Castonguay, Kelly, Mauro, and Rae 1998; NRTEE 1999; Oge 1999; Soloway 1999; Hill and Leiss 2001; Internal Trade Secretariat 2002; NAFTA Secretariat 2002.

Relevant Parts of AIT

Article 100: Objective
It is the objective of the Parties to reduce and eliminate, to the extent possible, barriers to the free movement of persons, goods, services and investments within Canada and to establish an open, efficient and stable domestic market. All Parties recognize and agree that enhancing trade and mobility within Canada would contribute to the attainment of this goal.

Article 101: Mutually Agreed Principles

... 3. c) Parties will reconcile relevant standards and regulatory measures to provide for the free movement of persons, goods, services and investments within Canada; ...

Article 200: Definitions of General Application

... **harmonization** means making identical or minimizing the differences between standards or related measures of similar scope ...

mutual recognition means the acceptance by a Party of a person, good, service or investment that conforms with an equivalent standard or standards-related measure of another Party without modification, testing, certification, re-naming or undergoing any other duplicative conformity assessment procedure; ...

Article 401: Reciprocal Non-Discrimination
1. Subject to Article 404, each Party shall accord to goods of any other Party treatment no less favourable than the best treatment it accords to:

(a) its own like, directly competitive or substitutable goods; and
(b) like, directly competitive or substitutable goods of any other Party or non-Party.

2. Subject to Article 404, each Party shall accord to persons, services and investments of any other Party treatment no less favourable than the best treatment it accords, in like circumstances, to:

(a) its own persons, services and investments; and
(b) persons, services and investments of any other Party or non-Party.

3. With respect to the Federal Government, paragraphs 1 and 2 mean that, subject to Article 404, it shall accord to:

(a) the goods of a Province treatment no less favourable than the best treatment it accords to like, directly competitive or substitutable goods of any other Province or non-Party; and
(b) the persons, services and investments of a Province treatment no less favourable than the best treatment it accords, in like circumstances, to persons, services and investments of any other Province or non-Party.

4. The Parties agree that according identical treatment may not necessarily result in compliance with paragraph 1, 2 or 3.

Article 402: Right of Entry and Exit
Subject to Article 404, no Party shall adopt or maintain any measure that restricts or prevents the movement of persons, goods, services or investments across provincial boundaries.

Article 403: No Obstacles
Subject to Article 404, each Party shall ensure that any measure it adopts or maintains does not operate to create an obstacle to internal trade.

Article 404: Legitimate Objectives
Where it is established that a measure is inconsistent with Article 401, 402 or 403, that measure is still permissible under this Agreement where it can be demonstrated that:

(a) the purpose of the measure is to achieve a legitimate objective;
(b) the measure does not operate to impair unduly the access of persons, goods, services or investments of a Party that meet that legitimate objective;
(c) the measure is not more trade restrictive than necessary to achieve that legitimate objective; and
(d) the measure does not create a disguised restriction on trade.

Article 405: Reconciliation
1. In order to provide for the free movement of persons, goods, services and investments within Canada, the Parties shall, in accordance with Annex 405.1, reconcile

their standards and standards-related measures by harmonization, mutual recognition or other means.

2. Where a difference, duplication or overlap in regulatory measures or regulatory regimes operates to create an obstacle to internal trade, the Parties shall, in accordance with Annex 405.2, cooperate with a view to addressing the difference, duplication or overlap.

Annex 405.1: Standards and Standards-Related Measures
13. In order to minimize potential obstacles to internal trade, the Parties shall establish mechanisms to consult and cooperate on matters relating to standards and standards-related measures.
14. Where a difference between a standard or standards-related measure of a Party and that of another Party is identified by a Party as operating to create an obstacle to internal trade, the affected Parties shall jointly conduct a review of the matter for the reconciliation of those standards or standards-related measures and make the results available.

Annex 405.2: Regulatory Measures and Regulatory Regimes
9. Where differing regulatory measures or regulatory regimes of several Parties operate to create a substantial obstacle to internal trade, the affected Parties shall jointly conduct a review of the aspects of the regulatory measures or regulatory regimes that are creating the obstacle ...

Article 606: Corporate Registration and Reporting Requirements
The Parties shall endeavour to reconcile extra-provincial corporate registration and reporting requirements for enterprises incorporated under the law of any Party. The Parties shall, no later than July 15, 1995, prepare an implementation plan for consideration by the Committee ...

Article 708: Recognition of Occupational Qualifications and Reconciliation of Occupational Standards
Subject to Article 709, each Party undertakes to mutually recognize the occupational qualifications required of workers of any other Party and to reconcile differences in occupational standards in the manner specified in Annex 708. The Red Seal program shall be the primary method through which occupational qualifications in regulated trades are recognized. [Article 709 describes Legitimate Objectives in language similar to Article 404 above.] ...

Article 807: Reconciliation of Consumer-Related Measures and Standards
1. For the purposes of Article 405 (Reconciliation), the Parties shall, to the greatest extent possible, reconcile their respective consumer-related measures and standards listed in Annex 807.1 to a high and effective level of consumer protection. No Party shall be required by such reconciliation to lower the level of consumer protection that it maintains as at the date of entry into force of this Agreement.

2. The list of measures and standards in Annex 807.1 may be expanded in accordance with Article 809 ...

Article 1007: Reconciliation
1. For the purposes of Article 405 (Reconciliation), each Party shall endeavour, where practicable, to undertake to reconcile, through harmonization or other means, standards-related measures such as labeling and packaging regulations and requirements and oenological practices ...

Article 1105: Reconciliation
1. The Parties shall make every effort to reconcile, in accordance with Annex 405.1, their measures that have an impact on trade in the processing of natural resources.
2. Further to Annex 405.1, the reconciliation of measures adopted or maintained for a legitimate objective, such as the protection of health or safety or the protection of the environment, in accordance with this Chapter shall be based on criteria including, but not limited to, the following:

(a) a reasonable level of scientific and technical evidence;
(b) an assessment of the economic and environmental costs of the non-implementation of the measure; and
(c) the economic feasibility of the measure.

3. For greater certainty, a measure referred to in paragraph 2 shall not be considered to be inconsistent with this Agreement by reason solely of the lack of full scientific certainty regarding the need for the measure ...

Article 1408: Reconciliation
1. Further to Article 405 (Reconciliation), the Parties shall reconcile, by harmonization, mutual recognition or other means, their regulatory and standards-related measures in accordance with Annexes 405.1 and 405.2 and their measures listed in Annex 1408.1 in accordance with that Annex.
2. Article 1415 and Chapter Seventeen (Dispute Resolution Procedures) do not apply to disputes relating to compliance with this Article ...

Article 1508: Harmonization
1. The Parties shall endeavour to harmonize environmental measures that may directly affect interprovincial mobility and trade, following principles such as those set out in the "Statement of Interjurisdictional Cooperation on Environmental Matters" (Winnipeg: CCME, 1991) and "Rationalizing the Management Regime for the Environment: Purpose, Objectives and Principles" (Winnipeg: CCME, 1994) any other applicable principles established by the Council, and this Agreement.

2. In harmonizing environmental measures, the Parties shall maintain and endeavour to strengthen existing levels of environmental protection. The Parties shall not, through such harmonization, lower the levels of environmental protection.

3. In the event of an inconsistency between Article 405 (Reconciliation) and this Article, this Article prevails to the extent of the inconsistency ...

Source: AIT 2002

Participants in the AIT Panel Hearings

The Panel
Clay Gilson, c.m. – chair
Claude Castonguay, c.c., o.q.
Kathleen Kelly
Arthur Mauro, o.c., q.c.
Bob Rae, p.c., q.c

Mark Newman – Counsel to the Panel
Fillmore Riley .

For Alberta
Internal Trade Representative
   James Ogilvy – Intergovern-
   mental & Aboriginal Affairs

For Canada
Internal Trade Representative
   Tom Wallace – Industry

Counsel
   Lorne Ternes – Justice

Counsel
   Brian Evernden – Justice
   John Tyhurst – Justice

Other Officials
Doug Younie – Environmental
Protection
Fulvio Fracassi – Environment
Irving Miller – Justice

Other Officials
Frank Vena – Environment

For Québec
Acting Internal Trade Representative
   Barry Le Blanc – Canadian
   Intergovernmental Affairs

For Saskatchewan
Internal Trade Representative
   Robert Perrin – Intergovernmental &
   Aboriginal Affairs

Counsel
  Jean-François Jobin – Justice

Counsel
  Linda Zarzecny – Justice

Other Officials
Claude Sauvé – Environment &
Wildlife
Françoise St -Martin – Natural
Resources Management
Raynald Archambault – Natural
Resources

Other Officials
Scott Robinson – Environment &
Resource

Internal Trade Secretariat
André Dimitrijevic, Executive Director   Gord Greasley, Policy Advisor
SOURCE: Gilson, Castonguay, Kelly, Mauro, and Rae 1998

Copy of Letter from U.S. Corporations to U.S. Trade Representative

19 April 2001
The Honorable Robert Zoellick
United States Trade Representative
600 17th St. NW
Washington, DC 20508

Dear Ambassador Zoellick:

We are writing to affirm the business community's support for the inclusion of effective investment provisions in the proposed Free Trade Agreement of the Americas (FTAA) and in free trade agreements with Chile and Singapore.

International investment is a sine qua non for U.S. firms to compete successfully in today's globalized economy. Investment is a principal catalyst for economic growth in developing countries and helps to ensure that globalization is an inclusive, rather than an exclusive process.

Investment agreements facilitate the objective by helping to create stable business environments, which in turn generate substantial growth opportunities. To that end, we endorse investment provisions, modeled on NAFTA, to achieve the following:

- removal of barriers to entry;
- 100 percent foreign ownership of investments permitted;
- non-discriminatory and fair and equitable treatment guaranteed;
- elimination of performance requirements;
- protection of assets from direct or indirect expropriation, to include protection from regulations that diminish the value of investors' assets;

- guarantee that investor disputes with host governments can be brought to arbitration panels such as those offered by the World Bank's Center for Dispute Settlement; and transparency in government rulemaking.

Recently, u.s. investment agreements have come under attack. Citing recent cases, critics argue that NAFTA's investment rules, and the findings of 'secret' arbitration panels impede a government's ability to promote environmental protection. We respectfully disagree. Investment treaty provisions are no bar to, but can compliment [sic] strong, effective, and transparent regulations to protect the environment, as well as worker safety and health. Indeed, investment treaty protection serves to encourage international investment which frequently includes the transfer of environmental technologies and practices. We would be pleased to work with you to develop ideas to address these issues.

Identical letters are being sent to Secretaries Powell, Evans and O'Neill.

Thank you for consideration of our views.

Sincerely,
American Chemistry Council
American Forest and Paper Association
Caltex Corporation
Chevron
Chubb Corporation
Daimler-Chrysler
The Dow Chemical Company
E.I. Du Pont De Nemours and Company
Eastman Chemical Company
Emergency Committee for American Trade
The Estée Lauder Companies, Inc.
Ford Motor Company
General Electric
General Motors Corporation
Hills and Company
Honeywell International Inc.
International Paper
3M
Metalclad Corporation
Motorola Inc.
National Association of Manufacturers
National Foreign Trade Council
Pacific Basin Economic Council, u.s. Committee
PricewaterhouseCoopers LLP
Procter & Gamble

Texaco Inc.
U.S. Chamber of Commerce
United States Council for International Business
United Parcel Service
(Published in World Trade Online, the electronic service of Inside U.S. Trade)

SOURCE: Sinclair 2001

References

Abbott, F.M., 2000. "The political economy of NAFTA Chapter 11: Equality before the law and the boundaries of North American integration." *Hastings International and Comparative Law Review* 23: 303–9.

Abouchar, J.A. and R.J. King, 1999. "Environmental laws as expropriation under NAFTA." *Review of European Community and International Environmental Law* 8(2): 209–14.

Abraham, B. and J.F. Lawless, 1995. *Analysis of 1988 and 1992–93 Ethyl Corporation Test Fleet HC and NOₓ Emissions.* Waterloo: Institute for Improvement in Quality and Productivity, University of Waterloo.

Adler, U. (ed.), 1995. *Automotive Electric/Electronic Systems.* Stuttgart: Robert Bosch Gmbh.

AIT 1998a. *Agreement on Internal Trade, Dispute Regarding the Manganese-based Fuel Additives Act, Submission by the Complaining Party, The Government of Alberta, Supporting Documents, Volumes 1 and 2.*

– 1998b. *Agreement on Internal Trade, Dispute Regarding the Manganese-based Fuel Additives Act, Submission of the Responding Party, The Government of Canada, Supporting Documents, Volume 2.*

– 2002. *Agreement on Internal Trade.* http//www.intrasec.mb.ca/eng/it.htm.

AIT Hearings 1998a. *The Agreement on Internal Trade, Article 1704 Panel Hearings Concerning a Dispute between Alberta and Canada regarding the Manganese-Based Fuel Additives Act, Volume 1.* Wednesday, 15 April 1998.

– 1998b. *The Agreement on Internal Trade, Article 1704 Panel Hearings Concerning a Dispute between Alberta and Canada regarding the Manganese-Based Fuel Additives Act, Volume 1A.* Wednesday, 15 April 1998.

– 1998c. *The Agreement on Internal Trade, Article 1704 Panel Hearings Concerning a Dispute between Alberta and Canada regarding the Manganese-Based Fuel Additives Act, Volume 2.* Thursday, 16 April 1998.

Albo, G., 1994. "'Competitive austerity' and the impasse of capitalist employment policy." In R. Miliband and L. Panitch (eds), *Between Globalism and Nationalism: The Socialist Register 1994*. London: Merlin Press.

Alliance of Automobile Manufacturers 2002a. *MMT Program Part 1 Report*. July 29. www.autoalliance.org.

– 2002b. *MMT Program Part 2 Report*. July 29. www.autoalliance.org.

Alliance for Responsible Trade et al., 1999. *Alternatives for the Americas: Building a People's Hemispheric Agreement*. Ottawa and Don Mills: Canadian Centre for Policy Alternatives and Common Frontiers.

Allison, J.R., 1986. "Arbitration of private antitrust claims in international trade: A study in the subordination of national interests to the demands of a world market." *New York University Journal of International Law and Politics* 18(2): 361–439.

Appleton, B., 1994. *Navigating NAFTA: A Concise User's Guide to the North American Free Trade Agreement*. Scarborough, Ontario: Carswell.

– 1996. *Notice of Intent to Submit a Claim to Arbitration under Section B of Chapter 11 of the North American Free Trade Agreement, Ethyl Corporation (Investor) v. Government of Canada (Party)*. September 10.

– 1997a. *Notice of Arbitration Under the Arbitration Rules of the United Nations Commission on International Trade Law and the North American Free Trade Agreement Between Ethyl Corporation (Claimant/Investor) v. Government of Canada (Respondent/Party)*. April 14.

– 1997b. *Statement of Claim Between Ethyl Corporation (Claimant/Investor) v. Government of Canada (Respondent/Party)*. October 2.

Aristotle, 1925. *Ethica Nichomachea*. W.D. Ross (trans). Oxford: Clarendon Press.

Asik, J.R. and D. Anglin, 1997. "Spark knock." *McGraw-Hill Encyclopedia of Science and Technology*. New York: McGraw-Hill. 176–8.

Audley, J., 2002. "Environment's new role in U.S. trade policy." *Trade, Equity and Development* 3: 1–8, September. Carnegie Endowment for International Peace.

– D.G. Papademetriou, S. Polaski, and S. Vaughan, 2003. *NAFTA's Promise and Reality: Lessons from Mexico for the Hemisphere*. Washington: Carnegie Endowment for International Peace. Accessed at www.ceip.org/pubs.

Baier, G., 2003. "The law of federalism: judicial review and the division of powers." In F. Rocher and M. Smith (eds), *New Trends in Canadian Federalism*. Peterborough: Broadview Press. 111–34.

Benson, J.D. and G. Dana, 2002. "The impact of MMT gasoline additive on exhaust emissions and fuel economy of low emission vehicles (LEV)." *SAE Technical Paper Series*, 2002–01–2894.

Bentham, J., 1789. *An Introduction to the Principles of Morals and Legislation.* Oxford.

Bernstein, S., 2002. *The Compromise of Liberal Environmentalism.* New York: Columbia University Press.

– and N. Cashore, 2002. "Globalization, internationalization, and liberal environmentalism: Exploring non-domestic sources of influence on Canadian environmental policy." In D.L. VanNijnatten and R. Boardman (eds), *Canadian Environmental Policy Context and Cases.* Second edition. Oxford: Oxford University Press. 212–32.

Bhuie, A.K. and D.N. Roy, 2001. "Deposition of Mn from automotive combustion of methylcyclopentadienyl manganese tricarbonyl beside the major highways in the greater Toronto area, Canada." *Journal of the Air and Waste Management Association* 51: 1288–301.

Boardman, R., 2002. "Milk-and-potatoes environmentalism: Canada and the turbulent world of international law." In D.L. VanNijnatten and R. Boardman (eds), *Canadian Environmental Policy: Context and Cases.* Don Mills: Oxford University Press. 190–211.

Böckstiegel, K.-H., C.N. Brower, and M. Lalonde, 1998. *Award on Jurisdiction in the NAFTA/UNCITRAL Case between Ethyl Corporation (Claimant) and the Government of Canada (Respondent) before the Tribunal consisting of Prof. Dr. Karl-Heinz Böckstiegel (Chairman), Mr. Charles N. Brower (Arbitrator), Mr. Marc Lalonde (Arbitrator).* June 24.

Braadbaart, O., 1998. "American bias in environmental economics: Industrial pollution abatement and 'incentives versus regulations'." *Environmental Politics* 7(2): 134–52.

Breton, A., 1995. "A comment." In M.J. Trebilcock and D. Schwanen (eds), *Getting There: An Assessment of the Agreement on Internal Trade.* Toronto: C.D. Howe Institute. 90–4.

Brouillard, C.F., 1995a. Letter to the Honourable Sheila Copps. February 1. *Agreement on Internal Trade, Dispute Regarding the Manganese-based Fuel Additives Act Submission of the Responding Party, The Government of Canada, Supporting Documents, Volume 2.*

– 1995b. Letter to the Honourable Sheila Copps. February 15. *Agreement on Internal Trade, Dispute Regarding the Manganese-based Fuel Additives Act Submission of the Responding Party, The Government of Canada, Supporting Documents, Volume 2.*

Brower, C.N., 1994. "Evidence before international tribunals: The need for some standard rules." *The International Lawyer* 28(1): 47–58.

– and L.A. Steven, 2001. "Who then should judge?: Developing the international rule of law under NAFTA Chapter 11." *Chicago Journal of International Law* 2: 193–202.

Canada 1998. *Agreement on Internal Trade, Dispute Regarding the Manganese-based Fuel Additives Act, Submission of the Respondent Party, The Government of Canada.* January 26.

CCME 1991. *Statement of Interjurisdictional Cooperation on Environmental Matters.* Winnipeg: CCME.

– 2002a. *About CCME.* http//www.ccme.ca/le_about/le.htm. January 31.

– 2002b. *A Canada-Wide Accord on Environmental Harmonization.* http//www. ccme.ca/3e_priorities/3ea_harmonization/3ea1_accord/3eal.htm.February 5.

– 2002c. *CCME History.* Winnipeg: CCME.

CCPA 2001. "NAFTA investor rights plus: An analysis of the draft investment chapter of the FTAA." *Briefing Paper Series: Trade and Investment* 2(5): 1–12. Ottawa: Canadian Centre for Policy Alternatives.

CEPA 1999. *Canadian Environmental Protection Act, 1999.* http//laws.justice.gc.ca/ en/C–15.31/text.htrr.

Chatterjee, P. and M. Finger, 1994. *The Earth Brokers.* New York: Routledge.

Chibueze, R.O., 2001. "The adoption and application of the Model Law in Canada: Post-Arbitration Challenge." *Journal of International Arbitration* 18(2): 191–209.

Clarke, H.A., 1997. *Affidavit of H.A. (Tony) Clarke: Ontario Court (General Division) between Ethyl Canada Inc. (Plaintiff) and the Attorney General of Canada and the Minister of the Environment (Defendants).* August 28.

– and M. Barlow, 1998. *MAI Round 2: New Global and Internal Threats to Canadian Sovereignty.* Toronto: Stoddart Publishing.

Clarkson, S., 2002a. *Uncle Sam and Us: Globalization, Neoconservatism, and the Canadian State.* Toronto: University of Toronto Press.

– 2002b. "Systemic or surgical? Possible cures for NAFTA's investor-state dispute process." *Canadian Business Law Journal* 36(3): 368–87.

– 2003. *Ontario Superior Court of Justice, Between: The Council of Canadians, and Dale Clark, Deborah Bourque, and George Kuehnbaum on their own behalf and on behalf of all members of the Canadian Union of Postal Workers (Applicants) and Her Majesty in Right of Canada, as Represented by the Attorney General of Canada (Respondents), Affidavit, Court File No. 01-CV-208141.* May.

Clendenning, E.W. and R.J. Clendenning, 1999. *A Comparative Study of the Structure, General Rules, Dispute Settlement Mechanisms and Sectoral Provisions of the Agreement on Internal Trade (AIT) with those of the NAFTA and WTO Agreements.* Ottawa: Internal Trade, Consultations and Federal-Provincial Relations, Industry Canada).

Coase, R.H., 1960. "The problem of social cost." *The Journal of Law and Economics* 3: 1–44.

Coe, J.J., 2002. "Domestic court control of investment awards: Necessary evil or Achilles heel within NAFTA and the proposed FTAA?" *Journal of International Arbitration* 19(3): 185–207.

Cohen, D., 1995. "The Internal Trade Agreement: Furthering the Canadian economic disunion." *Canadian Business Law Journal* 25(2): 257–79.

Commission on Lead in the Environment 1985. *Lead in Gasoline: A Review of the Canadian Policy Issue, Interim Report.* September 30. Ottawa: Royal Society of Canada.

– 1986. *Lead in the Canadian Environment: Science and Regulation, Final Report.* September. Ottawa: Royal Society of Canada.

Commissioner of the Environment and Sustainable Development 2001. *Petition No. 32 – Fuel additive MMT.* http//www.oag-bvg.gc.ca/domino/petition... iewe1.0/704B3377E8CAOCB285256C5600689A6. Accessed 4 November 2003.

Copeland, B., 1998. *Interprovincial Barriers to Trade: An Updated Review of the Evidence.* Victoria: BC Ministry of Employment and Investment.

Copps, S., 1994. Letter to Mr. Toshio Kunii, President Toyota Canada Inc. *Agreement on Internal Trade, Dispute Regarding the Manganese-based Fuel Additives Act Submission of the Responding Party, The Government of Canada, Supporting Documents, Volume 2.*

Cordes, M., 1997. "Leapfrogging the Constitution: the rise of State takings legislation." *Ecology Law Quarterly* 24(2): 187–242.

Cosbey, A., 2004. *A Capabilities Approach to Trade and Sustainable Development: Using Sen's Conception of Development to Re-examine the Debates.* Winnipeg: International Institute for Sustainable Development.

Court 1995. *United States Court of Appeals for the District of Columbia Circuit, No. 94–1505, Ethyl Corporation, Petitioner v. Environmental Protection Agency, et al., Respondents, American Automobile Manufacturers Association, Ferroalloys Association, Intervenors, On Petition for Review of an Order of the Environmental Protection Agency.* Argued 13 January 1995; Decided 14 April 1995.

Cox, R.W., 1987. *Production, Power and World Order: Social Forces in the Making of History.* New York: Columbia University Press.

CPPI 1994a. Letter to Ms. Maureen Kempston-Darkes. October 26. *Agreement on Internal Trade, Dispute Regarding the Manganese-based Fuel Additives Act Submission of the Responding Party, The Government of Canada, Supporting Documents, Volume 2.*

– 1994b. Letter to the Honourable Sheila Copps. November 11. *Agreement on Internal Trade, Dispute Regarding the Manganese-based Fuel Additives Act Submission of the Responding Party, The Government of Canada, Supporting Documents, Volume 2.*

CPPI Technical Task Force 1995. *Review of* MMT *Claims made by* MVMA, AIAMC *and Ethyl.* Ottawa: CPPI. February 28.

Cruz, M.A.G. and R. Schwentesius, 2003. "NAFTA's impact on Mexican agriculture: an overview." In K. Hansen-Kuhn and S. Hellinger (eds), *Lessons from* NAFTA: *The High Cost of "Free Trade."* Ottawa: Canadian Centre for Policy Alternatives. 49–63.

de Champlain, P., 2004. *Mobsters, Gangsters and Men of Honour.* Toronto: Harper-Collins Publishers Ltd.

de Mestral, A., 1995. "A comment." In M.J. Trebilcock and D. Schwanen (eds), *Getting There: An Assessment of the Agreement on Internal Trade.* Toronto: C.D. Howe Institute. 95–7.

Desjardins, M., 1995. *Briefing Note on Removal of* MMT *from Gasoline in Canada.* March 1. Transport Canada.

Dewar, E., 1997. "Breathless (What's wrong with the air in Toronto?)." *Toronto Life* 31(2): 50–9.

Dezalay, Y. and B.G. Garth, 1996. *Dealing in Virtue: International Commercial Arbitration and the Construction of a Transnational Legal Order.* Chicago: University of Chicago Press.

Dobbin, M., 2007. "Elite's 'deep integration' plot coming out of the shadows." *The* CCPA *Monitor* 14(3): 1, 6.

Doern, G.B. and M. MacDonald, 1999. *Free-Trade Federalism: Negotiating the Canadian Agreement on Internal Trade.* Toronto: University of Toronto Press.

– and B.W. Tomlin, 1992. *Faith and Fear: The Free Trade Story.* Toronto: Stoddart Publishing.

Drache, D., 1993. "Assessing the benefits of free trade." In R. Grinspun and M.A. Cameron (eds), *The Political Economy of North American Free Trade.* Montreal: McGill-Queen's University Press. 73–88.

Duhem, P., 1906. *La Théorie physique: Son objêt et sa structure.* Paris: Chevalier et Rivière.

DuPuy, R.K. (ed.), 2000. *Fuel Systems and Emission Controls.* Sunnyvale, California: Chek-Chart.

Durbin, P.T. (ed.), 1980. *The Culture of Science, Technology and Medicine.* New York: The Free Press.

Easson, A., 1995. "Harmonization of legislation: Some comparisons between the Agreement on Internal Trade and the EEC Treaty." In M.J. Trebilcock and D. Schwanen (eds), *Getting There: An Assessment of the Agreement on Internal Trade.* Toronto: C.D. Howe Institute. 119–50.

Eggleton, A.C., 1996. Letter to The Honourable Sergio Marchi, P.C. February 23. *Agreement on Internal Trade, Dispute Regarding the Manganese-based Fuel*

Additives Act Submission by the Complaining Party, The Government of Alberta, Supporting Documents, Volume 2.

Eklund, C.D., 1994. "A primer on the arbitration of NAFTA Chapter Eleven investor-State disputes." *Journal of International Arbitration* 11(4): 135–71.

EPA 1999. *Response to Ethyl Corporation Petitions Denying Reconsideration of Three EPA Regulations: CAP 2000, Heavy Duty Gasoline, and OBD/IM.* May 4. http //www.epa.gov/orcdizux/regs/ld-hwy/cap2000,respo717.pdf.

– 2007. *Comments on the Gasoline Additive MMT (methylcyclopentadienyl manganese tricarbonyl).* http//www.epa.gov/otaq/regs/fuels/additive/ mmt_cmts.htm.

Ethanol Advisory Panel 2002. *Ethanol Made In Manitoba: A Report by the Ethanol Advisory Panel to the Government of Manitoba.* Winnipeg: Manitoba Energy Development Initiative.

Ethyl Canada 1997. *Ontario Court (General Division), Between Ethyl Canada Inc. (Plaintiff) and the Attorney-General of Canada and the Minister of the Environment (Defendants), Statement of Claim.* June 23.

Federal Register

FR 1994. "Fuels and Fuel Additives: Waiver Decision/Circuit Court Remand." *Federal Register*, Vol. 59, No. 158. Wednesday, 17 August 1994. 42,227–61.

– 2000. "Final Notification of Alternative Tier 2 Requirements for Methylcyclopentadienyl Manganese Tricarbonyl (MMT)." *Federal Register*, Vol. 65, No. 139. Wednesday, 19 July 2000. 44,775–6.

Finn, E., 2004. "Filling our tanks (and brains) with the wrong fuel: Lament for an election in which the crucial issue was ignored." *The CCPA Monitor* 11(4): 4–5.

Foster, J.W. and J. Dillon, 2003. "NAFTA in Canada: The era of a supra-constitution." In K. Hansen-Kuhn and S. Hellinger (eds), *Lessons from NAFTA: The High Cost of "Free Trade."* Ottawa: Canadian Centre for Policy Alternatives. 83–116.

Frey, B., 2001. "Cultural economics – history and theory." *Culture, Society and Market* 6: 143–53.

Frumkin, H. and G. Solomon, 1997. "Manganese in the U.S. gasoline supply." *American Journal of Industrial Medicine* 31: 107–15.

Gill, S., 1992. "The emerging world order and European change." In R. Miliband and L. Panitch (eds), *New World Order? The Socialist Register 1992.* London: Merlin. 157–96.

– 1996. "Globalization, democratization, and the politics of indifference." In J.H. Mittelman (ed.), *Globalization: Critical Reflections.* Boulder: Lynne Rienner Publishers. 205–28.

– 1997. "Global structural change and multilateralism." In S. Gill (ed.), *Globalization, Democratization and Multilateralism*. New York: St. Martin's Press. 1–17.

Gilson, C., C. Castonguay, K. Kelly, A. Mauro, and B. Rae, 1998. *Report of the Article 1704 Panel Concerning a Dispute between Alberta and Canada Regarding the Manganese-Based Fuel Additives Act*. Winnipeg, Manitoba: June 12, File No. 97/98 – 15 – MMT – P058.

Gioia, D.A., 1992. "Pinto fires and personal ethics: a script analysis of missed opportunities." *Journal of Business Ethics* 11: 379–89.

Goldring, J., 1998. "Consumer protection, globalization and democracy." *Cardozo Journal of International and Comparative Law* 6(1): 1–83.

Gould, E., 2007. "TILMA is a radical, regressive experiment in deregulation." *The CCPA Monitor* 13(8): 8–9.

Gourley, D., 2002. Personal correspondence with the author.

Government of Alberta 1997. *Agreement on Internal Trade, Dispute Regarding the Manganese-based Fuel Additives Act, Submission by the Complaining Party, The Government of Alberta*. December 1.

Government of Québec 1997. *Agreement on Internal Trade, Dispute Concerning the Manganese-Based Fuel Additives Act, Brief from Québec, Interested Party*. December 19.

Graham, W.C., 1987. "International commercial arbitration: the developing Canadian profile." In R.K. Paterson and B.J. Thompson (eds), UNCITRAL *Arbitration Model in Canada: Canadian International Commercial Arbitration Legislation*. Toronto: Carswell. 77–111.

Greider, W., 2002. "The right and us trade law: Invalidating the 20th century." *The Nation* October 15. 1–11.

Griffin, K. and A.R. Khan, 1992. *Globalization and the Developing World: An Essay on the International Dimensions of Development in the Post-Cold War Era*. Geneva: U.N. Research Institute for Social Development.

Grinspun, R. and M.A. Cameron (eds), 1993. *The Political Economy of North American Free Trade*. Montreal: McGill-Queen's University Press.

Grinspun, R. and R. Kreklewich, 1994. "Consolidating neoliberal reforms: 'Free trade' as a conditioning framework." *Studies in Political Economy* 43, Spring: 33–61.

Grinspun, R. and Y. Shamsie (eds), 2007. *Whose Canada? Continental Integration, Fortress North America and the Corporate Agenda*. Montreal: McGill-Queen's University Press.

Hansen-Kuhn, K. and S. Hellinger (eds), 2003. *Lessons from NAFTA: The High Cost of "Free Trade."* Ottawa: Canadian Centre for Policy Alternatives.

Harding, S.G. (ed.), 1976. *Can Theories be Refuted?* Dordrecht: D. Reidel.

Harrison, K., 1996. *Passing the Buck: Federalism and Canadian Environmental Policy.* Vancouver: University of British Columbia Press.

Harrison, K., 2002. "Federal-provincial relations and the environment: Unilateralism, collaboration, and rationalization." In D.L. VanNijnatten and R. Boardman (eds), *Canadian Environmental Policy: Context and Cases.* Don Mills: Oxford University Press. 123–44.

Harrison, K., 2003. "Passing the environmental buck." In F. Rocher and M. Smith (eds), *New Trends in Canadian Federalism.* Peterborough: Broadview Press. 313–52.

Hart, M.M. and W.A. Dymond, 2002. "NAFTA Chapter 11: Precedents, Principles and Prospects." In L. Ritchie Dawson (ed.), *Whose Rights?: The NAFTA Chapter 11 Debate.* Ottawa: Centre for Trade Policy and Law, Carleton University. 129–70.

Hayford, S.L., 1996. "Law in disarray: Judicial standards for vacatur of commercial arbitration awards." *Georgia Law Review* 30: 731–842.

Health and Welfare Canada 1978. *Methylcyclopentadienyl Manganese Tricarbonyl (MMT), Assessment of the Human Health Implications of Its Use as a Gasoline Additive.* Ottawa: Environmental Health Directorate, Health Protection Branch.

Helliwell, J.F., 1996. "Do national borders matter for Québec's trade?" *Canadian Journal of Economics* 29: 507–22.

– 2002. *Globalization and Well-Being.* Vancouver: UBC Press.

– and G. Verdier, 2001. "Measuring international trade distances: a new method applied to estimate provincial border effects in Canada." *Canadian Journal of Economics* 34(5): 1,024–41.

Herrmann, G., 1987. "The British Columbia Enactment of the UNCITRAL Model Law." In R.K. Paterson and B.J. Thompson (eds), *UNCITRAL Arbitration Model in Canada: Canadian International Commercial Arbitration Legislation.* Toronto: Carswell. 65–76.

Hill, S. and W. Leiss, 2001. "MMT, a risk management masquerade." In W. Leiss, *In the Chamber of Risks: Understanding Risk Controversies.* Montreal and Kingston: McGill-Queen's University Press. 65–102.

Hirsch, F., 1976. *The Social Limits to Growth.* Cambridge: Harvard University Press.

Ho, S.P., 1989. "Global warming impact of ethanol versus gasoline." Paper presented at the 1989 National Conference on Clean Air Issues and America's Motor Fuel Business. October. Washington, D.C.

Hoberg, G., 2002. "Canadian-American environmental relations: a strategic framework." In D.L. VanNijnatten and R. Boardman (eds), *Canadian Environmental Policy Context and Cases.* Don Mills: Oxford University Press. 171–89.

Hodgson, B., 2001. *Economics As A Moral Science*. Berlin: Springer-Verlag.

Hoellering, M.F., 1987. "International commercial arbitration: the United States perspective." In R.K. Paterson and B.J. Thompson (eds), UNCITRAL *Arbitration Model in Canada: Canadian International Commercial Arbitration Legislation*. Toronto: Carswell. 17–24.

Hogg, P.W., 1997. *Constitutional Law of Canada*. Scarborough: Thomson and Carswell.

Hotz, M.C.B., 1986. *Alternatives to Lead in Gasoline*. February. Ottawa: Royal Society of Canada.

House Standing Committee on Environment and Sustainable Development HSCESD10/19 1995a. committees/sust/evidence/148_95–10–19/sust148_blk101.html. 1–34.

– 10/24 1995b. committees/sust/evidence/149_95–10–24/sust149_blk101.html. 1–48.

– 10/26 1995c. committees/sust/evidence/151_95–10–26/sust151_blk101.html. 1–3.

Howarth, R.B. and P.A. Monahan, 1996. "Economics, ethics, and climate policy: framing the debate." *Global and Planetary Change* 11: 187–99.

Howlett, M., 2002. "Policy instruments and implementation styles: the evolution of instrument choice in Canadian environmental policy." in D.L. VanNijnatten and R. Boardman (eds), *Canadian Environmental Policy: Context and Cases*. Don Mills: Oxford University Press. 25–45.

Howse, R., 1990. "The Labour Conventions Doctrine in an era of global interdependence: Rethinking the constitutional dimensions of Canada's external economic relations." *Canadian Business Law Journal* 16(2): 160–84.

– 1995. "Between anarchy and the rule of law: dispute settlement and related implementation issues in the Agreement on Internal Trade." In M.J. Trebilcock and D. Schwanen (eds), *Getting There: An Assessment of the Agreement on Internal Trade*. Toronto: C.D. Howe Institute. 170–95.

Hua, M.-S. and C.-C. Huang, 1991. "Chronic occupational exposure to manganese and neurobehavioral function." *Journal of Clinical and Experimental Neuropsychology* 13: 495–507.

Hubbard, C.P., J.S. Hepburn, and H.S. Gandhi, 1993. "The effect of MMT on the OBD II catalyst efficiency monitor." SAE *Technical Papers*, 932855.

Hufbauer, G.C. et al., 2000. NAFTA *and the Environment: Seven Years Later*. Washington: Institute for International Economics.

Hughes, V., B.R. Evernden, and J. Tyhurst, 1997. *Statement of Defence in the Matter of an Arbitration under Chapter 11 of the North American Free Trade Agreement Between Ethyl Corporation (Claimant/Investor) v. Government of Canada (Respondent/Party)*. November 27.

Hurley, R.G., W.L.H. Watkins, and R.C. Griffis, 1989. "Characterization of automotive catalysts exposed to the fuel additive MMT." *SAE Technical Papers*, 890582.

IISD/WWF 2001. *Private Rights, Public Problems: A Guide to NAFTA's Controversial Chapter on Investor Rights*. Winnipeg: International Institute for Sustainable Development and World Wildlife Fund.

Internal Trade Secretariat 2002a. *CGA Canada – The Roundtable on the Agreement on Internal Trade Proceedings and Recommendations*. 26 March 1996. Ottawa. http //www.intrasec.mb.ca/eng/lib/study5.htr.

– 2002b. *Overview of the Agreement on Internal Trade*. 3 January 2002. http// www.intrasec.mb.ca/eng/overview.htm.

Iregren, A., 1990. "Psychological test performance in foundry workers exposed to low levels of manganese." *Neurotoxicology and Teratology* 12: 673–7.

– 1994. "Using psychological tests for the early detection of neurotoxic effects of low level manganese exposure." *Neurotoxicology* 15: 671–7.

Jackson, A., 2003. *From Leaps of Faith to Hard Landings: Fifteen Years of "Free Trade."* Ottawa: Canadian Centre for Policy Alternatives.

Jackson, A. and M. Sanger, 1998. *Dismantling Democracy: The Multilateral Agreement on Investment (MAI) and Its Impact*. Ottawa and Toronto: Canadian Centre for Policy Alternatives and James Lorimer and Company Ltd.

Jakubowski, J., 1982. "Reflections on the philosophy of international commercial arbitration and conciliation." In J.C. Schultsz and A.J. Van Den Berg (eds), *The Art of Arbitration: Essays on International Arbitration Liber Amicorum Pieter Sanders 12 September 1912–1982*. Deventer, Netherlands: Kluwer Law and Taxation Publishers. 175–88.

James, W., 1909. *The Meaning of Truth: A Sequel to Pragmatism*. New York: Longmans, Green and Co.

Juanós i Timoneda, J., 1997. "The legal dynamics of the regulation of MMT: Air quality standards and the Salt Lake City airshed." *Journal of Land, Resources and Environmental Law* 17(2): 283–342.

Kant, I., 1788. *Critique of Practical Reason*. Riga. Königsberg.

– 1797. *Metaphysics of Ethics*.

Keeney, D.R. and T.H. DeLuca, 1992. "Biomass as an energy source for the midwestern U.S." *Journal of Alternative Agriculture* 7: 137–43.

Kraucher, W.M., 1993. *Ford Motor Company's Concerns with Ethyl's Fourth Waiver Request*. August 6. Submission to EPA, Public Docket A–93–26.

– 1994. *Section 211 (C): Vehicle Verification Test Program*. April 29. Ford Motor Company.

Kuhn, T.S., 1957. *The Copernican Revolution*. Cambridge: Harvard University Press.

– 1977. *The Essential Tension.* Chicago: University of Chicago Press.

Kukucha, C., 2003. "Domestic politics and Canadian foreign trade policy: Intrusive interdependence, the WTO and the NAFTA." *Canadian Foreign Policy* 10(2): 59–86.

Law Commission of New Zealand 1991. *Report No. 20 Arbitration.* Wellington: Law Commission of New Zealand.

Law Reform Commission of British Columbia 1982. *Report on Arbitration.* Vancouver: Law Reform Commission of British Columbia.

Leavitt, R., 1996. "Diagnosing O_2 sensor problems." *The Analyser* (News for the Auto Repair Industry) 2: 1–3.

Lee, M., 2000. "In search of a problem: the future of the Agreement on Internal Trade and Canadian Federalism." *Briefing Paper Series* 1(4). October. Vancouver: Canadian Centre for Policy Alternatives.

Leiss, W., 2001. *In the Chamber of Risks: Understanding Risk Controversies.* Montreal and Kingston: McGill-Queen's University Press.

Lenihan, D.G., 1995. "When a legitimate objective hits an unnecessary obstacle: Harmonizing regulations and standards in the Agreement on Internal Trade." In M.J. Trebilcock and D. Schwanen (eds), *Getting There: An Assessment of the Agreement on Internal Trade.* Toronto: C.D. Howe Institute. 98–118.

Lillich, R. and C. Brower (eds), 1993. *International Arbitration in the Twenty-first Century: Towards 'Judicialization' and Uniformity.* Irvington, New York: Transnational Publishers.

Lindblom, C.E., 1959. "The science of 'muddling through'." *Public Administration Review* 19: 79–88.

– 1979. "Still muddling, not yet through." *Public Administration Review* 39: 222–33.

Lopez, D., 1997. "Dispute resolution under NAFTA: lessons from the early experience." *Texas International Law Journal* 32(2): 163–208.

Loranger, S. and J. Zayed, 1994. "Manganese and lead concentrations in ambient air and emission rates from unleaded and leaded gasoline between 1981 and 1992 in Canada: A comparative study." *Atmospheric Environment* 28: 1,645–51.

– 1995. "Environmental and occupational exposure to manganese: A multimedia assessment." *International Archives of Occupational and Environmental Health* 67: 101–10.

Lucchini, R. et al., 1995. "Neurobehavioral effects of manganese in workers from a ferroalloy plant after temporary cessation of exposure." *Scandinavian Journal of Work, Environment and Health* 21: 143–9.

Lund, T., 1995. Letter to the Honourable Sheila Copps. April 18. *Agreement on Internal Trade, Dispute Regarding the Manganese-based Fuel Additives Act*

Submission by the Complaining Party, The Government of Alberta, Supporting Documents, Volume 1.

Luz, M.A., 2000–01. "NAFTA, investment and the Constitution of Canada: Will the watertight compartments spring a leak?" *Ottawa Law Review* 31(1): 39–84.

Macaulay, R.W. and J.L.H. Sprague, 1996. *Hearings Before Administrative Tribunals.* Toronto: Carswell Legal Publications.

Macdonald, D., 2002. "The business response to environmentalism." In D.L. VanNijnatten and R. Boardman (eds), *Canadian Environmental Policy: Context and Cases.* Don Mills: Oxford University Press. 66–86.

Macpherson, C.B., 1965. *The Real World of Democracy.* Toronto: Canadian Broadcasting Corporation.

– 1973. *Democratic Theory: Essays in Retrieval.* Oxford: Oxford University Press.

– 1977. *The Life and Times of Liberal Democracy.* Oxford: Oxford University Press.

Magnet, J.E., 1980. "The presumption of constitutionality." *Osgoode Hall Law Journal* 18(1): 87–145.

Mann, F.A., 1984. "England rejects 'delocalised' contracts and arbitration." *International and Comparative Law Quarterly* 33: 193–9.

Mann, H., 2002. *Review of the Decision on Jurisdiction of the Methanex Tribunal.* August 5. http//www.iisd.org/pdf/2002/trade_methanex_analysis.pdf.

– and S. Porter, 2003. *The State of Trade and Environment Law 2003: Implications for Doha and Beyond.* Winnipeg: International Institute for Sustainable Development.

Marceau, G., 1999. "A call for coherence in international law: Praises for the prohibition against 'clinical isolation' in WTO dispute settlement." *Journal of World Trade* 33(5): 1–63.

March, J.G. and H.A. Simon, 1958. *Organizations.* New York: John Wiley and Sons, Inc.

Marsilio of Padua, 1324. *The Defender of Peace.* A. Gewirth (trans.). New York: Columbia University Press, 1952.

McBride, S., 2001. *Paradigm Shift: Globalization and the Canadian State.* Halifax: Fernwood Publishing.

– 2003, "Quiet constitutionalism in Canada: The international political economy of domestic institutional change." *Canadian Journal of Political Science / Revue canadienne de science politique* 36(2): 251–73.

McCloskey, J.C., 1995. *Memorandum to the Minister* [of the Environment]. N95–16506–69408.

McConnaughay, P.J., 1999. "The risks and virtues of lawlessness: A 'second look' at international commercial arbitration." *Northwestern University Law Review* 93(2): 453–523.

McCullough, H.B. (ed.), 1995. *Political Ideologies and Political Philosophies.* Second edition. Toronto: Thompson Educational Publishing, Inc.

McGuire, K., 2002. "Commentary." In L. Ritchie Dawson (ed.), *Whose Rights?: The NAFTA Chapter 11 Debate.* Ottawa: Centre for Trade Policy and Law, Carleton University. 171–4.

McMurtry, J., 1999. *Unequal Freedoms: The Global Market As An Ethical System.* Toronto and Westport: Garamond and Kumarian Press.

– 2002. *Value Wars: The Global Market versus the Life Economy.* London: Pluto Press.

Meek, M.E. and I. Bogoroch, 1978. *Methycyclopentadienyl Manganese Tricarbonyl (MMT): Assessment of the Human Health Implications of Its Use as a Gasoline Additive.* 78–EHD–21. Ottawa: Environmental Health Directorate, Health Protection Branch, Health and Welfare Canada.

Memorandum of Understanding 1992. *Agreement on Internal Trade, Dispute Regarding the Manganese-based Fuel Additives Act Submission of the Responding Party, The Government of Canada, Supporting Documents, Volume 1.*

Mergler, D. et al., 1994. "Nervous system dysfunction among workers with long-term exposure to manganese." *Environmental Research* 64: 151–80.

Merrett, C.D., 1996. *Free Trade: Neither Free nor about Trade.* Montreal: Black Rose Books.

Michalos, A.C., 1969. *Principles of Logic.* Englewood Cliffs: Prentice-Hall.

– 1970a. *Improving Your Reasoning.* Englewood Cliffs: Prentice-Hall.

– 1970b. "Cost-benefit versus expected utility acceptance rules." *Theory and Decision* 1: 61–88.

– 1971. *The Popper-Carnap Controversy.* The Hague: Martinus Nijhoff.

– 1972. "Efficiency and morality." *The Journal of Value Inquiry* 6: 137–43.

– 1973. "Rationality between the maximizers and the satisficers." *Policy Sciences* 12: 229–44.

– 1978. *Foundations of Decision Making.* Ottawa: Canadian Library of Philosophy.

– 1979. "The loyal agent's argument." In T. Beachamp and N. Bowie (eds), *Ethical Theory and Business.* Englewood Cliffs: Prentice-Hall. 247–53.

– 1980a. "Philosophy of science: historical, social and value aspects." In P.T. Durbin (ed.), *The Culture of Science, Technology and Medicine.* New York: The Free Press. 463–502.

– 1980b. "A reconsideration of the idea of a science court." In P.T. Durbin (ed.), *Philosophy and Technology: An Annual Compilation of Research, Vol. 3.* New York: JAI Press. 10–28.

– 1981a. *North American Social Report, Volume Four: Environment, Transportation and Housing.* Dordrecht: D. Reidel.

– 1981b. "Technology assessment, facts and values." In P.T. Durbin (ed.), *Research in Philosophy and Technology, Vol. 4.* New York: JAI Press. 59–81.

– 1985. "Multiple discrepancies theory (MDT)." *Social Indicators Research* 16: 347–413.

– 1989. *Militarism and the Quality of Life.* Toronto: Science for Peace.

– 1990. "The impact of trust on business, international security and the quality of life." *Journal of Business Ethics* 9: 619–38.

– 1992. "Ethical considerations in evaluation." *Canadian Journal of Program Evaluation* 7: 61–75.

– 1995. "The case against the North American Free Trade Agreement." In A.C. Michalos, *A Pragmatic Approach to Business Ethics.* Thousand Oaks: Sage Publications Inc. 188–235.

– 1997a. "Combining social, economic and environmental indicators to measure sustainable human well-being." *Social Indicators Research* 40: 221–58.

– 1997b. "Issues for business ethics in the nineties and beyond." *Journal of Business Ethics* 16(3): 219–30.

– 1997c. *Good Taxes: The Case for Taxing Foreign Currency Exchange and other Financial Transactions.* Toronto: Science for Peace and Dundurn Press.

– 2001. "Ethics counselors as a new priesthood." *Journal of Business Ethics* 29: 3–17.

– 2003a. *Essays on the Quality of Life.* Dordrecht: Kluwer Academic Publishing.

– 2003b. "Identifying the horse, the cart and their proper order in sustainable development." Paper presented at a meeting of the Italian Society of Interdisciplinary Studies, Bari, Italy. May 2003.

Midwest Research Institute 1987. *Health Effects of Exposure to the Gasoline Octane Booster Methylcyclopentadienylmanganese Tricarbonyl (MMT) and Its Major Combustion Product Mn_3O_4, Final Report.* March 30. Ottawa: Environmental Health Directorate, Health Protection Branch, Department of National Health and Welfare.

Mill, J.S., 1859. *On Liberty.* London.

– 1861. *Utilitarianism.* London.

Miller, I., 1995. "Dispute resolution: an interprovincial approach." In M.J. Trebilcock and D. Schwanen (eds), *Getting There: An Assessment of the Agreement on Internal Trade.* Toronto: C.D. Howe Institute. 151–69.

Mitchell, W.C., 1918. "Bentham's felicific calculus." *Political Science Quarterly* 33: 161–83.

Monahan, P.J., 1984. "At doctrine's twilight: The structure of Canadian federalism." *University of Toronto Law Journal* 34: 47–99.

– 1995. "'To the extent possible': A comment on dispute settlement in the Agreement on Internal Trade." In M.J. Trebilcock and D. Schwanen (eds), *Getting There: An Assessment of the Agreement on Internal Trade.* Toronto: C.D. Howe Institute. 211–18.

– 1997. *Brief to the Standing Senate Committee on Energy, Environment and Natural Resources Respecting Bill C–29, The Manganese-Based Fuel Additives Act.* 18 February 1997.

– 2006. *Constitutional Law.* Toronto: Irwin Law Inc.

Moore, J., 2001. "Defending NAFTA's Chapter 11." May 1. Press release of a speech in the House of Commons.

MVMA/AIAMC 1995. *The Impact of Manganese-Based Fuel Additives on Vehicle Emission Control Technology in Canada: A Report Prepared by the Motor Vehicle Manufacturers Association and the Association of International Automobile Manufacturers of Canada for Submission to the [House] Standing Committee on Environment and Sustainable Development.* 24 October.

NAFTA 2002. *North American Free Trade Agreement.* http//www.nafta-sec-alena.org/ english/nafta/htm.

NAFTA Secretariat 2002. *General Information.* http//www.nafta-sec-alena.org/ english/home.htm.

Nantais, M. and T.R. Clapp, 1994. Letter to M. Desjardins and Tony Clarke. October 12. *Agreement on Internal Trade, Dispute Regarding the Manganese-based Fuel Additives Act Submission of the Responding Party, The Government of Canada, Supporting Documents, Volume 1.*

Nemetz, N.T., 1987. "Dispute resolution." In R.K. Paterson and B.J. Thompson (eds), UNCITRAL *Arbitration Model in Canada: Canadian International Commercial Arbitration Legislation.* Toronto: Carswell. 3–6.

Newman, S., 2000. "Globalization and democracy." In M. Th. Greven and L.W. Pauly (eds), *Democracy Beyond the State? The European Dilemma and the Emerging Global Order.* Toronto: University of Toronto Press.

National Round Table on the Environment and the Economy

NRTEE 1999. *Methylcyclopentadienyl Manganese Tricarbonyl (MMT) Case Study.* Ottawa: NRTEE.

– 2001. *Managing Potentially Toxic Substances in Canada: A State of the Debate Report from the National Round Table on the Environment and the Economy.* Ottawa: NRTEE.

OECD 1994. *Managing the Environment: The Role of Economic Instrument.* Paris: OECD.

– 1997. *The World in 2020.* Paris: OECD.

Oge, M.T., 1999. Letter to Donald R. Lynam, Vice President, Air Conservation, Ethyl Corporation. http//www.epa.gov/otaq/regs/fuels/additive/ mmtprop5.pdf. January 25.

Okun, A., 1975. *Equality and Efficiency: The Big Tradeoff*. Washington, D.C.: Brookings Institution.

Olson, M., 1965. *The Logic of Collective Action*. Cambridge: Harvard University Press.

Pal, L.A. and J. Maxwell, 2004. *Assessing the Public Interest in the 21st Century: A Framework*. Paper prepared for the External Advisory Committee on Smart Regulation. January 2004. Ottawa: Canadian Policy Research Networks Inc.

Panitch, L., 1996. "Rethinking the role of the state." In J.H. Mittleman (ed.), *Globalization: Critical Reflections*. Boulder: Lynne Rienner Publishers. 83–113.

Park, W.W. and J. Paulsson, 1983. "The binding force of international arbitral awards." *Virginia Journal of International Law* 23: 253–85.

Parliamentary Debates

PD9/19: 1995a.

/35/1/parlbus/chambus/house/debates/226_95–09–19/226g03e.html. 1–20.

- 9/19: 1995b.

/35/1/parlbus/chambus/house/debates/226_95–09–19/226g02e.html. 1–10.

- 9/22: 1995c.

/35/1/parlbus/chambus/house/debates/226_95–09–22/229g01e.html. 1–10.

- 9/26: 1995d.

/35/1/parlbus/chambus/house/debates/231_95–09–26/231g01e.html. 1–17.

- 11/8: 1995e. english/hansard/previous/257_95–11–08/257g01e.html. 1–5.

- 11/8: 1995f.

/35/1/parlbus/chambus/house/debates/257_95–11–08/257g02e.html. 1–19.

- 11/9: 1995g.

/35/1/parlbus/chambus/house/debates/258_95–11–09/258g01e.html. 1–39.

- 9/25: 1996a.

/35/2/parlbus/chambus/house/debates/074_96–09–25/074gole.html. 1–28.

- 9/27: 1996b. /english/hansard/076_96–09–076g02e.html. 1–15.

- 10/11: 1996c.

/35/2/parlbus/chambus/house/debates/086_96–10–11/086g02e.html. 1–2.

- 10/11: 1996d. /english/hansard/086_96–10–11/086gole.html. 1–10.

- 10/22: 1996e.

/35/2/parlbus/chambus/house/debates/088_96–10–22/088g02e.html. 1–12.

- 10/28: 1996f.

/35/2/parlbus/chambus/house/debates/091_96–10–28/091gole.html. 1–17.

- 11/29: 1996g./35/2/parlbus/chambus/house/debates/110_96–11–29/110gole.html. 1–12.

Paterson, R.K., 1987. "International Commercial Arbitration Act: An Overview."
In R.K. Paterson and B.J. Thompson (eds), UNCITRAL Arbitration Model in
Canada: Canadian International Commercial Arbitration Legislation. Toronto:
Carswell. 113–25.

– and B.J. Thompson (eds), 1987. UNCITRAL Arbitration Model in Canada:
Canadian International Commercial Arbitration Legislation. Toronto:
Carswell.

Perez, A., 1997. Affidavit of Alain Perez. Sworn June 25: Ontario Court (General
Division), Between Ethyl Canada Inc. (Plaintiff) and The Attorney-General of
Canada and the Minister of the Environment (Defendants).

Perrin, R. and L. Zarzeczny, 1998. Agreement on Internal Trade, Dispute
Regarding the Manganese-Based Fuel Additives Act, Submission on Behalf of
the Government of Saskatchewan. January 15.

Physicians for Social Responsibility 1996. Resolution on MMT in the United States
Gasoline Supply. April 16. http//psr.igc.org/mmt.htm.

Picard, A.A., 2003. "NAFTA in Mexico: promises, myths and realities." In
K. Hansen-Kuhn and S. Hellinger (eds), Lessons from NAFTA: The High
Cost of "Free Trade." Ottawa: Canadian Centre for Policy Alternatives.
23–48.

Pimentel, D., 1991. "Ethanol fuels: energy security, economics and the
environment." Journal of Agricultural and Environmental Ethics 4: 1–13.

– 2001. "The limits of biomass utilization." Encyclopedia of Physical Sciences
and Technology, Volume 2. Third edition. San Diego: Academic Press. 159–71.

– 2003. "Ethanol fuels: energy balance, economics, and environmental impacts
are negative." Natural Resources Research 12(2): 127–34.

Plutarch, 1998. Greek Lives. R. Waterfield (trans.). Oxford: Oxford University
Press.

Polanyi, K., 1957. The Great Transformation: The Political and Economic
Origins of Our Time. Boston: Beacon Press.

Polaski, S., 2003. "Jobs, wages and household income." In J. Audley, D.G.
Papademetriou, S. Polaski, and S. Vaughan (eds), NAFTA's Promise and Reality:
Lessons from Mexico for the Hemisphere. Washington: Carnegie Endowment
for International Peace. 11–37.

Province of British Columbia 1995. Clean Vehicles and Fuels for British
Columbia: A Policy Paper. Victoria: Ministry of Environment, Lands and
Parks.

– 1997. AirCare: Vehicle Emissions Inspections and Maintenance. Fifth edition.
Victoria: Student Study Guide.

Public Citizen 2001. NAFTA Chapter 11 Investor-to-State Cases: Bankrupting
Democracy. Washington: Public Citizen's Global Trade Watch.

- 2004a. *NAFTA at Ten Series: U.S., Mexican and Canadian Farmers and Agriculture.* http//www.citizen.org/publications/release.cfm?ID=7295. Accessed 20 January 2004.
- 2004b. *NAFTA at Ten Series: U.S. Workers' Jobs, Wages and Economic Security.* http //www.citizen.org/publications/release.cfm?ID=7295. Accessed 20 January 2004.
- 2004c. *NAFTA at Ten Series: Undermining Sovereignty and Democracy.* http // www.citizen.org/publications/release.cfm?ID=7295. Accessed 20 January 2004.

Ranney, D., 2003. "NAFTA at 10: an assessment." In K. Hansen-Kuhn and S. Hellinger (eds), *Lessons from NAFTA: The High Cost of "Free Trade."* Ottawa: Canadian Centre for Policy Alternatives. 65–81.

Rees, W.E., 1994. "Pressing global limits: trade as the appropriation of carrying capacity." In T. Schrecker and J. Dagleish (eds), *Growth, Trade and Environmental Values.* London, Ontario: Westminster Institute for Ethics and Human Values. 29–56.

Reichenbach, H., 1949. *The Theory of Probability.* Berkeley: University of California Press.

Reitan, M., 1998. "Ecological modernization and 'realpolitik': Ideas, interests and institutions." *Environmental Politics* 7(1): 1–26.

Robinson, I., 2003. "Neo-liberal trade policy and Canadian federalism revisited." In F. Rocher and M. Smith (eds), *New Trends in Canadian Federalism.* Peterborough: Broadview Press. 197–242.

Rodrik, D., 1999. *The New Global Economy and Developing Countries: Making Openness Work.* Washington, D.C.: Overseas Development Council.

Roels, H. et al., 1987. "Epidemiological survey among workers exposed to manganese: Effects on lung, central nervous system, and some biological indices." *American Journal of Industrial Medicine* 11: 307–27.

- 1992. "Assessment of the permissible exposure level to manganese in workers exposed to manganese oxide dust." *British Journal of Industrial Medicine* 49: 25–34.

Roos, J.W., D.L. Lenane, B.F. Fort, D.G. Grand, and K.L. Dykes, 1992. "The effect of manganese oxides on OBD II catalytic converter monitoring." *SAE Technical Papers*, 942056.

Roos, J.W., D.P. Hollrah, G.H. Guinther, and L.J. Cunningham, 2002. "A peer-reviewed critical analysis of SAE Paper 2002–01–2894 'The impact of MMT gasoline additive on exhaust emissions and fuel economy of low emission vehicles (LEV)'." *SAE Technical Papers*, 2002–01–2903.

Rosen, J.F., 1986. Letter to F. Kenneth Hare, Chair of the Commission on Lead in the Environment. September 24. Attached to the Final Report of the Commission with "Dissenting Opinion by US Researchers."

Royal Commission on the Economic Union and Development Prospects for Canada, 1985. *Report*. Ottawa: Minister of Supply and Services.

RTI 1998. *Final Report: Manganese Exposure Study (Toronto)*. Research Triangle Park, North Carolina: Research Triangle Institute.

Rugman, A.M, J. Kirton, and J. Soloway, 1997. "NAFTA, environmental regulations, and Canadian competitiveness." *Journal of World Trade* 31(4): 129–44.

Runnalls, D., 1994. "Trade and sustainable development: Friends or enemies?" In T. Schrecker and J. Dagleish (eds), *Growth, Trade and Environmental Values*. London: Westminster Institute for Ethics and Human Values. 57–79.

Sands, P., 1994. "The 'greening' of international law: Emerging principles and rules." *Indiana Journal of Global Legal Studies* 1(2): 293–323.

Schneiderman, D., 1999. "MMT promises: How the Ethyl Corporation beat the federal ban." Parkland Institute. *The Post* 3(1): 1–5.

Schubert, G.A., 1960. *The Public Interest: A Critique of the Theory of a Political Concept*. Glencoe: Free Press.

Schwanen, D., 1995. "Overview and key policy issues." In M.J. Trebilcock and D. Schwanen (eds), *Getting There: An Assessment of the Agreement on Internal Trade*. Toronto: C.D. Howe Institute. 1–19.

– 2000. "Happy birthday, AIT!" *Policy Options/Politiques* 21(6): 51–5.

– 2002. "Commentary." In L. Ritchie Dawson (ed.), *Whose Rights?: The NAFTA Chapter 11 Debate*. Ottawa: Centre for Trade Policy and Law, Carleton University. 44–6.

Senate 1988. *Constitutional Jurisdiction Pertaining to Certain Aspects of the Free Trade Agreement*. Senate of Canada, Proceedings of the Standing Committee on Foreign Affairs. Wednesday, May 4. Issue No. 21.

Senate Standing Committee on Energy, Environment and Natural Resources SSCEENR 2/11: 1996. /english/senate/com-e/enrg-e/10ev-e.htm. 1–33.

– 2/4: 1997a. /english/senate/com-e/enrg-e/05ev-e.htm. 1–47.

– 2/4: 1997b. /english/senate/com-e/enrg-e/06ev-e.htm. 1–41.

– 2/5: 1997c. english/senate/com-e/enrg-e/07ev-e.htm. 1–13.

– 2/5: 1997d. english/senate/com-e/enrg-e/08ev-e.htm. 1–62.

– 2/6: 1997e. english/senate/com-e/enrg-e/09ev-e.htm. 1–44.

– 2/19: 1997f. english/senate/com-e/enrg-e/11ev-e.htm. 1–8.

– 2/19: 1997g. english/senate/com-e/enrg-e/12ev-e.htm. 1–57.

– 2/20: 1997h. english/senate/com-e/enrg-e/13ev-e.htm. 1–2.

– 2/20: 1997i. english/senate/com-e/enrg-e/13ev-e.htm. 1–24.

– 3/4: 1997j. english/senate/com-e/enrg-e/14ev-e.htm. 1–9.

– 3/4: 1997k. *Interim Report Concerning Bill C–29*. /36/1/parlbus/commbus/senate/com-e/enrg-e/rep-e/c29-e.htm. 1–11.

– 3/4: 1997l.*The Minority Opinion.* http//www.parl.gc.ca/english/senate/com-e/enrg-e/rep-e/c29-a-e.htm. 1–16.

Shapouri, H., J.A. Duffield, and M. Wang, 2002. *The Energy Balance of Corn Ethanol: An Update.* USDA, Office of Energy Policy and New Uses, Agricultural Economics. Report No. 813.

Shrybman, S., 1999. *A Citizen's Guide to the World Trade Organization.* Toronto: Canadian Centre for Policy Alternatives and James Lorimer and Co. Ltd.

Siegl, P. and K.-D. Bergert, 1982. "Eine frudiagnostische Uberwachungsmethode bei Manganexposition [A method of early diagnostic monitoring in manganese exposure]." *Zeitschrift für die gesamte Hygiene und ihre Grenzgebiete: Arbeitsmedizin, Epidemiologie, Sozialmedizin, Umweltmedizin* 28: 524–6.

Sierra, P. et al., 1995. "Occupational and environmental exposure of automobile mechanics and nonautomotive workers to airborne manganese arising from the combustion of methylcyclopentadienyl manganese tricarbonyl (MMT)." *American Industrial Hygiene Association Journal* 56: 713–16.

Simon, H.A., 1945. *Administrative Behavior.* New York: Macmillan Co.

– 1957. *Models of Man.* New York: John Wiley and Sons, Inc.

– 1978. "Rationality as process and as product of thought." *American Economic Review* 68: 1–16.

Sinclair, S., 1994. *Shifting Powers, Depressing Standards: An Analysis of the Internal Trade Agreement.* November 1. Ottawa: Canadian Centre for Policy Alternatives.

– 2001. "Canadian government retreats on NAFTA investor-state concerns." *Briefing Paper Series: Trade and Investment* 2(3) June 11. Ottawa: Canadian Centre for Policy Alternatives.

– 2007. NAFTA Chapter 11 Investor –State Disputes (to March 2007). Ottawa: Canadian Centre for Policy Alternatives. https//policyalternatives.ca/index.cfm?act=search&search type=simple&search=nafta+&submit=go

Sjogren, B. et al., 1996. "Effects on the nervous system among welders exposed to aluminium and manganese." *Occupational and Environmental Medicine* 53: 32–40.

Smith, A., 1776. *The Wealth of Nations.* London.

Soloway, J.A., 1999. "Environmental trade barriers under NAFTA: The MMT fuel additives controversy." *Minnesota Journal of Global Trade* 8: 55–95.

– 2000. "Environmental regulation as expropriation: the case of NAFTA's Chapter 11." *Canadian Business Law Journal* 33: 92–127.

– 2003. "NAFTA's Chapter 11: Investor protection, integration and the public interest." *Choices* 9(2):1–47.

Sono, K., 1987. "The Japanese experience." In R.K. Paterson and B.J. Thompson (eds), UNCITRAL *Arbitration Model in Canada: Canadian International Commercial Arbitration Legislation.* Toronto: Carswell. 25–30.

Sornarajah, M., 2003. *Ontario Superior Court of Justice, Between: The Council of Canadians, and Dale Clark, Deborah Bourque, and George Kuehnbaum on their own behalf and on behalf of all members of the Canadian Union of Postal Workers (Applicants) and Her Majesty in Right of Canada, as Represented by the Attorney General of Canada (Respondents), Affidavit, Court File No.01-CV-208141. April.*

Stevenson, G., 2004. "Federalism and intergovernmental relations." In M.S. Whittington and G. Williams (eds), *Canadian Politics in the 21st Century.* Scarborough: Nelson. 79–104.

Swenarchuk, M., 1998. "Stomping on the Earth: Trade, Trade Law, and Canada's Ecological Footprints." Canadian Environmental Law Association. *Trade and Environment.* May. http//www.cela.ca/international/buffalo.htm.

Swinton, K., 1995. "Law, politics, and the enforcement of the Agreement on Internal Trade." In M.J. Trebilcock and D. Schwanen (eds), *Getting There: An Assessment of the Agreement on Internal Trade.* Toronto: C.D. Howe Institute, 196–210.

Tatarkiewicz, W., 1976. *Analysis of Happiness.* The Hague: M. Nijhoff.

Thomas, J.C., 2002. "The experience of NAFTA Chapter 11 Tribunals to date: A practitioner's perspective." In L. Ritchie Dawson (ed.) *Whose Rights?: The NAFTA Chapter 11 Debate.* Ottawa: Centre for Trade Policy and Law, Carleton University. 98–128.

Tollefson, C., 2003. "NAFTA's Chapter 11: The case for reform." *Choices* 9(2): 48–58.

Trebilcock, M.J., 2001. "The Supreme Court and strengthening the conditions for effective competition in the Canadian economy." *Canadian Bar Review* 80(1 and 2): 542–604.

– 2002. "Trade liberalization and regulatory diversity." http//www.library.utoronto.ca/envireform/conference/nov2002/trebilcock.paper.pdf.

– and R. Behboodi, 1995. "The Canadian Agreement on Internal Trade: Retrospect and Prospects." In M.J. Trebilcock and D. Schwanen (eds), *Getting There: An Assessment of the Agreement on Internal Trade.* Toronto: C.D. Howe Institute. 20–89.

– and D. Schwanen (eds), 1995. *Getting There: An Assessment of the Agreement on Internal Trade.* Toronto: C.D. Howe Institute.

UNCITRAL 2002. *United Nations Commission on International Trade Law.* http//www.uncitral.org/english/commiss/geninfo.htm.

– 2003. UNCITRAL *Model Law on International Commercial Arbitration (1985).* http//www.jus.uio.no/lm/un.arbitration.model.law.1985/toc.htm.

– 2004. *United Nations Commission on International Trade Law.* http//www.uncitral.org/english/commiss/geninfo.htm.

UNCSD 1996. *Report of the Secretary-General, Financial Resources and Mechanisms, Addendum.* United Nations Commission on Sustainable Development, Fourth Session. April 18-May 3. E/CN.17/1996/4/Add.1. 22 February 1996.

UNDP (United Nations Development Programme) 2003. *Making Global Trade Work for People.* London: Earthscan.

U.S. Department of Energy 1999. "Ethanol: Separating fact from fiction." *Biofuels: Ethanol for Sustainable Transportation.* April. National Renewable Energy Laboratory.

U.S. EPA 1984. *Health Assessment Document for Manganese.* EPA 600/8-83-013F.

Valiante, M., 2002. "Legal foundations of Canadian environmental policy: underlining our values in a shifting landscape." In D.L. VanNijnatten and R. Boardman (eds), *Canadian Environmental Policy: Context and Cases.* Don Mills: Oxford University Press. 3-24.

VanderZwaag, D., 1998. "The precautionary principle in environmental law and policy: elusive rhetoric and first embraces." *Journal of Environmental Law and Practice* 8: 355-75.

- 1999. "CEPA and the Precautionary Principle/Approach." http//www.ec.gc.ca/cepa/ip18/e18_01.htm.

VanDuzer, J.A., 2002. "NAFTA Chapter 11 to date: The progress of a work in progress." In L. Ritchie Dawson (ed.), *Whose Rights?: The NAFTA Chapter 11 Debate.* Ottawa: Centre for Trade Policy and Law, Carleton University. 47-97.

VanNijnatten, D.L., 2002. "The bumpy journey ahead: provincial environmental policies and national environmental standards." In D.L. VanNijnatten and R. Boardman (eds), *Canadian Environmental Policy: Context and Cases.* Don Mills: Oxford University Press. 145-70.

- and W.H. Lambright, 2002. "Canadian smog policy in a continental context: looking south for stringency." In D.L. VanNijnatten and R. Boardman (eds), *Canadian Environmental Policy: Context and Cases.* Don Mills: Oxford University Press. 253-73.

Vaughan, S., 2003. "The greenest trade agreement ever? Measuring the environmental impacts of agricultural liberalization." In J. Audley, D.G. Papademetriou, S. Polaski, and S. Vaughan (eds), *NAFTA's Promise and Reality: Lessons from Mexico for the Hemisphere.* Washington: Carnegie Endowment for International Peace. 61-87.

Veeder, V.V., 2003. Letter to C.F. Dugan, M.A. Clodfelter. June 2. http//www.naftaclaims.com.

Veenhoven, R., 1984. *Conditions of Happiness.* Dordrecht: D. Reidel.

Vogel, D., 1995. *Trading Up: Consumer and Environmental Regulation in a Global Economy.* Cambridge: Harvard University Press.

Wagner, J.M., 1999. "International investment, expropriation and environmental protection." *Golden Gate University Law Review* 29: 465–527.

Walker, B., 2002. "Big Oil's MTBE Cover-Up." Alternet.org. October 10. http //www.alternet.org/story.html?StoryID=1427.

Wang, M., C. Saricks, and D. Santini, 1999. "Effects of fuel ethanol use on fuel-cycle energy and greenhouse gas emissions." Argonne National Laboratory, Center for Transportation Research, Energy Systems Division (ANL/ESD–38).

Waters, M., 1995. *Globalization*. New York: Routledge.

Weiler, T., 2000. "The *Ethyl Arbitration*: First of its kind and a harbinger of things to come." *The American Review of International Arbitration* 11 (1–2): 187–201.

Wennberg, A. et al., 1991. "Manganese exposure in steel smelters a health hazard to the nervous system." *Scandinavian Journal of Work, Environment and Health* 17: 255–62.

Wheare, K.C., 1963. *Federal Government*. London: Oxford University Press.

Wilberforce, R., 1987. "Resolving international commercial disputes: the alternatives." In R.K. Paterson and B.J. Thompson (eds), UNCITRAL *Arbitration Model in Canada: Canadian International Commercial Arbitration Legislation*. Toronto: Carswell. 7–14.

Williamson, W.B., H.S. Gandhi, and E.E. Weaver, 1982. "Effects of fuel additive MMT on contaminant retention and catalyst performance." SAE *Technical Papers*, 821193.

Wittgenstein, L., 1961. *Tractatus Logico-Philosophicus*. D.F. Pears and B.F. McGinnes (trans). London: Routledge and Kegan Paul.

Wood, G. and M. Egyed, 1994. *Risk Assessment for the Combustion Products of Methylcyclopentadienyl Manganese Tricarbonyl (MMT) in Gasoline*. December 6. Ottawa: Health Canada, Environmental Health Directorate.

Zayed, J., 2001. "Use of MMT in Canadian gasoline: Health and environmental issues." *American Journal of Industrial Medicine* 39:426–33.

– et al., 1994. "Occupational and environmental exposure of garage workers and taxi drivers to airborne manganese arising from the use of methylcyclopentadienyl manganese tricarbonyl in unleaded gasoline." *American Industrial Hygeine Association Journal* 55:53–8.

Index